1 Timothy

1 Timothy

A Charge to God's Missional Household

Volume 3

Paul S. Jeon

PICKWICK *Publications* • Eugene, Oregon

1 TIMOTHY
A Charge to God's Missional Household
Volume 3

Copyright © 2017 Paul S. Jeon. All rights reserved. Except for brief quotations in critical publications or reviews, no part of this book may be reproduced in any manner without prior written permission from the publisher. Write: Permissions, Wipf and Stock Publishers, 199 W. 8th Ave., Suite 3, Eugene, OR 97401.

Pickwick Publications
An Imprint of Wipf and Stock Publishers
199 W. 8th Ave., Suite 3
Eugene, OR 97401

www.wipfandstock.com

PAPERBACK ISBN: 978-1-5326-1727-0
HARDCOVER ISBN: 978-1-4982-4187-8
EBOOK ISBN: 978-1-4982-4186-1

Cataloguing-in-Publication data:

Names: Jeon, Paul S.

Title: 1 Timothy : a charge to God's missional household : vol. 3 / by Paul S. Jeon.

Description: Eugene, OR: Pickwick Publications, 2017 | Includes bibliographical references.

Identifiers: ISBN 978-1-5326-1727-0 (paperback) | ISBN 978-1-4982-4187-8 (hardcover) | ISBN 978-1-4982-4186-1 (ebook)

Subjects: LCSH: Bible. Timothy, 1st—Commentaries. | Bible. Timothy, 1st—Criticism, interpretation, etc.

Classification: LCC BS2745.3 J4 2017 (print) | LCC BS2745.3 (ebook)

Manufactured in the U.S.A.   12/13/17

To Brian Forman, with appreciation and admiration

Contents

Preface | ix
Acknowledgments | xi
Abbreviations | xiii

1 Synopses of Volumes 1 and 2 | 1

2 1 Timothy 5:1—6:2: Godly Conduct from All Members of God's Household (B' Unit) | 4

3 1 Timothy 6:3–21: The Teaching that is According to Godliness Is Great Gain for Eternal Life (A' Unit) | 126

Bibliography | 267

Preface

I HAD PLANNED TO COMPLETE this book on 1 Timothy not long after completing my dissertation on Titus. At the time, I figured that I had "academic momentum," a rhythm that one picks up from constantly researching and writing in the final season of a Ph.D. Given that I had worked with the 1 Timothy letter for many years and already developed what I thought was a solid outline, I thought that this book would be churned out in a matter of one or two years. That was the fall of 2011. Between then and now, much has transpired—so much that I wondered if I would ever be able to complete this project. Still, the unexpected delay gave me an extended season to dwell on the letter and gain certain insights that can come only with time. During the intervening years, I had ample opportunities both to lecture on 1 Timothy while teaching at Reformed Theological Seminary and to preach on it at my church (NewCity) and occasional conferences. Regular dialogue with students, colleagues, and parishioners opened new angles into understanding the message of 1 Timothy, a letter that unfortunately tends to be treated somewhat plainly as a sort of church-manual.

I write commentaries in hope that they might be of some service to those who want to better understand the Bible. My desire has never been to write *the* commentary on any given work in the New Testament. Rather, I see myself as entering into a dialogue that has been taking place for many centuries about the meaning of the text. In this sense, I feel deeply privileged to offer my brief comments on 1 Timothy. My goal is that the reader will feel like he or she has a better grasp of the meaning and import of the letter and, in turn, will experience a degree of the benefits that I have experienced from sitting down with this letter—indeed, sitting under it—for almost six years now.

Acknowledgments

First, as always, I want to thank my parents. They know that I have no idea how much they have sacrificed for me. Second, I want to thank my research assistant, Brian Forman, who meticulously reviewed the text and enhanced the overall commentary in more ways than I can fully express. Third, though we have never met, I want to readily acknowledge Philip Towner, who served as both my guide and conversationalist through his wonderful commentary for over six years. In more ways than I can count, he pointed me away from exegetical fallacies and towards more promising interpretations. Finally, I want to thank my church NewCity and my family—especially my wife, Geena—for making life and ministry a delight.

Abbreviations

1 Tim	1 Timothy
ABCS	Africa Bible Commentary Series
ANTC	Abingdon New Testament Commentaries
BDAG	W. Bauer, W. F. Arndt, and F. W. Gingrich (3rd ed.; rev. by F. W. Danker), *Greek-English Lexicon of the New Testament*
BDF	F. Blass, A. Debrunner, and R. W. Funk, *A Greek Grammar of the NT*
Bib	*Biblica*
BrazTCB	Brazos Theological Commentary on the Bible
BSac	*Bibliotheca Sacra*
BTCB	Belief: A Theological Commentary on the Bible
CBQ	*Catholic Biblical Quarterly*
CCSS	Catholic Commentary on Sacred Scripture
COP	*Colloquium Oecumenicum Paulinum*
CTST	*Current Trends in Scripture Translation*
DLNT	*Dictionary of the Later New Testament and Its Developments*
EBib	Études bibliques
ESV	*English Standard Version*
ExTim	*Expository Times*
HB	Human Biology
HNTC	Harper's New Testament Commentaries
HTR	*Harvard Theological Review*
ICC	International Critical Commentary

ICNT	India Commentary on the New Testament	
JSNTSup	JSNT, Supplement Series	
JSOT	*Journal for the Study of the Old Testament*	
KJV	King James Version	
LXX	Septuagint	
MNTC	MacArthur New Testament Commentary	
NAC	New American Commentary	
NASB	*New American Standard Bible*	
NCBC	New Collegeville Bible Commentary	
NCBNT	New Clarendon Bible, New Testament	
NCCS	New Covenant Commentary Series	
NIBC	New International Biblical Commentary	
NIGTC	New International Greek Testament Commentary	
NIV	*New International Version*	
NovT	*Novum Testamentum*	
NRSV	*New Revised Standard Version*	
NSBT	New Studies in Biblical Theology	
NT	New Testament	
NTC	New Testament Commentary	
NTL	New Testament Library	
NTS	*New Testament Studies*	
OT	Old Testament	
PE	Pastoral Epistles	
PS	Pauline Studies	
PTMS	Princeton Theological Monograph Series	
RNBC	Readings: A New Biblical Commentary	
RSV	*Revised Standard Version*	
SBLDiS	SBL Dissertation Series	
SBLSBS	Society of Biblical Literature Sources for Biblical Study	
TCGNT	B. M. Metzger, *A Textual Commentary on the Greek New Testament*	
TCH	The Church in History	

TynNTC	Tyndale New Testament Commentaries
TZ	*Theologische Zeitschrift*
UBS	United Bible Societies lexicon
WBC	Word Biblical Commentary
WGRW	Writings from the Greco-Roman World
WUNT	Wissenschaftliche Untersuchungen zum Neuen Testament

1

Synopses of Volumes 1 and 2

Synopsis of Volume 1

IN VOLUME 1, CHAPTER 1, I provided an overview of the 1 Timothy letter regarding its main message, authorship, and historical background; in addition, my commentary's text-centered, literary-rhetorical, and audience-oriented approach to the 1 Timothy letter was explicated. Overall, the message of 1 Timothy is summarized in the title of this book, *1 Timothy: A Charge to God's Missional Household*. Regarding authorship and the historical background, the 1 Timothy letter was composed by the apostle Paul to address the problem of false teaching overseers within the mid-sixties Ephesian church. For the approach of my commentary, I demonstrated how the public, performative aspect of 1 Timothy as a first-century letter shapes the way in which a modern audience is to understand, experience, and analyze the apostle Paul's message.[1]

In volume 1, chapter 2, I analyzed the performative aspect of 1 Timothy according to the ancient linguistic structuring device of *chiasm*—a rhetorical method of organizing a letter's content to enable its oral delivery and aural comprehension. In ancient letters, a chiasm conveyed a parallel structure in language that intentionally led the audience through introductory themes toward a central point (or points); at the central point, the chiasm pivoted and moved the audience's attention toward a cumulative conclusion that recalled and developed aspects of the introductory themes. I demonstrated that the 1 Timothy letter is organized into one overall chiastic arrangement, referred to in this commentary as a *macro*chiasm. I also demonstrated that there are six literary units that comprise and arrange the 1 Timothy macrochiasm, which are referred to in this commentary as *micro*chiasms. Still, within each microchiasm of 1 Timothy, there are smaller

---

1. For a detailed explanation of the main message, authorship, historical background, and performance of 1 Timothy as a communal letter, see volume 1, chapter 1.

literary units, referred to as *mini*chiasms. The aggregation of the minichiasms, microchiasms, and macrochiasm of 1 Timothy effectively build and convey meaning to the audience.

Also in volume 1, chapter 2, I provided an in-depth explanation of my translation methodology. The basis of my English translation of 1 Timothy in this commentary seeks to maintain the dynamic sense of the original Greek words and to demonstrate how these Greek words were instrumental to the performance and rhetorical strategy of the letter.[2]

In volume 1, chapters 3 and 4, I analyzed the first two microchiasms according to their rhetorical organization, content, and themes. In volume 1, chapter 3, I demonstrated that the first microchiasm—the A unit of the 1 Timothy letter (1:1–20)—established an inseparable link of authority from God and Jesus to Paul and Timothy (1:1, 2, 11, 18). In contrast, a group of "some" within the Ephesian church who "teach-different" (1:3) were identified by Paul as both the problem and motivation of the letter; over and against Paul, this group was teaching "some-thing different" that "lies-opposed to the sound teaching" (1:10b).

In volume 1, chapter 4, I demonstrated that the second microchiasm—the B unit of the 1 Timothy letter (2:1–15)—highlighted the proper lifestyle of "godliness" (2:3, 10) that flows from Paul's sound teaching. Interrelated, there was a sustained emphasis on salvation—God's desire and activity to enable humans to be saved (2:3–6)—and the Ephesian church's missional duty to attract others to Jesus Christ for salvation. To this end, the apostle Paul identified the unique roles of men and women in the church (2:8–12, 15) that ulitimately derived from the creational roles of men and women by God (2:13–14).[3]

Synopsis of Volume 2

In volume 2, chapters 2 and 3, I analyzed the second two microchiasms according to their rhetorical organization, content, and themes. In volume 2, chapter 2, I demonstrated that the third microchiasm—the C unit of the 1 Timothy letter (3:1–16)—outlined the qualifications for church leadership as a result of the unqualified overseers in the Ephesisan church. An emphasis was placed on the sacrificial manner in which an overseer cherishes his wife and on his leadership within his own home. The theme of God's church as a familial household was explicitly conveyed to the audience (3:15; cf.

---

2. For the establishment of 1 Timothy as a macrochiasm, clarifications of terminology, and an explanation of my translation methodology, see volume 1, chapter 2.

3. For a detailed explanation of 1 Timothy 1–2, see volume 1, chapters 3 and 4.

3:5). Finally, we heard the pivot point of the overall 1 Timothy macrochiasm in the Christ hymn (3:16), which initated a movement toward the letter's conclusion.

In volume 2, chapter 3, I demonstrated that the fourth microchiasm—the C' unit of the 1 Timothy letter (4:1–16)—oriented the audience's attention to the problem of "some" in the Ephesian church. Specifically, I articulated the dichotomy between the group of "some" and Timothy via comparison: the lifestyle of "some" who were "holding-toward deceitful spirits and teachings of demons" (4:1) was defined by ascetic "bodily training" (4:8a); in stark contrast, the lifestyle of Timothy who was "being-nourished in . . . the commendable teaching" (4:6) was defined by training "toward godliness" (4:7b). The C' unit concluded by challenging the audience to consider whether or not they were listening to Timothy and "the teaching" (4:16).

2

1 Timothy 5:1—6:2: Godly Conduct from All Members of God's Household

(B' Unit)

THIS CHAPTER EXAMINES THE B' unit of the macrochiasm—the fifth of six microchiasms within the 1 Timothy letter.[1] Within the fifth microchiasm (5:1—6:2), five minichiasms are heard (5:4–8; 5:11–16; 5:17–19; 5:20–25; 6:1–2).

The Fifth Microchiasm

The 5:1—6:2 microchiasm is composed carefully of four elements (A-B-B'-A'); linguistic parallels identifying chiastic arrangements are indicated by the Greek text:

> A. ¹ An elderly-man (πρεσβυτέρῳ) do not rebuke-violently; rather exhort (παρακάλει) as a father, younger-men as brothers (ἀδελφούς), ² elderly-women (πρεσβυτέρας) as mothers, younger-women as sisters (ἀδελφάς), in all purity.
>
> > B. ³ Honor widows—those truly widows (ὄντως χήρας). ⁴ But if some widow has (ἔχει) children or those-from-parents, they must learn (μανθανέτωσαν) first (πρῶτον) to be-godly to their own household (οἶκον) and to give-return repayments to their parents; for this is acceptable in the sight of God. ⁵ But she who is truly a widow (ὄντως χήρα) and who is left-remaining has hoped upon God and remains in the

---

1. For the establishment of 1 Timothy as a macrochiasm, clarifications of terminology, and an explanation of my translation methodology, see volume 1, chapter 2.

supplications and the prayers night and day, ⁶ but she who is self-indulgent—living—is dead. ⁷ And these charge, that they might be irreproachable. ⁸ But if someone does not provide-for those of his own and especially for household-members (οἰκείων), he has denied the faith (πίστιν) and is worse-than the without-faith (ἀπίστου). ⁹ A widow must be-enrolled not being less than sixty years, woman of one man,

> C. ¹⁰ᵃ in commendable works (ἔργοις) testified:
>> D. ¹⁰ᵇ if she raised-children, if she has shown-hospitality, if the feet of the holy-ones she washed, if the afflicted she assisted,
> C'. ¹⁰ᶜ if she followed in all good work (ἔργῳ).

B'. ¹¹ But younger widows reject; for when they are impassioned from Christ, they desire to marry ¹² holding condemnation because the first (πρώτην) faith (πίστιν) they rejected; ¹³ but simultaneously also they learn (μανθάνουσιν) to be idlers, going about the houses (οἰκίας), but not only idlers; rather also gossips and busybodies, speaking what is not necessary. ¹⁴ I want, therefore, younger-women to marry, to child-parent, to master-households, to give no occasion to the opponent for maligning. ¹⁵ For already some have turned-aside after Satan. ¹⁶ If some faithful-woman has (ἔχει) widows, she must assist them and the church must not be-burdened, that it might assist those who are truly widows (ὄντως χήραις).

A'. ¹⁷ The elders (πρεσβύτεροι) who lead commendably must be considered-worthy of double honor, especially those who toil in word and teaching. ¹⁸ For the writing says, "A threshing ox you shall not muzzle," and, "Worthy is the laborer of his pay." ¹⁹ Do not accept an accusation against an elder (πρεσβυτέρου), except upon two or three testifiers. ²⁰ Those who sin in the sight of all reprove, that also the rest might hold fear. ²¹ I testify in the sight of God and of Christ Jesus and of the elect angels, that these-things you might guard without prejudice, doing nothing according to favoritism. ²² Lay hands quickly on none, nor share in others's sins; keep yourself pure. ²³ No-longer drink water; rather a little wine use because of your stomach and frequent illnesses. ²⁴ The sins of some humans are conspicuous, preceding them for judgment, but for some they also follow. ²⁵ Likewise also the commendable works are conspicuous, and those having otherwise do-not have-the-power to be-hidden. ⁶:¹ Those who are under the yoke as slaves must consider their own masters worthy of all honor, that the name of God and the teaching might not be-blasphemed. ² But those who have faithful masters must not look-down because they are brothers (ἀδελφοί); rather all-the-more they must serve-as-slaves, because faithful and beloved are those who receive the beneficial-work. These-things teach and exhort (παρακάλει).

1 Timothy 5:1–2: Proper Conduct toward All Members of God's Household

(A Element)

In the A element (5:1–2) of the fifth microchiasm, Paul addresses the way that Timothy is to engage those in God's household.² Immediately, the audience hear: "An elderly-man do not rebuke-violently" (5:1). The term "An elderly-man" (πρεσβυτέρῳ) recalls "the presbytery" (τοῦ πρεσβυτερίου) in 4:14 of the preceding microchiasm. Though it is possible that the audience hear "An elderly-man" in reference to one of the men in "the presbytery," it is most likely that the term would be understood as a general reference to older men, that is, relative to the age of those in God's household and of Timothy.³ Furthermore, the fact that Timothy is to "not rebuke-violently"

---

2. Towner, *Letters*, 329, makes an important observation about the entire section of this chapter—the fifth microchiasm—which reinforces that 1 Timothy is directed both to Timothy and the broader Ephesian audience: "The continuation of the second-person singular imperatives . . . underscores Timothy's role as apostolic representative in the church as primary recipient of the letter . . . otherwise, third-person singular and plural verbs show that the teaching concerning widows (5:3–16), elders and their assessment (5:17–25), and slaves (6:1–2a) is to be received and acted on by members of the groups addressed and, in some cases, by the larger community as a whole."

3. Knight, *PE*, 214: "The singular is generic, as is evidenced by the plurals used for the following three groups ["younger-men," "elderly-women," "younger-women"] . . . πρεσβύτερος . . . designates both age and office . . . Although some have thought that πρεσβύτερος is used here for church officers . . . most commentators have recognized that the corresponding categories of 'younger men' (νεωτέρους) and 'older women' (πρεσβυτέρας) point to this as a category of age and sex rather than of office." Merkle, *40 Questions about Elders and Deacons*, 220: "The word translated 'older man' (*presbuteros*) is the same word translated 'elder' in 1 Timothy 5:17. However . . . the context must decide. In 1 Timothy 5:1, it is clear that the office of elder is not in view because the following verses refer specifically to age categories." See Horrell, "Disciplining Performance," 115; Witherington, *Letters*, 264; Marshall, *PE*, 573.

It may also be worth noting that later in the fifth microchiasm, the audience are told

an elderly-man would convey several implications for the audience. The term "rebuke-violently" (ἐπιπλήξῃς) connotes harsh dealing as though being hit or struck.[4] Also, the negative particle "not" (μή) recalls its prior occurrences in association with the activities of the false teachers.[5] As such, that Timothy is to "not rebuke-violently" an elderly-man may indicate that the false-teaching overseers in the Ephesian church had been doing so and that Timothy's leadership must be markedly different from the false leadership of "some."[6] Indeed, where Timothy is to "not (μή) rebuke-violently (ἐπιπλήξῃς)" in 5:1 recalls Paul's statement that qualified overseers are "not (μή) violent (πλήκτην)" in 3:3, the audience clearly hear Paul's polemical rhetoric against "some" who are unqualified, false-teaching overseers. Here, then, not only is the polemical contrast in the fourth microchiasm between Timothy and the false teachers carried forward into the fifth microchiasm, but the overall macrochiastic polemic against the false teachers is also advanced: in the same way that Timothy is to "charge some not (μή) to teach-different, nor (μηδέ) to hold-toward myths" (1:3–4), and just as qualified leaders in the church are "not (μή) addicted-to-wine, not (μή) violent" (3:3), "Not (μή) a young-plant" (3:6), do "not (μή) fall into disgrace" (3:7), and are "not (μή) holding-toward much wine, not (μή) avaricious" (3:8), so too Timothy—the qualified leader in Ephesus (1:1, 18; 3:15; 4:6–14)—must "not (μή) rebuke-violently" an elderly-man (5:1). Timothy's leadership must be unlike the presumably harsh dealings of the false teachers.

The polemical continuaton from the fourth to the fifth microchiasm would also be heard through the seamless movement—via transitional words—from "strongly-remain" (ἐπίμενε, 4:16) in the A' element of the fourth microchiasm to "rebuke-violently" (ἐπιπλήξῃς, 5:1) in the A element of the fifth microchiasm.[7] What is more, given the localized cluster of

---

that a legitimate widow must not be less than sixty years (5:9). However, the use of this age for the "elderly-man" is speculative.

4. See Marshall, *PE*, 573. Knight, *PE*, 213.

5. See 1:3, 4, 7; 3:3, 6, 7, 8; 4:12.

6. That the false teachers are overseers in the church, see discussion in volume 1, chapter 1 regarding Acts 20:28–30. See also discussion in volume 2, chapter 2 regarding 1 Timothy 3:1–7.

7. The aural emphasis on the verbal prefix (ἐπί) would be apparent. The ἐπί prefix in the verb "Strongly-hold" (ἔπεχε, 4:16) would strengthen the connection and linguistic transition between the fourth and fifth microchiasms.

It may be worth noting (see *italics*) that the terms "teaching" (διδασκαλίᾳ) in 4:16 and "exhort" (παρακάλει) in 5:1 would likely also be heard with aural similarities, which would further strengthen the unified movement from the fourth microchiasm to the fifth microchiasm.

Regarding the function of *transitional words*, see volume 1, chapter 2.

intensified, compound verbs—"Strongly-hold" (ἔπεχε, 4:16), "strongly-remain" (ἐπίμενε, 4:16), and "rebuke-violently" (ἐπιπλήξῃς, 5:1)—the twofold reason for Timothy's actions in the fifth microchiasm would be clear. On the one hand, Timothy's call is to "Strongly-hold" and "strongly-remain" in his personal nourishment of "the teaching" of the church (4:13, 16), "the commendable teaching" that he has followed (4:6b), and "the sound teaching" in accordance with the gospel that exhibits God's radiance and results in blessing toward him (1:10–11); in this way, therefore, Timothy's call to "not rebuke-violently" an elderly-man is derived from the teaching. On the other hand, therefore, the audience understand that the rhetorical force of these connected compound verbs indicates that the apostle Paul is just as concerned for Timothy to "not rebuke-violently" an elderly-man (5:1) as he is for Timothy to "Strongly-hold" and "strongly-remain" (4:16) in the teaching. To be sure, to "rebuke-violently" an elderly-man would not only indicate a failure to "Strongly-hold" and "strongly-remain" but also a rejection of the teaching of the church, as "some" who teach-different have done. In short, the audience understand that Paul is equally forceful about Timothy's godly interactions in 5:1 as he is with Timothy's spiritual duties of truth in 4:16—both are connected, and one leads to the other.[8] Indeed, Timothy's personal duties to grow in godliness according to his devotion to the teaching (4:16) must translate to a public expression, namely his interactions with those in God's household (5:1).

A further rhetorical nuance would hardly go unnoticed. Throughout the macrochiasm, the audience have heard Paul's public polemic against the false teachers: the consistently negative connotation ascribed to the indefinite pronoun "some" and its cognates (1:3, 6, 8, 10b, 19; 3:1, 5; 4:1); the discrediting use of "myths" to describe the unverifiability of their teachings (1:4; 4:7a); and the implication that they are "falsifying" (2:7) are indications that they are "false-worders" (4:2) who are privy to God's just judgment upon "falsifiers" (1:10). For all intents and purposes, Paul—the apostolic authority of the church—has been continuously demonstrating that the false teachers are unqualified to lead the Ephesian church. Yet, even still he has not intended to "rebuke-violently" as perhaps the false-teaching overseers have done; instead, Paul has declared their errors, provided correction, and invited them to come to a knowing-embrace of truth, namely that the Savior God desires all humans to be-saved—including "some."

In this context, Paul's next statement is significant: "rather exhort as a father." The term "rather" (ἀλλά) connotes an emphatic contrast. Thus "rather" than rebuking an elderly-man, the focus is on Timothy's action to

---

8. See discussion in Towner, *Letters*, 330–31.

"exhort as a father." The verb "exhort" (παρακάλει) recalls its earlier occurrences in the macrochiasm and would be heard with a cumulative effect. In 1:3 of the first microchiasm, the apostle "exhorted" (παρεκάλεσά) Timothy to remain in Ephesus. Paul did not merely suggest that Timothy should remain in Ephesus; instead, he instructed his genuine child "in faith" (1:2) to do so. That is, Paul has authority over Timothy, but he and Timothy also share the same purpose—they are partners "in faith." Similarly, in 2:1 of the second microchiasm, the audience heard Paul "exhort" (παρακαλῶ) them to pray on behalf of all humans. Again, Paul was not offering a suggestion. Instead, he was drawing upon his authority as an apostle—hence something more akin to a command—but in the context of his, Timothy, and the audience's shared interest in God's missional desire for all humans to be-saved. In both 1:3 and 2:1, Paul's exhortations conveyed a respectful tone, communicating a sense of authority yet a unified concern to maintain God's missional household by preserving the teaching and promoting godliness.[9] Here, then, in 5:1 it is this same twofold nuance of authority and respect that Timothy must observe as he carries out the difficult task of respectfully correcting "an elderly-man."[10] To be sure, the contrast in 5:1 between "rubuke-violently" and "exhort" indicates that Timothy's leadership of those "in faith"—those living in the household of God (1:4)—does not entail adopting a harsh tone but "rather" involves respect. Such respect is not only undergirded by a shared interest but also—and much more fundamentally—by a unified existence "in faith," that is, "in Christ Jesus" (3:13) as a family.[11]

Moreover, the qualifying phrase "as a father" further emphasizes and nuances the connotations of authority and respect within the framework of family. The term "father" (πατέρα) in 5:1 recalls "God the Father" (πατρός) in 1:2 of the first microchiasm, clearly indicating that the elderly-man in view

---

9. The *ESV* translation "urge" helpfully indicates the aspect of respect but loses the balanced aspect of authority that the verb conveys.

10. Undoubtedly, a balance between asserting his unique authority and showing proper respect to the elderly would have required much wisdom on the part of Timothy. The difficulty of the implied situation would clearly convey the "messiness of ministry," a reality that necessitates practical wisdom for knowing how to apply universal truth to specific and various contexts.

11. This is not to suggest that Paul's commands here on the appropriate demeanor of Timothy is more unique than practices of the first-century Greco-Roman period. Parallel instructions can be found in other ancient literature (see Marshall, *PE*, 572–73), and given the missional call of God's household, it was a general practice for the apostle Paul not to create undue social skepticism; see volume 1, chapter 4. Still, Paul's command here in 5:1 (and 5:2) was likely both to contrast the way in which the false teachers looked down on Timothy because of his youth (4:12) and to emphasize the way that God's family is to respect one another at all ages.

is related to Timothy and the audience as family "in faith."[12] Significantly also, where such an elderly-man "in faith" is to be regarded in reverence "as a father" (5:1) by others who are "in faith," he is to revere and submit to God the Father of the household "in faith" (1:2), that is, to the household-law of God "in faith" (1:4). In short, the elderly-man "in faith" who is to be regarded "as a father" is simultaneously expected to adhere to the respectful authority of the apostle Paul and also, therefore, of the younger Timothy who is the entrusted leader of God's household in Ephesus (1:18; 4:6–16).

For Timothy, the term "father" in 5:1 would be reminiscent of his relationship to Paul as a "genuine child in faith" (1:2). In effect, though neither Paul (1:2) nor an elderly-man (5:1) are Timothy's actual father, Timothy is to display loyalty, respect, and deference to both men as if they were his father.[13] Indeed, given the proper reverence for all those "in faith" toward God the "Father" (1:2), so must Timothy's dynamic with "a father" (5:1) in God's household be defined by reverence and humility.[14] In effect, Paul intends for Timothy to exhort an elderly-man "as a father" with the same degree of caution, respect, and admiration with which he would hypothetically exhort the apostle Paul himself.[15]

Continuing the introductory A element, Paul conveys that Timothy must exhort "younger-men as brothers, elderly-women as mothers, younger-women as sisters, in all purity" (5:1–2).[16] Two implications are immediately heard by the audience. First, the cohesion of the A element is

---

12. Given that such "an elderly-man" is viewed "as a father"—part of God's household—the audience would understand that the "elderly-man" in 5:1 is not to be grouped with the false teachers—those not "in faith." This seems to strengthen the contrast between the way in which church leaders (Paul and Timothy) are to rebuke "some" versus the way that church leaders are to exhort those "in faith."

13. Marshall, *PE*, 574: "ὡς πατέρα expresses the thought 'with the respect appropriate to a father.'"

14. Towner, *Letters*, 331: "Timothy is called on to treat even older men in need of correction with a certain deference and politeness that will ensure that the correction is unifying rather than divisive." Barclay, *1 & 2 Tim*, 150: "Older men are to be treated with the respect and dignity due to them because of their age. Timothy is not to rebuke them in a sharp or severe way. That does not mean, however, that he should not minister to them at all. In keeping with his calling, even older men are under his pastoral care. Therefore, Paul instructs Timothy to 'exhort' an older man, implying a softer tone, as opposed to a harsher, more domineering rebuke."

15. Such a concept of familial reverence toward the elderly is not only sentimental and theological but also practical: just as biological kin are organized according to age and gender, so too is the household of God to be characterized by structure. See Osiek and Balch, *Families in the New Testament World*, 165–66.

16. The verb "exhort" from 5:1 is carried through to the end of verse 5:2.

heard in the obvious symmetry and repetition of the conjunction "as" (ὡς).[17] The rhetorical effect would not only emphasize the familial aspect of God's household—those "in faith" are to be viewed "as" fathers, brothers, mothers, and sisters—but also, therefore, its unity, namely that an elderly-man, younger-men, elderly-women, and younger-women are all united as one family.[18] Second, the continued juxtaposition of authority and familial relations would be further emphasized for the audience. That is, where the authorized leaders "in faith" are to exhort others "in faith" as members of a family, the audience understand that authority in God's household is closer to the authority that a loving parent has over a child or an older sibling has over a younger one.[19] Indeed, rather than the authority of taskmasters, the audience understand that leadership in the church—namely Paul and Timothy's—has familial love as the methodology of the household-law of God (1:4–5). Paul's point is to underscore for the audience that legitimate authority in God's household is properly viewed only in light of Christ Jesus, the one who enables love to beyond-abound (1:14), that is, the mediator of God and humans (2:5) who brings old and young together in God's presence (4:5) as one family (5:1–2).

In this highly emphasized familial context, Timothy is to exhort "younger-men as brothers." The adjective "younger-men" (νεωτέρους) recalls Timothy's "youth" (νεότητος) in 4:12 of the fourth microchiasm. Here, then, as much as none must look-down-on Timothy's "youth" (4:12), neither are the "younger-men" in God's household (5:1). Indeed, rather than contrasting Timothy's "youth" in 4:12 against the "younger-men" in 5:1, the audience understand that Paul is concerned with a dual dynamic among the faithful in God's household: church leaders are to be respected (3:13; 4:12), and church leaders are to equally respect those under their care, namely as family members (5:1). The term "younger-men" (νεωτέρους) also recalls "a

---

17. It may be helpful to visualize the symmetrical arrangement of 5:1–2:
"An elderly-man . . . as (ὡς) a father,"
"younger-men as (ὡς) brothers,"
"elderly-women as (ὡς) mothers,"
"younger-women as (ὡς) sisters, in all purity."
It may be worth noting that the symmetry is somewhat broken by the prepositional phrase attached to the last group ("in all purity"). This was likely intentional, drawing attention to Timothy's interaction with younger-women (see below).

18. Towner, *Letters*, 330, translates ὡς with the adjective "fictive." To be sure, even within this microchiasm, the apostle distinguishes between those connected through biological kinship (5:4, 16) versus spiritual kinship (5:1–2). However, "fictive" may be too forceful because it suggests the idea of inauthenticity—certainly Paul intends his audience "in faith" to view themselves as a "genuine" family (1:2).

19. Barcley, *1 & 2 Tim*, 150: "In all of Timothy's dealings with God's people, he is to be guided by the fact that the church is the family of God."

young-plant" (νεόφυτον) in 3:6 of the third microchiasm. Here, however, a contrast would be intended: Timothy's authoritative interactions with the "younger-men" in God's household are to further distinguish his leadership from the "young-plant" false teachers who, ironically, look-down-on Timothy's "youth" and, presumably, upon the "younger-men," too.

The term "brothers" (ἀδελφούς) in 5:1 recalls 4:6 of the previous microchiasm where, in response to the incorrect, ascetic prohibitions of the false teachers, Timothy was to provide authoritative, corrective instruction to the "brothers" (ἀδελφοῖς).[20] Thus in 5:1, both Timothy's sustained *authority* in relation to the "brothers"—"Instructing" (4:6), "exhort" (5:1)—and his sustained view of them as *family* underscores the framework in which his church authority is exercised. In stark contrast to the false teachers who are not "in faith" and thus do not respect "youth"—even leaders such as Timothy—nor "younger-men" as family members (4:12; 5:1), the audience understand that Timothy leads the "younger-men" in God's household by treating them as "brothers" (5:1), that is, as equals who are not looked down upon.[21] It is quite apparent that Paul intends to carry forward his polemic into the fifth microchiasm: the manner in which Timothy exerts authority must be qualitatively different from the harsh practices of the false-teaching overseers.

Within the same framework as Timothy's authority toward the men in God's household, Paul commands Timothy to exhort "elderly-women as mothers" (5:2). That Timothy must respect and treat "elderly-women as mothers" (πρεσβυτέρας ὡς μητέρας) would have come as no surprise, certainly corresponding to Timothy's respectful authority toward an elderly-man as a father (5:1)—thus clearly being a general reference to

---

20. In 5:1–2, Paul identifies "brothers" distinctly from "sisters"; this may corroborate the notion that "brothers" in 4:6 had specifically the men in view. See volume 2, chapter 3.

21. Barcley, *1 & 2 Tim*, 150: "Even as Timothy has pastoral care over them, he is to treat them as equals."

It may be worth noting that in the case that Paul's use of "brothers" in 4:6 is a general reference to all the men "in faith" among the audience—regardless of age—his use of "brothers" here in 5:1 is certainly qualified by age and would be understood as a nuance from its earlier occurrence. That is, while Timothy's "Instructing . . . the brothers" in 4:6 is an umbrella term applying (at the very least) to all the men, so too does Timothy's call in 5:1 to "exhort" both "An elderly-man . . . as a father" and "younger-men as brothers" encapsulate all of the men whom Timothy is instructing in 4:6.

At least in part, Marshall speaks to this nuanced application of "brothers": "Paul addresses his readers generally as brothers (fellow-believers) but describes them as (his) children when expressing affection and fatherly concern" (*PE*, 574). Where "brothers" in 4:6 refers to the faithful in general (perhaps only the men), "brothers" in 5:1 expresses the familial affection with which Timothy is to lead a specific group of the men.

elderly-women in the Ephesian church[22]—but also because of the way in which the broader Greco-Roman culture honored mothers.[23] In view of the latter, Timothy is commanded to exhibit proper respect to elderly-women in order to remove any obstacle to the missional call of God's household; any perception of disregard for the elderly would have hindered the reception of the gospel, the testimony, the mystery concerning Christ Jesus by the wider culture, namely those-outside God's household (3:7). In view of the former, Timothy's leadership of "elderly-women as mothers" would foster and emphasize the familial reality for those within God's household, namely the endearing and respectful bond between mothers and sons.[24] Still, in view of both, the sustained polemic against the false teachers would likely also be highlighted: in contrast to the unqualified "someone" who is a young-plant man and does not have a missional, commendable testimony from those-outside (3:1, 6, 7), and unlike those for whom the law is laid—namely "patricides and matricides" (πατρολῴαις καὶ μητρολῴαις, 1:9)—Timothy does not rebuke-violently a "father" (πατέρα) nor "mothers" (μητέρας) in God's household but rather exhorts them with respect, honor, and humility (5:1–2).[25]

As the final clause in the introductory A element, Timothy must exhort "younger-women as sisters, in all purity" (5:2). Similar to "brothers," Timothy's exhortations to "sisters" would convey his respect for them as equal family members. However, the inclusion of the prepositional phrase "in all purity" would break the perfect symmetry of verses 1 and 2, certainly drawing attention to the way that Timothy must specifically relate with "younger-women as sisters." Up to this point, the way in which Timothy must interact with the ages and genders of those within God's household has been implicit and without need for clarification—fathers with veneration,

---

22. Some commentators consider the "elderly-women" (πρεσβυτέρας) to be members of the presbytery (e.g., Grady, *Truth Sets Women Free*, 130); however, this would not account for the explicit context of age categories in 5:1–2. See above regarding "An elderly-man" (πρεσβυτέρῳ) in 5:1.

23. See the multiple references in Witherington, *Letters*, 264.

24. Barcley, *1 & 2 Tim*, 150–51: "Like Paul's reference to regarding older men as fathers, treating older women as 'mothers' means showing them proper honour and respect. But there is also a sense of endearment. The mother-son relationship is unique. Timothy is to treat older women with the respect and love that a son gives to his mother." This observation is certainly appropriate and highlights the disposition of loving respect that Paul intends to permeate the household of God.

25. This polemical contrast against the false teachers and the "father . . . mothers" (πατέρα . . . μητέρας) language of 5:1–2 would most likely be heard as an echo of the fifth commandment: LXX Exod 20:12: "τίμα τὸν πατέρα σου καὶ τὴν μητέρα." See Barcley, *1 & 2 Tim*, 150.

brothers with equality, mothers with endearment. Here, though, Paul is explicit about the appropriate manner for Timothy's interaction with "younger-women," namely "in all purity." The phrase "in . . . purity" (ἐν . . . ἁγνείᾳ, 5:2) recalls the previous microchiasm wherein Timothy is to be an example of the faithful "in word, in behavior, in love, in faith, in purity (ἐν ἁγνείᾳ)" (4:12). Undoubtedly, then, the audience understand that Timothy's exhortations and interactions with "younger-women" are to exemplify fidelity, that is, to uphold God's proper intention for sexuality specifically within the boundaries of marriage. Moreover, Timothy's "youth" (νεότητος) in 4:12 seems to have a direct bearing on the way in which Timothy must engage "younger-women" (νεωτέρας): Timothy's interaction with younger-women who are "in faith" must align with his own existence "in faith," that is, by remaining "in . . . purity" (4:12; 5:2) with regard to sexuality. Furthermore, given both the ascetic practices of the false teachers (4:3a) and that the "young-plant" (νεόφυτον, 3:6) false teachers who are being-puffed-up were looking-down-on Timothy's "youth" (νεότητος) with pride (4:12), Timothy's interactions with "younger-women" (νεωτρας, 5:2) were likely under explicit scrutiny. Clearly, the apostle Paul felt it necessary to underscore that Timothy must carry himself in an irreproachable manner, not only to remove any suspicion about his qualifications to lead the church "in purity" (4:12) but also to ensure his authoritative relationship toward younger-women "in . . . purity" (5:2).[26]

Paul's use of the intensifier "all" (πάσῃ) highlights that Timothy is to be completely pure in his exhortations toward the younger-women who are under his care in God's household. Indeed, given that Timothy is to treat younger-women as though they were his sisters, certainly both he and the audience would understand Paul's explicit point: there is not to be any hint of sexuality between them.[27] Still, the term "all" (πάσῃ) would recall the missional purpose of God's household throughout the macrochiasm, particularly in the parallel B unit (2:1, 2, 4, 6, 10)—the second microchiasm—and

---

26. Witherington nuances that any sexual interaction with younger women would cloud Timothy's ability to exhort them as the leader of the church: "Timothy might be attracted to such a woman and as a result be more lenient with her. Thus he is warned to keep his conduct circumspect" (*Letters*, 264).

27. By highlighting that younger women are to be viewed "as sisters" (5:1), the rhetorical effect may intend to highlight the heinousness of any improper sexual relations with those under Timothy's care. Brother-sister incest was discouraged by OT law (Lev 18:9) and by Roman law; see McCabe, *Incest*, 34; Plessis, *Roman Law*, 125. It may be noted that Greco-Roman Egypt practiced brother-sister marriages; see Shaw, "Explaining Incest," 267–99; however, such brother-sister relationships were viewed as contrary to natural order by both Jews and Romans; see Pearce, *Land of the Body*, 42–43; contra Frandsen, *Incestuous and Close-Kin Marriage*, 126–27.

most immediately in the preceding A' element of the fourth microchiasm where, in light of the living God who is the Savior of "all" (πάντων) humans (4:10), Paul commanded Timothy to be an example (4:12), lead the church in worship (4:13), and use his gift (4:14) so that his subsequent progression might be manifested to "all" (πᾶσιν, 4:15). Timothy's exhortations toward the younger-women, then, is not only to align with his exemplary leadership but is intended to have a missional dynamic that would make the household of God attractive to those-outside (cf. 3:7).[28] Thus while Timothy is to remove suspicions about his leadership, so too is he to remove any suspicions about the church.[29]

In sum, as the overall macrochiasm progresses, the audience hear that the sustained theme of Timothy's authority in the concluding A' element of the fourth microchiasm (4:11–14) is advanced forward into the introductory A element of the fifth microchiasm (5:1–2). Timothy's authority in the church is emphatically placed within the sustained theme of familial, household relations among those "in faith," thus progressing the sustained theme of God's household-law (1:4) via qualified leaders (3:1–13; 4:6–16).[30]

---

28. Where Timothy is called to reveal to all (4:15) that God's family is a safe place that fosters proper, respectful treatment of younger women—"in purity" (4:12; 5:2)—the church in Ephesus would be seen as a place of healing for those who have been mistreated.

29. Watson, *Insatiable Appetites*, 30: "In the first century CE, Christians were accused of both cannibalism and incest." Kesich, *Formation and Struggles*, 145 n. 9: "the secrecy of Christian meetings, their calling one another brother and sister, and the exchange of the kiss of peace may have given rise to the suspicion of incest." Mackay, *Ancient Rome*, 287: "the Eucharist formed part of a ceremony called a 'love feast' in which they celebrated their love of God in a common feast, referring to their fellow Christians as 'brothers and sisters.' This practice too was misinterpreted by analogy with disreputable pagan practices, being taken to signify promiscuous sex in general and incest in particular." See Middleton, *Radical Martyrdom*, 68; Cavill, "Anglo-Saxon Saints' Lives—and Deaths," 81; Wagner, *After the Apostles*, 133. Such a negative stigma attributed by Greco-Romans in the first century against supposed brother-sister incest among Christians suggests that it was, by and large, not an acceptable practice in Greco-Roman society.

Misconceptions about Christian brother-sister incest relations in the first century were also derived from Christian marriages. Early, *History of Christianity*, 24: "Christians were . . . accused of incest because Christian spouses often called each other 'brother' and 'sister.'" Andria, *Romans*, 25: "Still others thought that Christians committed incest because they called each other 'brother' and 'sister' although they were sometimes husband and wife, like Aquila and Priscilla." In this full context, it seems likely that Paul's explicit emphasis for Timothy to be an example "in purity" (4:12) and to exhort "sisters, in all purity" (5:2) would include an apologetic impetus, namely to have a commendable witness to those-outside God's household (3:7) regarding sexuality within the church as both non-promiscuous (4:12) and non-incestuous (5:2).

30. Swinson, *Letters to Timothy*, 75: "These instructions [5:1–2] supplement and

1 Timothy 5:3–9: Widows Who Are Truly Widows

(B Element)

In the B element, Paul provides an extensive discussion on the care and proper honoring of widows, beginning with the statement, "Honor widows—those truly widows" (5:3).[31] The term "honor" (τίμα) recalls the blessings of "honor (τιμή) and glory" that are given to the King of the eternities—the only God—in 1:17 of the first microchiasm. Here, then, the implication for the audience is that such "honor" given to widows would ultimately give "honor" to God.[32] Furthermore, given the way Paul has explicitly expanded the scope of God's household in 5:1–2 to include fathers, brothers, mothers, and sisters, the audience would likely understand that such "widows" (5:3), especially if elderly, are to be viewed as "mothers" (5:2). In this way, the term "honor" (τίμα) in 5:3 would undoubtedly bring the fifth commandment into view: "honor (τίμα) your father and your mother" (LXX Exod 20:12). Thus in addition to familial reverence and respect, the sort of "honor" that Paul has in view for the widows would include financial or material assistance to meet their physical needs in old age.[33] Here, then, the specific nuance of the verb "honor" has less to do with payment for work

---

provide guidance for the more forceful directives that typified the previous unit."

31. For a helpful summary discussion on the background to the situation on widows, see Towner, *Letters*, 333–37. In contrast to a speculative interpretation on the possible formation of a widows' group or office (e.g., Spencer, *1 Tim*, 125; Thurston, "1 Tim 5.3–16," 159; Dewey, "1 Tim," 600), Towner's thesis seems more plausible: "From Israel's earliest times, God was known as the defender of widows (Deut 10:18; 24:17). 'Doing justice' was at least partly measured by the treatment of widows (Isa 1:17). And honoring God's concern for widows became an instrinsic element in the keeping of the covenant, which the early church recognized as one of its responsibilities (Acts 6:1; Jas 1:27)." Similarly, see Knight, *PE*, 216. For further discussion, see Marshall, *PE*, 575–77.

32. That God himself cares for widows, see Exodus 22:22–24; Isaiah 1:17; James 1:27. Wall with Steele suggest that "Paul's code is an attempt to structure the congregation's welfare system according to Jewish practice (and the Torah) rather than Roman law" (*1 & 2 Tim*, 129).

33. Waltke, *OT Theology*, 426: "The fifth commandment . . . invests their aged parents—who may no longer have financial worth and have become a liability—with dignity and honor . . . to honor parents involves taking care of them . . . Jesus applies the commandment to caring for parents, in Matthew 15." Getz, *Material Possessions*, 97–98: "Furthermore, what Jesus taught about honoring father and mother would certainly have motivated these new believers to take care of their parents and other family members. But more generally, it would motivate these believers to view the church as an 'extended family'—a larger body of believers where individual members should be concerned about one another's earthly welfare." See Barcley, *1 & 2 Tim*, 151–52.

done and more to do with the practical implications of giving honor where honor is due.[34]

Furthermore, the audience hear that Paul's main focus in 5:3 is clearly not on the actual logistics of providing care but rather on the identification of those "those truly widows." The adverb "truly" (ὄντως) connotes "really" or "certainly" and functions as a qualifier. Its occurrence here underscores to the audience that while the apostle believes that the church should honor God by helping those who are distressed, he is not supportive of providing thoughtless care. Rather, prior to distributing material help, Paul's qualification challenges the audience of the Ephesian church to be proactive about identifying not merely "widows" (χήρας) in the general sense but those who are "truly" in need.[35] In this way, the qualifier "truly" prepares the audience for what follows by raising the natural question, "Who, then, should be counted as a true widow?"

1 Timothy 5:4–8: A Minichiastic Unit

Within the B element of the microchiasm (5:3–9), the audience hear 5:4–8 as a minichiasm in itself. Verses 5:4–8 are composed carefully of six sub-elements ("a"-"b"-"c"-"c'"-"b'"-"a'"); linguistic parallels identifying chiastic arrangements are indicated by the Greek text:

> "a". ⁴ᵃ But if some (εἰ δέ τις) widow has children or those-from-parents, they must learn first to be-godly to their own household (ἴδιον οἶκον) and to give-return repayments to their parents;
>
> > "b". ⁴ᵇ for this (τοῦτο) is acceptable in the sight of God.
> >
> > > "c". ⁵ᵃ But she who is truly a widow and who is left-remaining (μεμονωμένη) has hoped upon God
> > >
> > > "c'". ⁵ᵇ and remains (προσμένει) in the supplications and the prayers night and day, ⁶ but she who is self-indulgent—living—is dead.

---

34. See 5:17; Verner, *Household of God*, 163; contra Bartsch, *Die Anfänge urchristlicher Rectsbildungen*, 118.

35. Knight, *PE*, 216: "ὄντως is not being used to deny that others are widows in the normal sense of the word, but rather to signify those who qualify for the church's care."

In addition to the usual meaning of "widow" in reference to a woman who survives her husband, it is possible that the term "widows" (χήρας) included a broad scope. Kartzow, *Destabilizing the Margins*, 113: "In antiquity, also in Christian texts, χήρα covers a wide spectrum of women, including virgins, women living apart from their husbands, divorced women, and women whose husbands were dead." See Witherington, *Letters*, 265; Marshall, *PE*, 578; Bassler, "Limits and Differentiation," 138.

"b'". ⁷ And these (ταῦτα) charge, that they might be irreproachable.

"a'". ⁸ But if someone (εἰ δέ τις) does not provide-for those of his own (ἰδίων) and especially for household-members (οἰκείων), he has denied the faith and is worse-than the without-faith.

The first minichiasm of the 5:1—6:2 microchiasm is framed by Paul's concern for one's "own household" in the "a" and "a'" sub-elements, namely the proper activity of children who have widows in their families. The "b" and "b'" sub-elements are framed by Paul's concern with "this" and "these." The minichiasm gravitates around the criteria of those who are truly widows in the dual pivot "c" and "c'" sub-elements.

1 Timothy 5:4a: If Some Widow Has Children, They Must Learn to Be-Godly

("a" sub-element)

The "a" sub-element (5:4a) begins with the contrasting conjunction "but" (δέ). The rhetorical effect would draw attention to the linguistic disparity between widows—"those truly widows" (τὰς ὄντως χήρας) in 5:3 versus "some widow" (τις χήρα) in 5:4.³⁶ To be sure, much like Paul's use of "someone" (τις) in 3:1 of the third microchiasm, "some" (τις) in 5:3 would have a generic application, in effect, referring to "widows in general." Yet, given the cumulative progression of the macrochiasm, the audience would most likely understand that Paul does not only intend "some widow" as a neutral statement. As with Paul's use of "some" in 3:1, the indefinite pronoun "some" (τις) in 5:3 would likely convey a simultaneous pejorative reference to the false teachers. Indeed, throughout the macrochiasm, the audience have heard Paul's sustained emphasis that "some" (τισίν) teach-different (1:3), that is, "some-thing" (τι) different than the sound teaching, the gospel (1:10–11), namely "some" (τινες) men, of whom are Hymenaeus and Alexander (1:19–20), who were likely influencing women to teach and govern men in the church (2:12). Such men—"someone" (τις)—were doing so as unqualified overseers (3:1–7) who do not know how to lead their own households nor how to care-for the church of God (3:5); they were attempting to oversee the church as a young-plant without deep roots in the faith (3:7), thus "some" (τινες) had apostatized from the faith by holding-toward teachings of demons (4:1). Here in 5:4a, then, although the audience understand

---

36. The play on words—τάς (5:3) versus τις (5:4)—would be apparent.

that "some widow" is not directly a reference to the false-teaching men who were overseers in the church, surely there is a degree of association with "some."[37] Thus while "some" does not carry its full polemical application upon the "widow" in 5:4a, its juxtaposition with the adverb "truly" conveys a sense of hesitation and speculation as to whether the widow in view is qualified for material provisions from the church.

Paul's rationale for such hesitation is that some widow "has children or those-from-parents" (5:4a). Here, Paul is identifying that "some widow" is not truly alone, that is, not one of those who are "truly widows" (5:3); on the contrary, she "has children or those-from-parents"—that is, children or grandchildren—who can and ought to care for her.[38] The implication here would be that "children or those-from-parents" of "some widow" must honor her with material provisions according to the fifth commandment. Subsequently, the church would be able to "Honor widows—those truly widows" (5:3), namely those who only have children or those-from-parents "in faith," that is, in God's familial household to care for them. Thus where the "children or those-from-parents" honor their own widow as a mother (5:4a), the church is then able to honor its widows as mothers "in faith" (5:3), thereby giving honor to God (1:17) in accordance with the fifth commandment.

It is worth noting that much of Paul's language in 5:4a would remind the audience of his prior discussion in the third microchiasm concerning church leaders.[39] The phrase "But if some (εἰ δέ τις) widow" in 5:4a recalls

---

37. It must be noted that that while "some" in 3:1 of the third microchiasm included a polemical reference to the false teachers, it also had a specific application in reference to men; see volume 2, chapter 2 regarding 1 Timothy 3:2.

Given that the false-teaching men were likely influencing the women among the audience "to teach" and possibly "to govern" a man (2:12), and given the likely scenario that women were actually doing so (see volume 1, chapter 4 regarding 1 Timothy 2:12), it might be possible to surmise that "some widow" may have alluded to female false teachers. However, it would be clear to the audience is that Paul does not consider the women in 2:12 nor "some widow" in 5:4 to be the false teachers but rather the men who were influencing them. Where the false teachers in influential leadership positions were men (see 1:20; 3:2), Paul specifically has in view men who are leading others astray. Thus the pejorative association in view of "some widow" with "some"—the false teachers—would most likely be understood as the latter's influence on the former: "some" men were responsible for affecting the lives of "some widow."

38. Knight, *PE*, 217: "Those descendants are designated by two plural terms, τέκνα and ἔκγονα. τέκνον, 'child,' is used here in the plural of immediate descendants of a parent. ἔκγονα . . . placed alongside τέκνα with disjunctive ἤ, in a general sense means 'descendants' and more specifically 'grandchildren.'"

39. This is one reason why a few commentators conclude that "widows" refers to an office or to those who were elders; see Belleville, "Women in Ministry," 102–3; Spencer, *1 Tim*, 125; Thurston, "1 Tim 5.3–16," 159. Yet, if taken this way, the polemical language

"but if someone" (εἰ δέ τις) in 3:5. Paul's concern whether or not some widow "has children (τέκνα ... ἔχει) or those-from-parents" in 5:4a recalls the qualified church leaders in 3:4 who are "holding children" (τέκνα ἔχοντα) in submissiveness.[40] However, unlike Paul's concern for a man leading his own household in 3:4–5, the audience understand that Paul's concern for "some widow" in 5:4a is of a different sort. In 3:4, "holding children" denoted an overseer's unfailing, irreproachable commitment to protect his children amidst the danger of different teaching, that is, to both preserve the teaching and promote godliness in his own children. Here, however, the context does not suggest that "some widow" is seeking to protect her children or those-from-parents; if anything, "some widow" who "has children or those-from-parents" is clinging to them to protect her from material destitution. There is a clear shift in focus: Paul's concern is not merely with "some widow" but rather—and perhaps more so—with the activity of her children and those-from-parents to support her. Furthermore, as the audience heard with Paul's prior use of the term "if" (εἴ, 1:10b; εἴ, 3:1; εἰ, 3:5), the situation in Ephesus "if (εἰ) some widow has children or those-from-parents" (5:4) is not hypothetical or conditional but rather is a real and present circumstance within the church. That is, there are "children or those-from-parents" in the Ephesian church who are not caring for their own widows.

In this context, Paul commands that the children or those-from-parents "must learn first to be-godly to their own household and to give-return repayments to their parents" (5:4a). The sense of the verb "must learn" conveys learning through practice and experience. Moreover, a connection is heard through the linguistic arrangement of the entire 1 Timothy letter. The verb "must learn" (μανθανέτωσαν) here in the fifth microchiasm—the B' unit of the macrochiasm—recalls "must learn" (μανθανέτω) in 2:11 of the second microchiasm—the parallel B unit. Building upon this connection,

---

in the third microchiasm would necessarily identify "*some* widows" not as qualified officers or elders but rather as allies of the false teachers. Thus in the case that the "some widow" in the fifth microchiasm is to be understood in association with "some" in the third microchiasm, then Paul would be denouncing the widows as those who, along with the false teachers, have apostatized from the faith (4:1) and are against the sound teaching that the apostle Paul was commanded by God and sent by Christ Jesus to teach (1:1, 11, 12; 2:7). As will be shown below, rather than qualifying widows for an office, Paul's point in the 5:4–8 minichiasm is ultimately a polemic against the false teachers's ungodly influence upon individual households and, therefore, upon God's household. For further analysis, see Grudem, *Evangelical Feminism*, 255–57.

40. Although the English translation "has" (ἔχει) in 5:4 may introduce cognate confusion with other English translations—e.g., "has denied" (ἤρνηται, 5:8)—the sense of the Greek in this instance would not be accurately conveyed in English as "holds," which has otherwise been the consistent English translation of the verb throughout the letter.

where the disposition of proper conduct for women who profess "godliness" (θεοσέβειαν, 2:10) was in view for 2:11 of the B unit, the audience understand that Paul's command "they must learn . . . to be-godly" (εὐσεβεῖν) in the parallel B' unit intends for the widow's children or those-from-parents to have an outward disposition in accordance with what is proper for those "in faith."[41] Significantly, then, "they must learn . . . to be-godly" implies that the widow's children or those-from-parents are not godly nor acting properly toward her. Indeed, not only are they actively failing to honor her as a mother (5:2–3; LXX Exod 20:12) but in a sense they are also actively allowing her to die by not providing for her. In this case, there may be an allusion to "matricides" (1:9), that is, to "someone" who does not use the law lawfully (1:8), namely the false-teaching overseers. Thus more than "some widow," it seems that her "children or those-from-parents" are those who actually bear the most resemblance of "some." Certainly, where a subtle polemical connotation is heard in the phrase "some widow," it is enhanced or perhaps even defined by her relationship with and the activity of her ungodly "children or those-from-parents."

Throughout the macrochiasm, there has been a progressive theme of godly children in relation to godly parents: Paul's "genuine child (τέκνῳ) in faith" (1:2), that is, "child (τέκνον) Timothy" (1:18); the women's missional "child-parenting" (τεκνογονίας) of those "in faith" (2:15); and the "children" (τέκνα, 3:4; τέκνων, 3:12) in submissiveness according to the commendable leading of qualified men. In halting dissimilarity, however, the "children" (τέκνα) and "those-from-parents" (ἔκγονα) in 5:4a bear no such resemblance, and the cumulative impact of the macrochiasm would be observed. Because the children or those-from-parents of "some widow" are not godly—indeed, they must learn "to be-godly" (εὐσεβεῖν, 5:4a)—the missional duty of God's household to exhibit "godliness" (εὐσεβείᾳ, 2:2) would be hindered; thus, the confessedly great "mystery of godliness" (εὐσεβείας, 3:16) concerning Christ Jesus would not be exclaimed, and training for "godliness" (εὐσέβειαν, 4:7b) as the promise of life eternal with Christ Jesus in heaven would be altogether absent. In short, the devastation associated with the ungodliness of these children or those-from-parents in 5:4a would be far reaching: not only their salvation but also the salvation of others may be lost.[42]

---

41. The verb εὐσεβέω and its cognates are used in the letter to express authentic faith; see volume 1, chapter 4 regarding 1 Timothy 2:2. Belleville, "Christology, Greco-Roman," 227: "Εὐσέβια is something that must be put into practice (1 Tim 5:4) . . . Orthodoxy and orthopraxy are closely connected." See Towner, *Letters*, 339.

42. Where the verb εὐσεβέω and its cognates convey an outward expression of one's existence "in faith," its absence expresses the opposite.

For the faithful among the audience who profess godliness—both men and women—it is likely that Paul's statement in 5:4a would be heard as an alarm call. As much as the church is summoned to honor widows who do not have children or those-from-parents to care for them (5:3), certainly any godly man or woman in the church who has a widow in their own family must first care for her (5:4a). To refuse to do so would not only exhibit ungodliness but would also hinder the missional purpose of God's household. Certainly, the importance of caring for one's own household here in 5:4a emphasizes the apostle Paul's sustained message throughout the letter: as was the case with a qualified overseer, true godliness must first be conducted in the home toward one's own kin before it is demonstrated publicly. Significantly also, the audience understand that Paul's concern for both godliness and its corresponding missional effect undergirds the reason for Paul's imperative "they must learn . . . to be-godly." It is not just to prevent religious duplicity but also to prevent ineffective external witness: to a culture that placed a high premium on familial care—especially of the elderly—and to God who intends for mothers to be honored, it would have tainted the church's reputation if its constituents cared for the members within God's household while neglecting their own parents and grandparents, especially those who were widowed.[43]

The term "first" (πρῶτον) recalls its sustained, interconnected progression throughout the entire macrochiasm, connoting "lead, foremost, prominent." In the first microchiasm Paul was the "first" (πρῶτος, 1:15b; πρώτῳ, 1:16a)—lead—of sinners. In the second microchiasm the "first" (πρῶτον, 2:1)—lead—duty of the church was to pursue missional prayer and a life in all godliness, and Adam was the "first" (πρῶτος, 2:13)—lead—teacher and governor. In the third microchiasm, the "first" (πρῶτον, 3:10)—lead—importance for qualifiied deacons was their testing. Here, then, in the fifth microchiasm, the audience understand that the "first" (πρῶτον, 5:4a)—lead, foremost, prominent—action of children or those-from-parents of widows is to learn to be-godly, that is, to begin to honor their own widowed mother with material provisions (5:2–3). At the same time, the audience would understand that this lead activity to care for one's own family would equally

---

43. To be sure, Paul's concern is the progress of the gospel, which is impeded if the audience live in a less than commendable manner. Nevertheless, the inclusion of Paul's next statement, "for this is acceptable in the sight of God" (5:4b), reiterates the soteriological and theological underpinning of Paul's ethical instructions. Towner, *Letters*, 340: "The insistence on filial responsibilities pervaded traditional Greco-Roman society . . . But whatever this value might add to the appeal, Paul does not base this instruction on natural law or Greek philosophy. Rather, at this point Paul inserts for the second time in this letter a formulaic reason that makes the will of God as expressed in Torah the framework for ethics."

apply to the godly men and women: before honoring those who are "truly widows" (5:3), the lead familial duty for the faithful among the audience is to honor their own "widow" (5:4a).[44]

The specification that one's familial duty is to be-godly "to their own household" (τὸν ἴδιον οἶκον) in 5:4a recalls "his own household" (τοῦ ἰδίου οἴκου) in 3:5. Where Paul clearly draws a parallel between the two verses, the interconnected polemical implication is clear: in the same way that "someone" does not know how to lead "his own household" and, therefore, cannot care-for the church God (3:5), that is, God's household (3:15), so too the children or those-from-parents of "some widow" do not care for those in "their own household" (5:4a) and thus disable the church from caring for those in God's household. Such "children or those-from-parents" in 5:4a are certainly not aligned with the reading, the exhorting, and the teaching of the church (4:13); if they were, then they would be caring for their own household. At the very least, then, the implication is that these children or those-from-parents are not following Timothy and, thus, are not following the commendable teaching (4:6), that is, the sound teaching of the divinely appointed teacher, Paul (1:10b; 2:7).

Paul, therefore, summons such ungodly children or those-from-parents to begin following Timothy and the teaching of the church, namely by a definitive action: "and to give-return repayments to their parents" (5:4a). The conjuction "and" (καί) in 5:4 would most likely be understood epexegetically, specifying that "to be-godly to their own household" means "to give-return repayments to their parents." The alliterative juxtaposition of the alpha prefixes (α-) in the phrase "give-return repayments" (ἀμοιβὰς ἀποδιδόναι) would carry the sense of "render repayments." Here, the rhetorical effect would highlight the reciprocal duty expected of godly children or those-from-parents: in the same way that they have received care in different forms from their predecessors so now they are expected to give back to them what they have received—particularly in the form of material assistance, here, honoring their widowed mother according to the fifth commandment. Indeed, this dynamic of reciprocity would be strengthened through the rhetorical word-play of "those-from-parents" (ἔκγονα) and "parents" (προγόνοις) in 5:4a.[45] Still, the verb "to give-return" (ἀποδιδόναι)

---

44. Barcley, *1 & 2 Tim*, 152: "Taking care of one's own family is so basic to the Christian life that a few verses later Paul equates the failure to do so with unbelief (cf. 5:8). Care for the widows in one's own family is therefore central to true biblical faith and practice."

45. Knight, *PE*, 218: "the rendering 'parents and grandparents' (by *NEB* and *TEV*) accurately conveys the meaning of the word in this context, which refers here primarily to a widowed mother or grandmother. 'Parents' is an acceptable rendering if it is

in 5:4 recalls Christ Jesus, who "gave" (δούς) himself as a ransom on behalf of all (2:6). Thus in addition to the implication of the fifth commandment to honor one's father and mother, the audience understand why Paul is insistent that "to be-godly" for children or those-from-parents includes "to give-return repayments to their parents." That is, where Christ Jesus is the mystery of "godliness" (3:16), "to be-godly" (5:4) involves being like him: Christ "gave" himself (2:6), thus to be-godly is "to give-return" repayments to one's parents (5:4).

In sum, the attention that Paul gives to material provisions for "some widow" in the "a" sub-element conveys the inseparable relationship between a profession of godliness and its resultant expression in tangible good works.[46] Furthermore, Paul intends the audience to understand that there is a degree of distinction between biological and christological family bonds: the lead—"first"—activity of godliness must be toward one's own household (5:4a), then godly care follows toward those in God's household (5:3).

1 Timothy 5:4b: This is Acceptable in the Sight of God

("b" sub-element)

In the "b" sub-element, Paul goes on to declare: "for this is acceptable in the sight of God" (5:4b). As its prior occurrences throught the macrochiasm, the term "this" (τοῦτο) in 5:4b would be a reference to that which precedes, namely Paul's commands for a widow's children or those-from-parents to learn to be-godly toward their own household in 5:4a so that widows in the church may be provided for in 5:3.[47] Moreover, as its prior occurrences throughout the macrochiasm, the audience understand that the conjuction "for" (γάρ) in 5:4b marks the basis for the preceding 5:4a verse. In effect, the audience understand that the reason for children or those-from-parents to be-godly and to give-return repayments to their own household—widows, parents (5:4a)—is because it "is acceptable in the sight of God" (5:4b). Notably, the parallel arrangement of the overall macrochiasm would be underscored. The phrase "this is acceptable in the sight of God" (τοῦτο . . . ἀπόδεκτον ἐνώπιον τοῦ θεοῦ, 5:4b) here in the B' unit of the macrochiasm echoes Paul's statement in the parallel B unit: "This is . . . acceptable

---

understood to include more than one generation."

46. See volume 1, chapter 4 regarding 1 Timothy 2:10.

47. While it is possible that Paul has in view Timothy's exhortations among the elderly and young in the church, the placement of "this" (τοῦτο) within the minichiasm would have the godly conduct toward widows in view. See Knight, *PE*, 218.

in the sight of our Savior God" (τοῦτο . . . ἀπόδεκτον ἐνώπιον τοῦ σωτῆρος ἡμῶν θεοῦ, 2:3). Given both the movement of the phrase through the progression of the macrochiasm and its overarching parallel relation, the audience understand that its latter occurrence in 5:4b both carries forward and communicates the same significance. That is, where the focus in 2:3 of the B unit was on salvation, namely the "Savior (σωτῆρος) God" who desires all humans "to be-saved" (σωθῆναι, 2:4a), Paul intends his audience to understand that salvation is at stake in 5:4b of the parallel B' unit. The parallel activities in the B and B' units, therefore, highlight the same point and are meant to be heard together. In alignment with the Savior God's saving, missional purposes, the "first" (πρῶτον)—lead—activity of the church in the B unit of the macrochiasm was to missionally pray on behalf of all humans and to lead a life in all "godliness" (εὐσεβείᾳ); in parallel, the "first" (πρῶτον)—lead—activity of children or those-from-parents in 5:4b of the B' unit is "to be-godly" (εὐσεβεῖν) to their widows and parents. Such would missionally attract those-outside to God's household via the gospel's influence on their own households. Indeed, it would evidence that the children or those-from-parents have aligned themselves with the saving purposes of the one and same Savior God who is proclaimed throughout the OT and NT as being a warrior for the orphaned and widowed.[48]

As the "b" sub-element concludes, and as heard throughout the macrochiasm, Paul's twofold point is clear. On the one hand, salvation is evidenced by actions that are aligned with the Savior God. On the other hand, failure to comply with what is acceptable to the Savior God evidences the lack of salvation, that is, the rejection of God. For the children or those-from-parents among the audience—both those "in faith" and those evidently not—Paul is calling them to salvific action for others, if not also for themselves.

1 Timothy 5:5a: She Who Is Truly a Widow, Left-Remaining, Has Hoped Upon God

("c" sub-element)

As the first half of the minichiasm's pivot, the "c" sub-element begins, "But she who is truly a widow and who is left-remaining has hoped upon God" (5:5a). Just as "But" (δέ) contrasted "some widow" who has children or

---

48. E.g., Exod 22:22–24; Isa 1:17. Wall with Steele, *1 & 2 Tim*, 128: "The letter of James reflects this same concern and considers care for widows in their distress a hallmark of the religion approved by God (Jas 1:27; cf. Acts 6:1–7)."

those-from-parents in 5:4a versus "widows who are truly widows" (ὄντως χήρας) in 5:3, so too the disjunctive "But" (δέ) is heard again to contrast "she who is truly a widow" (ὄντως χήρα) in 5:5a with "some widow" who has children or those-from-parents in 5:4a. Furthermore, as in 5:4a, the conjuction "and" (καί) that immediately follows the phrase "truly a widow" in 5:5a would likely be heard epexegetically as a specifying term. In effect, the audience understand that "she who is truly a widow" refers to she "who is "left-remaining," undoubtedly a woman—contra "some widow"—who is literally alone without any children or those-from-parents. Two observations are worth noting. First, the passive voice of the participle "left-remaining" suggests that such a widow's situation is not of her own doing.[49] Given Paul's sustained contrast between the two types of widows, the implication for the audience may be that she who is "truly a widow" in 5:3 and 5:5a is unwillingly alone whereas "some widow" in 5:4a is in some way responsible for her situation.[50]

Second, the participle "left-remaining" (μεμονωμένη) is reminiscent of Paul's exhortation for Timothy "to remain" (προσμεῖναι) in Ephesus (1:3), Paul's instruction for women to "remain (μείνωσιν) in faith" to evidence their salvation (2:15), and Paul's command for Timothy to "strongly-remain" (ἐπίμενε) in his careful devotion to godliness and the teaching of the church (4:16). Given the sustained presence of the false teachers in the context of each prior occurrence and, therefore, the sure difficulty for Timothy and the women to "remain" and "strongly-remain" against such opposition, Paul's identification that she who is "truly a widow" and "left-remaining" would indicate to the audience that such widows are not only those—like Timothy and the women—who persevere against the opposition of "some"—the false teachers—but also who endure an extremely difficult situation, particularly the lack of material sustenance. Indeed, without any family to provide for them—likely as the result of being left alone through the death or

---

49. Hearon and Maloney suggest: "Probably women who had been abandoned by living husbands, especially if the cause of the breach was the woman's embrace of Christianity, were classed with the widows" ("Listen to the Voices of the Women," 43). Certainly, such abandoned women were unwillingly alone.

50. Where the term "widow" (χήρα) "covers a wide spectrum of women, including virgins, women living apart from their husbands, divorced women, and women whose husbands were dead" (Kartzow, *Destabalizing the Margins*, 113), Paul may be further narrowing his definition of the type of widows whom the church must honor (5:3). In this case, such widows are (1) only women who are alone without their own family to care for them and (2) only women who have not initiated their aloneness (e.g., not divorcing or living apart from their husbands unnecessarily). In the case that a widow was living apart from her husband or divorced, the implication would likely be that she should first seek to be reconciled to her husband.

abandonment of her husband or family—such a woman is "truly a widow" and in need of honor and care from the church (5:3). At the same time, given the explicit contrast between "truly a widow" and "some widow," the audience may hear a further implication intended by Paul. The fact that "some widow" is not "left-remaining" both indicates that she is not alone and—more significantly—that neither is she remaining "in faith" with Timothy (1:3; 4:16) and the women (2:15) against the false teaching of "some."

Having described the type of woman who is "truly a widow" in negative terms, Paul goes on to positively define her as she "who has hoped upon God" (5:5a). The phrase "has hoped upon God" (ἤλπικεν ἐπὶ θεὸν) recalls Paul and Timothy in the previous microchiasm who "have hoped upon the living God" (ἠλπίκαμεν ἐπὶ θεῷ ζῶντι, 4:10). Here, then, the audience understand that a woman who is "truly a widow" is not only allied with the apostle Paul and his authorized representative Timothy but also has the living God as her Savior (4:10). Thus as a widow who "has hoped" (ἤλπικεν) upon God (5:5a), along with Paul, Timothy, and the faithful in the audience, she shares in their common "hope" (ἐλπίδος), namely Christ Jesus (1:1). In short, Paul makes clear that "she who is truly a widow" exists in the realm "in faith," thus articulating why the church under Timothy's leadership is to "Honor widows—those truly widows" (5:3): surrounded by an entire family "in faith"—children (1:2, 18; 2:15), fathers and brothers (5:1), mothers and sisters (5:2)—widows who are truly widows live in God's household, the place where mothers are honored in the sight of God.

1 Timothy 5:5b–6: Remains in the Supplications and Prayers Night and Day

("c'" sub-element)

As the second half of the minichiasm's pivot, Paul continues his description of she who is truly a widow in the "c'" sub-element: "and remains in the supplications and the prayers night and day" (5:5a). The verb "remains" (προσμένει) in 5:5b of the "c'" sub-element recalls that she is "left-remaining" (μεμονωμένη) in 5:5a of the parallel "c" sub-element. In effect, Paul is doubly emphasizing the unswerving and unswaying disposition of "truly a widow" who exists "in faith." What is more, that she remains "in the supplications and the prayers night and day" draws out the force of the verb "remains," namely that she persists in beseeching God for help—the one upon whom she has hoped (5:5a)—thus displaying the sincerity of not only her hope but also her salvation. Still, the rhetorical juxtaposition of the passive verb "left-remaining" in the "c" sub-element and the active verb "remains" in the "c'" sub-element is certainly intentional, conveying to the audience that although she is biologically alone on no account of her own—she is completely passive in this sense—she is active in prayer and conversation with God, who is the Father of the household in which she lives (1:2).

Furthermore, the parallel arrangement of the overall macrochiasm would be underscored. The terms "supplications and prayers" (ταῖς δεήσεσιν καὶ ταῖς προσευχαῖς, 5:5b) in the fifth microchiasm—the B' unit of the macrochiasm—echoes Paul's exhortation for "supplications, prayers" (δεήσεις προσευχάς), 2:1) to be-done on behalf of all humans in the second microchiasm—the parallel B unit.[51] Given both the movement of the terms through the progression of the macrochiasm and their overarching parallel relation, the audience are to understand that the latter's occurrence in 5:5b both carries forward and communicates the same significance. That is, where the focus in 2:1 of the B unit was on the missional activity of the entire church, Paul intends his audience to understand that in 5:4b of the parallel B' unit she who is "truly a widow" embodies the prominent missional activity of what is expected for all who have been saved by the Savior God (2:3–4a). Indeed, such a widow who has hoped upon God (5:5a) remains in supplication and prayer not only—and perhaps not even primarily—for her own needs but rather for the salvation of all humans, that is, for the advancement and acceptance of the faithful word concerning Christ Jesus—the gospel.[52] Furthermore, that she does so "night and day" (νυκτὸς καὶ ἡμέρας) indicates her tireless constancy and dedication to bring those-outside into the household of God through supplication and prayer—in effect, her missional child-parenting as she remains "in faith" (2:15).[53] Here, then, much like Paul and Timothy who toil and agonize to preserve the teaching and promote godliness in God's missional household (4:10), the

---

51. For nuances of the terms "supplications" and "prayers," see volume 1, chapter 4 regarding 1 Timothy 2:1.

52. It may be observed that the widow who is "left-remaining" (μεμονωμένη) but who "remains" (προσμένει) in prayer (5:4) echoes—perhaps also paralleling—Timothy's calling to "remain" (προσμεῖναι) in Ephesus (1:3) and to "strongly-remain" (ἐπίμενε) in the teaching (4:16). Both Timothy and this widow remain in a specific circumstance, yet both continue in missional work. It seems that by remaining in Ephesus, Timothy is able to ensure that continual care is provided for the widow who is left-remaining so that she may do missional work, remaining in prayer.

53. The juxtaposition of the terms "night" and "day" would most likely be heard as a rhetorical merism, effectively including any and all possible times. Barclay, *1 & 2 Tim*, 153: "The phrase 'night and day' points not so much to the duration of prayers, but to their constancy." Contra Knight, *PE*, 219: "'Night and day' describes when the widow is involved in prayer."

audience understand that she who is truly a widow toils and agonizes in a similar way, that is, "night and day" in missional supplications and prayers as a vital member of God's household.

To conclude the "c'" sub-element, Paul states, "but she who is self-indulgent—living—is dead" (5:6). As in 5:4a and 5:5a, the audience again hear the disjunctive "but" (δέ) to signify a contrast. In effect, Paul pits the two types of widows against each other. While "she who is truly a widow" is without any material sustenance yet has hoped upon God and, for as long as she is alive, remains in the supplications and the prayers for the salvation—life eternal—of all humans (5:5a-b; cf. 2:1), in stark contrast, the other type of widow is "she who is self-indulgent—living—is dead" (5:6).[54] The present participle "self-indulgent" (σπαταλῶσα) describes a woman who continues to live in luxury.[55] Significantly, then, Paul's rhetorical arrangement of the overall macrochiasm would be heard: "self-indulgent" here in the B' unit of the macrochiasm would be reminiscent of Paul's description in the parallel B unit regarding the improper way for women who profess godliness to cosmetic themselves, namely with braids and gold or pearls or rich attire rather than with modesty and self-control and good works (2:9–10). Undoubtedly, "she who is self-indulgent" functionally requires no material assistance from the church—indeed, she is the antithesis of the "truly widows" who are in need and whom the church must honor (5:3, 5a–b). Positively, the audience are to understand that the "self-indulgent" widow in 5:6 of the B' unit is the archetype of a woman who does not do what is proper for women who profess godliness in the parallel B unit, spending her resources on "rich attire" (2:9) rather than on "good works" (2:10) that share God's desire for all humans to-be-saved (2:3–4a).

Indeed, as much as the children or those-from-parents of "some widow" are not aligned with God's purposes in 5:4a–b, so also the "self-indulgent" widow in 5:6 is not aligned with God's purposes. Instead of sharing the Savior God's desire for all humans to-be-saved (2:4a)—as does "she who

---

54. Knight, *PE*, 219: "The contrast with the godly widow is striking: The godly widow trusts in God and seeks first his kingdom; this widow lives only for herself."

55. For various interpretations of this term, see Collins, *1 & 2 Tim*, 138, who interprets it as a description of her refusal to share her possessions; Easton, *PE*, 152, who interprets it as a description of sexual promiscuity; Mounce, *PE*, 283, who interprets it to generalized self-absorption.

It may be worth noting that where the "self-indulgent" widow who lives in luxury (5:6) is "some widow" (5:4a), the implication may be that "some widow" not only has children or those-from-parents to care for her (5:4a) but also is over-indulging with the financial provisions she receives—possibly from the church. Hence, Paul's description qualifies what type of widow—to be sure, a godly woman who is alone—is to receive help from the church.

is truly a widow" who remains in the supplications and the prayers night and day for the salvation of all (2:1; 5:5)—"she who is self-indulgent" has no concern for missional child-parenting nor supplications and prayers. Thus the "self-indulgent" widow effectively evidences by her own actions that she is not "in faith," that is, will not be-saved (2:15). Such a dire implication is punctuated by the concluding phrase "living—is dead" (5:6). Undoubtedly, Paul intends for his audience to hear the full effect of such bleak irony: although the self-indulgent widow appears "living" (ζῶσα), she "is dead" (τέθνηκεν). Given the contrast to "she who is truly a widow" in 5:5 who has hoped upon God and thus exists in the realm "in faith," that is, with the only God, the King of the eternities (1:17), the audience understand that the self-indulgent widow "is dead" in an eternal sense because her hope is not upon God.[56] To be sure, antithetical to those who would-inevitably-come to have-faith upon Christ Jesus for "life (ζωήν) eternal" (1:16), who live in the church of "the living (ζῶντος) God" (3:15), who train for the promise of "life" (ζωῆς) for the present and for the inevitable-coming (4:8b), and who have hoped upon "the living (ζῶντι) God" (4:10), the audience understand that the self-indulgent widow is not "living" (ζῶσα) with the eternal God—she is eternally "dead" (τέθνηκεν).[57]

As the second half of the pivot concludes in the "c'" sub-element, the contrast between "she who is truly a widow" (5:3, 5) and "she who is self-indulgent" (5:4a, 6) echoes the sustained polemic throughout the macrochiasm between Paul, Timothy, and the faithful in the Ephesian church over and against "some" apostate false-teaching overseers who have not only become-shipwrecked regarding the faith (1:20) but also lead and influence the church to do the same. Thus as Paul's concern is for the audience to enhance their discernment of truth (2:4b, 7, 3:15, 4:3b) versus that which is false (1:10a; 2:7; 4:2) and also their allegiance to God, Christ Jesus, and the Spirit (1:1, 2; 2:5; 4:1) versus Satan, the devil, deceitful spirits, and demons (1:20; 3:6–7; 4:1), so too Paul intends for his audience to discern between these opposing types of widows.

---

56. Spencer aptly captures Paul's point: "In contrast to hoping on and praying to God is living luxuriously (5:6), which proleptically has already resulted in not eternal life but eternal death" (*1 Tim*, 125). Knight, *PE*, 219: "Although this widow would likely think that she is really 'living it up' and that the godly widow's life is really 'dead,' Paul's verdict is just the opposite. While being physically alive . . . she is as a matter of fact already spiritually dead."

57. The aural similarity between "dead" (τέθνηκεν) and "children" (τέκνα) may be worth noting. Given that neither the "children" in 5:4 nor the widow in 5:6 are described by Paul as existing "in faith," there may be a rhetorical implication between the "dead" widow who is not concerned with salvation and the ungodly "children" who do not honor her.

1 Timothy 5:7: Charge, That They Might Be Irreproachable

("b'" sub-element)

In the "b'" sub-element, Paul states, "And these charge, that they might be irreproachable" (5:7). As throughout the macrochiasm, "these" (ταῦτα) in 5:7 would be heard in reference to what precedes, namely Paul's discussion about caring for widows. Yet, its placement within the 5:4–8 minichiasm would provide a significance nuance. The demonstrative "these" (ταῦτα) in 5:7 recalls "this" (τοῦτο) in 5:4b of the parallel "b" sub-element wherein Paul's concern was specifically for the ungodly children or those-from-parents to do what is acceptable in the sight of God, namely that "they must learn first to be-godly to their own household and to give-return repayments to their parents" (5:4a). Here in 5:7, then, given the parallel connection of the "b" and "b'" sub-elements in the minichiasm, the audience understand that Paul has in view and is addressing the children or those-from-parents of "some widow" rather than the widow herself.[58] That is, in 5:7 Timothy is to charge "these"—the matters prescribed in 5:4—to the children or those-from-parents.[59] Such would undoubtedly have corollary implications upon both the church's ability to honor true widows (5:3, 5) and the self-indulgent widow (5:6) who, by her children or those-from-parents's newfound godly actions toward her (5:4a), may herself be influenced to live a life of godliness as a woman "in faith" rather than living a dead life (5:6).

The verb "charge" (παράγγελλε) recalls its earlier occurrences throughout the macrochiasm in direct application to "some": Timothy is to "charge" (παραγγείλῃς) some not to teach-different" (1:3); in view of "some" who have turned-aside from a without-hypocrisy faith, Paul specifies that the end of the "charge" (παραγγελίας) is love, namely intending the restoration of "some" to faith (1:5–6); Paul entrusts the "charge" (παραγγελίαν) to Timothy, that he might war the commendable war against "some" who regarding the faith have become-shipwrecked (1:18–19); and in view of "some" who are holding-toward teachings of demons and who promote ascetic bodily training (4:1, 3, 8), Timothy is commanded to correctively "Charge" (παράγγελλε) and teach the things concerning godliness and God's universal offer of salvation to all humans (4:11).[60] To be sure, Paul's

---

58. This observation is significant for the audience's understanding of the entirety of 5:7.

59. Knight suggests that "these" (ταῦτα) in 5:7 refers only to 5:4. I agree in part, acknowledging that the ripple effects of carrying out Paul's command in 5:7 would have direct implications for all of 5:3–6 (*PE*, 220).

60. It may be worth noting that the inclusion of the conjuction "And" (καί) at the

command for Timothy to "charge" in 5:7 would carry the same authoritative force. Yet, far more significantly, the further implication is that "these" matters in 5:7 concerning the children or those-from-parents to be-godly to their own household (5:4a) pertain to the same authoritative, corrective treatment—the "charge"—that concerned the false teachers in 1:3, 1:5, 1:18, and 4:11—the "charge." The rhetorical connection, therefore, would suggest to the audience that the ungodly children or those-from-parents whom Timothy must "charge" are either strongly influenced by the false teachers or are themselves young-plant false teachers who do not know how to lead their own household or care-for God's church (3:5–6).

Still, applied toward the children or those-from-parents of "some widow" (5:4a), the "charge" would convey an integrated outcome. On the one hand, it is the onus of the children or those-from-parents to be-godly and proactively provide for their own household—to give-return repayments to their parents and widows (5:4a)—so that the church can proactively provide for widows who are left-remaning (5:3, 5). On the other hand, there seems to be a correlation between the ungodly *children or those-from-parents* who selfishly do not provide for "some widow" (5:4a) and the *self-indulgent widow* who is entirely focused on herself (5:6). Indeed, where one seems to lead to the other in a cycle of ungodliness, it is fitting that some self-indulgent widow (5:4a, 6) has ungodly children or those-from-parents (5:4a) and vice versa. The command for Timothy to "charge" the children or those-from-parents (5:7), therefore, would not only intend to stir them toward godliness (5:4a) but also to stir "some" widow (5:4a), such that she would no longer be self-indulgent (5:6) but rather would have hope upon God and remain in supplication and prayer night and day (5:5). Indeed, Paul's intent is that the self-indulgent widow would not stay eternally dead but instead would be living eternally in God's household (cf. 5:6). The net result of Paul's command for Timothy to "charge" in 5:7 would effectively resolve the tension of the minichiasm and have a missional effect, enabling "truly widows" to be provided for (5:3, 5) while also transforming both the ungodly children or those-from-parents (5:4a) and the self-indulgent widow (5:6) to be a godly family. Such a godly family would be glad participants in what is acceptable in the sight of God (2:3; 5:4), thus evidencing their existence "in faith,"

---

beginning of 5:7 ("And these charge") may not be insignificant. Likely conveying "also," the conjunction would suggest that Paul's instructions here in the 5:4–8 minichiasm are not any less important than the other matters that Timothy must charge to the audience in the letter. The nearly identical repetition of 4:11 in 5:7 seems to corroborate that Paul's commands in 5:7 are equally important for God's missional household:

   4:11: "Charge these-things and teach" (παράγγελλε ταῦτα καὶ δίδασκε);
   5:7: "And these charge" (καὶ ταῦτα παράγγελλε).

that is, their salvation. Still, the far reaching implications of Paul's command would be apparent: not only would the now godly children or those-from-parents (5:4a) provide for the widows in their own household—namely those widows who were once self-indulgent (5:6; cf. 5:4a) but are now "in faith"—thereby making it possible for the church to honor "widows—those truly widows" (5:3, 5), but also, now as members of God's family, the godly children or those-from-parents themselves would use any of their additional resources to participate in the calling of the church to honor "widows—those truly widows" in God's household (5:3).

Paul concludes the "b" sub-element by explicitly stating the overall effect of charging the children or those-from-parents: "that they might be irreproachable" (5:7).[61] The term "irreproachable" (ἀνεπίλημπτον) recalls Paul's umbrella descriptor of a qualified overseer in 3:2 who must be "irreproachable" (ἀνεπίλημπτον) particularly in the way he leads his own household (3:2–5).[62] Here, then, the progression of the macrochiasm would advance the implication of the term: not only is it necessary for overseers of God's household to be "irreproachable," but Paul considers it equally important for the children or those-from-parents in God's household to be "irreproachable." Thus the audience understand that the household-law of God "in faith" is not only top-down but also bottom-up: church officers lead the "children" (τέκνα) of their own household (3:4) so that God's household may function as intended, and, in turn, "children (τέκνα) or those-from-parents" care for their own households (5:4) so that God's household may function as intended—in this case, by caring for "widows—those truly widows" (5:3). In short, both in God's household and in godly households, the older care for the young, and the younger care for the old.

In sum, given that Paul applies "irreproachable" to those on both ends of the spectrum—leaders and children—the audience understand that the rhetorical function of the term expresses Paul's concern for all those in God's household to be irreproachable, especially in matters pertaining to family

---

61. Where the "b" and "b'" sub-element parallelism of the minichiasm indicates that "children or those-from-parents" are in view of 5:7, it is evident that "they might be irreproachable" also refers the children or those-from-parents (5:4a). To be sure, there is disagreement on the subject of the verb "might be" (ὦσιν), with the suggestion that the "they" in view relates either to the audience or to the widows. However, given the structure of the minichiasm, with its focus on the families of the widows, there should be little doubt that "they" pertains specifically to the children or those-from-parents. For further support of this conclusion, see discussions in Knight, *PE*, 220; Marshall, *PE*, 589; Mounce, *PE*, 274.

62. The repetition of the verbal cognates "to be" (εἶναι) in 3:2 and "might be" (ὦσιν) in 5:7 would also be apparent: "to be irreproachable" (ἀνεπίλημπτον εἶναι, 3:2); "might be irreproachable" (ἀνεπίλημπτον ὦσιν, 5:7).

life within their own households. To be sure, such "irreproachable" lifestyles at home and thus in the church would enable all of the faithful—old and young alike—to be missional by having a commendable testimony from those-outside (3:7). Still, as the "b" sub-element concludes, the audience would perceive a faint but clear conceptual echo: in the same way that "if someone does not know how to lead his own household, how will he care-for the church of God?" (3:5), so also if the children or those-from-parents do not care for their own household, how will they care for the church of God? The health of one's own household and the health of the household of God are both integral and inseparable.

1 Timothy 5:8: If Someone Does Not Provide-for His Own, He has Denied the Faith

("a'" sub-element)

In the concluding "a'" sub-element, Paul conveys the severe, climactic implication of the minichiasm: "But if someone does not provide-for those of his own and especially for household-members, he has denied the faith and is worse-than the without-faith" (5:8). As heard throughout the current minichiasm, the disjunctive "But" (δέ) again signifies a contrast. In effect, unlike the result of children or those-from-parents's adherence to Timothy's charge—being godly to their own household (5:4), irreproachable in God's household (5:7), and thus indicating their existence "in faith"—the result of children or those-from-parents who do not adhere to Timothy's charge is the opposite. Indeed, the latter's result is clear: "if someone does not provide-for those of his own and especially for household-members, he has denied the faith and is worse-than the without-faith" (5:8).

Consistent with Paul's prior use of the term "if" (εἴ, 1:10; εἴ, 3:1; εἰ, 3:5; εἰ, 5:4) to indicate a real and present circumstance within the church, it is evident that "if (εἰ) someone" in 5:8 is not hypothetical or conditional but rather is already happening in the Ephesian church. That is, the children or those-from-parents are neither providing for their own families members nor for God's family members "in faith."[63] Furthermore, the phrase "But if someone" (εἰ δέ τις) in 5:8 of the "a'" sub-element recalls "But if some (εἰ δέ τις) widow" in 5:4 of the parallel "a" sub-element. Significantly, where "someone" (τις) in 5:8 is understood by the audience in reference to the

---

63. That "those of his own" refers to the biological families and "household-members" refers to those in God's household who exist in the familial realm "in faith, see discussion below.

children or those-from-parents in 5:7—thus to the children or those-from-parents in 5:4—the progression of the minichiasm corroborates that "some" (τις) in 5:4 does not primarily have the widow in view but rather her children or those-from-parents, that is, their impact upon her. Such is emphasized to the audience by the fact that the children or those-from-parents in 5:4 clearly do not provide-for "their own household" (ἴδιον οἶκον) in the same way that "someone" in 5:8 "does not provide-for those of his own (τῶν ἰδίων) and especially for household-members (οἰκείων)." Furthermore, given that the focus here is on those who neglect to provide-for their households, the audience likely recall that the phrase "But if someone (εἰ δέ τις) does not provide-for those of his own (τῶν ἰδίων) and especially for household-members (οἰκείων)" in 5:8 has in view the unqualified men in 3:5: "but if someone (εἰ δέ τις) does not know how to lead his own household" (ἰδίου οἴκου), how will he care-for the church of God?" Thus it seems that Paul's statement is polemical and intended against the false-teaching overseers, or at least those who are directly influenced by them. Furthermore, the false teachers seem to bear a striking resemblance to the children or those-from-parents whose first—lead—activity must be to learn to be-godly (5:4a), that is, to do what is actually acceptable in the sight of God (5:4b). In this case, just as children in submissiveness to Paul and Timothy's leadership in the church would evidence their familial relationship "in faith" to Paul, Timothy, and faithful among the audience (cf. 3:4), the audience understand that if the children or those-from-parents do not adhere to Timothy's charge (5:7), then it is clear that "if someone does not provide-for those of his own" (5:8) identifies those who are not children in submissiveness to Paul and Timothy and thus are not "in faith." Indeed, Paul goes on to declare that such children or those-from-parents have "denied the faith" (5:8). Undoubtedly, both the ungodly children or those-from-parents (5:4, 8) and the unqualified overseers (3:5) have a low view of one's own family, which is antithetical to the godly leadership and lifestyle that accords with the sound teaching of Paul.

Where the false teachers or those influenced by their teaching are in view, the audience would hear the phrase "those of his own and especially for household-members" in 5:8 with a twofold nuance. On the one hand, the pronoun "own" (ἰδίων) recalls "own" (ἴδιον) in 5:4a and "own" (ἰδίου) in 3:5. Here, if alluding to the false teachers, Paul is emphasizing that "someone"—the false teachers—are those who do not provide for their own widows and parents (5:4a) in the same way that they cannot lead their own household (3:5). On the other hand, the latter half of the phrase "and especially for household-members" would most likely be understood in reference to providing for widows who are truly widows, namely the godly, elderly widows "in faith" (5:3, 5). Although it is possible that "and" (καί) might be heard epexegetically as a specifying term—the sense being, "his own, that is, especially for his own household-members"—the qualifier "especially" seems to indicate a nuanced meaning.[64] The qualifying term "especially" (μάλιστα) recalls "especially" (μάλιστα) in 4:10 of the previous microchiasm wherein those "of the faithful"—those in God's household—were clearly in view. Here, then, in 5:8 the audience would likely understand "especially" not as specifying the members of one's own biological household but rather as referring to "of the faithful" (4:10), that is, the "household-members" of God (5:8). Thus similar to 4:10, Paul's statement "does not provide-for his own and especially for household-members" in 5:8 is highly polemical: those under the influence of the false teachers neither provide-for their own widows (5:4a, 8) nor for the truly widows in God's household (5:3, 5:5). To be sure, this dual neglect for one's own household—"those of his own"—and for God's household—"household-memebers"—in 5:8 is a precise echo of the unqualified men in 3:5 who cannot lead their own household and cannot care-for the church of God.

Certainly, it would come as no surprise to the audience that "someone" such as this "has denied the faith and is worse-than the without-faith" (5:8). The phrase "someone . . . has denied the faith" (τις . . . τὴν πίστιν ἤρνηται) echoes Paul's statement that "some will apostasy from the faith" (ἀποστήσονταί τινες τῆς πίστεως) in 4:1 of the previous microchiasm. The connection here seems to further imply that Paul has the false teachers in view of his command for Timothy to "charge" in 5:7. In this case, the audience understand that the apostate false teachers are those who neither provide-for those of their own household nor for God's own household. Furthermore, Paul intends to emphasize that such absence of a tangible expression of "the faith" toward one's own family and toward God's family is a clear indication that "someone" has *already* denied the faith.[65] In short, by failing to provide-for those belonging to God's household, that is "especially for household-members" (5:8), "someone" demonstrates that he himself does not belong to it. The audience understand that "someone" (τις) who "has denied the faith" (τὴν πίστιν) in 5:8 bears the mark of none other than "some" (τινες) who "regarding the faith (τὴν πίστιν)

---

64. Contra Knight, *PE*, 221; Marshall, *PE*, 590.

65. Notice the use of the perfect tense, "has [already] denied" (ἀρνέομαι).
Given the connection of 5:8 to 4:1, it may be worth noting that even with Paul's use of the future tense "will apostasy" (ἀποστήσονταί), the clear implication of the fourth minichiasm was that "some" had already apostatized; see volume 2, chapter 3 regarding 1 Timothy 4:4a.

have become-shipwrecked" (1:19)—to be sure, the false teachers in the Ephesian church.

Moreover, to further emphasize the dire implications of "someone" who has denied the faith, Paul continues with a description: "and is worse-than the without-faith" (5:8). Here, the weight of Paul's rhetoric doubles up: a denial of "the faith" (τὴν πίστιν) is worse-than simply being "without-faith" (ἀπίστου). To be sure, such was heard in the first microchiasm wherein the false teachers—unlike Paul who without-knowing did "in unfaithfulness" (ἀπιστίᾳ, 1:13)—were acting in ignorance even *after* having experienced the gospel that exhibits God's radiant glory. That is, the false teachers were not only acting like those "in unfaithfulness" but were doing so as those who once had faith.[66] It comes as no surprise, then, that "someone" who "has denied the faith," indeed, is worse than the "without-faith" (5:8), for they seem to be "some" who have actively turned-aside, rejected, and apostatized from the faith that they once had (1:6, 19; 4:1).

In sum of the 5:4–8 minichiasm, the audience hear that Paul's overarching point is that the faithful in God's household—those who exist "in faith"—both provide-for "those of their own" family members—widows, parents (5:4a, 8)—and for God's own familial "household-members"—widows who are truly widows (5:3, 5; cf. 5:8). Such dual care is not only an exhibition of godliness that is acceptable to God (4:4a–b) but is expected of everyone living in God's household.[67] The missional implication is straightforward: God's household cannot be attractive to those-outside (3:7) and those "without-faith" (5:8) when its family members do not even take care of each other or their own biological families. God's missional household must be-godly from the inside. Those who are ungodly must learn to provide-for those of their own and thus to provide-for God's own household-members.

1 Timothy 5:9: A Widow Must Be-Enrolled

(B Element, continued)

After the 5:4–8 minichiasm, Paul in 5:9 concludes the B element: "A widow must be-enrolled not being less than sixty years, woman of one man." (5:9). Where Paul is further qualifying the type of widow in God's household

---

66. See volume 1, chapter 3 regarding 1 Timothy 1:13.

67. Notably, rather than including the entire phrase "This is commendable and acceptable in the sight of our Savior God" (2:3), it may be that Paul intentionally omits the adjective "commendable" from 5:4b, effectively conveying that care for one's own family is such a basic duty that it would not command any admiration.

whom the church must honor with material provisions, the audience hear this concluding verse (5:9) as a conceptual parallel with the opening statement regarding widows who are truly widows (5:3). Several observations are worth noting. First, the passive verb "must be-enrolled" (καταλεγέσθω) suggests that the audience are to be proactive in the process of enrolling widows for material assistance.[68] That is, as much as she who is truly a widow was passive in the process by which she was left-remaining (5:5a), the church must be active to ensure that her needs are met. Second, Paul states a basic age requirement: a widow must be-enrolled "not being less than sixty years" (μὴ ἔλαττον ἐτῶν ἑξήκοντα γεγονυῖα). For the first-century audience, the minimum age of "sixty years" (ἐτῶν ἑξήκοντα) would not only suggest that she is too old to remarry and have children but also too old to work and provide sufficiently for herself.[69] Thus for Paul's audience who are to proactively enroll qualified widows to receive material sustenance, the explicit minimum age requirement would have been a criterion for discerning which widows were truly in need.[70] Third and finally, the qualifying phrase "woman of one man" (ἑνὸς ἀνδρὸς γυνή) in 5:9 echoes Paul's qualification for qualified overseers and deacons to be the "man of one woman" (μιᾶς γυναικὸς ἄνδρα, 3:2; μιᾶς γυναικὸς ἄνδρες, 3:12). Where marital fidelity was the concern of Paul's statement in 3:2 and 3:12, the audience understand that Paul considers the widow's fidelity—both previously as a married woman and now as an unmarried widow—to be a corresponding qualification of her godliness, that is, evidence that she lives in the household of God and is thus a widow who is truly a widow (5:3, 5).[71] In sum, the B element

---

68. That the purpose for widows being enrolled is to receive help—not for them to serve in the church—see Marshall, *PE*, 592.

69. Paul's specification "not being less than sixty years" is deliberate, functionally setting the maximum age at which a woman could remarry and biologically conceive children; see Amundsen and Diers, "The Age of Menopause," 79–86. Towner, *Letters*, 346: "Furthermore, given the typical life span of that culture and day, the age stipulation would mean that these real widows were in the closing years of their lives . . ." See also Kelly, *PE*, 115; Marshall, *PE*, 593.

70. It may worth noting that the phrase "not (μή) less than sixty years" recalls Paul's prior use of the negative particle "not" (μή) in reference to the false teachers, e.g., "not (μή) avaricious" (3:8). Given that "self-indulgent" widows (5:6) may have been receiving and abusing financial help from the church, Paul's criterion "not less than sixty years" may have implied to the audience that the self-indulgent were both less than sixty years and influenced by the false teachers.

71. That fidelity applies to both one's status as married or single, see volume 2, chapter 2 regarding 1 Timothy 3:2.

Not a few commentators suggest that the statement "woman of one man" conveys that a woman was only married once (e.g., Bellville, "1 Tim," 99; Hanks, *The Subversive Gospel*, 169; Montague, *First and Second Tim*, 109). "However," as Hanks observes, "this

of the microchiasm concludes with a summons to proactively help those who are truly widows in the church—those "in faith" who are part of God's family, are elderly, and do not have any other family to care for them.

1 Timothy 5:10a: In Commendable Works

(C Element)

As the microchiasm progresses forward, the C element continues to describe the widow whom the church must honor: "in commendable works testified" (5:10a). The prepositional phrase "in commendable works" (ἐν ἔργοις καλοῖς) indicates for the audience that a widow who must be enrolled for help is one who persisted or abided in that which is commendable as part and parcel of her life. Such a description would remind the audience of "she who is truly a widow . . . and remains in the supplications and the prayers night and day" (5:5)—supplications and prayers (2:1) being that which is "commendable" (καλόν) and acceptable in the sight of the Savior God in the parallel B unit of the macrochiasm (2:3). Furthermore, commendable "works" (ἔργοις, 5:10a) here in the B' unit of the macrochiasm recalls Paul's earlier statement in the parallel B unit that women in the church are to cosmetic themselves with "good works (ἔργων)" (2:10), wherein Paul was concerned with missional godliness for the sake of the women attracting outsiders to Christ Jesus. Here, then, as the audience discern whom among the widows must be honored as truly widows, the arrangement of the macrochiasm highlights the qualifying theme: in line with the missional activity of those in the church who pray (2:1) and promote missional godliness (2:2, 10) in the B unit of the macrochiasm, the church must honor those widows in the parallel B' unit who are immersed in such missional works of God's household.

Furthermore, here in the B' unit of the macrochiasm, the participle "testified" (μαρτυρουμένη) in 5:10 recalls its cognate noun in 2:6 of the parallel B unit, the "testimony" (μαρτύριον) concerning Christ Jesus. Given both the progression of the macrochiasm and the overarching parallel relation between the B and B' units, the audience understand a twofold implication. On the one hand, as much as the widow is immersed "in commendable works"—in a subjective sense, her own actions as proof—so also her works

---

would make it impossible for a remarried young widow who was widowed again to be supported by the church" (*The Subversive Gospel*, 169). It is highly unlikely that Paul had in view a "one-marriage woman"; rather, the immediate and overall context of the letter suggests that fidelity is the concern. See Knight, *PE*, 223; Marshall, *PE*, 594.

are "testified"—in an objective sense, others proving that she is or has been immersed in commendable works.[72] On the other hand, the content of the widow's "testified" works is evident (5:10), namely "the testimony" concerning Christ Jesus (2:6). That is, both the widow and others can testify to the fact that she actively attracts others to Christ Jesus. Further still, the phrase "in commendable (καλοῖς) works testified (μαρτυρουμένη)" in 5:10 recalls "a commendable testimony" (μαρτυρίαν καλὴν) of a qualified overseer in 3:7. Where it was necessary both for an overseer's subjective actions to be proof that he is commendable—that he is qualified—and for those-outside the church to provide objective proof that his actions are commendable (3:7), the audience understand that a widow who must be-enrolled is not only testified in commendable works within God's household but also by those-outside. Significantly, then, the widow whom the church must honor would be known by those-outside—she has not been insular within the church. In other words, such a widow exemplifies what it means to live in God's missional household: as her works have been testified, and even at the last stage of life, her commendable works were and are intended to attract and welcome "those-outside" into the household of God. The audience understand that this widow shares the Savior God's missional desire for all humans to be-saved (2:3–4a). As the C element concludes, Paul's description of the widow becomes even clearer: she must not only be at least sixty years (5:9), is left-remaining, and has hoped upon God (5:5), but is known to attract others to Christ Jesus—both within God's household and outside.

1 Timothy 5:10b: Examples of Commendable Works

(D Element)

In the pivot D element of the fifth microchiasm, the apostle Paul provides four further illustrations of what it means to be a widow who is testified in commendable works: "if she raised-children, if she has shown-hospitality, if the feet of the holy-ones she washed, if the afflicted she assisted" (5:10b). The fourfold repetition of the term "if" (εἰ) in 5:10b recalls its prior occurrences throughout the macrochiasm; here, however, the sudden absence of its rhetorical pairing with "some" would be striking. That is, in each prior occurrence of "if," the audience heard its immediate combination with the consistently polemical pronoun "some": "if (εἴ) some-thing (τι) different lies-opposed to the sound teaching (1:10); "if (εἴ) someone (τις) aspires

---

72. That both the subjective and objective sense are included, see volume 1, chapter 4 regarding 1 Timothy 2:6.

to the office of overseer (3:1); "if (εἰ) someone (τις) does not know how to lead his own household" (3:5); "if (εἰ) some (τις) widow has children or those-from-parents" (5:4); "if (εἰ) someone (τις) does not provide for his own and especially for household-members (5:8). In 5:10b, therefore, the absence of "some" would underscore a rhetorical contrast between "some" and a "widow" who is truly a widow, that is, who is testified in commendable works (5:10a). Moreover, where each occurrence of the term "if" indicated a real and present circumstance within the church (εἴ, 1:10; εἴ, 3:1; εἰ, 3:5; εἰ, 5:4; εἰ, 5:8), it is evident that Paul's fourfold repetition of "if" (εἰ) here in 5:10b defines the factitive activites—not hypothetical—by which a true widow is testified (5:10a).

To be sure, the audience would likely hear "if she raised-children" to indicate the widow's commitment to fulfill what would have been considered normal household duties of meeting the physical needs to rear children to adulthood.[73] Yet, given the arrangement of the overall macrochiasm, it is likely that Paul intends to convey a more significant implication. The phrase "if she raised-children (ἐτεκνοτρόφησεν)" in 5:10b of the fifth microchiasm—the B unit of the macrochiasm—echoes for the audience that a woman "will be-saved consistent-with child-parenting (τεκνογονίας)" in 2:15 of the parallel B unit. There, in the parallel B unit, the women who profess godliness were identified as those who evidence their salvation—their existence "in faith," that is, in God's household—by their commitment to missional "child-parenting"—bringing others into God's household. Thus in the B' unit of the macrochiasm, the audience would understand that a widow who must be-enrolled to receive help is not only a woman who has been active in salvific "child-parenting" but also has "raised-children" who themselves exist "in faith," that is, in God's household. The implication may be that not only her own children but also the children of other families "in faith" were directly influenced and "raised" by her example of godliness in the church.[74] In this case, the audience understand that just as a widow has cared for those in God's household, so now those in God's household are to

---

73. The aorist tense "raised-children" (ἐτεκνοτρόφησεν) suggests that Paul is describing the widow's past action of having nurtured children. However, Paul has already indicated that "she who is truly a widow . . . is left-remaining" (5:5), that is, does not have children or those-from-parents to care for her (cf. 5:4a). As such, Paul may be referencing the widow's care for other people's children "since by definition the widow has no children or grandchildren to look after her, and the other qualities are all concerned with service to other people" (Marshall, *PE*, 595); see Kelly, *PE*, 116–17.

74. The Ephesian church had only been established for ten to fifteen years (see volume 1, chapter 1); such would be substantial time for these elderly, godly widows to positively influence the children in the church.

honor and care for her. In sum, "if she raised-children" would denote both a physical, domestic component as well as a spiritual one.[75]

The second commendable work in which the widow is testified—"if she has shown-hospitality" (ἐξενοδόχησεν)—echoes the adjectival cognate "affectionate-of-stranger" (φιλόξενον) in 3:2 of the third microchiasm, which was a qualification expected of an overseer. Paul's intention is to highlight the missional activity of the widow who has modeled the missional household of God in her own house by warmly welcoming all and supporting the church's itinerant workers.[76] In effect, the audience understand that such a widow—"woman of one man, in commendable works testified" (5:9–10a)—would have been an effective partner of the church overseer—"man of one woman . . . affectionate-of-stranger" (3:2), "a commendable testimony" (3:7)—to preserve the teaching and promote godliness as God's missional household.[77]

The third commendable work—"if the feet of the holy-ones she washed"—underscores the tangible expression of the widow's humility, namely her willingness to care for "the holy-ones" through even the most menial of tasks. It is possible that the audience would understand this qualification as an extension of showing hospitality, in which case "the holy-ones" would refer to traveling Christians.[78] To be sure, washing feet was not a uniquely Christian practice;[79] nevertheless, there can be little doubt that Jesus's washing the feet of his disciples infused new significance into the act.[80] Undoubtedly, the phrase "feet . . . she washed" (πόδας ἔνιψεν) would

75. See Grudem, *Evangelical Feminism*, 256.

76. Towner, *Letters*, 347: "This too is a retroflection on her conduct as matron of the house, showing her practical participation in caring for traveling believers and in this way extending the church's mission." For missional connotations, see volume 2, chapter 2 regarding 1 Timothy 3:2.

77. Such a scenario would complementary. That godly men and women are to exhibit the same qualities in different roles, see volume 1, chapter 4 regarding 1 Timothy 2:1–4a, 8–15.

78. Collins, *1 & 2 Tim*, 140.

79. Towner, *Letters*, 347. Bauckham, *Testimony of the Beloved Disciple*, 203: "Outside of John 13 there is only one New Testament reference to a Christian practice of washing the feet of fellow Christians [1 Tim 5:10] . . . The association with hospitality is not unexpected in the light of the general evidence about footwashing from the ancient world, and tends to preclude the possibility that the footwashing here is a religious rite. Rather, among the good works expected of widows is that they should perform for their houseguests the footwashing that, had they not been Christians, they would have expected a slave or the guests themselves to perform."

80. Compare the Greek texts:
1 Tim 5:10b: "πόδας ἔνιψεν";
John 13:5: "νίπτειν τοὺς πόδας"; John 13:12: "ἔνιψεν τοὺς πόδας"; John 13:14:

be an archetypal embodiment of true Christian humility.⁸¹ Still, the forward movement of the overall macrochiasm would give further expression to the widow's testified works for "the holy-ones." The term "the holy-ones" (ἁγίων, 5:10b) in the B' unit of the macrochiasm recalls the cognate "holiness" (ἁγιασμῷ, 2:15) in the parallel B unit, which highlighted the women's existence "in faith," that is, in God's holy presence, in God's household. Thus here in 5:10b the audience understand that Paul is not only emphasizing that "the holy-ones" whose feet the widow washed are members of God's household—in which the widow herself lives—but also that the widow's existence in God's holy presence is testified by her specific care for those in God's presence.⁸² Furthermore, "the holy-ones" (ἁγίων) in 5:10b recalls 4:5 of the previous microchiasm wherein the mediator Christ Jesus was in view as the content of the word of God by which all creation is "made-holy" (ἁγιάζεται). In effect, for both the "the holy-ones" and the widow who exist in the familial realm "in faith" (1:2)—"in Christ Jesus" (3:13)—Paul is corroborating that both "the holy-ones" and the widow are part of one family who—unlike the false teachers's ascetic practices—enjoy all of creation in the holy presence of God.

The fourth commendable work—"if the afflicted she assisted"—further articulates why such a widow must be honored by the church. Where "she assisted" connotes material provisions for "the afflicted," Paul's sustained point throughout the microchiasm is apparent: just as the widow helped others in need, so must she be helped in her need.⁸³ It is possible that the audience hear a general reference to her compassion, namely that "she

---

"ἔνιψα ... τοὺς πόδας."

81. See Edwards, "Christological Basis," 367–83. Bauckham, *Testimony of the Beloved Disciple*, 203: "The fact that 1 Timothy 5:10 itself clearly presumes an established practice should be noted, and makes it very unlikely that it reflects the influence of the Fourth Gospel." To be sure, the date of composition for John ("almost any date between about 55 and 95 is possible") was most likely after 1 Timothy ("somewhere in the middle 60s") (Carson and Moo, *Introduction*, 264, 572, respectively). However, it is most likely that oral tradition was not only known by Paul—whom Christ Jesus directly sent and appointed for service (1:1, 12)—but also by the Ephesian church, which Paul founded at least ten years prior to 1 Timothy.

82. Certainly, Paul is not referring to the widow's servitude to men; "the holy-ones" (ἁγίων) would include both men and women and perhaps even emphasize the widow's humble care for other women who remain "in holiness" (ἁγιασμῷ) in 2:15 of the parallel B unit. Paul's point is that the widow cared for men and women indiscriminantly as those who are equally valuable.

83. Barcley, *1 & 2 Tim*, 160: "The verb for 'to give aid' is used again in verse 16 with regard to material, financial help, and so that, at least in part, seems to be in view here. The widow who is helped by and serves the church has already been one who has helped to meet the needs of others in their times of distress."

assisted" (ἐπήρκεσεν) all people—not merely "the holy-ones"—such that her commendable reputation is by those inside and outside God's household. Still, the participle "the afflicted" (θλιβομένοις) may also specify those within God's household who are suffering either from persecution or living in poverty.[84] Given either broad or narrow implication, what is clear to the audience is that the way in which "the afflicted she assited" was tangible, costly, and verifiable. In this sense, much like the testimony concerning Christ Jesus was tangible, costly, and verifiable (1:15; 2:6; 3:16), the widow who assisted the afflicted ultimately represents her service to Christ Jesus who is the Lord of the realm in which she lives (1:2).[85]

In sum, as the microchiasm advances around the pivot D element, the audience hear the progression of Paul's unified concern throughout each element: as the leader of the Ephesian church, Timothy—the youth (A' element of the fourth microchiasm)—must respect the elderly (A element of the fifth microchiasm); children or those-from-parents must be-godly and care for their own elderly, just as those in the household of God must care for God's own elderly (B element); elderly widows ought to have a reputation for commendable works (C element), namely their activity to influence the youth to live together as the missional household of God (D element). Paul's focus is the interconnected unity between the young and old both giving to and receiving from one another as family members—both in their own families as the result of receiving marriage as God's commendable creation (4:3–4) and in God's family through their common faith upon Christ Jesus (1:16). Moving into the concluding parallel elements of the microchiasm, the audience are prepared for Paul's advancement and expansion of the familial, missional theme.

1 Timothy 5:10c: If She Followed In All Good Work

(C' Element)

After hinging around the pivot D element of the microchiasm, Paul continues with the C' element: "if she followed in all good work" (5:10c). The adjective "all" (παντί) encompasses a totality, thereby indicating for the audience that the four works listed in the pivot D element were only illustrations. In effect, the widow in the C element (5:10a) who is testified in commendable works is testified in the parallel C' element (5:10c) by "all" that she has done. Furthermore, the phrase "in all" (ἐν παντί) recalls 3:11

---

84. E.g. 1 Thess 3:4; 2 Thess 1:6, 7; cf. 2 Cor 4:8; 7:5. See Marshall, *PE*, 597.
85. See Matthew 25:34–40.

of the third microchiasm, wherein the wives of qualified deacons were described as "faithful in all (ἐν πᾶσιν)," that is, as women "in faith" who are aligned with the apostle Paul's authority and model a missional lifestyle that has salvation in view.[86] Here, then, as heard throughout the fifth microchiasm, Paul's point is reiterated for emphasis: the widows whom the church must honor are missional "in all" (ἐν παντί) aspects, just as the Savior God, Christ Jesus, and the church are missional toward "all" (πάντων, 2:1, 6; πάντας, 2:4) humans in the parallel B unit. Still, "in all" (ἐν παντί) in 5:10c of the C' element recalls 5:2 of the A element within the current microchiasm, wherein "in all (ἐν πάσῃ) purity" was heard as a reference to Timothy's sexual conduct among younger-women. Perhaps implied, then, and echoing "woman of one man" in 5:9, widows who must be-enrolled are testified to have followed sexual propriety in their life, that is, fidelity according to their previous status as single or married women.

The phrase "good (ἔργῳ) work" here in 5:10c of the C' element echoes "commendable (ἔργοις) works" in 5:10a of the parallel C element. As noted, after hearing the four works in the D element and the qualifier "all" in the C' element, the audience hear the rhetorical movement of the microchiasm: the widow is testified in all "work," not just a few "works." What is more, the audience again hear the arrangement of the overall macrochiasm: the phrase "good work" (ἔργῳ ἀγαθῷ) here in 5:10c of the B' unit recalls "good works" (ἔργων ἀγαθῶν) in 2:10 of the second microchiasm—the parallel B unit. That is, unlike the self-indulgent widow in the B' unit of the macrochiasm (5:6) who was the archetype for women who do what is improper for a profession of godliness in the B unit (2:9), the widow who must be-enrolled (5:3, 5, 9, 10a–b) is one who cosmetics herself in what is proper for women who profess godliness: good works (2:10; 5:10c).[87] The verb "followed" (ἐπηκολούθησεν) connotes deep devotion, in this instance suggesting that "all good work" in 5:10c was a way of life, a guiding principle for the widow. That is, the widow's commendable reputation arose not from sporadic activities but a constancy marked by zeal and dedication to participate in God's missional purposes.[88] Still, the verb "followed" (ἐπηκολούθησεν)

---

86. That the wives of deacons are in view, see volume 2, chapter 2 regarding 1 Timothy 3:11.

87. It may be worth noting that the audience—particularly the women—now have a further understanding of the "good works" in which they are to cosmetic themselves (2:10), namely "all good work" (5:10c). In effect, the audience would understand that every aspect of life is a good work wherein it attracts others to Christ Jesus.

88. Given that the Ephesian church was ten to fifteen years old, it is unlikely that the widow in view—"not being less than sixty years" (5:9)—would have lived a full life of "good work." Yet, Paul's point is that the widow's life has followed a consistent pattern of "all good work" since coming to have-faith upon Christ Jesus and entering God's

recalls Paul's instructions to Timothy in 4:6 of the previous microchiasm regarding the words of the faith and of the commendable teaching that "you have followed" (παρηκολούθηκας). In this way, Paul's statement that "she followed in all good work" (5:10c) would not necessarily refer to the widow's way of life as her own natural disposition but—and perhaps rather—as that which has been nourished, fostered, and grown through the words of the faith and the commendable teaching (4:6). In short, such a widow whom the church must honor has been and is still committed to that which concerns Christ Jesus—the teaching (1:10b; 4:6, 13, 16), the gospel (1:11), the testimony (2:6), the mystery (3:9, 16)—precisely because she has been and still is "in faith," that is, "in Christ Jesus" (3:13) from the moment that she came to have-faith upon him (1:16).[89]

1 Timothy 5:11–16: Instructions concerning Young Widows

(B' Element)

Within the B' element of the microchiasm (5:11–16), the audience hear 5:11–16 as a minichiasm in itself.

1 Timothy 5:11–16: A Minichiastic Unit

As a minichiasm in itself, verses 5:11–16 of the B' element are composed carefully of four sub-elements ("a"-"b"-"b'"-"a'"); linguistic parallels identifying chiastic arrangements are indicated by the Greek text:

> "a". [11] But younger (νεωτέρας) widows (χήρας) reject; for when they are impassioned from Christ, they desire to marry (γαμεῖν) [12] holding condemnation because the first faith they rejected;
>
> "b". [13a] but simultaneously also they learn to be idlers (ἀργαί), going-about (περιερχόμεναι) the houses,
>
> "b'". [13b] but not only idlers (ἀργαί); rather also gossips and busybodies (περίεργοι), speaking what is not necessary.

---

household.

89. Tamez suggests that Paul's commitment to supporting widows "is predicated upon their obedience to the traditional Greco-Roman domestic code . . . their domestic role as defined by the patriarchal society" ("1 Tim," 513). See Portefaix, "'Good Citizenship,'" 155. However, Paul's emphasis to his first-century Ephesian audience is clearly on the widow's existence in and commitment to God's household, not in and to Greco-Roman standards.

GODLY CONDUCT FROM ALL MEMBERS OF GOD'S HOUSEHOLD 47

"a'". [14] I want, therefore, younger-women (νεωτέρας) to marry (γαμεῖν), to child-parent, to master-households, to give no occasion to the opponent for maligning. [15] For some already have turned-aside after Satan. [16] If some faithful-woman has widows (χήρας), she must assist them and the church must not be-burdened, that it might assist those who are truly widows (χήραις).

The second minichiasm of the 5:1—6:2 microchiasm is framed by Paul's concern for the younger widows in Ephesus in the "a" and "a'" sub-elements and the corrective instructions that will enable elderly widows to be assisted. The minichiasm gravitates around the ungodly activities of the younger widows in the "b" and "b'" sub-elements.

1 Timothy 5:11–12: Younger Widows Reject, the First Faith They Rejected

("a" sub-element)

Within the B' element, the introductory "a" sub-element of the 5:11–16 minichiasm immediately begins with a distinction from the godly, elderly widow in preceding C, D, and C' elements: "But younger widows reject" (5:11).[90] As heard consistently throughout the previous minichiasm, the disjunctive "But" (δέ) communicates a contrast, here between "younger widows" (5:11) and the widow who must be-enrolled to receive formal care from the church (5:9–10). The audience understand that "younger (νεωτέρας) widows" (5:11) is a relative contrast to widows who are "not being less than sixty years" (5:9).[91] As such, these "younger widows" must not be-enrolled. Whereas the elderly widow (5:9) of the first century was understood to be in the final stage of life and thus only able to participate in God's missional household by remaining in supplications and prayers (5:5), the audience understand that these "younger widows" (5:11) are still capable of doing the works that the elderly widow can no longer do, namely raising-children, showing-hospitality, washing the feet of the holy-ones, and assisting the afflicted (5:10b). Furthermore, where the implication in 5:9 was that the elderly widow was biologically too old to remarry and

---

90. To be sure, this contrast sustains the dichotomy between "widows—truly widows" and non-truly widows. Wall with Steele suggest a further distinction within the non-truly widows group, namely "those who should expect the financial support of their children (vv. 4, 8, 16); and those who are still young and should expect to remarry (vv. 11–15)" (*1 & 2 Tim*, 129).

91. See discussion in Marshall, *PE*, 598.

have children, the audience understand that these "younger widows" in 5:11 are still at a stage in life when having children or those-from-parents is possible. Still, Paul's use of the descriptive phrase "younger (νεωτέρας) widows" in 5:11 recalls "younger-women" (νεωτέρας) in 5:2 of the A element wherein Paul's concern was sexual propriety, perhaps between them and Timothy—"the youth" (νεότητος, 4:12). At least to a degree, then, the mention of "younger" in 5:11 would alert the audience that Paul is concerned with these women's sexuality.

The verb "reject" (παραιτοῦ) is forceful and recalls Paul's earlier command to "reject" (παραιτοῦ) the vile and silly myths (4:7a) in the fourth microchiasm. Positively, then, in the same way that the false teachers were influencing the audience to accept vile and silly myths, the implication is that the church was accepting younger widows to receive material support rather than elderly widows.[92] In regard to providing for these younger widows, therefore, Paul's command would be understood as non-negotiable. Furthermore, where Paul's command to "reject" younger widows is intended to be heard in relation to 4:7a, the surrounding context of 4:7a may indicate that Paul's command in 5:11 has a direct bearing on the younger women's ability to follow the words of the faith and of the commendable teaching (4:6b) and train for godliness (4:7b).

Such would likely be confirmed for the audience by Paul's next statement: "for when they are impassioned from Christ, they desire to marry" (5:11). Consistent with its prior occurrences throughout the macrochiasm (2:13; 3:13; 4:5, 8, 10, 16; 5:4), the audience understand that the conjuction "for" (γάρ) in 5:11 marks the basis for the preceding statement. In effect, the audience understand that the reason for Timothy and the audience to reject younger widows from enrolling to receive material provisions from the household of God—the realm "in faith" wherein Christ Jesus is Lord (1:2)—is because "they are impassioned from Christ, they desire to marry." The term "when" (ὅταν) indicates a conditional situation. However, the grammatical structure of the explanation, along with the apodosis being in the present tense ("they desire to marry"), indicates that Paul is depicting here an actual situation, namely that "they are [already] impassioned from Christ."[93] The verb "impassioned" (καταστρηνιάσωσιν) means "to be

---

92. The further implication seems to be that the ungodly children or those-from-parents—likely the fase teachers (5:4a, 8)—are using the church to provide for their own ungodly, self-indulgent widows (5:6), thereby stealing from the church's ability to provide for its members (5:8), that is, to honor widows who are truly widows in God's household (5:3, 5).

93. Marshall, *PE*, 599: "The present tense suggests that cases are already happening, as v. 15 confirms." See Towner, *Letters*, 350 n. 102.

drawn away by one's own sensuous impulses."[94] The audience would likely hear a twofold nuance. On the one hand, these younger widows are "impassioned from Christ" in the sense that they are the "self-indulgent" widow who "living—is dead" (5:6), that is, is not "in Christ."[95] In this case, they are living like the ungodly women in the second microchiasm—the parallel B unit of the macrochiasm—who cosmetic themselves "in braids and gold or pearls or rich attire" (2:9) rather than what is proper for women who profess godliness, consistent-with "good works" (2:10). As the clear antithesis of the elderly widow who "followed in all good work" (5:10c), such younger widows, therefore, must *not* be-enrolled, that is, Timothy and the audience must proactively "reject" them from receiving material assistance by the church (5:11). On the other hand, given the sexual connotation implied with the adjective "younger" in 5:2, the audience may also understand that the "younger widows" in 5:11 who are "impassioned from Christ" have a deeper desire for sexual interaction—perhaps with "younger-men" (5:2) and perhaps even with Timothy, the "youth" (4:12)—than they do for fidelity to their current situation of singleness as a "woman of one man" to Christ Jesus like the elderly widow (5:9).[96]

Given that these younger widows are impassioned from Christ, the audience would understand the phrase "they desire to marry" in this specific context. The verb "to marry" (γαμεῖν) in 5:11 recalls "to marry" (γαμεῖν) in 4:3 of the previous microchiasm wherein Paul was clearly upholding the reception of marriage as a commendable creation of God to be enjoyed in God's holy presence (4:3–5). Thus the audience understand that the problem in view is not at all related to marriage. Rather, where God created marriage for reception with thanksgiving "by the faithful and those who have knowingly-embraced the truth" (4:3), Paul's focus is on receiving marriage as those "in faith," as the faithful of whom God is the Savior (4:10). In other words, rather than an ungrounded "desire to marry," the younger widows's desire ought to be in line with the Creator of marriage, that is, for a marriage that would honor the One who created it (4:3). Emphasizing this point, the younger women's "desire" (θέλουσιν) in the B'

---

94. UBS, s.v. To be sure, the precise meaning of the verb is difficult to determine, given that it is a *hapax legomenon*. Knight's analysis is helpful: "καταστρηνιάζω . . . is a compound verb composed of στρηνιάζω and κατά, in the sense of 'against,' which requires that the object be genitive [τοῦ Χριστοῦ]" (*PE*, 226).

95. Such would adhere to Towner's analysis (*Letters*, 350) based on Revelation 18:7, 9 wherein the promiscuity in view relates to luxurious living.

96. Such would adhere to Marshall's observations: "The sense is that they 'feel sensuous impulses that alienate them from Christ' (BA), i.e., that their sexual impulses form a temptation that lead them away from devotion to Christ" (*PE*, 598–99).

unit of the macrochiasm is void of the Savior God in the parallel B unit of the macrochiasm who "desires" (θέλει) all humans to be-saved and to come to a knowing-embrace of truth (2:4). Indeed, much like the false teachers's "desiring" (θέλοντες) in 1:7, the audience understand that these younger widows's "desire" (θέλουσιν) in 5:11 is not what God "desires" (θέλει) in 2:4. In short, the younger widows that Paul has in view do not share the same interests as God, the implication being that they have not allowed him to be their Savior, that is, they are not of the faithful (4:10).

Such would be corroborated for the audience by Paul's next statement: "holding condemnation because the first faith they rejected." The verb "holding" recalls its prior occurrences throughout the macrochiasm in reference to clinging (1:19; 3:4, 9; 4:8, 16). Within the present microchiasm, "having" (ἔχουσαι) in 5:11 of the B' element recalls some widow who "has" (ἔχει) children or those-from-parents in 5:4 of the parallel B element. Where "some widow" in 5:4a was negatively impacted by the ungodly children or those-from-parents that she "has," the audience would likely be alerted to the negative implication of the "younger widows" who are "holding" in 5:11. Indeed, the rhetorical contrast from the other occurrences of the verb throughout the macrochiasm would be magnified: rather than aligning themselves with Timothy by "holding faith" (1:19), the younger widows are "holding condemnation" (5:12).[97] The term "condemnation" (κρίμα) in 5:12 recalls the "condemnation" (κρίμα) of the devil into which the being-puffed-up, young-plant false teaching overseers had fallen in 3:6 of the third microchiasm. Thus the audience would not only understand that the "younger (νεωτέρας) widows" (5:12) have fallen away from faith upon Christ Jesus but also that such falling away may be attributed to being "a young-plant" (νεόφυτον) with regard to the faith (cf. 3:6) or being under the influence of the "young-plant" overseers (3:6). In any case, that the younger widows are "holding condemnation" clearly indicates their status apart from Christ Jesus.

Paul goes on to emphasize the dire situation of these younger widows: "the first faith they rejected" (5:12).[98] The phrase "first faith" (πρώτην πίστιν) in the B' element recalls the arrangement of the minichiasm within the parallel B element, wherein the ungodly children or those-from-parents must learn "first" (πρῶτον) to be godly to their own household in the "a" sub-element (5:4a) precisely because they have denied "the faith" (πίστιν)

---

97. The force of the rhetorical contrast here seems similar to 4:13, where the negative implication of the verb "hold-toward" is jarringly switched to a positive one; see volume 2, chapter 3.

98. The conjuction "because" (ὅτι) in 5:12 ("because the first faith they rejected") would point to the reason for "holding condemnation," the sense being, "as a result of."

and are worse-than the "without-faith" (ἀπίστου) in the parallel "a'" sub-element (5:8). That is, just as the ungodly children or those-from-parents are misaligned with the "first" (πρῶτον)—lead, prominent—duty of being godly (5:4a) and thus have denied the "faith" (πίστιν) and are worse-than the "without-faith" (ἀπίστου) (5:8), so too are the ungodly younger widows in the parallel B' element misaligned with the "first" (πρώτην)—lead, prominent—duty of the "faith" (πίστιν) (5:12), namely a life of godliness that directly corresponds to having-faith upon Christ Jesus (1:16).[99] Indeed, such widows have "rejected" (ἠθέτησαν) the "faith" (πίστιν), which echoes the current situation of "some—rejecting (ἀπωσάμενοι)—regarding the faith (πίστιν) have become-shipwrecked" (1:19); for this reason Timothy and the audience are to "reject" such widows (5:11).[100]

Here, a further implication would likely be understood by the audience, namely that of allegiance. Where the younger widows are impassioned from Christ (5:11), the audience understand that such widows are estranged from Paul's opening statement concerning "Christ Jesus our Lord" (1:2). That is, not only is *the younger widows's* "desire" to marry (5:11) not what God "desires" (2:4), but *the man* whom they desire to marry does not himself align with "the first faith," that is, does not view Christ Jesus as "Lord."[101] In other words, the situation of younger widows being impassioned from Christ is evident by their desire to marry a non-Christian, which, functionally, displays a desire that has "rejected" Christ Jesus.[102] Thus in the introductory "a" sub-element (5:11–12), the audience would understand that the younger widows in view may not receive material provisions from the household of

---

99. Undoubtedly, Paul's consistent use of the term "first" throughout the macro-chiasm to connote "lead, foremost, prominent" (1:15, 16; 2:1, 13; 3:10; 5:4a) would be understood in the same way here. It has been suggested that "first faith" refers to an oath or pledge not to remarry once enrolled to receive material support from the church (e.g., Spencer, *1 Tim*, 130; Simpson, *PE*, 91; Coleman, *Delivering Women*, 101), but this proposal is unlikely.

100. The terms "rejected" (ἠθέτησαν) in 5:12, "rejecting" (ἀπωσάμενοι) in 1:19, and "reject" (παραιτοῦ) in 5:11 are not cognates. However, their conceptual and functional connotations would be apparent.

101. See volume 2, chapter 2 regarding 1 Timothy 3:2 in connection with Ephesians 5.

102. Paul's similar teaching regarding marriage with a non-Christian man is found in 1 Corinthians 7:39. Witherington, *Letters*, 270–71: "But perhaps there is an easier explanation: the strain that remarrying put on one's faith because most of the candidates for husband would be pagans . . . The real overarching concern is that younger women not feel that they have to abandon their faith commitment in order to remarry. Paul is thinking of the way a patriarchal household worked, whereby the gods of the head of the household became the gods of the family, and thus a woman wishing to remarry to a non-Christian might have a strong inclination to abandon her Christian faith." See also Winter, *Roman Wives*, 136–37.

God—the realm "in faith," which is entered by coming to have-faith upon Christ (1:16)—because such widows are "impassioned from Christ," thus "holding condemnation"—effectively bearing or incurring condemnation because they rejected their lead allegiance to Christ Jesus.

1 Timothy 5:13a: They Learn to be Idlers, Going-About the Houses

("b" sub-element)

In the "b" sub-element (5:13a) Paul elaborates further why Timothy and the audience are to reject younger widows from receiving material assistance from the church: "But simultaneously also they learn to be idlers, going-about the houses." The phrase "But simultaneously . . . also" (ἅμα δὲ καί) expresses a parallel situation.[103] Thus not only "they are impassioned from Christ" (5:11) but "they learn to be idlers, going-about the houses" (5:13). The term "idlers" (ἀργαί) would carry connotations of being lazy, ineffective, and not participating in any form of work. The verb "learn" (μανθάνουσιν) in 5:13 of the B' unit of the macrochiasm recalls 2:11 of the parallel B unit wherein women were to "learn" (μανθανέτω) in quietness, that is, with a peaceable disposition, in all submissiveness.[104] In other words, though both types of learning happen through a habitual practice, the sort of learning in view for 5:13 is experientially antithetical to the type of learning by women who profess godliness in 2:11: just as the younger widows are impassioned from Christ—functionally rejecting and not accepting the authority of Christ—so also they "learn" to be idlers—a continued rejection of godliness—through the habitual practice thereof. Still, within the current microchiasm "learn" (μανθάνουσιν) in 5:13 of the B' element recalls the ungodly children or those-from-parents in 5:4 of the parallel B element who must "learn" (μανθανέτωσαν) to be-godly to their own household, namely through action and experience. In effect, then,

---

103. Marshall, *PE*, 601: "At the same time as some are wanting to marry, others are learning to be lazy." This is not to suppose, however, that the younger widows divided neatly into two categories, one being inflamed with lust, the other being indolent. To be sure, the combination of terms within the phrase does not convey a rhetorical contrast as would "but" (δέ) on its own. Rather, as "simultaneously" implies, there was overlap. Knight, *PE*, 227: "'and at the same time also' (ἅμα δὲ καί) . . . 'denoting the coincidence of two actions in time.'"

104. Regarding 2:11, Towner succinctly explains: "this meant quiet and attentive listening (in quietness) and complete ("all") acceptance of the authority of the teacher to teach and the willingness to embrace what was being taught" (*Letters*, 216).

given the arrangements of both the overall macrochiasm and the current microchiasm, the audience understand the apostle Paul's main point in the "b" sub-element (5:13a): the younger widows, in their state of being unmarried, coupled with their reception of material assistance from the church, have habitually learned "to be idlers."[105] To be sure, where the audience may have intended to do good by helping every kind of widow—young and old, ungodly and godly alike—Paul's concern is that the church was inadvertently promoting in the younger widows a disposition of laziness, enabling them to be "idlers" while simultaneously disabling elderly widows from receiving care. With a compounding effect, the younger widows's disposition as "idlers" had likely fostered their ungodly lifestyle, namely as those who are impassioned from Christ (5:11), desire to marry without consideration of allegiance to Christ Jesus as Lord (5:12), and thus do not share God's missional desire, that is, do not participate in the commendable, good, missional work of the church to raise-children, show-hospitality, wash the feet of the holy-ones, and assist the afflicted (5:10).

Paul qualifies the younger women's activity as idlers: "going-about the houses" (5:13). The participle "going-about" (περιερχόμεναι) recalls the earlier verbal cognates throughout the macrochiasm: in the first microchiasm, Christ Jesus "came" (ἦλθεν) into the world to save sinners (1:15); in the second microchiasm, the Savior God desires all humans "to come" (ἐλθεῖν) to a knowing-embrace of truth (2:4b); in the third microchiasm, Christ Jesus's apostle Paul was hoping "to come" (ἐλθεῖν) to Timothy quickly to help bring-about the household-law of God (3:14–15); in the fourth microchiasm, Paul commanded Timothy in 4:13 to lead the church in Ephesus until "I come" (ἔρχομαι). Here, then, the audience would hear the emphasis of Paul's rhetoric: in stark contrast to the missional activities of Christ Jesus, God, Paul, and Timothy, the ungodly younger widows are "going-about" as idlers without any missional concern for the salvation of others or the well-being of the church. To be sure, it is possible that the younger widows were "going-about" in ways that disrupted and destabilized various households, akin to the divisive impact that the false teachers were having on the household-law of God (1:4).[106] Yet, the arrangement of the microchiasm

---

105. Paul's command to "reject" the younger widows in 5:11 implied that the Ephesian church was doling out provisions. See above.

106. This is not to suggest that the younger widows were false teachers. Contra Fee, *Listening to the Spirit in the Text*, 74: "these younger widows were going around from house to house passing on the foolishness of the false teachings." Furthermore, it has been suggested that "going-about the houses" in 5:13 indicates ministry work performed by these widows (e.g., Belleville, *Women in Ministry*, 99). However, in context, it is clear that the widows in view are the antithesis of Christian ministry workers—indeed, the implication is that they are not Christians (5:11, 12). That the younger widows

would likely provide the audience with a more precise understanding. Within the B element, the arrangement of minichiasm conveyed that Paul's concern was for children or those-from-parents to be-godly to "their own household" (τὸν ἴδιον οἶκον, 5:4) in the "a" sub-element by individually providing-for "those of their own" (τῶν ἰδίων, 5:8) family and also "especially for household-members" (μάλιστα οἰκείων, 5:8), that is, God's family in the parallel "a'" sub-element. Thus while all those "in faith" have a duty to all of the faithful, the audience understand that they also have a special, prominent duty to their own biological families. Indeed, such was the point in Paul's discussion of a qualified overseer wherein a man's ability to lead his "own household" (τοῦ ἰδίου οἴκου) was inseparably linked to his ability to care-for the church of God (3:5), that is, for "the household (οἴκῳ) of God" (3:15). Here in 5:13a, then, the younger widows's activity of going-about the "houses" (οἰκίας) presents a stark contrast from attending to one's own household and also, therefore, to God's household. Instead of being testified in commendable works within their own household (5:10c) such as continuing to raise-children, show-hospitality, wash the feet of the holy-ones, and assist the afflicted (5:10b), these younger widows are idlers in regard to all good work (5:10c), for they are "going-about the houses"—effectively neglecting both their own household and the household of God. In sum, as the "b" sub-element concludes, the audience understand that the younger widows are failing to adopt the sort of missional lifestyle expected for all who belong to the household of God; they do not cosmetic themselves in what is proper for women who profess godliness—good works (2:10)—but rather in what is proper for "idlers."

1 Timothy 5:13b: Gossips, Busybodies, Speaking What is Not Necessary

("b'" sub-element)

In the "b'" sub-element (5:13b) Paul continues to describe the younger widows in view: "but not only idlers; rather also gossips and busybodies, speaking what is not necessary." Similar to the phrase "But simultaneously ... also" (ἅμα δὲ καί) in 5:13a of the parallel "b" sub-element, the entirety of the terms within the phrase "but not only" (οὐ μόνον δέ) would not introduce a contrast but rather a continuation.[107] The term "idlers" (ἀργαί) in

---

are "idlers"—a disposition to not work—would not define their activity of "going-about the houses" as a form of ministry but rather the opposite.

107. Marshall, *PE*, 603: "The phrase οὐ μόνον δέ ... ἀλλὰ καί ('and not only ... but

5:13b of the "b'" sub-element recalls "idlers" (ἀργαί) in 5:13a of the parallel "b" sub-element. The rhetorical force of the repetition would impress upon the audience that the idle preoccupations of these younger widows results in a downward spiral of further non-missional, ungodly activities—certainly, a real and present danger upon the missional purpose of household of God in Ephesus.

Paul indicates that the younger widows's progressive idleness and its habitual impact results in "gossips and busybodies." The audience would hear the irony: on the one hand, as the younger widows learn to be "idlers" (ἀργαί, 5:13a)—the absence of works—but, on the other hand, they are "going about" (περιερχόμεναι) and are "busybodies" (περίεργοι, 5:13b).[108] Such irony would highlight that these younger widows encompass the full spectrum of ungodly activity: not only are they inactive with regard to godliness, but they are busy in regard to activities that disrupt the household of God.

Given the context of the minichiasm, the audience would likely understand the term "gossips" (φλύαροι) to imply conversations that were not godly, that is, not missional. Furthermore, given the sexual connotation of the "a" sub-element wherein the younger widows are impassioned from Christ and thus rejecting their allegiance to Christ Jesus as Lord, it seems that their corresponding activity may include an improper expression of sexuality, namely by gossiping on the topic.[109] Whatever the content may have been, the audience would understand that these women who are impassioned from Christ are not only drawn away from the type of conversation that contributes to the missional purpose of God's household—attracting outsiders to Christ Jesus—but also are actively engaged in conversation that hurts the reputation of the church, thus hindering its missional purpose. In short, that these younger widows are "gossips" in the B' element of the microchiasm is clearly an antithesis to "supplications and prayers," that is, the conversations of she who is truly a widow in 5:5 of the parallel B element.

Still, Paul's concluding participle phrase of the "b'" sub-element would have further implications of what it means for the younger widows to be

---

also . . .') introduces a worse aspect of the situation."

108. The aural similarity between "idlers" (ἀργαί) and "busybodies" (περίεργοι) would likely emphasize the rhetorical effect of the irony. Furthermore, the prepositional prefixes between "going about" (περιερχόμεναι) and "busybodies" (περίεργοι) would emphasize the downward spiral of ungodly activities as the result of being "idlers." A comparison of the Greek text may be helpful to visualize Paul's rhetoric (see *italics*):
5:13a: "ἅμα δὲ καὶ ἀργαὶ μανθάνουσιν *περιερχόμεναι* τὰς οἰκίας";
5:13b: "οὐ μόνον δὲ ἀργαὶ ἀλλὰ καὶ φλύαροι καὶ *περίεργοι*, λαλοῦσαι τὰ μὴ δέοντα."

109. See Winter, *Roman Wives*, 133–36, who provides a more detailed analysis for why the gossip in view likely was in reference to sexuality.

gossips: "speaking what is not necessary" (5:15b). While the term "speaking" (λαλοῦσαι) would draw the audience's attention to the younger women's act of gossiping, the phrase "is not necessary" (μὴ δέοντα) would likely be understood as a polemical contrast. The negative particle "not" (μή) recalls its prior occurrences throughout the macrochiasm in relation to the adverse activity of the false teachers.[110] Similarly, the audience understand that the activity of these younger women—likely due to the influence of the false teachers—has adversely affected the missional purpose of God's household. Furthermore, the verb "is . . . necessary" (δέοντα) recalls its triple occurrence in the third microchiasm to identify men who are qualified to lead and model behavior for everyone in the missional household of God (3:2, 7, 15).[111] Thus where the consistent sense of the verb in the third microchiasm conveyed a lifestyle that is applicable to all those in God's household, Paul's point in 5:13b, is not that the younger widows are merely engaged in gratuitous "speaking" but rather that their "speaking" does not accord with the missional lifestyle of those "in faith."[112] At the conclusion of the "b" sub-element, the audience understand that as the younger widows are going about as idlers (5:13a), not only are they adversely affecting and destabilizing individual households as gossips but are—emphatically—living in a way that sabotages the missional household of God.

1 Timothy 5:14–16: Younger-Women to Marry, the Church Must Not Be-Burdened

("a'" sub-element)

In the concluding "a'" sub-element (5:14–16) of the 5:11–16 minichiasm, Paul gives instructions to resolve the situation with younger widows in the Ephesian church, beginning with the statement: "I want, therefore, younger-women to marry, to child-parent, to master-households, to give no occasion to the opponent for maligning" (5:14). The phrase "I want, therefore"

---

110. See 1:3, 4, 7; 3:3, 6, 7, 8; 4:12. This is not to suggest that the younger widows are the false teachers but rather the impact of the false teaching upon them.

111. That the qualifications for leadership in the church in the third microchiasm would be understood by Paul's audience in reference to men—not women—see volume 2, chapter 2 regarding 1 Timothy 3:2; see also volume 1, chapter 4 regarding 1 Timothy 2:12–14.

112. It might be suggested that "not necessary" functions to identify the younger widows as the false teachers, particularly in third microchiasm. However, this is most unlikely for many reasons—e.g., the false teachers are "forbidding to marry" (4:3), yet these younger widows "desire to marry" (5:13).

(βούλομαι οὖν) in 5:14 of the B' unit of the macrochiasm recalls "I want, therefore" (βούλομαι οὖν) in 2:8 of the parallel B unit, wherein the phrase was Paul's cumulative response to the missional calling of the church (2:1–2), the desire of the Savior God (2:3–4), the sacrifice of Christ Jesus (2:6), and Paul's own appointment as an authorized apostolic teacher (2:7). Thus, given the unified arrangement and progression of the overall macrochiasm, the audience would hear the same connotations carried forward in 5:14, namely in regard to missional activity as a command from the authority of Paul. Indeed, given that the activity of the younger widows in the current minichiasm is that which hinders the missional activity of the church, the audience would certainly hear "I want, therefore" as a corrective response. Where the younger widows are impassioned from Christ in 5:11 of the "a" sub-element, the apostle Paul—who was taught and sent by Christ Jesus (1:1, 12)—is conveying that which will bring these younger widows back to Christ. Again, the audience hear Paul's missional, restorative purpose.

The term "younger-women" (νεωτέρας) in 5:14 recalls "younger-women" (νεωτέρας) in 5:2. Yet, given the immediate context and arrangement of the current minichiasm, undoubtedly the audience would hear "younger-women" (νεωτέρας) in 5:14 of the "a'" sub-element in a parallel relation to "younger (νεωτέρας) widows" in 5:11 of the parallel "a" sub-element.[113] That is, Paul's instructions for "younger-women" (5:14) are concerned specifically with "younger widows" (5:11). For these younger widows, the audience understand that the corrective activities to draw them back to Christ Jesus are "to marry, to child-parent, to master-households" (5:14).

The verb "to marry" (γαμεῖν) in 5:14 recalls the teachings of the apostates in the fourth microchiasm who were "forbidding to marry" (γαμεῖν) in 4:3. Notably, Paul's instruction in 5:14 is for the younger widows to do exactly the opposite of what the false teachers would have them do. The audience again hear that Paul is clearly setting himself and "the teaching" (4:13, 16; cf. 1:10b, 4:6) in an antithetical relation to the unqualified apostate overseers who "teach-different" (1:3) and are holding-toward "teachings of demons" (4:1). Paul is underscoring again that marriage is not to be rejected but to be received with thanksgiving by the faithful—those who come to have-faith upon Christ Jesus (1:16)—because marriage was created by God, is commendable, and is to be enjoyed as a holy activity (4:3–5). The younger widows's activity "to marry" would certainly bring them—at least to a degree—in alignment with Christ Jesus. Still, that the apostle Paul wants younger widows "to marry" (γαμεῖν) in 5:14 of the "a'" element recalls that

---

113. The term "younger-women" (νεωτέρας, 5:14) in the B' element of the microchiasm is not arranged as a parallel linguistic pair with "younger-women" (νεωτέρας, 5:2) in the A element.

the younger widows desire "to marry" (γαμεῖν) in 5:11 of the parallel "a" sub-element. Yet, where the younger widows had a desire to marry according to a rejection of the first faith (5:12), that is, a desire to marry a man who is not allied to Christ Jesus—thus being impassioned from Christ (5:11)—the audience understand that Paul's instruction "to marry" in 5:14 has in view a man for whom—along with Paul, Timothy, and all those who are "in faith"—Christ Jesus is Lord. Thus as much as Paul in the fourth microchiasm instructed the audience about the proper reception of marriage—in purity, where sexuality is expressed within the boundaries of marriage (4:12)—here in the fifth microchiasm Paul's teaching concerns the proper expression of marriage, namely "in faith." The audience understand, therefore, that the younger widows—who themselves desire to marry (5:11)—are certainly "to marry" (5:14), that is, to tangibly demonstrate their allegiance to Christ Jesus by marrying a man who is allied to Christ Jesus. Indeed, such a man has been described throughout the macrochiasm: he is a sinner for whom Christ Jesus came to save (1:15), a man who has come to have-faith upon Christ Jesus for life eternal (1:16), a man for whom Christ Jesus gave himself as a ransom (2:7), a man who prays without anger or word-quarreling (2:8), who intends to lead his household sacrificially and with fidelity as Christ Jesus himself leads the church (3:2), who trains himself for godliness to be in heaven with Christ Jesus for eternity (4:7b–8), and who is godly to his own parents or widowed mother (5:4). The audience understand that Paul's corrective, restorative instructions have the younger widows's best interest in mind, namely their salvation and eternal existence in the holy presence of God—"in faith," "in Christ Jesus," in God's household.

In this context of marrying a man "in faith" for the purpose of restoring the impassioned younger widow back to Christ, Paul also instructs these same younger widows "to child-parent." The verb "to child-parent" (τεκνογονεῖν) here in the B' unit of the macrochiasm recalls "child-parenting" (τεκνογονίας) in 2:15 of the parallel B unit, wherein the women evidenced their own salvation—their existence "in faith"—through their organic, missional activity to bring outsiders into the household of God. Thus in 5:14, the audience understand that as the result of marrying a godly man who will continually lead her to Christ Jesus, the younger widow—now a married younger woman—will be able to remain "in faith" (2:15) and evidence her salvation, that is, "to child-parent" those who are "in faith." Indeed, heard within the fifth microchiasm, such activity in 5:14 of the B' element "to child-parent" (τεκνογονεῖν) those who exist "in faith" would prevent ungodly, non-missional activities by the "children" (τέκνα) or "those-from-parents" (ἔκγονα) in 5:4a of the parallel B element.[114]

In this context, Paul also instructs the younger widows "to master-households" (5:14). The verb "to master-households" highlights the result of marrying a godly man and being committed to missional child-parenting, especially of one's own children. At the same time, therefore, "to master-households" (οἰκοδεσποτεῖν) would also identify the antithetical trajectory from where the younger widows once were: impassioned from Christ (5:11), having rejected the faith (5:12), idlers, going-about "the houses" (οἰκίας) as gossips and busybodies (5:13). In short, the audience understand that the end result of adhering to Paul's instructions in 5:14 will be a complete reversal: the once impassioned younger widows will no longer be going-about "the houses" with ungodly, missionally hindering activities but rather will "master-households."

Certainly, the result of Paul's instructions "to master-households" (οἰκοδεσποτεῖν) echoes the "household-law (οἰκονομίαν) of God in faith" (1:4), thus indicating that these once "younger widows" will not only exist "in faith" but will be an integral part of God's household-law.[115] To be sure, "to master-households" would have conceptual echoes of a qualified man in the audience who is "leading his own household commendably" (3:4), knows how "to lead his own household" (3:5), and is "leading children commendably and their own households" (3:12). In this way, where the women's call "to master-households" (οἰκοδεσποτεῖν, 5:14) combines with their husbands's call "to lead" (προστῆναι, 3:5) and be "leading" (προϊστάμενον, 3:4; προϊστάμενοι, 3:12) their own "household" (οἴκου, 3:4, 5; οἴκων, 12), the audience understand that Paul has in view the integrated, harmonized actions of men and women "in faith"—not only within individual households but also within the design of "the household-law (οἰκονομίαν) of God in faith" (1:4). Paul's point is that both men and women "in faith" are to live according to inherently equal, harmonizing roles to preserve and promote the proper functioning of godly households in order to preserve and promote the proper functioning of God's household.[116] The audience

---

114. The linguistic connection between Paul's instruction "to child-parent" (5:14) and "children or those-from-parents" (5:4) would be apparent (see *italics*):

"*children*" (*τέκνα*, 5:4); "to *child*-parent" (*τεκνογονεῖν*, 5:14);

"those-from-*parents*" (ἔκ*γονα*, 5:4); "to child-*parent*" (τεκνο*γονεῖν*, 5:14).

115. Linguistically, the connection would be apparent: both terms fuse together two ideas:

1:4: "household" (οἶκος), "law" (νόμος);

5:14: "households" (οἶκος), "to master" (δεσποτέω).

116. See Oden, *First and Second Tim*, 158, who rightly notes that far from disparaging the role of women, the 1 Timothy letter—particularly 5:14—summons women

understand that such requires both men and women who exist "in faith" to refrain from activities that would hinder their own household-law, that is, to refrain from that which would be a misrepresentation of God's creational design for his own household. To be sure, should the younger widows refuse "to master-households" (5:14), the "household-law of God in faith" (1:4) will be adversely affected.

To summarize, where the progressive problem in the current minichiasm is both the rejection of salvation by the younger widows and the hindered missional purpose of God's household, the audience understand that Paul's resolutive instructions in 5:14 of the concluding "a'" sub-element function to correct both. The proper functioning of individual Christian households—men, women, and children "in faith"—results in the proper functioning of God's missional household—men, women, and children "in faith." What is more, given that Paul is concerned with the proper dynamic of men and women in the current B' unit of the macrochiasm, the audience are to understand its unified, integrated signifance according to the parallel B unit, which shares the same concern. The proper dynamics of men and women according to God's creational design (2:13) are to have harmonizing and inseparable effects upon the individual households (5:14) and the household of God (2:12, 15). On the one hand, God's design was intended to preserve and promote blessing, protection, and care for women; for this reason the men lead and sacrifice themselves for the sake of the women, both in their individual household and in God's household (3:5, 15). On the other hand, God's design was intended to preserve and promote missional child-parenting (2:15; 5:14) and raising-children (5:10b); for this reason men lead households (3:4, 12) and women master-households (2:15; 5:10b, 14) together toward one purpose, both in their individual household and in God's household (3:5, 15; 5:14). Such would convey the integrated function of God's design (2:12–13) for the household-law of God (1:4): for those who live in God's household, it is expected that they live accordingly.

After stating his restorative instruction positively, the apostle Paul conveys its negative consequent: by adhering to Paul's instructions to marry, to child-parent, and to master-households, the younger widows are thus "to give no occasion to the opponent for maligning" (5:14b).[117] The verb "to give" (διδόναι) here in 5:14 of the B' element recalls its prior cognate

---

to play pivotal roles in their households. See also Methuen, "'Virgin Widow,'" 285–98; Thurston, *The Widows*, 36–55.

117. Knight, *PE*, 228–29: "The infinitive διδόναι, 'to give,' is used in a parallel construction with the preceding infinitives, but in meaning it is dependent on them in the sense that, if the first three things are done (marry, bear children, and manage one's home, especially the first), then 'no occasion for reproach' is left to be given."

occurrence in 5:4 of the parallel B element: children or those-from-parents to are be-godly by learning "to give-return (ἀποδιδόναι) repayments to their parents" (5:4). In this way, the systemic connection between parents and children and children or those-from-parents is strengthened: younger widows are "to child-parent" (τεκνογονεῖν) and thus "to give" (διδόναι) no occasion to the opponent for maligning (5:14) in the same way that the "children" (τέκνα) or "those-from-parents" (ἔκγονα) of "some widow" are "to give-return" (ἀποδιδόναι) repayments to their parents (5:4). Still, Paul's use of the verb "to give" (διδόναι) in 5:14 recalls its prior cognate occurrences throughout the macrochiasm: Paul had "given-over" (παρέδωκα) the false teachers Hymenaeus and Alexander to Satan (1:20); Christ Jesus "gave" (δούς) himself as a ransom on behalf on all (2:7); the divine gift "was given" (ἐδόθη) to Timothy (4:14). Here, then, Paul's instruction for the younger widows "to give" would likely also be understood in the framework of God's divine purposes that have in view the salvation of all humans through the proper functioning of God's missional household. That the younger widows are "to give no occasion to the opponent for maligning" suggests that their lifestyle should not hinder the missional purpose of God's household.

Within the phrase "no occasion to the opponent for maligning," the adjective "no" (μηδεμίαν) echoes the cognate "no" (μή), which the audience have heard throughout the macrochiasm in reference to the activity of the false teachers and anyone who is associated with them. In effect, the suggestion may be that by not adhering to Paul's instructions, the younger widows are adhering to the influence of the false-teaching overseers. To be sure, that the younger widows are to give no "occasion" (ἀφορμήν) does not imply perfection, as though they will never stumble in their godly marriages, child-parenting, and role to master-households.[118] Yet, Paul's instruction here does convey deliberation and intentionality: those of the faithful—those who come to have-faith upon Christ (1:16) and thus live corresponding missional lives of godliness (2:1–2, 8–11, 15; 3:7)—exist in a household whose purpose is to make the Christian faith attractive. In short, the younger widow will have a critically important and irreplaceable role in God's missional household if she realigns her desire to marry (5:11) according to Paul's instructions (5:14), thus transitioning from being impassioned to Christ to participating in the missional activities that invite others come into the household of God.

It is possible that the audience would hear "the opponent" (ἀντικειμένῳ) as a general reference to any of the non-Christian pagans

---

118. Marshall, *PE*, 604: "ἀφορμή is a 'starting point, opportunity', hence an 'occasion' or 'pretext' for doing something."

in the surrounding Ephesian community.[119] However, the participle "the opponent" (ἀντικειμένῳ) echoes Paul's polemic against "some" who teach-different the first microchiasm, namely "some" who teach some-thing different that "lies-opposed" (ἀντίκειται) to the sound teaching (1:10b).[120] With either a wide or more narrow understanding, Paul's point is clear: the younger widows—after adhering to Paul's restorative instructions to marry, child-parent, and master-households (5:14)—must purposefully strive to give no occasion for "the opponent" who is actively looking for one. The phrase "for maligning" (λοιδορίας χάριν) indicates verbal abuse on the occasion of the younger widow's ungodly behavior.[121] In light of Paul's corrective instructions, the younger widows's integration into both a godly family life and the familial household of God would not only prevent "maligning" by the opponent but also promote the lifestyle of godliness that gives no occasion for it.[122]

Paul's next statement would grab the audience's attention: "For already some have turned-aside after Satan" (5:15). The term "already" (ἤδη) here in the "a" sub-element indicates an actual reality and would, therefore, be heard as a conceptual echo of "when" (ὅταν) in 5:11 of the parallel "a" sub-element—a present reality in which the younger widows were already impassioned from Christ. As such, "already" would be heard to amplify the

---

119. That any opponent of the faith is in view, see Witherington, *Letters*, 272. This could include "the enemy," that is, Satan, "who operates against the community in concert with the criticism of those outside" (Towner, *Letters*, 357).

120. The participle "the opponent" (ἀντικειμένῳ) could also be describing the false teachers as a collective; see Towner, *Letters*, 357.

121. The preposition "for" (χάριν, 5:14) is not a cognate of "grace" (χάρις, 1:2; χάριν, 1:12): the two terms share no similar connotation. Yet, it may be worth noting that the aural similarity between "for" (χάριν, 5:14) and "grace" (χάρις, 1:2; χάριν, 1:12) would likely enhance the rhetorical effect of Paul's instruction to the younger widows: where "grace" was understood as a divine blessing from God (1:2) that is mutally given back to him upon its reception (1:12), the audience would understand that for a younger widow to disregard Paul's instructions would positively give an occasion for maligning "grace."

122. Paul's instructions for the younger widows to follow the normal course of a godly family life in 5:14 would certainly not be restrictive or oppressive. Not only would it contribute to their salvation, but it would also have a missional component to those outside. Witherington, *Letters*, 273: "Lest we think that Paul's concern about younger widows is merely an example of patriarchal polemics, we would do well to consult Dio Cassius's *Roman History* . . . in which he recounts how the new cult of Ises (in Rome and elsewhere) was brought into disrepute because of strong suspicions backed by some evidence that young (and even married) women were engaging in sexually suggestive behavior in the rites of the cult. The fledgling Christian faith could not afford to have that reputation, especially in Ephesus, where there was already more than enough sexual scandal going around, some of which was connected with organized religion."

urgency of Paul's instructions.[123] Furthermore, as heard throughout the macrochiasm, the conjuction "for" (γάρ) in 5:15 marks the basis for the preceding statement. In effect, the audience understand that the reason for younger widows to heed Paul's instructions is because "some have turned-aside after Satan." The urgency of the situation would be enhanced by the parallel arrangement of "for" (γάρ) in both 5:11 and 5:15 of the parallel "a" and "a'" sub-elements. In this way, the overall rhetorical sense of Paul's instructions in the arrangement of the minichiasm would likely be heard as: "Younger widows are impassioned from Christ, that is, already have turned-aside after Satan. As such, reject these younger widows so that they give no occasion to the opponent for maligning."

Moreover, the urgency of Paul's instructions is further heard through the evident commonalities between the younger widows and the false teachers, namely the devastating impact upon their salvation. That "some (τινες) have turned-aside after Satan" in 5:15 recalls both that "some (τινες) will apostasy from the faith" (4:1) and that "some (τινες)—rejecting—regarding the faith have become-shipwrecked" (1:19). Also, that "some (τινες) have turned-aside (ἐξετράπησαν)" in 5:15 recalls that "some (τινες) . . . have turned-aside (ἐξετράπησαν) for useless-words" in 1:6. What is more, that "some" have turned-aside after "Satan" (σατανᾶ) recalls Hymenaeus and Alexander, whom Paul had given-over to "Satan" (σατανᾷ) in 1:20. Undoubtedly, then, Paul intends his audience to hear the sinister strategy and influence of the false teachers to pursue and gain the allegiance of these younger widows who do not have godly husbands to lovingly and sacrificially protect them.[124] The overall parallel arrangement of the macrochiasm would be heard. In 2:12-14 of the B unit of the macrochiasm, the false teachers were likely influencing the women to teach and govern a man in the household of God, as did the serpent in the garden (Gen 3:1-6; cf. 1 Tim 2:14), and Paul was correctively instructing the women to display their allegiance to God by not rejecting his creational design (2:12, 13). Here in 5:14-15 of the parallel B' unit, the false teachers have influenced the younger widows to

---

123. The adverb "already" (ἤδη) should elucidate for the contemporary reader why 1 Timothy lacks an opening prayer or introduction that is typically found in Paul's other letters. Apparently, the situation had already become so dire through the influence of the false teachers that the apostle felt it was urgent to jump into matters without the usual niceties.

124. It would be evident to the audience that Paul is not concerned that the younger widows are themselves the false teachers. Clearly, the younger widows who "desire to marry" (5:11) are not the false teachers who are "forbidding to marry" (4:3). As such, Paul's instruction for the younger widows "to marry" (5:14) would indeed be a way for them to not only protect themselves from the false teachers but also to effectively divorce themselves from the destructive influence of the false teachers.

turn-aside after Satan (5:15), and Paul is correctively instructing the women to realign themselves with Christ Jesus by marrying a godly man who will lead and protect her from false teaching, by child-parenting together with him, and by mastering the household together in harmony with his leading to raise godly children in a godly household that will actively participate in the design of God's missional household "in faith." Thus in both the B and B' units of the macrochiasm, the audience understand that Paul's concern is for the protection and salvation of the women in the audience. For this reason, he wants the younger-women to marry a man who will protect her in the way that Christ protects the church (5:14).[125]

The phrase "after Satan" (ὀπίσω τοῦ σατανᾶ) in the "a'" sub-element would be especially forceful, given Paul's statement in the parallel "a" sub-element regarding the younger widows who "are impassioned from Christ . . . holding condemnation because the first faith they rejected" (5:11–12). Paul is highlighting a stark polarity between Christ and Satan, and subsequently between those who give their allegiance to the former and the latter.[126] In this way, Paul's further implication is clearly understood: where the apostate false teachers are holding-toward teachings of demons (4:1), the younger widows's allegiance to "some" indicates their allegiance to one, Satan.[127] Conversely, therefore, Paul—the apostle of Christ Jesus (1:1)—in 5:14 wants the younger widows to align themselves with the teaching of the

---

125. See volume 2, chapter 2 regarding 1 Timothy 3:2.

126. The phrase "after Satan" (ὀπίσω τοῦ σατανᾶ) is likely not insignificant. In Mark's Gospel, Jesus contrasts two groups. On the one hand, there are those who desire "after" (ὀπίσω) Jesus (8:34). On the other hand, there are those who attempt to make Jesus follow them, to whom Jesus replies, "Go, after (ὀπίσω) me, Satan (σατανᾶ)" (8:33). To "have turned aside after (ὀπίσω) Satan" in 1 Timothy 5:15, then, seems to indicate both an allegiance to Satan and an opposition to following Christ.

It may also be worth noting the overall linguistic similarities of Paul's statements in 5:11, 15 of the parallel "a" and "a'" sub-elements in comparsion to Jesus's statement in Mark 8:33–34:

1 Tim 5:11: "impassioned from Christ, they desire (θέλουσιν) to marry" (5:11);

1 Tim 5:15: "some (τινες) have already turned aside after Satan (ὀπίσω τοῦ σατανᾶ)" (5:15);

Mark 8:33–34: "Go, after me, Satan (ὀπίσω μου σατανᾶ) . . . If someone desires after me (εἴ τις θέλει ὀπίσω μου) to follow . . ."

127. In Paul's final words to the Ephesian overseers in Acts 20, the false-teaching overseers whom Paul predicted in Acts 20:30 are described by Paul as "pulling-away the disciples *after* (ὀπίσω) *themselves*" (emphasis added). It seems relevant—and extremely polemical—for Paul in the 1 Timothy letter to now describe the influence of the false teachers upon the women in Ephesus who "have turned-aside *after* (ὀπίσω) *Satan*" (5:15, emphasis added). In other words, similar to the way that Jesus addresses Peter as "Satan" in Mark 8:33 (". . . and to Peter he said, 'Go after me, Satan'"), Paul seems to be doing the same with the false teachers in Ephesus.

church (1:10b; 4:6, 13, 16) and thereby transition their allegiance to another, Christ. Indeed, the audience understand that 5:15 summarizes the devastating impact that the false teachers have already had among the audience, particularly among the younger widows.[128] Where the salvation of the younger widows is at stake, the urgency of Paul's instruction resounds. The overall impetus of the letter has been for the entire audience to align themselves with Timothy, the apostle, and thus Christ Jesus and God; thus what is clearly implied here in the concluding "a'" sub-element is that if anyone in the audience—not merely the younger widows—refuses to heed the apostle's salvific instructions that accord with the sound teaching—the gospel, the testimony, the mystery concerning Christ Jesus (1:11; 2:6; 3:16)—then the situation is bound to only get worse, namely more shipwrecked faith (1:19), more apostasy (4:1), and more turning-aside after Satan (5:15).

In the concluding verse of the "a'" sub-element of the minichiasm and the B' element of the microchiasm, Paul begins: "If some faithful-woman has widows" (5:16). Several observations are worth noting. First, in the same way that Paul's prior use of the term "if" indicated a real and present circumstance within the church (εἴ, 1:10; εἴ, 3:1; εἰ, 3:5; εἰ, 5:4; εἰ, 5:8), it is evident that "if (εἴ) some faithful-woman" in 5:15 is not hypothetical or conditional but rather is already a current state of affairs in Ephesus. Moreover, Paul's return to the formulaic combination of "if" and "some" in regard to the younger widow here in 5:14 would highlight the contrast to the fourfold use of "if" in reference to the factitive activities of the true widow in 5:10. Second, the indefinite pronoun "some" (τις) in 5:16 recalls "some" (τινες) in 5:15 of the current "a'" sub-element who have already turned-aside after Satan. Here, then, the audience are to understand that Paul still has in view the younger widows in the minichiasm who are impassioned from Christ (5:11), have turned-aside after Satan (5:15), and whom Paul, therefore, wants restored to faith through their adherence to his instructions (5:14). Third, the term "faithful-woman" (πιστή) in 5:16 of the "a'" sub-element recalls the younger widows in 5:12 of the parallel "a" sub-element who had rejected "the first faith" (πίστιν). Combined with the immediate implication of "some" (5:15, 16), the audience understand that the phrase

---

128. Such would lend further credence to Paul's instructions in 2:12 of the parallel B unit, wherein the influence of the false teachers upon the women in the audience was clearly in view. Paul highlights for the audience that heeding the false teachings of the false teachers results in turning aside after Satan (5:15); certainly this is clear because it has already happened to the false teachers themselves (1:6, 19, 20; 4:1). Thus it is evident why Paul's instructions in 2:12 are of paramount importance: as in 5:15, salvation is at stake in 2:12, and failure to listen to Paul would be a repeat of 2:14, that is, of the human choice to turn aside after Satan (Gen 3:1–13) rather than wanting to follow God's design (2:13).

"some faithful-woman" carries a strong, pejorative irony: to be sure, "some faithful-woman" is not "in faith" (cf. 1:2, 4; 2:15; 3:13; 4:12) nor is "of the faithful" (cf. 4:3b, 10, 12) but rather is a younger widow who is impassioned from Christ (5:11), that is, who already has turned-aside after Satan (5:15). At the same time, therefore, given Paul's want for the younger widow to be restored to faith (5:14), the sense is that Paul's statement would equally carry a restorative implication, the sense being: "If some woman wants to be faithful, then she certainly can be."[129]

Fourth, that "some faithful-woman"—the younger widows—"has widows" in 5:16 would likely imply that "some faithful-woman" is young in age relative to the presumably elderly widows who she "has." The phrase "if (εἰ) some (τις) faithful-woman has (ἔχει) widows (χήρας)" in 5:16 of the B' element would recall 5:4 of the parallel B element wherein "if (εἰ) some (τις) widow (χήρα) has (ἔχει) children or those-from-parents."[130] In effect, then, the audience would hear 5:16 as a parallel advancement of 5:3, yet flowing in the reverse direction.[131] The overall sense would be that "some faithful-woman" who has widows (5:16) is herself an ungodly child who must learn first to be-godly to her own household and to give-return repayments to her parents, namely "some widow" (5:4). Thus while alluded to in 5:4a, the interconnected cycle of ungodliness between parent and child is corroborated for the audience here in 5:16 through the parallel arrangement of the microchiasm. That is, just as "some (τις) widow" in the B element did not raise her children or those-from-parents to be-godly (5:4a), so also her children or those-from-parents—now "some (τις) faithful-woman," a

---

129. The traditional understanding of 5:16—that Paul is addressing believing women—is possible. In this case, "If some faithful-woman" (5:16) would be heard according to an affirming, general application to "any faithfulful-woman"—as did "If someone aspires to overseer" (3:1). However, as in 3:1, to disregard the simultaneously polemical force of "some" in 5:16 would certainly miss the overall force of Paul's letter, which consistently dichotomizes two groups: those allied to Timothy, Paul, Christ Jesus, and God versus those who are not. Given the immediate context of the 5:11–16 minichiasm, it seems to be most natural that the audience would understand "some faithful-woman" as a rhetorical irony referring to the younger ungodly widows rather than a sudden switch to a discussion of all believing women.

Regarding other interpretations of the identity of "faithful-woman" (5:16), it has been suggested that Paul is addressing affluent women in Ephesus (e.g., Kelly, *PE*, 121), but the traditional interpretation is that Paul is addressing believing women with family members who are widows (e.g., Marshall, *PE*, 606; Knight, *PE*, 229).

130. As in 5:4, the English translation "has" for the verb ἔχει in 5:8 is most fitting for the context, rather than the translation "holds," which has been been consistently applied to translations of the verb throughout the letter.

131. Here, a visual comparison of the verses is helpful:
5:4: "εἰ δέ τις χήρα τέκνα ἢ ἔκγονα ἔχει";
5:16: "εἴ τις πιστὴ ἔχει χήρας."

younger widow herself—is ungodly to the elderly widows whom she has (5:16), namely "some widow" (5:4a). Thus in the same way that the ungodly children or those-from-parents in 5:4 of the B element must learn to care for their widows, so also "some faithful-woman" in 5:16 of the parallel B' element must learn to do the same. Put positively, Paul's point is fully integrative and concerned with individual family life: a "faithful-woman" who is actually "in faith" is identified as such by her assistance of the widows whom she has (5:16), which is the same way that "godly" children or those-from-parents who are actually "in faith" are identified by giving-return repayments to their parents (5:4a).[132]

Fifth and finally, the audience hear that the apostle Paul wants specifically some "faithful-woman" (πιστή)—note, not men—to care for the widows that she has, that is, for women to care for women.[133] Evidently and similar to Timothy's interaction with "younger-women in all purity" (5:2), the audience understand that Paul intends to establish winsome boundaries between men and women. Such would practically prevent circumstances in which a godly man from the church might fall into sexual temptation while trying to provide direct care to widows, thereby protecting the women and giving no occasion to the opponent for maligning (5:14).[134] Furthermore, Paul's instructions would highlight an essential role that godly women must fill in the proper functioning of individual households and ultimately God's household: especially women are uniquely suited to attend to other women.[135]

The two imperatives "she must assist them" and "the church must not be-burdened" are tied to each other,[136] so much that the "and" (καί) between them could be conveyed as "so that." In effect, the audience understand that

---

132. A similar positive and negative connotation was heard in 3:1. Positively, it is commendable to aspire to the office of overseer; negatively, if "someone" aspires to the office of overseer, then they must be qualified to do so.

133. The term πιστή is feminine. The textual manuscript variant that provides the longer reading "faithful man or woman" (πιστὸς ἢ πιστή) is improbable and likely an attempt to include believing men in the responsibility of caring for widows; see Metzger, *TCGNT*, 642; Marshall, *PE*, 581. This longer reading seems to miss the point, namely that Paul wanted especially the women to attend to widows.

134. Where "some faithful-woman has widows" refers to a setting in which both a younger widow and elderly widow are in view, Paul's concern would likely pertain to a man's unavoidable interaction with "some faithful-woman"—a younger widow—while trying to provide for the elderly widows.

135. The intended bond between older women and younger women is also alluded to in Titus 2:3–4. See also volume 1, chapter 4 regarding 1 Timothy 2:12.

136. Contra *ESV*: "If any believing woman has relatives who are widows, let her care for them. Let the church not be burdened, so that it may care for those who are really widows."

a primary way to help the church, that is, to advance the missional calling of God's household, is first and foremost to care for their own households well; such would enable the church to help those who otherwise have no one to help them.[137] The verb "assist" (ἐπαρκείτω) recalls for the audience Paul's earlier description of an elderly widow who is testified in commendable works, namely having "assisted" (ἐπήρκεσεν) the afflicted (5:10). Its occurrence here in 5:16 would likely be heard with a twofold nuance. On the one hand, that some faithful-woman "must assist" her widows indicates that her lifestyle will align with the elderly, godly widow of 5:10. That is, when "*some faithful-woman*" actually becomes a "faithful-woman"—one of "the faithful" (4:3b, 10)—by heeding Paul's instructions to marry, to child-parent, and to master-households (5:14), she will likewise raise-children, show-hospitality, wash the feet of the holy-ones, and assist the afflicted (5:10b). Furthermore, given the connection between "the afflicted she assisted" (5:10b) and "she must assist" (5:16), Paul may be qualifying a specific group of "the afflicted" whom the younger widow specifically "must assist," namely their own afflicted widows (5:16). On the other hand, Paul's command that some faithful-woman "must assist" in 5:16 of the B' element echoes Paul's command in 5:4a of the parallel B element wherein children or those-from-parents "must learn" to be-godly to their own household and to give-return repayments to their parents. Such would not only strengthen the integrated, cyclical connection between parent and child—"some widow" (parent) and "some faithful-woman" (child)—but also indicate that Paul's command in 5:16 intends to restore "some faithful-woman" to godliness, that is, to do what is acceptable in the sight of God (5:4b). Thus, positively, the audience hear that Paul wants "some" woman to actually become a "faithful-woman" who is testified in commendable works.

Adherence to Paul's first command that some faithful-woman "must assist" her widows enables the fulfillment of Paul's second command: "the church must not be-burdened" (5:16). The connection of the two commands in 5:16 of the B' element echoes the connection of Paul's statement in 5:8 of the parallel B element, namely that failing to provide for one's own family results in failing to provide for God's family. Furthermore, strengthening this implication, by specifying "the church" (ἐκκλησία) in 5:16, the audience would recall Paul's earlier statement in 3:5 that someone cannot care-for "the church" (ἐκκλησίας) of God if he does not know how to lead his own household. Even more, "the church" (ἐκκλησία) in 5:16 would recall the household of God, which is "the church" (ἐκκλησία) of God (3:15). The occurrence

---

137. Horton aptly captures the nuance by discussing "the importance of staying at our posts to which God has called us: as children, parents, extended family, neighbors, coworkers, and citizens" (*Ordinary*, 190).

of "the church" here in 5:16, then, would frame Paul's command to "some faithful-woman" within the macrochiasm's interconnected household imagery: where "the church"—God's household—"must not be-burdened," it is because individual families are performing their basic Christian duty to be godly to their own household (5:4a). To be sure, Paul's concern that the church must not "be-burdened" (βαρείσθω) does not indicate that it is exhausting or irksome for the church to care for widows; rather, Paul's concern is that widows who can and should be cared for by others—namely their own family members—should not unnecessarily use church resources that could otherwise be used for widows who have no one else to care for them.

Indeed, Paul makes this clear by stating the purpose for which the church must not be-burdened: "that it might assist those who are truly widows" (5:16). The immediate repetition of "might assist" (ἐπαρκέσῃ) after "she must assist" (ἐπαρκείτω) would emphasize their inseparable connection: individual families "must assist" their own widows so that the church "might assist" those who are truly widows (5:16). What is more, such would be punctuated for the audience by Paul's rhetorical arrangement of the B and B' elements: the opening statement of the B element was for the church to honor widows, namely "those truly widows" (τὰς ὄντως χήρας, 5:3), and the final statement of the B' element allows the church to assist "those who are truly widows" (ταῖς ὄντως χήραις, 5:16).

In sum, the audience understand that Paul's instructions are thoroughly integrated: home life and church life are interconnected, and godly women are invaluable to the proper functioning of both. Significantly also, the proper dynamic of care that is acceptable to God (5:4b)—the younger caring for the elderly, children caring for their parents—is part of the way that the household of God can fulfill its fundamental, missional calling. Thus when "some faithful-woman" becomes a godly woman "in faith" who cares for her own family (5:4a, 16), she will certainly be following in a good work (5:10c) that ought to be viewed as an integral part of directly fulfilling God's redemptive purposes toward all humans.[138] Moreover, the further implication is that when "some faithful-woman" enters the realm "in faith"—the household of God, which is the church of the living God (3:15)—she will want to assist her widows (5:16) because she herself is a participant of the

---

138. Towner, *Letters*, 359, correctly highlights the missional dimension of Paul's entire discussion about identifying the true widow: "The complexity of the situation facing the Ephesian church should not be missed. It emerges in various ways, but above all we see how Paul walks the fine line between dealing with what might be regarded as a church-specific problem and the wider society's evaluation of the church. The bottom line is that in this case, too, behavior adopted in the church or sanctioned by the church ultimately affects how those on the outside regard the church."

church's missional call and, therefore, would not want anything to hinder its missional purpose (5:16).

1 Timothy 5:17—6:2: Instructions concerning Elders and Slaves

(A' Element)

Within the concluding A' element of the microchiasm (5:17—6:2), the audience hear three minichiasms (5:17-19; 5:20-25; 6:1-2). In this section, each of the three minichiasms will be examined.

1 Timothy 5:17-19: A Minichiastic Unit

As a minichiasm in itself, verses 5:17-19 of the A' element are composed carefully of four sub-elements ("a"-"b"-"b'"-"a'"); linguistic parallels identifying chiastic arrangements are indicated by the Greek text:

> "a". ¹⁷ᵃ The elders (πρεσβύτεροι) who lead commendably must be considered-worthy of double honor,
>
> > "b". ¹⁷ᵇ especially those who toil in word (λόγῳ) and teaching.
> >
> > "b'". ¹⁸ For the writing says (λέγει), "A threshing ox you shall not muzzle," and, "Worthy is the laborer of his pay."
>
> "a'". ¹⁹ Do not accept an accusation against an elder (πρεσβυτέρου), except upon two or three testifiers.

The third minichiasm of the 5:1—6:2 microchiasm is framed by Paul's discussion of elders among the audience in the "a" and "a'" sub-elements. The minichiasm gravitates around authoritative words in the "b" and "b'" sub-elements.

1 Timothy 5:17a: Elders who Lead Commendably, Worthy of Double Honor

("a" sub-element)

In the introductory "a" sub-element of the 5:17-19 minichiasm, Paul commands that a specific group of among the audience should be treated by the church in a specific way: "The elders who lead commendably must be considered-worthy of double honor" (5:17a). The plural term "The elders" (πρεσβύτεροι) in 5:17a of the A′ element recalls "An elderly-man" (πρεσβυτέρῳ) and "elderly-women" (πρεσβυτέρας) in 5:1–2 of the parallel A element. It may be possible, then, that audience hear Paul speaking in general terms about the elderly-men and elderly-women in the church. However, "elders" (πρεσβύτεροι) in 5:17a also recalls "the presbytery" (πρεσβυτερίου) in 4:15 of the preceding microchiasm, namely the authorized church council that was comprised of leaders of the church at large. Therefore, it is immediately apparent to the audience that Paul may intend "The elders" to be understood as the members of "the presbytery." Undoubtedly, it is evident that Paul is referring to the leaders of the church—the elders within the presbytery—by the way he describes "The elders" with the participle "lead" (προεστῶτες) and the adverb "commendably" (καλῶς).[139] The elders who "lead commendably" (καλῶς προεστῶτες) in 5:17a recalls the church overseer in the third microchiasm who is qualified for the "commendable" (καλοῦ) work (3:1) of an overseer by "leading . . . commendably" (καλῶς προϊστάμενον) his own household (3:4) as a demonstration of his ability "to lead" (προστῆναι) the church (3:5). Given these explicit connections, the audience are to understand that Paul's discussion of "The elders" in 5:17a has in view church leaders, likely an "overseer" from 3:1–7.[140] Furthermore, that Paul intends for the elders who "lead commendably" (καλῶς προεστῶτες) in 5:17a to be understood as men in leadership positions in the church would be corroborated by the fact that the other leaders of the Ephesian church—qualified deacons—are "leading . . . commendably" (καλῶς προϊστάμενοι) both children and their own households (3:12).[141] Still, where Paul's discussion

---

139. See Knight, *PE*, 231. Ibid., 232: "προΐστημι occurs only in Paul, and six out of his eight uses of the verb refer to officers and their activity in the church (Rom. 12:8; 1 Thes. 5:12; 1 Tim. 3:5; 5:17)."

Given the parallelism to 5:1–2, it may be worth noting that this leading group of "elders" did not necessarily consist entirely of elderly men. That younger men were likely included, see below regarding 5:17b of the "b" sub-element.

140. As noted, commentators view the terms "overseer" and "elder" interchangeably; see volume 2, chapter 2 regarding 1 Timothy 3:1. While many commentators cite Acts 20:17, 28, Titus 1:5, 7, and 1 Peter 5:1–2 as proof texts—indeed they are—it is evident that the 1 Timothy letter itself establishes the connection. To be sure, it would be audible and apparent to Paul's first-century audience that "The elders" in 5:17 and the "overseer" in 3:1–7 overlap as leaders of the church. See discussion in Merkle, *Why Elders?*, 19–22.

141. Given that Paul's discussion of church leaders in 3:1–13—particularly in relation to 2:12–14—identified for the audience that leadership positions in the church are held by qualified men who sacrificially lead (see volume 2, chapter 2), it would be apparent for the audience that Paul has men in view as "The elders" in the 5:17–19 minichiasm.

of leadership qualifications in the third microchiasm was simultaneously accompanied by a rhetorical polemic against "some" men who were unqualified for the office of overseer,[142] the audience would likely also perceive a subtle polemic here to distinguish between qualified and unqualified elders in the Ephesian church.[143] That is, Paul seems to be indicating that there are qualified men in Ephesus who "lead (προεστῶτες) commendably" (5:17; cf. 3:5) as elders—likely as overseers. At the same time, the connection to 3:5 simultaneously indicates that there are unqualified men in Ephesus who do not lead commendably as elders, namely the man who "does not know how to lead (προστῆναι) his own household" (3:5; cf. 5:17).

Concerning this particular group of leaders in the church, Paul declares that they "must be considered-worthy of double honor" (5:17a). The term "honor" (τιμῆς) recalls 5:3 of the current microchiasm wherein the church is called to "Honor (τίμα) widows—those truly widows." The repetition of "honor" reinforces the overall concern of the fifth microchiasm that various members of God's household must display proper respect toward one another. In 5:17a, just as a widow who is testified in commendable works must be-enrolled to receive care from the church (5:9–10), so too the elders who lead commendably must be considered-worthy of double honor. Furthermore, "honor" (τιμῆς) also recalls the blessings of "honor (τιμή) and glory" that are given to God in 1:17 of the first microchiasm. Here, then, the audience understand that considering the elders worthy of double "honor" would ultimately give "honor" to God. Moreover, that "double (διπλῆς) honor" is in view suggests that the audience's adherence to Paul's command would be a tangible way for God to receive, in effect, "double honor." To be sure, just as the "honor" for widows in 5:3 was concerned with material provisions, so also the audience understand that the "double honor" in 5:17a is not merely dispositional but also material, namely in the form of tangible—presumably monetary—recompense.[144]

---

142. The indefinite pronoun τις is used only in reference to the overseers, not deacons; see 3:1, 5.

143. Not a few a commentators suggest that the participle phrase "lead commendably" does not distinguish "The elders" in 5:17a from those that do not lead commendably. Knight, *PE*, 232: "As in the other occurrences, καλῶς connotes no pejorative comparison of others, but is simply the evaluation of one person's performance by itself." See discussion in Marshall, *PE*, 611. However, this would not account for the overall polemic of the letter against the false teachers nor the specific polemic that is sustained alongside Paul's description of qualified overseers.

144. Merkle, *Why Elders?*, 83: "Although the normal meaning of the word translated 'honor,' refers to the respect or worth given to someone, in this context it clearly includes the idea of financial support. In 1 Timothy 5:3, Paul commands the church, 'Honor widows who are truly widows,' which clearly refers to financial support." See

As the "a" sub-element concludes, a further significance would be heard. The verb "must be considered-worthy" (ἀξιούσθωσαν) recalls the cognate term "worthy" (ἄξιος) in regard to the faithful word concerning both Christ Jesus's entrance into the world to save sinners (1:15) and the proper reception of God's creation in the present life in view of the life to come (4:9). Clearly, both 1:15 and 4:9 have salvific implications in regard to the truth about Christ Jesus and the godly practice thereof. Thus Paul's command to the audience in 5:17a that the elders who lead commendably "must be considered-worthy" of double honor would not be heard as a passing nicety but rather as a weighty declaration: to not consider the elders "worthy" of double honor (5:17a) would also tangibly signify that the faithful word is not "worthy" of all acceptance (1:15; 4:9). Therefore, to the faithful among the audience Paul expects that they will consider the elders "worthy" as they also accept that the faithful word is "worthy." In short, as heard throughout the macrochiasm, 5:17a demonstrates that allegiance to Paul's command evidences allegiance to Christ Jesus and thus one's existence "in faith."

1 Timothy 5:17b: Those who Toil in Word and Teaching

("b" sub-element)

In the "b" sub-element the apostle provides a qualifying statement about those whom the church must consider-worthy of double honor: "especially those who toil in word and teaching" (5:17b). Several observations are worth noting. First, the adverb "especially" (μάλιστα) recalls its prior two occurrences in the letter. In 4:10 of the previous microchiasm, the audience heard "especially" (μάλιστα) as an emphatic reference to the universal offer of salvation by the living God to all humans over and against the delimited view of salvation by the false teachers. In 5:8 of the current microchiasm, "especially" (μάλιστα) denoted the "household-members" in the household of God, namely the faithful for whom God is the Savior. Here in 5:17b, then,

---

Fee, *1 & 2 Tim*, 129; Meier, "*Presbyteros*," 327; Knight, *PE*, 232. Contra Kirk, "Did 'Officials' in the New Testament Church Receive a Salary?," 105–8; Towner, *Letters*, 363–64 n. 18. For further discussion, see Marshall, *PE*, 613.

It has been suggested that "double honor" in 5:17a evidences "double standards" in regard to financial provisions for widows in comparision to elders; see Gench, *Tyrannical Texts*, 130; Krause, *1 Tim*, 109–10. Yet, as will be shown below, Paul's point is not about paying male elders more than female widows; to be sure, elders who are not teaching elders do not to receive "double honor"; see below regarding 5:17b. Rather, Paul's point is about paying those who "toil"; see below regarding 1 Timothy 5:18.

the likely implication would not only be that the elders in 5:17a are saved but also that these elders "who lead commendably" have been leading God's missional household toward the universal acceptance of the faithful word concerning Christ Jesus by all humans. At the same time, given the polemical use of "especially" in 4:10, a subtle polemic would likely also be intended here in 5:17b against any elder who distorts the "word and teaching."

The precise sense in which the adverb "especially" was heard by the audience is difficult to pinpoint, connoting either "namely" or "above all."[145] The former sense—"namely"—would specify that the elders "who toil in word and teaching" must be considered-worthy of double honor to the exclusion of elders who do not toil in word and teaching.[146] The latter sense—"above all"—would convey that all of the elders who lead commendably must be considered-worthy of honor, but double honor must be given over and above to "those who toil in word and teaching."[147] The ambiguity seems fitting here. On the one hand, given the overarching context of "some" who teach-different (1:3; 10b), it may be that Paul is commanding the audience to show double honor specifically to elders "who toil in word and teaching"—namely "teaching elders"—as a way of materially sustaining them while they effectively war against the different teaching of "some" (1:3; 1:10b). On the other hand, such a limited application seems to unduly disregard "the elders who lead commendably" (5:17a) yet are not teaching elders, that is, not those who toil in word and teaching. Certainly, such non-teaching elders would still be considered-worthy of honor in the estimation of the apostle. Thus, the nuanced sense heard by the audience would most

---

145. USB, s.v.

146. Marshall, *PE*, 612: "'namely', identifying those who lead well with those who teach." In the same way, Knight suggests that if "μάλιστα can at times have the meaning 'that is,' then Paul is giving here a further description of those he has already mentioned" (*PE*, 232).

147. Either sense may be heard in 4:10 and 5:8, but the former—"namely"—is more likely. A comparison between each connotation may be helpful:

4:10 ("namely"): "the living God, who is the Savior of all humans, *namely* of the faithful." Here, "namely" specifies "the faithful" as those for whom God is the Savior, yet without implying partiality on God's part.

4:10 ("above all"): "the living God, who is the Savior of all humans, *above all* of the faithful." Here, "above all" implies partiality on God's part toward "the faithful," thus missing the point that God is equally the Savior of all humans.

5:10 ("namely"): "if someone does not provide-for those of his own and *namely* for household-members." Here, "namely" specifies that "household-members" are to be provided for by someone, yet without implying partiality by the provider.

5:10 ("above all"): "if someone does not provide-for those of his own and *above all* for household-members." Here, "above all" implies partiality on behalf of the provider toward "household-members" over and above "those of his own," thus missing the point that someone must provide for both.

likely be that all of "The elders who lead commendably" in the household of God are to be honored according to their leadership duties, and for this reason, teaching elders are to be honored in a particular manner according to their additional duties to "toil in word and teaching."

The verb "toil" (κοπιῶντες) in 5:17 recalls for the audience Paul and Timothy's "toil" (κοπιῶμεν) in 4:10 of the fourth microchiasm to promote the faithful word that is worthy of all acceptance.[148] The elders in view, then, are those who share in the apostle Paul and Timothy's collective endeavor to preserve the teaching over and against the unqualified apostate overseers who teach some-thing different (1:10b). Furthermore, due to the cumulative progression of the macrochiasm, here in 5:17 of the fifth microchiasm the terms "word" (λόγῳ) and "teaching" both have well-established connotations. In 1:15 of the first microchiasm, the audience heard "Faithful is the word" (λόγος) concerning Christ Jesus's entrance into the world to save sinners. In 3:1 of the third microchiasm, "Faithful is the word" (λόγος) delineated the missional leadership of the church in godliness. In the fourth microchiasm, the audience heard that all creation of God is made-holy consistent-with the "word" (λόγου) of God (4:5), that is, the "words" (λόγοις) of the faith in which Timothy is being-nourished (4:6), the faithful "word" (λόγος) that is worthy of all acceptance (4:9), and the "word" (λόγῳ) of which Timothy is to be an example (4:12). Still, the term "word" (λόγῳ) in 5:17 would also recall its verbal cognates: Paul is "saying" (λέγω) the truth (2:7) and the Spirit explicitly "says" (λέγει) that some will apostasy from the faith (4:1). Undoubtedly, then, the audience understand that the elders in 5:17 who toil in "word" (λόγῳ) are those who are participatory allies with Timothy, the apostle Paul, and thus Christ Jesus, God, and the Spirit. Such elders stand in stark contrast to the false teachers who are "false-worders" (ψευδολόγων, 4:2), have turned-aside for "useless-words" (ματαιολογίαν, 1:6), and are not understanding what "they-are-saying" (λέγουσιν, 1:7).

The term "teaching" (διδασκαλίᾳ) in 5:17 would also recall its progression throughout the macrochiasm. In the first microchiasm, Paul preserves the sound "teaching" (διδασκαλίᾳ) that accords with the gospel of the glory of the blessed God (1:10–11). In the fourth microchiasm, Timothy is being-nourished by the commendable "teaching" (διδασκαλίας) that he has followed (4:6), is to hold-toward the "teaching" (διδασκαλίᾳ), and is to strongly-hold the "teaching" (διδασκαλίᾳ, 4:16). The term "teaching" (διδασκαλίᾳ) in 5:17 would also recall its cognates: Paul is a "teacher" (διδάσκαλος) "in faith" and truth (2:7) of the testimony concerning Christ Jesus (2:6); qualified

---

148. The explicit connection between "toil" (κοπιῶντες) in 5:17b and "toil" (κοπιῶ μεν) in 4:10 would further emphasize the connection between "must be considered-worthy" (ἀξιούσθωσαν) in 5:17a and "worthy" (ἄξιος) in 4:9; see above.

overseers are "able-to-teach" (διδακτικόν, 3:2); Timothy is commanded to "teach" (δίδασκε) the truth regarding godliness, the promise of life, and God's universal offer of salvation to all humans (4:10–11). Again, the audience understand that the elders in 5:17 who toil in "teaching" (διδασκαλίᾳ) are those who are participatory allies with Timothy, thus the apostle Paul, and thus Christ Jesus, God, and the Spirit.[149] Such elders stand in stark contrast to the false teachers who "teach-different" (ἑτεροδιδασκαλεῖν, 1:3), are desiring to be "law-teachers" (νομοδιδάσκαλοι, 1:7), and are holding-toward "teachings" (διδασκαλίαις) of demons (4:1).

In sum, therefore, due to the sustained association of both "word" and "teaching" throughout the macrochiasm, the audience would understand that the two terms are synonyms, the sense being that Paul is referring to elders "who toil in word, that is, in teaching."[150] In short, Paul is identifying elders who "toil in teaching," hence teaching elders. These elders toil in the teaching of "the gospel" that exhibits the radiant glory of God and results in blessing toward him (1:10–11), "the testimony" concerning Christ Jesus who gave himself as a ransom on behalf of all (2:6), and "the mystery" of godliness regarding Christ, who was manifested in flesh and was taken-up in glory.[151] Certainly, then, the audience understand that these specific elders in 5:17 are men who are "able-to-teach" (διδακτικόν, 3:2), whom the apostle Paul positively permits "to teach" (διδάσκειν) and govern in the church (cf. 2:12); they are men who do not abdicate their creational roles to lead (cf. 2:13)—indeed, they lead commendably (3:4, 5; 5:17a)—and who exhibit irreproachable fidelity to their wives in the form a sacrificial, loving leadership (3:2). Thus the elders who toil in "teaching" are those whom Paul intends the audience to view as their protectors, namely from the shipwrecking influence of different teachings (1:10), that is, of the teachings of demons (4:1), which result in turning-aside after Satan (5:15). Given such implications, it is fitting for the audience to give special honor—double

---

149. Regarding the relationship of the Spirit to "teaching," see volume 2, chapter 3 regarding 1 Timothy 4:1.

150. This was already made explicit in 4:6, wherein the conjuction "and" (καί) was heard epexegetically to specify "the words of the faith" as synonymous with "the commendable teaching"; see volume 2, chapter 3. Contra Towner, who suggests that "word" is distinguished from "teaching," arguing that the former applies to those who have yet to embrace the gospel, namely unbelievers, and the latter applies to those who already belong to the household of faith and are merely in need of edification (*Goal*, 121–24). However, as Paul makes clear in the 1 Timothy letter, both terms are interwined and equally applicable to both those who would-inevitably-come to have-faith upon Christ Jesus (1:16) and those of the faithful (4:3b, 10).

151. The "sound teaching" in 1:10 is defined by its direct relation "according to the gospel" (1:11); see volume 1, chapter 3 regarding 1 Timothy 1:11a.

honor—to the elders who both lead commendably and teach in the church, namely the men who are qualified overseers in Ephesus. Over and against "some" who are unqualified false-teaching overseers in the Ephesian church, Paul is identifiying that it is these qualified teaching elders in 5:17—overseers—who alongside Timothy are able to lead the audience to preserve the teaching and promote godliness as God's missional household.

1 Timothy 5:18: For the Writing Says

("b'" sub-element)

In the "b'" sub-element, Paul states, "For the writing says, 'A threshing ox you shall not muzzle,' and, 'Worthy is the laborer of his pay'" (5:18). Consistent with its prior occurrences throughout the macrochiasm (2:13; 3:13; 4:5, 8, 10, 16; 5:4, 11, 15), the audience understand that the conjuction "for" (γάρ) in 5:18 marks the basis for the preceding statement in 5:17. In effect, the audience understand that the reason why the teaching elders must be considered-worthy of double honor (5:17) is because "the writing says" (5:18). Such an explanation would indicate a break from the way that Paul had given his prior commands in the fifth microchiasm. In regard to Timothy's call to exhort an elderly-man (5:1), the audience's call to honor widows who are truly widows (5:3, 5, 9, 10), and the ungodly younger widow's call to assist the widows she has (5:16; cf. 5:4), Paul uses practical applications of missional godliness that are informed by indirect and implicit references to scriptural commands, namely to honor one's parents. However, regarding the audience's call to consider the teaching elders worthy of double honor, Paul's command is informed by a direct and explicit reference to "the writing" without any further explanation. For sure, "the writing" (ἡ γραφή) would be understood by the audience as Paul's reference to God's very own authoritative, written revelation.[152] Simply and clearly, then, Paul's point is that teaching elders must be considered-worthy of double honor because God says it in his divine revelation, "the writing" (5:18). It is possible that the apostle's reason for this explicit reference to "the writing" was in response to doubt and speculation by the audience regarding how they ought to relate to their leaders, particularly in light of the false teachers who were evidently vying for leadership positions (3:1–7). With some among the audience aligning themselves with the false teachers's leadership (5:15; cf.

---

152. Knight, PE, 233: "γραφή . . . means in general 'writing' but is used 'in the NT exclusively with a sacred meaning, of Holy Scriptures' (BAGD s.v. 2 . . .) . . . Paul regards ἡ γραφή as holy scripture, i.e., as God directly speaking."

2:12) and others maintaining allegiance to the teaching of Paul and Timothy's leadership, the remaining group may have been tempted to adopt an attitude of indifference or perhaps even suspicion toward any form of leadership within the Ephesian church. As a result and to make certain beyond all doubt, Paul states plainly that all those who live in God's household—the realm "in faith," the church—should adhere to the basic view that "the writing" calls them to give honor to those for whom it is due.

Still, the particular rhetorical force of Paul's statement "For the writing says" would not go unnoticed by the audience. Paul's reference to "the writing" (ἡ γραφή) in 5:18 recalls Paul's reference to his own letter in 3:14: "These-things to you I write (γράφω)." Where "the writing" (5:18) explicitly has God's revelation in view, Paul's rhetorical implication may intend to emphasize that the 1 Timothy letter that "I write" (3:14) as "an apostle . . . according to the command of God" (1:1) is to be considered part of "the writing," that is, part of divine revelation from God (5:18). What is more, Paul's explicit reference to "the writing" in 5:18 is unnecessary to support his command in 5:17: Paul's command is at once authoritative according to his divine appointment as an apostle of Christ Jesus by the command of God (1:1; 1:12; 2:7). By referencing what "the writing says" (5:18), therefore, Paul's command would almost be doubly authoritative: it is not only what the apostle Paul says in his writing (5:17; cf. 3:14), but it is also what God clearly says in "the writing" (5:18). It would thus be understood that Paul is going out of his way to emphasize that adherence is expected: there is no possible reason for anyone in the audience to doubt or to disregard that the elders who lead commendably and toil in word and teaching must be considered-worthy of double honor (5:17).

The verb "says" (λέγει) not only recalls the cognate "word" (λόγῳ) in 5:17b of the parallel "b" sub-element but also—and more importantly—conveys that like the "word" that is worthy of all acceptance (1:15; 4:9), so also is the content of what the Scripture "says" to be accepted. That is, even as the "word" concerning Christ Jesus is faithful and worthy of all acceptance for salvation, godliness, holiness, nourishment, eternal life, and example (1:15; 3:1; 4:5, 9, 12) and is authoritative because it is of God (4:5), so too Paul's command from what the writing "says" is equally authoritative concerning reverence for the teaching elders in the expression of double honor (5:17). For the elders who toil in "word" (λόγῳ, 5:17), Paul intends to impress upon the audience the need to revere such leaders in the church who handle and teach what the writing "says" (λέγει)—the very "word" (λόγου) of God (4:5). Here, too, Paul's statement in 5:18 that the writing "says" (λέγει) recalls that the Spirit "says" (λέγει) in 4:1 of the fourth microchiasm. Not only, therefore, would the audience hear a connection between "the writing" and "the

Spirit," but they would also understand that Paul's command is equally and fully aligned with both "the writing" and "the Spirit."[153] In effect, what Paul is "saying" (λέγω, 2:7) is both what the writing "says" (λέγει, 5:18) and what the Spirit "says" (λέγει, 4:1).[154]

Paul goes on to state what the writing says: "'A threshing ox you shall not muzzle,' and, 'Worthy is the laborer of his pay'" (5:18). The first scriptural citation "A threshing ox you shall not muzzle" in 5:18a clearly references LXX Deuteronomy 25:4: "You shall not muzzle a threshing ox."[155] Here, the audience understand that Paul has the OT in view of "the writing" (5:18). Yet, the second scriptural citation "Worthy is the laborer of his pay" in 5:18b is not an OT citation; rather, it refers to a saying by Jesus Christ written in Luke 10:7: "Worthy is the laborer of his pay."[156] Indeed, such could only be understood by the audience as part of "the writing" insofar as it affirms either a written collection of Jesus's sayings or Luke's Gospel as a written text.[157] Significantly, therefore, the audience understand that Paul is

---

153. Where "the writing" would have been understood by the audience as the word of God to humans preserved in written form, the connection of "the Spirit" (4:1) in relation to "the writing" would not only indicate the Spirt's direct involvement with the writing but also the Spirit's direct relation to God.

154. This is not to suggest that Paul's statement regarding the Spirit in 4:1 is bound to a statement found in the writing —e.g., what "the Spirit . . . says" in 4:1 comes from what "the writing says." Rather, the suggestion is the opposite: what "the writing says" is what "the Spirit . . . says." In other words, just as the personal source of Paul's statement in 4:1 is "the Spirit," so too is "the Spirit" the personal source of Paul's statement in 5:18. Implied, then, is that "the Spirit" is the author of "the writing."

155. Compare the Greek texts; note that the word order is slightly different:
1 Tim 5:18a: "βοῦν ἀλοῶντα οὐ φιμώσεις";
LXX Deut 25:4: "οὐ φιμώσεις βοῦν ἀλοῶντα."

156. Compare the Greek texts; with exception of the conjunction γάρ, notice the precise similarity:
1 Tim 5:18b: "ἄξιος ὁ ἐργάτης τοῦ μισθοῦ αὐτοῦ";
Luke 10:7: "ἄξιος γὰρ ὁ ἐργάτης τοῦ μισθοῦ αὐτοῦ."
Wolfe, "Sagacious Use of Scripture," 213: "First Timothy 5:18 does omit γαρ ('for'), but this omission is more likely to confirm the role of the quotation as Scripture . . . he omitted γὰρ and simply connected the two sayings [LXX Deut 25:4 and Luke 10:7] with καί. First Timothy 5:18 appears to be a direct citation of Luke 10:7."
Here, it may be worth noting the OT influence on Jesus's saying in view of Luke 10:7. Translations (*ESV*) of each text are shown here for comparison:
Luke 10:7: "And remain in the same house, eating and drinking what they provide, for the laborer deserves his wages."
Num 18:31 (*ESV*): "And you may eat it in any place, you and your households, for it is your reward in return for your service in the tent of meeting."

157. Lea and Griffin, *1, 2 Tim*, 156: "The second reference resembles the words of Christ in Luke 10:7. It is not likely that Paul was quoting the Gospel of Luke, a document whose date of writing is uncertain. Paul may have been referring to a collection

definitively widening the authority of "the writing" to not only include the OT canon but also Jesus's words.[158] Throughout the macrochiasm, Paul has underscored the primacy of authority—particularly his own—as defined in relation to Christ Jesus and God. In the opening statement of the letter, Paul identified himself as an apostle—authoritative representative—of Christ Jesus by the command of God our Savior (1:1). Continuing in the first microchiasm, Paul not only reiterated his authoritative connection to God—that he was considered-faithful with the gospel of the glory of the blessed God (1:11)—but also to Christ Jesus—the "Lord"—who appointed Paul for service (1:12). In the second microchiasm, Paul underscored his divine appointment as a proclaimer, apostle, and teacher (2:7). Further still, in the fourth microchiasm, Paul defined Timothy's leadership as a deacon in direct relation to Christ Jesus (4:6). Cumulatively, then, in addition to the clear authority that the OT would have for the church in Ephesus, the sustained theme of Paul's letter is undoubtedly to highlight Christ Jesus's authority. It would come as no surprise to the audience, then, that here in 5:18 the apostle intends to uphold the Jesus-saying as authoritative Scripture. In sum, Paul's concern for the audience is not to maintain a closed view of "the writing" as simply the authoritative canon of the OT but rather that all authority ultimately derives from Christ Jesus.

Hearing both scriptural citations as authoritative, the audience now discern the interrelated meaning of each. The different word order of Paul's first citation (5:18a) in relation to Deuteronomy 25:4 may be instructive. In the Deuteronomy text, the emphasis falls on the recipients of the command: "*You* shall not muzzle a threshing ox"; however, in the 1 Timothy text, the

---

of Jesus' sayings, some of which appear in Luke's Gospel." Knight, *PE*, 234: "Since, however, γραφή usually refers to what is written and recognized as scripture and since the words quoted are found verbatim in Luke's Gospel, Paul's dependence on that Gospel is the only alternative that fits all the data . . . Uncertainties about dating should not automatically rule this conclusion out . . . since the necessary dates are both possible and plausible, even with 1 Timothy dated in the early 60s."

158. Patterson and Kelley, "1 Tim," 682: "Paul gave equal authority to the words of the Old Testament and the words of Jesus and referred to both as Scripture." See Collins, *1 & 2 Tim*, 145–46; Guthrie, *PE*, 105; Spicq, *Les Épîtres Pastorales*, 176–77. Contra, some commentators argue that the audience would only have understood "the writing" as a reference to the OT and, therefore, that the Jesus-saying would not have been received by the audience as part of "the writing" but rather as further substantiation of the basic point that elders are worthy of double honor (e.g., Fee, *1 & 2 Tim*, 93; cf. Kelly, *PE*, 126). Marshall aptly summarizes: "Although many commentators think that the reference is purely to Deut 25.4 with v. 18b added as a kind of afterthought or backup from another source, it is quite possible that both quotations are envisaged as coming from 'Scripture'. If so, this is early evidence for the conferral of scriptural status on a collection of sayings of Jesus . . . In any case, for the author the second citation had equal authority with the OT" (*PE*, 615).

emphasis is placed on the one who works: "*A threshing ox you shall not muzzle.*"[159] The change in word order would likely highlight to the audience that, like a threshing ox, the teaching elders toil. The application of the OT verse would be resounding: if God commands his people to effectively "honor" to an assiduous animal, how much more must this be true for a hard-working human and particularly for the elders who toil in teaching God's own word in God's own household![160] In the same way, the accent of the Jesus-saying in 5:18b would apply to and underscore the inherent value of the teaching elders: "*Worthy is the laborer is of his pay.*" Where in both citations the apostle underscores the identity and worthiness of the animal or person laboring, the implication is that the audience are expected to hear the same emphasis in his own statement in 5:17 regarding the elders who toil.[161] Indeed, the term "Worthy" (ἄξιος) in the 5:18b citation recalls the verbal cognate "must be considered-worthy" (ἀξιούσθωσαν) in 5:17 of the current minichiasm, thus emphasizing the way in which the audience are to view the teaching elders. Still, the term "Worthy" (ἄξιος) in 5:18b—which was said by Jesus—would recall the faithful word that is "worthy" (ἄξιος) of all acceptance—which concerns Christ Jesus's entrance into the world (1:15). Here, then, the matter of allegiance and authority would be in view: to not consider the teaching elders "worthy" of double honor (5:17) would be the same as not considering the authoritative word of Christ Jesus "Worthy" (5:18b). Moreover, upon hearing the term "pay" (μισθοῦ), the clear suggestion—according to Jesus's own word—is that the "double honor" in view for teaching elders is tangible, likely taking the form of remuneration.[162]

As the "b'" sub-element concludes, the audience understand that Paul—the apostle of Christ Jesus (1:1)—is presenting a plain fact: the person whom they call "our Lord" (1:2, 12)—Christ Jesus himself—indicates

---

159. Marshall, *PE*, 615–16: "the allusion is to the practice of driving oxen over a threshing floor to trample the corn with their hooves, separating the wheat from the chaff. The law laid down that the farmer must not prevent the animal from taking its share of the harvest." Ngewa, *1 & 2 Tim*, 127: "This prohibition was meant to keep the animal from being starved while it worked."
For the historical background to the Jewish exegesis of this verse, see Instone-Brewer, "A Literal Interpretation," 554–65.

160. Spencer, *1 Tim*, 136: "When an ox works, it should be fed . . . Analogously, if elders were indeed working, they too should be nourished by being honored (5:17)."

161. Wall with Steele, *1 & 2 Tim*, 133: "And this is hard work! The word used for 'labor' [in 5:17] is not *ergon* as we might expect but κοπιάω (*kopiaō*), which envisages the kind of sweaty exertion that exacts a physical toll on a daily laborer."

162. Phillips, *Exploring the PE*, 162: "Evidently, Paul envisioned elders being paid for their service to the local church because the word translated 'reward' means literally 'pay' . . . elders are expected to earn their financial support by sheer hard work and are to be remunerated accordingly."

that the audience ought to "pay" double honor to the elders who toil in word and teaching. Such would be fitting, given that those who toil in word and teaching work to preserve the teaching concerning Christ Jesus. Conversely, it would be equally clear that "some" who teach-different (1:3), who promote that which is false (4:2; cf. 1:10a; 2:7) rather than the truthful testimony about Christ Jeus (2:6), and who cause others to turn-aside after Satan (5:15) ought not to be honored but disregarded. In short, by providing for the qualified teaching elders in Ephesus, the audience understand that they themselves will play a key role alongside Paul and Timothy to preserve the teaching, thus to promote godliness, and thus to enable the missional purpose of God's household, namely the salvation of all humans.[163]

1 Timothy 5:19: An Accusation Against an Elder, Two or Three Testifiers

("a'" sub-element)

In the concluding "a'" sub-element, Paul continues his concern for the audience to show reverence to elders: "Do not accept an accusation against an elder, except upon two or three testifiers" (5:19). The term "elder" (πρεσβυτέρου) recalls for the audience its occurrence in the parallel "a" sub-element where Paul highlighted that "elders" (πρεσβύτεροι) who lead commendably must be considered-worthy of double honor. Not only, then, do the audience understand that Paul has in view the same church leaders in 5:17 but also their worthiness of honor. To be sure, the parallel "b" and "b'" sub-elements underscored the necessity to honor such elders. The appropriate response, therefore, when it comes to the matter of "an accusation against an elder" (5:19) is to protect their reputation against any baseless charges. Furthermore, where the audience have heard the negative particle "not" (μή) through the macrochiasm in association with the activities or influence of the false teachers, Paul's statement "Do not (μή) accept an accusation against an elder" in 5:19 likely indicates that to do so would be conformity to a practice in line with the false teaching overseers.[164] Indeed,

---

163. Ngewa aptly captures Paul's point: "while it is true that God provides, the Bible makes it clear that the standard way in which God does this is through the people whom the pastor ministers to. They have a responsibility to support the pastor, and in so doing to contribute to building the kingdom of God" (*1 & 2 Tim*, 127).

164. The command "do not accept" (μὴ παραδέχου) is somewhat ambiguous. It could be translated as a general principle on how to handle accusations brought against elders (the interpretation presented here) or it could be more specific ("Stop receiving charges"), suggesting Timothy and the audience have already gone about the

the overall context of the letter suggests that the "accusation" in view was understood by the audience in relation to some sort of collusion with the apostate false teachers.

In this context, the audience hear Paul's qualifying statement: "except on two or three testifiers" (5:19). The phrase "two or three testifiers" finds its basis in Deuteronomy 19:15.[165] Certainly, in the case that the false teachers are in view, the polemical irony of the situation would be magnified: where the false teachers bring an accusation against an elder (5:19) yet are those desiring to be law-teachers (1:7), it is evident that they fail to understand the law in Deuteronomy 25:4 (cited in 1 Tim 5:18a); thus Paul uses the law in Deuteronomy 19:15 (cited in 1 Tim 5:19) to undermine their credibility and, therefore, the accusation itself. The term "testifiers" (μαρτύρων) would draw attention to the observable proof that an accusation must bear, recalling its prior cognates throughout the macrochiasm: the godly widow who is "testified" (μαρτυρουμένη) in commendable works (5:10), the qualified overseer who has a commendable "testimony" (μαρτυρίαν) from those-outside (3:7), and the "testimony" (μαρτύριον) that Christ Jesus gave himself as a ransom on behalf of all (2:6). In all of these prior instances, Paul's emphasis was on the tangible, factual basis that could be proved: people saw a godly widow's commendable works (5:10) in the same way that they saw an overseer's repeated lifestyle (3:7) and saw Christ Jesus publically give himself (2:6). The suggestion seems to be that the false teachers's accusations against the qualified elders— perhaps the qualified overseers in Ephesus—had no verifiable proof; such would be fitting for their devotion to vile and silly—unverifiable—myths (4:7a; 1:4).

It is noteworthy that Paul would have to remind the audience—particularly the false teachers standing among them—of a procedure that they would have been familiar with throughout Jewish writings and even in the Jesus tradition; such may suggest that the basic principle of assuming

---

disciplinary process incorrectly. Either way Paul sees the need to either clarify or correct how accusations are to be considered.

165. Compare the relevant portions of the Greek texts:
1 Tim 5:19: "ἐπὶ δύο ἢ τριῶν μαρτύρων";
LXX Deut 19:15: "ἐπὶ στόματος δύο μαρτύρων καὶ ἐπὶ στόματος τριῶν μαρτύρων." It may also be worth noting the Jesus himself alludes to the same OT text in Matthew 18:16. In the case that this Jesus-saying was known and accepted (as the Jesus-saying in Luke 10:7; see 1 Tim 5:18b), Paul's reference here in 5:19 would seem to corroborate that Paul is highlighting Jesus's authority. Compare the relevant portion of the Greek text:
Matt 18:16: "ἐπὶ στόματος δύο μαρτύρων ἢ τριῶν."
For a more detailed analysis of Paul's use of the Deuteronomy texts, see Towner, *Letters*, 367–70.

innocence until proven guilty had in some way been negated. As in 5:18, Paul's use of the OT in 5:19 may have been another reminder to the audience that only God's revelation—in keeping with the OT and Christ Jesus—via the divinely authorized apostle Paul—not the unauthorized false teachers—is to be authoritative within God's household.[166] In this way, it is possible that the false-teaching overseers had set aside this basic OT procedure (5:19) and used their own false authority to, ironically, introduce a new disciplinary process. Still, Paul's citation of the OT may have been a response to the heated situation in Ephesus, which had affected the audience to the extent that they were weary of anyone claiming authority and sought to become their own. Paul may even have anticipated that his polemical tone throughout the letter would have unwittingly suggested to the audience that they had license to raise accusations against the leaders. Whatever the actual situation into which Paul was speaking, his basic concern in the 5:17–19 minichiasm is clear: an elder who leads commendably is worthy of honor—payment in the case of a teaching elder—and must be protected against accusations through the due process that God already established in the OT. As such, the audience are not to take any administrative cues from the false teachers or the apparent exigencies of the given situation but rather from the authority of Paul (5:17) and the writing (5:18–19), that is, the authority of God, Christ Jesus, and the Spirit.

1 Timothy 5:20–25: A Minichiastic Unit

As a minichiasm in itself, verses 5:20–25 of the A' element are composed carefully of four sub-elements ("a"-"b"-"b"-"a"); linguistic parallels identifying chiastic arrangements are indicated by the Greek text:

> "a". ²⁰ Those who sin in the sight of all reprove, that also the rest might hold (ἔχωσιν) fear. ²¹ᵃ I testify in the sight of God and of Christ Jesus and of the elect angels, that these-things you might guard without prejudice (προκρίματος),
>
>> "b". ²¹ᵇ doing nothing (μηδέν) according to favoritism. ²² Lay hands quickly on none (μηδενί), nor (μηδέ) share in others's sins (ἁμαρτίαις); keep yourself pure.

---

166. Phillips, *Exploring the PE*, 162: "Any accusations against an elder must be received only when they are submitted properly. That is the rule. To accept accusations without proper proof is to undermine the authority of God-appointed leaders and to act contrary to God's Word."

"b'". ²³ No-longer (μηκέτι) drink water; rather a little wine use because of your stomach and frequent illnesses. ²⁴ᵃ The sins (ἁμαρτίαι) of some humans are conspicuous,

"a'". ²⁴ᵇ preceding them for judgment (προάγουσαι εἰς κρίσιν), but for some they also follow. ²⁵ Likewise also the commendable works are conspicuous, and those having (ἔχοντα) otherwise do-not have-the-power to be-hidden.

The fourth minichiasm of the 5:1—6:2 microchiasm is framed by the concept of divine justice in the "a" and "a'" sub-elements. The minichiasm gravitates around Timothy's dutiful call in the "b" and "b'" sub-elements to purge the church of false teachers through his objective and impartial leadership, which is held in view of divine justice.

1 Timothy 5:20–21a: Reprove Those Who Sin in the Sight of All

("a" sub-element)

Lest any in the audience suppose that the apostle Paul was minimizing the significance of disciplinary action in 5:19, he provides further instruction of church discipline in 5:20-25. In the introductory "a" sub-element, Paul begins with a stern exhortation: "Those who sin in the sight of all reprove, that also the rest might hold fear" (5:20). The transition between 5:19 and 5:20 seems relatively clear. Whereas the former concerned the situation in which an accusation against an elder should be accepted—"except upon two or three testifiers" (5:19)—here Paul is concerned with what should be done in the case that an accusation against an elder—"Those who sin"—is accepted, presumably on the verifiable basis of two or three testifiers.[167] The present participle "Those who sin" (τοὺς ἁμαρτάνοντας) suggests an unrepentant disposition such that the elder in view is a man who unashamedly persists in sinning.[168] Given that the immediate context within the A' element focuses on elders who toil in word and teaching—overseers—it is probable that the particular "sin" relates in some way to

---

167. That Paul intends "Those who sin" (τοὺς ἁμαρτάνοντας) in reference to elders (5:17, 19) rather than to the audience in general, see Knight, *PE*, 236; Towner, *Letters*, 370; Marshall, *PE*, 618. To be sure, as ibid. notes: "the principle was presumably extended to the rest of the congregation."

168. Ngewa, *1 & 2 Tim*, 129: "*those who are sinning*. The form of the verb indicates that he is referring to those who sin habitually as opposed to those who commit a sin on just one accasion." See Patterson and Kelley, "1 Tim," 682; Spencer, *1 Tim*, 138.

teaching elders—unqualified overseers—who teach-different (1:3), which, in turn, promotes ungodliness (4:3a, 7a, 8a; cf. 2:12) and brings-about controversial-speculations and upheaval within God's household (1:4). Indeed, "Those who sin" (ἁμαρτάνοντας) recalls the polemical reference to "sinners" (ἁμαρτωλοῖς) for whom the law is laid (1:9), that is, those who are not "in faith," namely the false-teaching overseers.[169] Furthermore, where "those who sin" (ἁμαρτάνοντας) recalls that Christ Jesus came into the world to save "sinners" (ἁμαρτωλούς, 1:15), it is evident that those who unashamedly persist in sinning have not come to a knowing-embrace of truth (2:4b; 4:3b), that is, have not been saved by Christ Jesus. Thus in 5:20 where both teaching elders—overseers—and unsaved sinners are in view, the audience likely understand that Paul is referring to "someone" who is already an overseer (3:1), "someone" who was unable to care-for the church of God (3:5), and "some" who have apostatized and become-shipwrecked regarding the faith (1:20; 4:1).[170] Evidently, the testifiable impact of "some," that is, "Those who sin" as leaders within the Ephesian church—notably upon the women in the audience (2:12; 5:15)—would call for an accepted accusation against them (5:19) and the corresponding, appropriate punitive action.

Indeed, Paul goes on to define such action: "in the sight of all reprove" (5:20). The prepositional phrase "in the sight of all" indicates that the reproof in view must be public.[171] Such would expose "those who sin" in full view, explicating the wrongs they have done, and reprimanding them according

---

169. See discussion in volume 1, chapter 3 regarding 1 Timothy 1:13.

170. That "elders"—and specifically "overseers"—are in view here in 5:20 is corroborated by Paul's final statement to the Ephesian church in Acts 20:29-30, where Paul, specifically addressing the "overseers" (ἐπισκόπους, v. 28) in Ephesus, declared: "I know that with my departure fierce wolves will come into you-all, not sparing the flock, and *from you-all yourselves will arise men saying twisted-things* pulling-away the disciples after themselves" (my emphasis). See volume 1, chapter 1. Given that the Ephesian overseers themselves heard these departing words by Paul, surely they—listening to the performance of the letter—would understand that Paul has in view those who arose to the office of overseer after his departure.

To be sure, such was already implied in Paul's discussion of qualified overseers in 3:1-7, wherein there was simultaneously a polemic against "some" who were unqualified, unable to care for the church, and presumably had fallen into the condemnation and snare of the devil; see volume 2, chapter 2 regarding 1 Timothy 3:1-7. The fact that the false teachers were likely "a young-plant" (3:7) seems to enhance Paul's statement in Acts 20:29-30: the false teachers in Ephesus are not the overseers whom Paul addressed before his departure but rather are those who became overseers afterward. It would be fitting, therefore, that the polemic in 3:1-7 includes "Those who sin" in 5:20, and vice versa.

171. See Knight, *PE*, 236; Ngewa, *1 & 2 Tim*, 129; Patterson and Kelley, "1 Tim," 682.

to the authority and instruction of the apostle.[172] If any among the audience supposed from a misunderstanding of 5:19 that a testifiable accusation is to be taken lightly, here in 5:20 it becomes abundantly clear that unrepentant people "who sin" in God's household—even if they are elders—will be publicly reproved. Notably, the phrase "in the sight of all" (ἐνώπιον πάντων) recalls Paul's command in the current microchiasm for children or those-from-parents to learn to be-godly to their own household, which is acceptable "in the sight" (ἐνώπιον) of God (5:4). The connection would seem to relate "Those who sin" with the ungodly children or those-from-parents: just as the children or those-from-parents must learn first to be-godly to their own household, so too must "Those who sin" be reproved for being ungodly in God's household. Furthermore, "in the sight of all" (ἐνώπιον πάντων) in 5:20 of the fifth microchiasm—the B' unit of the macrochiasm—recalls the parallel B unit wherein the missional prayers on behalf of "all" (πάντων) humans (2:1, 2) was commendable and acceptable "in the sight" (ἐνώπιον) of God our Savior (2:3), who desires "all" (πάντας) humans to be-saved (2:4). In effect, given both the progression of the macrochiasm and the overarching parallel relation between the B and B' units, the audience understand that Paul has salvation in view of the public reproof for "Those who sin." Where the false teachers are to be reproved in the sight of all, the outcome is for their restoration to faith, that is, repentance.

The term "reprove" (ἔλεγχε) highlights the severity of the action.[173] Conceptually, it is reminiscent of 1:20 of the first microchiasm wherein Paul had publically given-over Hymenaeus and Alexander to Satan so that they might be-disciplined not to blaspheme (1:20), that is, be restored to faith. Heard in combination with the missional thrust of the letter, therefore, the audience would most likely understand that to "reprove" in the sight of all would be a form of punishment directed toward those who sin yet fundamentally with their salvation in view.[174]

Paul goes on to describe the impact that such public reproof will, in turn, have upon others: "that also the rest might hold fear" (5:20). The

---

172. It is worth noting that again (or still) the apostle is drawing from the OT, specifically the principles established in Deuteronomy 19:15–21. Verse 17 indicates that an accused person and his accuser must both appear before the Lord, the priests, and the judges who will determine the merits of the accusation. Verses 18–19 state that a careful inquiry is to be made and that if the accuser is found out to be a malicious witness, he is to be purged from the Israelites. The difference in the 1 Timothy text is that the accuser is found to be true and thus "Those who sin" are to be disciplined. In either case, the general process, outcome, and purpose are the same.

173. See Marshall, *PE*, 618–19.

174. Patterson and Kelley, "1 Tim," 682: "The emphasis here seems to be on an exposure of sin leading to repentance and changed behavior."

purpose—"that" (ἵνα)—of the public censure is not only to lead to repentance for "Those who sin" but also to inspire "fear" (φόβον) among "the rest" (οἱ λοιποί). To be sure, this twofold purpose is drawn out by the inclusion of the conjunction "and" (καί), which underscores that both "Those who sin" and "the rest" will benefit from the public reproof.[175] The meaning of the entire clause is made clear by the related OT passage in Deuteronomy 19:18–20:

> [18] The judges shall inquire diligently, and if the witness is a false witness and has accused his brother falsely, [19] then you shall do to him as he had meant to do to his brother. So you shall purge the evil from your midst. [20] And the rest (οἱ ἐπίλοιποι) shall hear and fear (φοβηθήσονται), and shall never again commit any such evil among you.

The thematic and linguistic overlap between 1 Timothy 5:20 and Deuteronomy 19:20 would be apparent. Given this connection, the "fear" (φόβον) that Paul has in view would convey two components: first, the audience are to understand that persistent sin will not be tolerated in God's household (5:20a) and second, therefore, they will resolve to "never again commit any such evil among you" (Deut 19:20; cf. 5:20b). Furthermore, that such fear would result in a committed resolve is emphasized by the verb "might hold" (ἔχωσιν), which recalls its prior occurrences throughout the macrochiasm in reference to clinging tightly.[176] In this way, where the intended outcome of Paul's command is so that the rest "might hold" fear in 5:20, it is evident that the public reproval of "Those who sin" would have a deeply lasting effect, which would not easily be let go.[177]

In sum of 5:20, the audience have heard Paul underscore two aspects of the judicial process. First, over and against the ungrounded, incorrect beliefs and practices of the false teachers, Paul highlights that the OT functions as the authorized canon for what the audience are to believe and how they are to live. Second, Paul's instructions for Timothy to reprove false teachers in leadership positions—to stop their different teaching and to

---

175. It is possible to take the conjunction "and" (καί) to mean "even, indeed," shifting the accent slightly toward the audience, that they may learn from this example that persistent sin will not be tolerated within God's household.

176. E.g., Timothy was instructed to war the commendable war, "holding" (ἔχων) faith and a good conscience (1:19); qualified overseers were "holding" (ἔχοντα) children in submissiveness with all respectability (3:4); qualified deacons were "holding" (ἔχοντας) the mystery of the faith in a pure conscience (3:9); godliness was "holding" (ἔχουσα) the promise of life for the present and for the inevitable-coming (4:8b).

177. Knight, *PE*, 237: "ἔχω is used here in the sense of 'have as one's own,' i.e., so that they have φόβος as an appropriate inner characteristic in the face of sin and discipline."

GODLY CONDUCT FROM ALL MEMBERS OF GOD'S HOUSEHOLD   89

initiate their repentance unto salvation—succinctly identifies the apostle's overarching concerning in the 1 Timothy letter to preserve the teaching and promote godliness within God's missional household. In short, where salvation is at stake, 5:20 conveys to the audience that both different teaching and persistent sin will not go unchecked. As the Ephesian church experience Paul's words here in the performance of the letter, a solemn mood would likely pervade across the faces of those in attendance.

Within this setting, Paul continues the introductory "a" sub-element: "I testify in the sight of God and of Christ Jesus and of the elect angels, that these-things you might guard without prejudice" (5:21a). Here, the audience understand that Paul is speaking primarily to Timothy.[178] Furthermore, a strong connection between Timothy in 5:20 and Paul in 5:21a would be heard immediately: just as Timothy must reprove those who sin "in the sight" (ἐνώπιον) of all (5:20), so now Paul testifies "in the sight" (ἐνώπιον) of God, Christ Jesus, and the elect angels about Timothy's dutifull and impartial execution of his calling.[179] In effect, that Paul testifies to Timothy's leadership is intended to guarantee it: the audience understand that "Those who sin" will not be overlooked by Timothy. Certainly, Timothy would feel the gravity of Paul's words: upon hearing "I testify" in regard to Timothy's leadership, it is apparent that the solemnity of the minichiasm is being squarely placed upon him.[180] Still, it would be evident that Paul intends for his words to be verifiable. The verb "I testify" (διαμαρτύρομαι) recalls its prior cognates throughout the macrochiasm: the "testifiers" (μαρτύρων) required for accepting an accusation (5:19); the godly widow who is "testified" (μαρτυρουμένη) in commendable works (5:10); the qualified overseer who has a commendable "testimony" (μαρτυρίαν) from those-outside (3:7); and the "testimony" (μαρτύριον) that Christ Jesus gave himself as a ransom on behalf of all (2:6). In short, not only will Paul's statement here in 5:21a be subjectively proven as true in and of itself—Paul is saying the truth (2:7)—but it will be objectively proven by the person who observes Timothy's leadership.

Significantly, then, that Paul testifies "in the sight of God and of Christ Jesus and of the elect angels" would greatly enhance the weightiness of

---

178. The verb "you might guard" (φυλάξῃς) occurs in the second person singular; see below.

179. The connection between 5:20 and 5:21a would be further strengthened by the aural similarities (see *italics*) between "I testify" (δι*α*μ*α*ρτύρομ*αι*) and "Those who sin" (*ἁ*μ*α*ρτ*ά*νοντ*α*ς).

180. Towner, *Letters*, 372: "First, the verb means 'to charge, warn, or adjure' in this context, and in these letters signifies the very serious nature of the tasks Timothy is given in the community (2 Tim 2:14) and as the apostle's delegate (2 Tim 4:1)."

Paul's statement. According to Paul, it is God, Christ Jesus, and the elect angels who will be the ultimate verifiers of his statement (or not) in regard to Timothy.[181] It is worth noting that where "God" (θεοῦ, 5:20) recalls "God (θεοῦ) the Father" (1:2), and where "Christ Jesus" (Χριστοῦ Ἰησοῦ, 5:20) recalls the "mediator of God and humans, the human Christ Jesus" (Χριστὸς Ἰησοῦς, 2:5), the audience might have expected to hear a trinitarian formula to include "the Spirit (πνεῦμα, 4:1)—or perhaps the more common formula referring both to God and Christ Jesus (1:1, 2; 2:5-6), or perhaps the even more common reference to God (1:4, 11, 17; 2:3; 3:5, 15; 4:10; 5:4, 5). In other words, Paul's mention here of not merely angels but "elect angels" (τῶν ἐκλεκτῶν ἀγγέλων) is somewhat surprising.[182] Although the audience might understand that angels are to play some role in eschatological judgment,[183] here in 5:21a the rhetorical purpose seems clear: Paul is orienting the attention of both Timothy and the audience to God's divine courtroom in heaven. Undoubtedly, Paul's reference to elect "angels" (ἀγγέλων) in 5:21 recalls that Christ Jesus was seen by "angels" (ἀγγέλοις) in the pivotal Christ-hymn of the macrochiasm in 3:16. Such would emphasize here that Paul clearly has the heavenly court in view. Yet, it would also draw further attention to the literal reality that Paul has been emphasizing throughout the macrochiasm: in fact, the one mediator of God and humans, the human Christ Jesus who came into the world, was literally manifested in flesh, and he is now literally "in glory," being seen by angels in heaven as an active judge in God's courtroom (1:15; 2:5; 3:16). Paul is highlighting the unavoidable fact that Christ Jesus presides as "Lord" (1:2, 12) alongside God the Father in the company of the elect angels. The net

---

181. Given Paul's explicit reference to the divine throne-room—the celestial court—in heaven, such would seem to strengthen the audience's understanding of Paul's placement within the tradition of the OT prophets who were summoned to the throne-room of God; see volume 1, chapter 3 regarding 1 Timothy 1:12. Wall with Steele, *1 & 2 Tim*, 134: "The appropriation of a familiar OT trope in which the prophet cross-examines Israel before a heavenly court that includes God, who then renders the verdict and executes the punishment, functions here as a cautionary note to Timothy not to preside over a kangaroo court."

182. For a possible explanation of Paul's inclusion of "elect angels," see Fuller, "Of Elders and Triads," 258–63. Not a few commentators suggest that the "elect angels" refers to those in heaven who are allied to God's purposes in contrast to fallen angels who are allied to Satan (e.g., Jude 6; 2 Pet 2:4); see Knight, *PE*, 238; Patterson and Kelley, "1 Tim," 682; Phillips, *Exploring the PE*, 163).

See Frame, *Systematic Theology*, 771–80 for a succinct but helpful discussion on angels in the Bible. He rightly notes: "Scripture is more explicit about the work of angels than about their nature" (772).

183. E.g., 1 Thessalonians 4:16. Similarly, in the OT angels appear to play a role as witnesses in God's "divine court" (e.g., LXX Job 1:6).

GODLY CONDUCT FROM ALL MEMBERS OF GOD'S HOUSEHOLD 91

effect would be clear: Timothy is not to be intimidated by the prospect of reproving "some" elders in authority, that is, "Those who sin" in the sight of all (5:20), nor even by the thought of reporting to the authority of the apostle Paul upon his arrival (3:14; 4:13); rather, given that Timothy's duty is being testified by Paul in the sight of God, Christ Jesus, and the elect angels, Timothy is to be far more concerned that he must ultimately give an account to the highest authority in heaven (5:21a).[184]

Paul has been plainly drawing attention to the gravity of Timothy's calling to reprove the unrepentant elders—the false teachers. Yet, his reason for doing so is clearly connected to the overall purpose of the letter: Timothy was exhorted to remain in Ephesus that he might charge "some" not to teach-different (1:3); Timothy was entrusted with the charge, that he might war the commendable war, holding faith and a good conscience (1:18–19). Indeed, where the end of the charge was love (1:5), such would bring-about the household-law of God in faith (1:4) so that qualified men—those who sacrificially love their wives and lead commendably in their own households (3:2, 4, 5)—might actually care-for the church of God as commendable overseers (3:1, 5). Indeed, where God is the Father of the household and Christ Jesus is Lord, Paul's testimony in their sight (5:21a) articulates exactly how pressing it is for Timothy and the audience to understand that "Those who sin" are unfit to lead God's household. The disqualified elders, therefore, must be publicly reproved in the sight of all, not only so that they may stop sinning in God's own household against God the Father and Christ Jesus but also so that "the rest" may resolve in fear to not commit any such evil (5:21a).

The conjunction "that" (ἵνα) identifies the purpose of the verb "I testify" and introduces the content of Paul's warning: Timothy is to "guard these-things" (5:21a).[185] The term "these-things" (ταῦτα) would likely be heard by the audience specifically to include the instructions regarding elders that began in 5:17 at the beginning of the A' element.[186] Further-

---

184. Couser, "Sovereign Savior," 116: "this ἐνώπιον formulation asserts that the divine imprimatur drives the conduct enjoined . . . where Paul directs an adjuration toward Timothy (5:21; 6:13), an even more immediate involvement of God is emphasized. God is present as a witness at the declarations and, in accordance with the different ways God is referred to in the adjurations, he will stay involved up until the age in monitoring (5:21) and enabling (6:13) Timothy with respect to the behavior enjoined."

185. Knight, *PE*, 238: "ἵνα is used in a subfinal sense . . . to give the content of the charge."

186. Cf. Knight, *PE*, 237: "The 'things' in view (ταῦτα), being plural, refer back to vv. 19 and 20 . . . and not just to v. 20. Because of the seriousness of the charge, with its own implications of judgment . . . ταῦτα probably does not refer back to vv. 17 and 18, although this cannot be absolutely ruled out."

more, the second person singular verb "you might guard" (φυλάξῃς) not only makes clear to the audience that Timothy is the person about whom Paul is testifying but also, therefore, seems to echo the military language in the beginning of the letter that was specifically addressed to Timothy, namely that "you might charge" (παραγγείλῃς) in 1:3 and that "you might war" (στρατεύῃ) in 1:18.[187] The sense, then, is not merely that Timothy is to make every effort to observe these instructions—for example, "that you might keep"—but rather, as a soldier would, he is to both protect "these-things" from violation (5:17-19) and execute "these-things" when necessary (5:20) against transgressors who threaten and endanger the household of God, namely the false-teaching overseers.

Still, the force of Paul's command to "guard"—protect and execute—"these-things" is squarely placed on the manner in which Timothy is to do so. Leaving no room for misunderstanding, the apostle qualifies his instructions: Timothy must guard "without prejudice" (5:21a). The term "without" (χωρίς) here in the B' unit of the macrochiasm recalls Paul's instructions for the men to pray in the parallel B unit "without" (χωρίς) anger and word-quarreling (2:8). The connection of the parallel B and B' units would have a significant impression upon the audience. In the same way the men in the church are to both purposefully pray "without" anger—they are not to seek retribution, nor harbor bitterness, nor refuse to reconcile among themselves—and "without" word-quarreling—their speech and attitudes are to be nothing like the fase teachers—so too must Timothy purposefully protect and exectute "these-things" in 5:17-20 "without" any hint of vengeance or divisive speech. Furthermore, where the noun "prejudice" (προκρίματος) is a legal term connoting "prejudgment," the audience understand that Paul's main focus is, positively, for Timothy to guard with absolute objectivity.[188]

Still, the term "prejudice" (προκρίματος) echoes both the younger widow's "condemnation" (κρίμα) in 5:12 of the preceding B' element and the "condemnation" (κρίμα) of the young-plant overseers who are being-puffed-up in 3:6 of the third microchiasm. In other words, the audience understand that Paul is highlighting a stark contrast. Whereas Timothy is to be "without prejudice" (5:21a), the opposite is true for the young-plant false teachers who will—if not already—"fall into the condemnation" of the devil (3:7) and the younger widows who are currently "holding condemnation"

---

187. The evident connection between all three verbs would be corroborated by the consistent "that" (ἵνα) construction: "that (ἵνα) you might charge" (1:3); "that (ἵνα) you might war" (1:18); "that (ἵνα) these-things you might guard" (5:21a).

188. Knight, *PE*, 238-39: "προκρίματος (a biblical hapax, but already known as a legal technical term in the second century BC; see BAGD and MM) means 'prejudgment' or 'discrimination,' i.e., preconceived judgment or prejudice." See Marshall, *PE*, 620.

because the first faith they rejected (5:12). Notably, Timothy is to be "without prejudgment" toward those who have, in effect, already brought judgment upon themselves. Indeed, such a godly manner by Timothy in the completion of his duties would underscore for the audience the ungodly nature of "some."

1 Timothy 5:21b–22: No Favoritism, Slow to Lay Hands, Keep Yourself Pure

("b" sub-element)

The "b" sub-element continues the apostle's concern for impartial treatment, beginning with the participial phrase: "doing nothing according to favoritism" (5:21b). The sense of "favoritism" (πρόσκλισιν) is "bias" or "favorable disposition." The aural similarity between "favoritism" (πρόσκλισιν) in 5:21b and "prejudice" (προκρίματος) in 5:21a would not go unnoticed, and it is possible that the audience heard this second phrase in 5:21b as either a clarification or supplementation of the first phrase in 5:21a.[189] Either way, the overarching point is clear: where all judgments are to be made without pre-knowledge and favoritism, Timothy is to carry out his duties with respect to elders impartially—both ensuring their honor (5:17–19) and their reproval (5:20). Moreover, given the implied exclusivity of the false teachers throughout the macrochiasm, and given that the term "nothing" (μηδέν) echoes the activities of the false teachers ("not"; μή, e.g., 1:3, 4, 7), the further indication is that "doing nothing according to favoritism" is to endorse Timothy as the antithesis of "some." The verb "doing" (ποιῶν) recalls the saving implications of "doing" (ποιῶν) in 4:16 of the prior microchiasm. That is, by "doing" nothing according to favoritism (5:22), the audience understand that Timothy will be "doing" that which will save himself and those who hear him (4:16). What is more, the conceptual echo between Christ Jesus's impartiality in 2:6 of the B unit and Paul's call for Timothy's impartiality in 5:20 of the parallel B' unit would likely be apparent. Thus in line with the impartial act of Christ Jesus who gave himself as a ransom on behalf of all (2:6), so also Timothy is not to act with any partiality (5:20)—even toward the false teachers who are opposing him, Paul, the sound teaching, and thus Christ Jesus.[190]

---

189. Marshall, *PE*, 620: "The language appears repetitious, but in fact the first phrase says that one is not to come with pre-formed opinions, the second that one is not to be ruled by partiality to one party or the other."

190. Similarly, Ngewa, *1 & 2 Tim*, 137, applies the same concept to the appointment

To be sure, the apostle's concern for Timothy's impartiality does not represent an allegiance to abstract moralism. Rather, the whole of 5:21 draws Timothy and the audience's attention toward the heavenly court, reminding them of God's own impartial judgment: he gives to each according to what each has done, Jew or Gentile; such is God's just judgment according to the commendable law (1:8–10). For Timothy, then, the audience understand that it is strictly proper for the household of God to preserve God's character of impartial judgment, particularly in the matters of honoring and reproving. In such a contentious context with the false teachers in Ephesus, Timothy certainly must have experienced great pressure and been tempted to be passive or reactive in his own leadership. However, as Paul's genuine child (1:2, 18) who is uniquely entrusted and recognized to serve as the apostle's representative (1:3, 18; 3:14–15; 4:13), the audience understand that it is particularly incumbent for Timothy to lead God's household not only according to God's truth but also God's justice.

Paul continues the "b" sub-element in 5:22: "Lay hands quickly on none, nor share in others's sins." Immediately, through the repeated cognates "nothing" (μηδέν) in 5:21b and "none, nor" (μηδενὶ ... μηδέ) in 5:22a, it is apparent to the audience that 5:21b and 5:22a share and emphasize a strong cohesion within the "b" sub-element. The deliberate word choice of these two verses makes explicit for the audience that doing "nothing" according to favoritism (5:21b) applies specifically to the matter of appointing "none" to the leadership position of an elder according to favoritism (5:22a).[191] In other words, just as Timothy is to be impartial and unbiased in honoring elders who lead commendably (5:17–19) and reproving elders—particularly overseers—who are unrepentant in sinning (5:20), so too is Timothy to be impartial and unbiased in the appointment of new elders—presumably overseers.[192]

---

of elders: "Just as Christ is unbiased and impartial, treating all sinners the same, so Timothy must be careful to not show favoritism when appointing people as elders." See 5:22 below.

191. It may be worth noting that Paul's specification in 5:22a may not be insignificant. Given that the false teachers were most likely "Those who sin (5:20), that is, overseers who arose from within the Ephesian church after Paul's departure (Acts 20:28–30), it seems that Paul's statement here in 5:22a may shed light on how the false teachers arose to the office of overseer, perhaps by favoritism. Consequently, it seems that newly converted men (3:7), who were not loving, sacrificial husbands toward their wives (3:2) and who did not lead their children nor their households commendably (3:4–5) had been appointed as overseers in Ephesus. In this case, Paul's instructions here in the "b" sub-element (5:21b–22) are, therefore, intended to be corrective and preventative.

192. Towner suggests that verse 22 is given "to address the contingency of appointing new elders to replace those dismissed as a result of the discipline process" (*Letters*,

The command "Lay hands (χεῖρας . . . ἐπιτίθει) quickly on none" in 5:22b recalls "the-laying of hands" (ἐπιθέσεως τῶν χειρῶν) of the presbytery upon Timothy in 4:14 of the prior microchiasm. As much as "the-laying of hands" in 4:14 was a public declaration by an authorized church council—the presbytery—to convey that a particular individual or group of individuals was officially sanctioned to uniquely lead in God's church, so also would Paul's statement in 5:22a refer to same authorized public declaration. Indeed, given both the sustained context of 5:17-21 in regard to "The elders" (οἱ . . . πρεσβύτεροι, 5:17) and the prior context of 4:14 in regard to "the presbytery" (τοῦ πρεσβυτερίου), it is apparent that the official action to "Lay hands" in 5:22a is in reference to "the presbytery" toward the appointment of new elders.[193] The specification against laying hands "quickly" (ταχέως) is intriguing given the urgency of the letter. Paul does not include any sort of standard greeting but immediately launches into pressing matters, "to charge some not to teach-different" (1:3).[194] That hands are not to be laid "quickly" (ταχέως, 5:22a) seems counterintuitive given that the disruption caused by the false teachers is serious enough for Paul himself to come to Timothy in "quickness" (τάχει, 3:14). Still, not only with the rise and influence of the false teachers but also with the forthcoming public reproval of such false-teaching elders, it seems that the apostle would have wanted Timothy to appoint new elders—particularly teaching elders, overseers—quickly. Much rather, the audience understand that the apostle is far more concerned with aspiring overseers undergoing a thorough examination—specifically according to the objective standards listed in 3:1-7—prior to any public authorization of their leadership.[195] Specifically, Paul's command to "Lay hands quickly on none" would be heard to correspond with the qualification that an aspiring overseer is "Not a young-plant" (3:6): enough time to assess a man's maturity in the faith (3:6)—as much as his missional leadership ability (3:2-5, 7)—would be part and parcel of appointing qualified men as new overseers in Ephesus. In this way, Paul's command in 5:22 seems to imply that the false teachers who arose from among the overseers after Paul's departure (Acts 20:28-30) were not thoroughly assessed by the current leaders in Ephesus: hands were laid quickly before exposing the men's unqualified status to lead (cf. 3:2-7). The slow pace that Paul advocates would be remedial to avoid the long-term

---

373). Such would affirm the need for Paul's discussion of objective qualifications for the office of overseer in 3:1-7; see volume 2, chapter 2.

193. As Towner observes, it is highly improbable that "Lay hands" in 5:22a has anything to do with restoring those that had fallen from grace (*Letters* 374, esp. n. 72).

194. For the urgency of the letter, see volume 2, chapter 2 regarding 1 Timothy 3:2

195. See Spencer, *1 Tim*, 139.

possibility of having to face unqualified false teachers yet again. In short, the audience understand that the same sort of circumspection for identifying true widows in God's household (5:3–16) equally applies to the selection of future leaders in God's household.

The further instructions "nor share in others's sins" (5:22a) would have related implications. Where other's "sins" (ἁμαρτίαις) recalls "Those who sin" (ἁμαρτάνοντας) in 5:20, Paul has in view a participatory effect between Timothy and the false teachers. That is, the careless or non-impartial appointment of elders who are unqualified would render Timothy complicit in the "sins" of "Those who sin."[196] At least to a degree—and at least until Paul's arrival (3:14; 4:13)—the audience understand that Paul is making Timothy liable for any appointment of unqualified elders, that is, future false teachers. Furthermore, the close connection between the act of laying hands—the public appointment of church leaders—and sharing in others' sins—the appointment of future false teachers—is clearly heard by the audience through the back-to-back repetition of "none, nor" (μηδενὶ . . . μηδέ) in relation to both laying hands and sharing in others's sins. Where the connotation of the negative particle "not" (μή) and its cognates was consistently heard in relation to the false teachers, the cumulative impact of the macrochiasm would be particularly felt: Timothy is to "charge some not (μή) to teach-different, nor (μηδέ) to hold-toward myths and genealogies without-limit" (1:3–4), namely "some" who are "not (μή) understanding either (μήτε) what they-are-saying or (μήτε) regarding some-things they-are-insisting" (1:7); indeed, "some" in leadership positions must "not" (μή) be addicted-to-wine, "not" (μή) violent, "Not" (μή) a young-plant (3:3, 6) so that they might "not" (μή) fall into the condemnation and snare of the devil (3:6, 7). In short, that Timothy is to be doing "nothing" (μηδέν) according to favoritism (5:21), is to lay hands quickly on "none" (μηδενί), "nor" (μηδέ) share in other's sins (5:22a) would have clear consequences: if Timothy were to do the oppositive, he himself would demonstrate a participatory association with the false teachers.

Still, the specific imperative to not "share in others's sins" (κοινώνει ἁμαρτίαις ἀλλοτρίαις) would likely suggest that the apostle's concern is more than just the careless—or non-impartial—appointment of *future* unqualified men to the office of overseer. Given the positive urgency of the letter for Timothy to charge "some" not to teach-different (1:3), the audience hear that Paul has in view the "sins" of *current* elders in the Ephesian church (5:19–20)—"Those who sin." By allowing "Those who sin" to continually serve as leaders of God's household, Timothy would, in effect,

---

196. See Ngewa, *1 Tim*, 132.

"share in others's sins" (5:22a). Furthermore, Paul's imperative here in 5:22 may also have been a subtle reminder for Timothy to not actually partake in their "sins," that is, to not succumb to their influence to teach some-thing different than the sound teaching that accords with the gospel (1:10–11). Whatever may have been the specific nuance intended by the apostle, the basic point is simple: Timothy is Paul's genuine child "in faith" who has been entrusted as the authorized household manager of God's church in the apostle's absence (1:2, 18; 3:14–15; 4:13–14); therefore, Timothy will be held liable—not only to Paul but also to God and Christ Jesus in the heavenly court (5:21)—on all accounts for the rash appointment of unqualified men as elders, his passive willingness to allow currently unqualified elders to continue leading as those who sin, or his partaking in the sins of such false-teaching elders.

The "b" sub-element concludes with another command: "keep yourself pure" (5:22b). The verb "keep" (τήρει) carries the notion of "protect" or guard."[197] Here, a twofold nuance would convey the full spectrum of Timothy's active diligence: in order to positively stay pure, Timothy must do so by simultaneously protecting and guarding himself from stepping into impurity. Moreover, the specificity of this command for Timothy to keep himself "pure" (ἁγνόν) in 5:22 recalls 4:12 of the previous microchiasm wherein Timothy was commanded to be an example of those of the faithful in word, behavior, faith, love, and "purity" (ἁγνείᾳ). Moreover, the term "pure" (ἁγνόν, 5:22) here in the A' element of the microchiasm recalls Paul's command in the parallel A element for Timothy to exhort younger-women as sisters in all "purity" (ἁγνείᾳ, 5:2). The audience would understand that Paul likely has in view Timothy's sexuality. However, given the progressive movement of the fifth microchiasm across the A-B-C-D-C'-B' elements toward the concluding A' element, it would also be clear to the audience that Paul is not merely concerned with sexual propriety but intends a further, nuanced implication. The catastrophic impact of the false teachers upon the women in Ephesus—particularly the younger widows—had accumulated immediately prior to the A' element: the women's association with the false teachers had not only led to ungodly treatment toward their own family members and the pooling of church resources away from widows who truly needed material support (5:16), but it had also resulted in turning aside after Satan (5:15). Thus given Paul's attention to the false teachers in the current A' element, Paul's command for Timothy to "keep yourself pure" (5:22b) would likely have a polemical quality against the false teachers who have so drastically devastated the salvation

---

197. See Marshall, *PE*, 622.

of the women in Ephesus. In other words, rather than sharing in "others's sins" (5:22a)—for example, causing the women to turn aside after Satan (5:15)—Timothy is to do the exact opposite. By reproving "Those who sin" (5:20)—the false-teaching overseers—and by laying hands quickly on none to prevent future false-teaching overseers (5:22a), Timothy will certainly not share in others's sins (5:21a) and will also keep himself "pure": he will keep the women in Ephesus safe from the deceptive influence of "some" who are holding-toward teachings of demons (4:1).

It is also likely that the audience would understand Paul's command for Timothy to "keep yourself pure" in light of the pronoun "yourself": Timothy is to foster personal activity that is antithetical to the false teachers. The term "yourself" (σεαυτόν) recalls Paul's command in the prior microchiasm for Timothy to "train yourself (σεαυτόν) for godliness" (4:7b); such was pitted against the vile and silly myths (4:7a) and ascetic bodily training (4:8a) of the false teachers. Similarly, in 4:16 Paul commanded Timothy to "Strongly-hold yourself (σεαυτῷ) and the teaching . . . for doing this you will save yourself (σεαυτόν) and those who hear you." Timothy's personal actions have a direct bearing upon others—this includes the women in Ephesus. In short, over and against the false teachers, Paul's command underscores that Timothy's actions will *not* lead others to turn-aside after Satan (cf. 5:15).

In sum, Timothy's call to "keep yourself pure" is a continuation of his call to be example "in purity"; he is to handle all matters—and particularly matters pertaining to elders—with impartiality. Even for "Those who sin" (5:20), Timothy must not accept an accusation against such elders except on two or three testifiers (5:19). Even if a man seems qualified for an overseer, Timothy is to be impartial according to the objective standards provided in 3:1–7. Timothy is to lay hands quickly on none, nor is he to share in others's sins through any sort of passivity that would allow "Those who sin" to continue leading and influencing God's household (5:22). In a word, Timothy is to safeguard the church: Paul's command for Timothy to "keep yourself pure" will enable God's entire household to keep itself pure, that is, to preserve the teaching and promote godliness as God's missional household.

1 Timothy 5:23–24a: A Little Wine Use,
the Sins of Some Are Conspicous

("b'" sub-element)

In the "b'" sub-element of the minichiasm, Paul begins with a continued command for Timothy: "No-longer drink water; rather a little wine use because of your stomach and frequent illnesses" (5:23). Given the sustained imperatives throughout the A' element toward Timothy in regard to the false teachers in Ephesus, the audience would undoubtedly hear the imperative in 5:23 not as personal advice from Paul to Timothy but rather as a relevant command for Timothy in view of the false teachers.[198] The adverb "No-longer" (μηκέτι) both establishes the parallelism between the "b" and "b'" sub-elements (μηδέν, 5:21; μηδενὶ ... μηδέ, 5:22) and conveys a strong connection between the two. That is, where Timothy is commanded to be doing "nothing" (μηδέν) according to favoritism (5:21), to lay hands quickly on "none" (μηδενί), "nor" (μηδέ) share in others's sins (5:22), the audience understand that Paul's immediate command to "No-longer (μηκέτι) drink water" (5:23) is to be heard as a qualification of Timothy's pure leadership against the false teachers. In dramatic rhetorical fashion, the blast repetition of the cognates "nothing," "none," "nor," and "No-longer" would signify that 5:21, 22, and 23 are not only connected but are to be understood together and centered around Paul's command to "keep yourself pure"—the pivotal statement in the movement from the "b" sub-element to the "b'" sub-element.

In view of Paul's discussion in the fourth microchiasm, the command "keep yourself pure" (5:22b) and its qualifier "No-longer drink water; rather a little wine use" (5:23) may have in view the ascetic practices of the false teachers. In this way, Paul would be clarifying to Timothy and the audience what it means to be "pure" in light of Christ Jesus, the mediator through whom all of God's commendable creation is made-holy (4:5). That is, Timothy is to "No-longer drink [just] water" (μηκέτι ὑδροπότει) as though there were something inherently unclean with wine (cf. 4:3); "rather" (ἀλλά) he is commanded to deliberately use "a little wine" (οἴνῳ ὀλίγῳ).[199] Indeed,

---

198. Not a few commentators interpret 5:23 as a parenthetical, personal comment to Timothy outside of the letter's context (e.g., Knight, *PE*, 240; Phillips, *Exploring the PE*, 166; Ngewa, *1 Tim*, 132), and a few translations either initiate a new paragraph or enclose the verse with parentheses to demarcate it from the surrounding context; see *TNIV* and *ESV*. However, given the deliberate purpose of everything heard thus far in the letter, it is unlikely that the audience would understand Paul's words as a new, unrelated statement.

199. Barcley, *1 & 2 Tim*, 173–74: "Paul essentially exhorts him, perhaps with the false teachers in view, that his previous call to purity does not entail abstinence. Quite the contrary. Paul does not simply tell Timothy that it is permissible to drink wine; he actually exhorts him to do so." Wall with Steele, *1 & 2 Tim*, 135: "Indeed, the asceticism that Paul has already demonized (4:1–4) may be the subtext here. That is, perhaps the problem is not Timothy but the congregation or the misguided teachers ... who are once again reminded that wine, like food and marriage, is the good gift of a benevolent Creator."

Marshall, *PE*, 624: "'to drink [only] water', seems to be used always as the opposite to

where the descriptor "little" (ὀλίγῳ) recalls that the false teachers's ascetic bodily training is for "little" (ὀλίγον) profitability (4:8a), Paul's command here in 5:23 to use "a little wine" seems not only intentional but also polemic. Furthermore, the verb "use" (χρῶ) recalls its earlier occurrence in the first microchiasm wherein Paul correctively declares over and against the false teachers that "the law is commendable if someone uses (χρῆται) it lawfully" (1:8). Here, then, in regard to the use of wine, a similar corrective implication would be intended, the sense being: "As part of God's commendable creation (4:4), wine is commendable if someone uses it as intended." Still, where the term "wine" (οἴνῳ) in 5:23 recalls its prior cognates in regard to leadership qualifications—overseers are not "addicted-to-wine" (πάροινον, 3:3); deacons are not holding-toward much "wine" (οἴνῳ, 3:8)—it seems that Paul intends for Timothy to use "a little wine" in order to positively exemplify what it means to be a "pure" leader who enjoys God's commendable creation over and against the ascetic false teachers.[200] That is, where Paul commands Timothy to "keep yourself pure" (5:22b) in immediate combination with "a little wine use" (5:23), the audience likely understand that Timothy is to showcase what it means to lead as a man both "not addicted-to-wine" (3:3) and "not holding-toward much wine" (3:8). In short, Timothy's leadership is to undercut both ungodly extremes of asceticism *and* over-indulgence.

The further specification for Timothy to use a little wine "because of your stomach and frequent illnesses" would not be surprising for the audience. As made evident through the cumulative progression of the macrochiasm, the audience understand—as they themselves have observed first-hand—that Timothy is under immense pressure. Not only is Timothy alone and outnumbered by the influential false teachers of the church who actively undermine Timothy's leadership (4:12), but the salvation of the audience is upon his shoulders (4:16). Moreover, not only will Timothy be held accountable by his father "in faith" (1:2, 18; 4:13)—the divinely authorized apostle Paul—but Paul has underscored that Timothy's actions are answerable to the heavenly court—God, Christ Jesus, and the elect angels (5:21). Undoubtedly, the gravity of the stressful situation in Ephesus combined with

---

drinking wine. Hence the command is not to stop drinking water (!) but to not drink only water." See Knight, *PE*, 240.

200. In passing, given the leadership qualifications in 3:3 and 3:8, it is possible that Timothy may have been tempted to over-compensate by abstaining from wine altogether. However, given the clear implication of 3:3 and 3:8—that Paul does not have abstinence in view—and given that Paul had effectively raised Timothy in regard to godliness and the proper training thereof (4:7b), it seems unlikely that Timothy would have misconstrued Paul's instructions in 3:3 and 3:8 or felt the need to avoid wine altogether.

the weighty implications of failure would have profound psychological and, therefore, corresponding physiological effects upon him—"the stomach and your frequent illnesses." Thus as much as Timothy's use of a little wine is corrective against the false teachers's asceticism, Paul is also specifying to his child "in faith" that a little wine is to be used for its evident curative properties.[201] Timothy is not only to exemplify "pure" leadership against any extreme notions of asceticism or excess, but he is also to practically benefit from the use of a little wine as a direct result of the physical toll that Timothy's leadership in Ephesus is having and will have upon him. Indeed, such would be affirmed to the audience by Paul's use of "because." The occurrence of the term "because" (διά) with the accusative "stomach" (στόμαχον) in 5:23 would not carry the same sense as the prior occurrences of the term, which was heard with a genitive construction; hence, "consistent-with" (διά, 1:16a; δι', 2:10; διά, 2:15; διά, 4:5). Given the strict context of the physical descriptions about Timothy's "stomach" (στόμαχος) and "frequent illnesses" (πυκνάς ... ἀσθενείας), the sense is that Timothy is commanded by Paul to use a little wine "because of the physiological impacts of ministry." To be sure, Paul highlights that the judicious use of wine, which is not inherently evil, should be appropriated not as an escape but for Timothy's health benefit and longevity.[202] Perhaps as a further implication for any empathetic listener in the audience, Paul's statement would be heard as a summons to relieve Timothy's burdens by aligning with and supporting his leadership against the false teachers.

Continuing the "b'" sub-element, verse 5:24 begins, "The sins of some humans are conspicuous." Notably, the grammatical placement of the indefinite pronoun "some" (τινῶν) within the construction of the sentence

---

201. For ancient sources that affirm the medicinal value of wine, see Towner, *Letters*, 376 n. 82; Wall with Steele, *1 & 2 Tim*, 135. Not a few commentators suggest that Paul's instructions were a remedy in regard to the polluted drinking water of the first-century (e.g., Ngewa, *1 & 2 Tim*, 133; Phillips, *Exporing the PE*, 166). Though certainly applicable, Paul's main point here seems to focus on both the proper exhibition of wine consumption (see 3:3, 8; 4:3a) and its medicinal benefits in response to the physical detriment incurred by Timothy's obedient service in Ephesus.

202. See Spencer, *1 & 2 Tim*, 140 esp. n. 102 regarding Jesus's positive use of and attitude toward wine.

The contemporary reader of 1 Timothy should not interpret 5:23 as a miscellaneous and passing remark but as an important point of clarification that functions within this minichiasm to explain more fully the meaning of "purity." Verse 5:23 seems especially instructive for pietistic movements that either implicitly or explicitly promote a sort of spirituality that looks more akin to asceticism than biblical Christianity. Basically, 5:23 is a concrete application of the principle enunciated in 4:4 that everything created by God is good and to be received with thanksgiving and in moderation—"a little" (ὀλίγῳ). See Wall with Steele, *1 & 2 Tim*, 135.

is unusual.²⁰³ As the initating term, its priority would have rhetorical significance and instruct the audience how they are to understand Paul's statement regarding "some humans" (τινῶν ἀνθρώπων). The indefinite pronoun "some" (τινῶν) recalls its prior, sustained, and ongoing occurrences throughout the macrochiasm as a subtle or explicit polemical reference to the false teachers and anyone who is either aligned with or influenced by them.²⁰⁴ Given the immediate context in 5:20–23 concerning Timothy's leadership over and against the false teachers who are in leadership positions, the audience understand that "some humans" does not merely refer to a generic group of "humans" but rather to a specific group of humans, namely "some"—the false teachers in the Ephesian church.

Still, although "humans" is qualified in this way, its occurrence within the overall arrangement of the macrochiasm would equally have its own qualifying effect upon "some." The term "humans" (ἀνθρώπων) here in 5:24 of the B' unit of the macrochiasm recalls it repetition in the parallel B unit: Paul exhorts the audience to pray on behalf of all "humans" (ἀνθρώπων) in 2:1; the Savior God desires all "humans" (ἀνθρώπους) to be-saved in 2:4a; and the one mediator of God and "humans" (ἀνθρώπων), the "human" (ἄνθρωπος) Christ Jesus gave himself as a ransom on behalf of all [humans] in 2:6. Here in 5:24, then, the rhetorical juxtaposition between the polemical connotations of "some" and the missional connotations of "humans" would have a particular effect. Beyond any doubt, Paul intends the audience to understand that God's desire is to save all humans—even "some." It is for this reason that Christ Jesus gave himself as a ransom on behalf of all—even "some." Thus not only are the audience to pray on behalf of all humans, even "some," but "some humans" are those specifically for whom the audience ought to missionally pray.

Indeed, in view of the cumulative progression of the macrochiasm, the overwhelming missional implication of the 1 Timothy letter would be considerably emphasized here in 5:24. In the A unit of the macrochiasm, "some" teach-different (1:3), that is, "some-thing" different than the sound teaching concerning Christ Jesus who came to save them (1:10–11, 15) and are starkly opposed to Christ Jesus's very own authorized representative—the apostle Paul (1:1, 12). In the B unit, the false teachers are influencing the audience to do that which brought sin into the world (2:12–14). In the C unit, "some" are unqualified both to lead their own

---

203. BDAG, s.v. Cf. Knight, *PE*, 241: "τινῶν ἀνθρώπων, 'of some men,' placed first for emphasis, indicates an indefinite quantity." While Knight identifies the deliberate rhetorical placement of τινῶν, its rhetorical connotation throughout the macrochiasm is not observed.

204. See esp. 1:3, 6, 8, 19; 3:1, 5; 4:1; 5:4, 8, 15, 16.

household and care-for the church of God (3:1–7). In the C' unit, "some" have apostatized from the faith, are holding-toward teachings of demons, and rejecting God's commendable creation through ungrounded ascetic practices (4:1, 3, 7a, 8a). In the current B' unit, "some" have influenced "some" among the audience to follow in their footsteps by turning-aside after Satan (5:15). Remarkably, then, despite the sustained ungodly activity of "some" throughout the unified progression of the A-B-C-C'-B' units, the fundamental point of Paul's letter is made abundantly clear by the phrase "some humans": by the authoritative sound teaching of the apostle Paul, as received directly by Christ Jesus and according to the command of God (1:1, 12; 2:7), all humans—universally and without distinction—may be-saved by Christ Jesus's substitutionary and representative sacrifice (2:6) by coming to have-faith upon him (1:16) because the living God is the Savior of all humans (4:10) and desires for all humans to be-saved (2:3–4a). With this emphatic missional context, the audience are reminded that the false-teaching "some"—though they are opposed to Christ Jesus and the salvation he offers—are still "humans" (5:24), that is, those in need of the gospel (1:11), the testimony (2:6), the mystery concerning Christ Jesus (3:16).

In regard to "some humans," Paul declares that their "sins . . . are conspicuous" (5:24a). Where the term "conspicuous" (πρόδηλοί) connotes that which is obvious to everyone, it is possible that the audience understand the phrase "the sins of some humans are conspicuous" as a polemical echo regarding the ironic imbecility of the false teachers. The false teachers are desiring to be law-teachers while not understanding either what they-are-saying or regarding some-things they-are-insisting (1:7), and they do not know the lawful use of the law (1:8–10a). Similarly, given that their "sins (ἁμαρτίαι) . . . are conspicuous," it is possible that Paul intends to highlight that the false teachers's sins are so obvious with respect to the law that any accusations brought against them (5:19) will not require any amount of intense reflection or nuancing; rather, it will be evident to any human—certainly at least two or three (5:19)—that "Those who sin" (ἁμαρτάνοντας) must be publically reproved by Timothy in the human court in Ephesus.

Still, the arrangement of the minichiasm would likely convey a further implication to the audience. The term "sins" (ἁμαρτίαι) here in 5:24a of the "b'" sub-element recalls others's "sins" (ἁμαρτίαις) in 5:22 of the parallel "b" sub-element. There, Timothy was called to prevent the appointment of future false teachers in the Ephesian church. Given this parallel connection, the phrase "sins . . . are conspicuous" would underscore that the appointment of unqualified leaders will become quickly apparent to all with a twofold nuance. On the one hand, Timothy and the other commendable leaders's "sins" will be quickly obvious if they do not adhere to Paul's instructions (5:21–22) and qualifications (3:1–7) regarding the appointment of future elders. On the other hand, the "sins" of unqualified men (cf. 3:1–7) who are appointed as overseers will become quickly obvious by the end result, namely their false teaching and subsequent ungodly, unmissional lifestyle.

As the "b'" sub-element concludes, the net effect of 5:24a with respect to what precedes it in the 5:20–25 minichiasm is that Timothy and the audience need not dwell or preoccupy themselves with the outcome of those who sin (5:20–22). Rather, they need only to concentrate on keeping themselves pure, that is, adhering to Paul's instructions. In short, Timothy and the audience may live out their calling as the faithful over and against the false teachers because "the sins of some humans are conspicuous" and will be easily discerned.

1 Timothy 5:24b–25: Judgment, Commendable Works are Conspicuous

("a'" sub-element)

In the concluding "a'" sub-element, Paul begins by describing the conspicuous sins of the false teachers, which are "preceding them for judgment" (5:24b). Several observations are worth noting. First, the aural similarity between "preceding" (προάγουσαι) in 5:24b and "conspicuous" (πρόδηλοί) in 5:24a would emphasize the flow from and connection between the "b'" and "a'" sub-elements.[205] Second, the participle "preceding" (προάγουσαι) recalls for the audience its earlier occurrence in 1:18 of the first microchiasm wherein Timothy was encouraged to war the commendable war against the false teachers by remembering the prophecies "preceding" (προαγούσας) upon him, that is, the divine nature of his calling. Here in 5:24b of the minichiasm, then, the audience understand that Paul specifically has in view God's divine activity, namely that all actions that were heard pertaining to false-teaching elders in 5:20–24a are ultimately assessed in the divine, heavenly court of justice (5:21a).[206] Third and emphasizing the second observation, within the current minichiasm a clear connection is heard between the term "prejudice" (προκρίματος, 5:21a) in the "a" sub-element and the participle phrase "preceding them for judgment" (προάγουσαι εἰς κρίσιν, 5:24b) in the parallel "a'" sub-element.[207] Where Timothy's actions "without

---

205. The shared prepositional prefix πρό would be apparent.

206. A similar idea of divine justice is found in LXX Isaiah 58:8b: "your righteousness shall go before you (προπορεύσεται) and the glory of God shall defend you."

207. The rhetorical play on words (see *italics*) between the prepositional prefix "*pre*"

prejudice" were rooted in the divine, heavenly court "of God and of Christ Jesus and of the elect angels" (5:21a), the implication for the phrase "preceding them for judgment" (5:24b) is that it does not merely refer to a human court but to the very impartial judgment of God in the divine, heavenly court.[208] As such, the rhetorical logic of the minichiasm would resound for Timothy and the audience: God's ultimate, divine "judgment" (5:24b) in the "a'" sub-element is the same divine justice that is "without prejudice" (5:21a) in the parallel "a" sub-element; thus, the very basis for observing the apostle's commands regarding "Those who sin" (5:20) in the "a" sub-element is the same basis for Timothy's impartial leadership amidst "the sins of some humans" (5:24b) in the parallel "a'" sub-element. In short, Paul underscores that God's divine "judgment" (5:24b) is "without prejudice" (5:21a).

Such parallelism within the minichiasm would also highlight that Timothy's judgments in the church are to mirror the impartiality of God's eschatological, heavenly court. Furthermore, by remembering that God himself is the ultimate judge for everything that transpires in the church, which is God's very own household, Timothy is free to lead, reprove, and appoint with impartiality in the human court (5:20–22) precisely because God and Christ Jesus do so in the divine court (5:21a, 24b). Indeed, where the living God upon whom Timothy hopes is impartial toward all humans (4:10), and where Christ Jesus upon whom Timothy has faith gave himself impartially on behalf of all humans (1:16; 2:6), Timothy's relationship "in faith" with God and Christ Jesus ought to shape and inform his own impartiality in God's household according to the sovereign rule of God the Father and Christ Jesus the Lord (1:2).

Although Paul has emphasized that God's eschatological divine judgment may be reflected here and now in the human court by Timothy, his next statement clarifies that judgment here and now may not always happen: "but for some they also follow." The repetition of "some" (τισὶν) in 5:24b would emphasize the full, unified scope of Paul's statement regarding "some" (τινῶν) in 5:24a. That is, the latter half of 5:24 is meant to provide a balanced realism to the first half, the sense being, "The sins of some humans are *not* conspicuous, following after them for judgment." The audience are to understand that perhaps a fraction of "some" false-teaching elders in Ephesus will experience God's divine "judgment" here and now through the mirrored judgment in the human court on earth (5:24a); yet, so also

---

(πρό) in "*pre*judice" and "*pre*ceding" (προκρίματος, 5:21a; προάγουσαι, 5:24b) and of the cognate terms for "*pre*judice" and "*judgment*" (προκρίματος, 5:21a; κρίσιν, 5:24b) would be apparent.

208. See Marshall, *PE*, 625. Contra Knight, who suggests that "judgment" refers to a human decision/court (*PE*, 241).

will a residual "some" false-teaching elders receive no judgment here and now on earth but rather only in the divine courtroom, that is, in the full presence of God and Christ Jesus with the elect angels as witnesses. In this way, therefore, the sense of the grouped conjunctions "but . . . also" (δὲ καί) may have been heard as "but indeed," which would accurately capture the force of Paul's statement in 5:24b: judgment may be delayed, "but indeed" it will inevitably take place.

Paul's use of the verb "follow" (ἐπακολουθοῦσιν) is noteworthy. Its occurrence was heard in 5:10 to describe the godly widow who has "followed" (ἐπηκολούθησεν) in all good work. Moreover, the verb recalls Timothy who in 4:6 of the fourth microchiasm was being-nourished in the words of the faith and the commendable teaching that he has "followed" (παρηκολούθηκας). Where the verb has conveyed an empirical, reliable consistency, the audience understand that Paul intends the same nuance here in 5:24b: though "the sins of some" may not immediately be apparent and precede them for judgment, indeed the sins of "some" will unfailingly "follow" the false teachers unto God's final judgment. Furthermore, a stark contrast would be highlighted: whereas the godly widow has "followed" in good work (5:10) and Timothy has "followed" the commendable teaching (4:6), the false-teachers have done neither—much rather, their sins "follow" them (5:24b). Taken as a whole, the net rhetorical effect of 5:24 upon the audience is that sometimes judgment is swift, sometimes it is slow—but it is never absent. It is out of this conviction that Timothy must lead the church impartially (5:21), keeping himself pure (5:22) irrespective of the immediate and perhaps unjudged actions of "some" (5:24).

Concluding the "a'" sub-element, Paul states in 5:25: "Likewise also the commendable works are conspicuous, and those having otherwise do-not have-the-power to be-hidden." The term "Likewise" (ὡσαύτως) recalls its prior occurrences throughout the macrochiasm to indicate similar yet distinct categories (2:9; 3:8, 11). Here, then, Paul intends the audience to hear the obvious symmetry between 5:24 and 5:25 with a particular nuance, namely that he is applying the same principle in 5:24 but to a different group of people in 5:25.[209] Indeed, given the repeated emphasis regarding "some" in 5:24, the sudden absence of the pronoun "some" in 5:25 would draw attention to Paul's rhetorical nuance between "some" in 5:24 and the new group in 5:25. In short, the audience understand that Paul intends a

---

209. Where "likewise" (ὡσαύτως) indicates a parallelism between 5:24 and 5:25, Knight observes that "vv. 24 and 25 are symmetrical and state the same truths, first about sin and then about good deeds" (*PE*, 242).

comparative contrast between the false-teaching elders and their adherents in 5:24 versus Timothy and the faithful among the audience in 5:25.[210]

Such is corroborated for the audience by the content of Paul's statement in 5:25 in comparison to 5:24. Over and against "the sins of some" (5:24), the phrase "the commendable works" (τὰ ἔργα τὰ καλά) in 5:25 recalls the godly widow in 5:10 who was testified in "commendable works" (ἔργοις καλοῖς) over and against "some" younger widows who had turned-aside after Satan (5:15). Furthermore, over and against "someone" who is an unqualified overseer, it is only qualified men who lead "commendably" (καλῶς, 3:4) and have a "commendable" (καλήν, 3:7) testimony from those-outside the church who are fit for the "commendable work" (καλοῦ ἔργου, 3:1) of an overseer. Indeed, over and against the reproval of "Those who sin" (5:20), the elders who "lead commendably" (καλῶς προεστῶτες, 5:17) must be considered-worthy of double honor. Undoutedly, then, Paul's point is that "the commendable works" here in 5:25 are to be understood in stark contrast to "The sins of some" in 5:24. In effect, where the "sins of some" have consistently led to swerving-from a without-hypocrisy faith, shipwrecked faith, apostasy, and turning-aside after Satan (1:5–6, 19; 4:1; 5:15), the commendable "works" of Timothy and the faithful are to flow from a without-hypocrisy faith (1:5) that preserves the teaching and promotes godliness as part in God's missional household to attract those-outside to Christ Jesus (3:7). With respect to the minichiasm, then, the specific sense of "the commendable works" in 5:25 would certainly denote adherence to the apostle Paul's instructions regardings elders, particularly their appointment according to the stipulations provided in 3:1–7. Furthermore, those of the faithful in God's household who align themselves with Timothy in "the commendable works" may rest assured that God will not only—negatively—bring judgment against "Those who sin" (5:20) and the "sins of some humans" (5:24), but he will also—positively—honor those whose commendable works support God's household: their works "also" (καί) precede or follow them. Therefore, while the fruit of Timothy and the audience's faithful adherence to Paul's instructions may be readily "conspicuous" (πρόδηλα, 5:25) here and now, Timothy and the audience understand that they are ultimately to find their prize in the upward vision of God's divine court—if not now, then indeed later.

Verse 5:25 concludes: "and those having otherwise do-not have-the-power to be-hidden." In relation to "the commendable works" (τὰ ἔργα τὰ

---

210. Given Paul's purposeful use of the pronoun "some" throughout the letter as a polemical reference to the false teachers, it is unlikely, contra Towner, *Letters*, 378, that the absence "makes [verse 25] an even more general statement" or that the "shift is apparently stylistic."

καλά) in the first half of the verse, it would be clear that "those" (τά) refers to "the commendable works."[211] Furthermore, where the term "otherwise" (ἄλλως) is heard in the context of commendable works that are "conspicuous," the audience understand that "those otherwise" refers to the commendable works that are *not* conspiciuous. Thus the meaning of the unique verbal-adverb pairing "and those having otherwise" would effectively convey the continuation of Paul's thought from the first half of 5:25: ". . . and those [commendable works] that *are* [not conspicuous] . . ."[212] Moreover, by clarifying that such inconspicuous commendable works "do-not have-the-power to be-hidden" (κρυβῆναι οὐ δύνανται), the audience understand the explicit twofold implication of 5:25. On the one hand, there are commendable works that are conspicuous here and now; on the other hand, the remaining commendable works, that is, those that are not immediately conspicuous will nevertheless be acknowledged and rewarded—they "do-not have-the-power to be-hidden." Still, the uniqueness of the phrasing "and those having otherwise" would hardly go unnoticed by the audience, likely drawing attention to its unnecessary rhetorical construction—notably the use of "having." Functioning as the concluding statement of the minichiasm, the participle "having" (ἔχοντα) here in 5:25 of the "a'" sub-element recalls its earlier occurrence in 5:20 of the parallel "a" sub-element wherein the repoval of those who sin was intended to cause the rest to "hold" (ἔχωσιν) fear, that is, resolve not to do evil.[213] In this way, the deliberate use of the verb "having" in 5:25 would not only be heard to bracket the minichiasm but also, therefore, to underscore the comprehensive quality of God's eschatological judgment. In the end, bad or good—sins (5:20) or commendable works (5:25)— will be assessed in the divine courtroom without prejudice (5:21) by God's judgment (5:24).

In sum, the verses of the 5:20–25 minichiasm seem to function as a sort of qualification, "a concession to human fallibility in the matter of identifying sin and merit."[214] As much as Timothy strives to keep the apostle's instructions without prejudice (5:20–21), as much as he seeks to avoid the future appointment of disqualified elders in the church (5:22), as much as he tries to keep himself and the church pure (5:22), as much as he appropriates wine judiciously, correctively, and healthfully (5:23), in the end—on account of sin—there are no guarantees that all will end well here

---

211. The repetition of τά would be apparent.

212. See Towner, *Letters*, 378 n. 96; also BDAG, s.v.

213. For English readability purposes, the participle ἔχοντα in 5:25 was translated as "having" instead of "holding," which is the consistent translation for the verb throughout the letter.

214. Towner, *Letters*, 376.

and now. Unqualified elders—future false teachers—may be appointed or allowed to continue in leadership roles (cf. 5:22), and accusations will be brought against Timothy and other commendable leaders irrespective of how baseless the allegations are (cf. 5:19). However, overarching and undergirding the balanced contrast between "sins" and "commendable works" (5:24–25) is the fundamental framework of God's divine court (5:21, 25). Thus, even though "the sins of some humans" may seem to prevail in Ephesus here and now, the overall rhetorical impact of the minichiasm is that Timothy and his allies are to reprove and select leaders (5:20) always bearing in mind the divine court "of God and of Christ Jesus and of the elect angels" (5:21a). That is, given the apostle's clear instructions and the unavoidability of God's judgment, Timothy and the audience must pursue "the commendable works" impartially and purely while nevertheless being sober about the messiness of ministry. Timothy and the faithful will strive to do their best, yet sin will persist: faithfulness will not always result in immediate fruitfulness. Ultimately, the source of Timothy and the audience's encouragement amidst the sea of neverending sin is that God, the impartial One, will give to each person according to what they have done, whether evil or good.

1 Timothy 6:1–6:2: A Minichiastic Unit

As a minichiasm in itself, verses 6:1–2 of the A' element are composed carefully of four sub-elements ("a"-"b"-"b'"-"a'"); linguistic parallels identifying chiastic arrangements are indicated by the Greek text:

"a". ⁶:¹ᵃ Those who are (εἰσίν) under the yoke as slaves (δοῦλοι)

"b". ⁶:¹ᵇ must consider their own masters (δεσπότας) worthy of all honor, that the name of God and the teaching might not (μή) be-blasphemed.

"b'". ⁶:²ᵃ But those who have faithful masters (δεσπότας) must not (μή) look-down

"a'". because they are (εἰσιν) brothers; rather all-the-more they must serve-as-slaves (δουλευέτωσαν), because faithful and beloved are (εἰσιν) those who receive the beneficial-work. These-things teach and exhort.

This fifth and final minichiasm of the 5:1—6:2 microchiasm is framed by the godly activity of Christian slaves in the "a" and "a'" sub-elements. The minichiasm gravitates around the Christian slaves's relationship with both non-Christian and Christian masters in the "b" and "b'" sub-elements.

1 Timothy 6:1a: Those Under the Yoke as Slaves

("a" sub-element)

The introductory "a" sub-element identifies those among the audience whom Paul is specifically addressing: "Those who are under the yoke as slaves" (6:1a).[215] Paul uses the general term "Those" (ὅσοι), which could be translated "as many as."[216] It is unlikely, then, that Paul has in mind a specific group of slaves—for example, elders who are slaves[217]—but rather is referring to all of the faithful among the audience who "are" (εἰσίν) currently "slaves" (δοῦλοι).[218] While slaves themselves fulfilled a full range of functions and, therefore, did not all fit the same mold,[219] one common denominator between all slaves is that they were counted as the property of their masters.[220] The inclusion of the prepositional phrase "under the yolk"

---

215. The issue of slavery seemed to pose difficulty for the early church, especially as slaves sought to elevate their position to freedom or equality; see Bartchy, "Slave, Slavery," 1098–1102. It must be remembered, however, that in the context of 1 Timothy the apostle's primary concern was the missional calling of God's household versus emancipation. Thus, his concern in what follows is how the attitude and actions of Christian slaves could misrepresent the church's witness to those-outside (cf. 3:7).

216. See Marshall, *PE*, 628.

217. Contra Barrett, *PE*, 82.

218. Given the context of the next verse (6:2), more than likely Paul in 6:1 has in view Christian slaves under non-Christian masters; see especially Towner, *Goal*, 175–80. While the specification provided in 6:2a clearly refers to "those who have faithful masters," that is, Christian masters, the implication of 6:1a suggests that Paul is addressing slaves of non-Christian masters, in effect, "those who have faithless masters." See Knight, *PE*, 244; Barcley, *1 & 2 Tim*, 179. Phillips, *Exploring the PE*, 168: "In the early days of the church, a high percentage of believers were slaves, most of whom had unsaved masters."

219. For more background on the identity and function of slaves during the NT period, see Ferguson, *Backgrounds*, 45–48. See also Spencer, *1 Tim*, 142–43.

220. It is worth noting that slavery in the first-century is not to be understood in terms of its more modern forms. Harrill, "Paul and Slavery," 583: "Roman slaves were not segregated from freeborns in work or type of job performed, with the notable exceptions of military service and mining. This integration of slaves into all levels of the ancient economy marks an important contrast with modern slavery. Modern slavery, for example, often required slave illiteracy by law, whereas ancient masters prized educated slaves. In cities throughout the Mediterranean, slaves were trained and served as physicians, engineers, artisans, shopkeepers, architects, artists, thespians, magicians, prophets (e.g., Acts 16:16–24), teachers, professional poets, and philosophers . . .

(ὑπὸ ζυγόν) seems deliberate, conveying the apostle's recognition of such slaves's difficult situation. The term "yolk" is found regularly throughout the OT to connote suffering and injustice.[221] Furthermore, the placement of the prepositional phrase "under the yolk" prior to the term "slaves" may have been the apostle's subtle, public recognition that their status as "slaves" represented one of the persisting realities of sin and, therefore, does not accord with the new, restorative reality created by Christ Jesus's ransom payment to set sinners free (2:6).

1 Timothy 6:1b: Slaves Honor Their Masters, the Name of God Not Be-Blaspehemed

("b" sub-element)

In the "b" sub-element, the audience hear that Christian slaves who now belong to the household of God "must consider their own masters worthy of all honor" (6:1b). Given Christian slaves's newfound freedom by coming to a knowing-embrace of truth concerning Christ Jesus in the parallel B unit (2:4–6), there may have been a newfound thought to view their masters apart from their present duty as slaves. In contrast, for slaves who have come to have-faith upon Christ Jesus and been set free from God's just judgment for their sin, Paul uses key terms that have occurred throughout the macrochiasm to define the way they ought to view their masters—particularly their non-Christian masters. The phrase "their own masters" (τοὺς ἰδίους δεσπότας) would be understood to limit the application of Paul's command.[222] Throughout the macrochiasm, the majority of the occurrences of the adjective "own" (ἴδιος) were heard in relation to an individual family household, and such would seem to be the implication here.[223] Furthermore, Paul's focus on the individual household would be emphasized by the term "masters" (δεσπότας), which echoes the younger women's call "to

---

Because slaves could be found at all economic levels of society, they had no cohesion as a group and lacked anything akin to class consciousness." Bartchy, *First-Century Slavery*, 87: ". . . the person in Greek or Roman slavery in the first century A. D. led an existence which differs in many significant ways from the slavery practiced in modern times. Perhaps the most significant difference between ancient slavery and modern slavery is the manumission [freedom] anticipated by first-century slaves." To be sure, this is not to suggest that slavery in the first-century was good or without tragedy; see Bryant, *Paul and the Rise of the Slave*, 28–30.

221. E.g., Deuteronomy 28:48; 47:6; 58:6; see also comments by Mounce, *PE*, 326.
222. See Knight, *PE*, 245.
223. See 3:4, 5, 12; 5:4, 8. The only exception is 2:6 in regard to God's "own" times.

master-households" (οἰκοδεσποτεῖν, 5:14) in the context of marriage and children. While the audience understand that Paul is not placing boundaries on those whom Christian slaves are to show honor,[224] it is evident that Paul's command to Christian slaves is confined in its application to their specific masters: they are not to generalize this command as a call to subservient living but rather to ordinary obedience in their everyday duty in life.[225] Given that such obedience would be shown from a Christian slave—likely to a non-Christian master—it seems that the purpose of Paul's command for ordinary obedience may intend extraordinary missional effects.

The phrase "must consider . . . worthy of all honor" would likely corroborate Paul's missional impetus. Each term here is rich with meaning. First, the adjective "all" (πάσης) recalls its prior occurrences throughout the macrochiasm—particularly in the parallel B unit (2:1, 2, 4, 5)—and draws attention to the missional calling of the church. Furthermore, where "all" (πάσης) recalls a godly woman's calling to be "faithful in all" (πᾶσιν, 3:11), that is, to model a missional lifestyle, it is evident that Paul's command to Christian slaves intends a missional impact. Paul's command is for the Christian slaves in Ephesus to steward their present situation uniquely in a way that others in the audience cannot. As slaves, they are to exhibit the freedom of their existence "in faith"—"in Christ Jesus" (3:13), "in glory" (3:16). That is, by honoring their own masters here and now in the B' unit of the macrochiasm, the slaves who have been set free by Christ Jesus's ransom

---

224. E.g., the entire audience are to "honor" the King of the eternities (1:17), "honor" widows who are truly widows (5:3), and "honor" elders who lead commendably (5:17). See below.

225. It is important to be both sensitive and culturally aware of the modern connotations that the terms "slaves" (6:1a) and "serve-as-slaves" (6:2b) may convey. Not a few commentators describe the awful misapplication of Paul's words that have occurred throughout history. Krause, "1 Tim," 438: "the writer's claim of women's subservient status [2:11-12] and call for slaves to submit to their masters [6:1-2] . . . have stood and continue to stand in many parts of the church as fences to full participation and justification for human degradation." Here, Harrill's comments are helpful: "Indeed, scriptural justification was the central pillar in the eighteenth-century proslavery argument while at the same time, abolitionist clergy found evidence in the Bible to justify the opposite and thus support their antislavery theology. In evaluating the merits of either position for scholarly biblical exegesis, we must appreciate the difference between ancient and modern slavery. We must also consider the tension between our time and the biblical period and not absolve slavery or downplay its significance in ancient life" ("Bible," 80). See MacArthur, *1 Tim*, 229-30.

As will be demonstrated below, clearly human degradation in any form is antithetical to the apostle Paul's commands where "brothers" (6:2a) and "beloved" (6:2b) are in view between masters and slaves. Also noted below, Paul's command for Christian "slaves" (6:1) to "serve-as-slaves" (6:2) is rooted in Christ Jesus himself who certainly did not intend human degredation (Mark 10:44-15; Phil 2:6-7).

will show their own masters the "peaceable and quiet life . . . in all (πάσῃ) godliness and respectability" (2:2), which is commendable and acceptable in the sight of the Savior God who desires "all" (πάντας) humans to be-saved (2:3–4a). Along with the entire audience (2:1–2) in the parallel B unit—the godly men in "all" (παντί) place (2:8) and the godly women in "all" (πάσῃ) submissiveness (2:11)—the slaves's godly lifestyle of showing "all" (πάσης) honor toward their own masters in the B' unit stems from sharing God's missional desire for all humans to come to a knowing-embrace of truth concerning Christ Jesus. Undoubtedly, although "all" would connote its basic meaning—"completely"—its rhetorical use throughout the macrochiasm underscores to the audience that Paul's command in 6:1b intends salvation for the slaves's masters.

Second, the term "honor" (τιμῆς) recalls its cognate occurrences throughout the macrochiasm: recipients of the gospel are to show "honor (τιμή) and glory" to the King of the eternities (1:17), must "honor" (τίμα) widows who are truly widows (5:3), and must show double "honor" (τιμῆς) to teaching elders who lead commendably (5:17). In this way, Paul's command identifies that the "honor" which slaves are to show to their own masters in 6:1b is simply the consistent outworking of their reception of the gospel that exhibits God's radiance and results in blessing toward him (1:11). The audience understand that the "honor" shown by Christian slaves to their own masters will ultimately give "honor" to God.

Third, the term "worthy" (ἀξίους) recalls its cognate occurrences throughout the macrochiasm: the faithful word concerning the entrance of Christ Jesus into the world to save sinners is "worthy" (ἄξιος) of all acceptance (1:15); the faithful word concerning the proper reception of God's creation in the present life in view of the life to inevitably-come (4:8)—that is, consistent-with faith upon Christ Jesus (1:16; 4:5)—is "worthy" (ἄξιος) of all acceptance (4:9); and the teaching elders who lead commendably "must be considered-worthy" (ἀξιούσθωσαν) of double honor (5:17) because Jesus himself said that the laborer is "worthy" (ἄξιος) of his pay (5:18). The force of Paul's command in 6:1b that Christian slaves must consider their own masters "worthy" of all honor would, therefore, be heard with a twofold implication. On the one hand, negatively, to not consider their own masters "worthy" of all honor would tangibly undermine the Christian slaves's profession that the faithful word is "worthy" of all acceptance (1:15; 4:9) and that God views people as inherently "worthy" (5:17, 19). On the other hand, positively, to consider their own masters "worthy" of all honor would tangibly demonstrate—particularly to any non-Christian masters—that the faithful word concerning Christ Jesus is "worthy" of all acceptance (1:15; 4:9) and that the laborer is "worthy" of his pay (5:17, 19). Thus the audience understand that Paul's command is both missional and beneficial for the slaves. By the ordinary gesture of showing "honor" to their own masters, Paul indicates that Christian slaves in Ephesus play an integral role in God's missional household: they are uniquely positioned to show their own masters on a daily basis both that in everday, ordinary life the faithful word is "worthy" of all acceptance and the laboring slaves themselves are "worthy" of honor (5:17, 19). Paul has the salvation of "their own masters" in view as well as the benefit of those who are under the yoke as "slaves" (6:1).

Fourth and finally, the verb "consider" (ἡγείσθωσαν) would certainly be fascinating and significant to the audience. Its only other occurrence was heard in regard to Christ Jesus the Lord who "considered" (ἡγήσατο) Paul faithful, appointing him for service, though firstly being a blasphemer, persecutor, and hubristic-person in unfaithfulness (1:12–13). Here in 6:1b, then, the apostle Paul's command highlights not only his own experience of the gospel directly from Christ Jesus but also the ensuing disposition that all recipients of the same gospel are to exhibit: although their own masters may not merit honor, nevertheless they should be honored by Christian slaves, that is, by those who did not merit salvation yet freely received it by grace (1:2, 14). In sum of the command that "Those under the yoke as slaves must consider their own masters worthy of all honor" (6:1a–b), the audience understand that any perspective that is accepted by the Christian slaves other than the one offered by the apostle would impact the church's ability to exist as God's missional household.

Continuing the "b" sub-element, Paul states the purpose clause: "that the name of God and the teaching might not be-blasphemed" (6:1b). Corroborating its missional impetus, the purpose clause of Paul's command underscores to the Christian slaves that their existence "in faith"—"in Christ Jesus," in God's household—should not primarily focus on their individual identity but rather on their corporate calling as family members to protect "the name of God and the teaching." Again, what is plain to the audience here is Paul's concern for all of the faithful in God's missional household to conduct themselves in light of the household-law of God "in faith" (1:4), namely to share the common purpose God, who is the Father of the household "in faith" (1:2), that is, the Savior God who desires all humans to be-saved (2:3–4a).

For Paul's Ephesian audience, the purpose clause in 6:1b—"that the name (ὄνομα) of God and the teaching might not be-blasphemed (βλασ φημῆται)"—would be a clear allusion to God's declaration in LXX Isaiah 52:5: ". . . all the day my name (ὄνομά) is blasphemed (βλασφημεῖται) in the

Gentiles."²²⁶ The apostle applies the OT verse by comparing the Christian slaves to the Jews and the unbelieving masters to the Gentiles.²²⁷ Paul's point is that disobedience and recalcitrance on the part of Christian slaves would result in the dishonoring of God among the unbelieving masters. Furthermore, within this OT background, the phrase "the name of God" (τὸ ὄνομα τοῦ θεοῦ) would obviously be heard in reference to God's renown, the reputation which he establishes particularly through the Exodus narrative and safeguards throughout the OT as exemplified in the third commandment of the Decalogue.²²⁸ In this regard, Paul is suggesting that God's renown goes forth in tandem with the missional purpose of God's household, not through any particularly fancy evangelistic method but rather through ordinary obedience to God's revealed will by the apostle Paul. In effect, it is by Christian slaves honoring their non-Christian masters that God's desire for all humans to be-saved is realized.

Of equal concern to Paul is that "the teaching might not be-blasphemed" (6:1b). The significance of the term "the teaching" (ἡ διδασκαλία) would not go unnoticed, given its progressive and sustained occurrence throughout the movement of the macrochiasm. In the A unit, in contrast to "some" who "teach-different" (ἑτεροδιδασκαλεῖν, 1:3), it is only "the (τῇ) sound teaching (διδασκαλίᾳ)" that accords with the gospel and thus exhibits God's radiance (1:10b–11). In the B unit, against the influence of the false teachers who are suggested to be "falsifying" (2:7) and influencing the godly women to reject God's creational design (2:12–14), it is Paul's divine appointment as an authorized proclaimer, apostle, and "teacher" (διδάσκαλος, 2:7) that enables him to correct the false teachers's influence regarding who is permitted "to teach" (διδάσκειν) in the church (2:12). In the C unit, a man who is qualified for an overseer is "able-to-teach" (διδακτικόν, 3:2) and knows how to lead and care-for the church of God. In the C' unit, over and against the apostatized false teachers who are holding-toward "teachings" (διδασκαλίαις) of demons (4:1), it is Paul's authorized representative Timothy who has followed "the (τῆς) commendable teaching (διδασκαλίας)" (4:6), who must hold-toward "the teaching" (τῇ διδασκαλίᾳ, 4:13), and must strongly-hold "the teaching" (τῇ διδασκαλίᾳ, 4:16). Finally, here in the B' unit, in line with honoring the elders who lead commendably by their toil in

---

226. Compare the relevant portions of the Greek texts:
1 Tim 6:1b: "ἵνα μὴ τὸ ὄνομα τοῦ θεοῦ καὶ ἡ διδασκαλία βλασφημῆται";
LXX Isa 52:5: "δι' ὑμᾶς διὰ παντὸς τὸ ὄνομά μου βλασφημεῖται ἐν τοῖς ἔθνεσιν."

227. The Jews are mentioned in the first half of LXX Isaiah 52:5—"my people" (ὁ λαός μου)—but also in the surrounding context (vv. 4 and 6).

228. Exodus 20:7; Deuteronomy 5:11: "You shall not take the name of the Lord your God (τὸ ὄνομα κυρίου τοῦ θεοῦ σου) in vain..."

"teaching" (διδασκαλίᾳ, 5:17), it is the Christian slaves who must honor their non-Christian masters to effectively preserve "the teaching" (ἡ διδασκαλία) from being blasphemed (6:1b). In short, the audience understand that Paul's missional command toward the Christian slaves is fully derived from the sound teaching—the gospel—concerning Christ Jesus and the freedom that his ransom achieved on their behalf.

The verb "be-blasphemed" (βλασφημῆται) recalls for the audience its earlier occurrence in 1:20 where Paul had given-over Hymenaeus and Alexander to Satan, that they might be-disciplined not "to blaspheme" (βλασφημεῖν). Furthermore, where the negative particle "not" (μή) has been heard with a polemical association to the activity or behavior of the false teachers, it seems that for God's name to "not (μή) be-blasphemed" (6:1b) would convey a twofold implication. On the one hand, negatively, the Christian slaves's poor attitude and conduct toward their own masters is as dangerous to the preservation of the teaching and promotion of godliness as are the false teachers and their corresponding ungodly, unmissional conduct. On the other hand, positively, Christian slaves's godly attitude toward their own masters will not only remove any reason for God's reputation to be-blasphemed but will also actively and personally advance God's renown to those-outside God's household, namely the non-Christian masters.

In sum, the movement of the minichiasm from the "a" sub-element to the "b" sub-element is clear. In 6:1a the audience understand that Paul expresses sympathy toward those who are under the yoke and thus experience the effects of Adam's sin (2:14) in a unique way. However, at the same time Paul does not let them off the hook: their less than ideal circumstances do not allow them to misapply their ultimate freedom from God's just judgment. In light of Christ Jesus—their ransom (2:6)—the Christian slaves in Ephesus must not act in any way that would cause the name of God and the teaching to be-blasphemed (6:1b). With an integral role in the missional purpose of God's household, the audience understand that Christian slaves are to act in a way that advances God's renown, that is, the reputation of their very own Savior God (1:2, 2).

1 Timothy 6:2a: Those Who Have Faithful Masters Must Not Look-Down

("b'" sub-element)

Advancing the scope of Paul's command in the "b" sub-element, Paul declares in the parallel "b'" sub-element: "But those who have faithful masters must not look-down because they are brothers" (6:2a). The pronoun "those" (οἱ) recalls "Those" (ὅσοι) in the parallel "b" sub-element and indicates that Paul is continuing his commands to Christian slaves. Given the explicit continuation, the weak adversative "But" (δέ) would not be heard to indicate a contrast but rather a shift in application, namely that the underlying principle in 6:1b remains the same for the slaves in 6:2a. The shift in application would be heard by the addition of the adjective "faithful" (πιστούς) to describe "masters" (δεσπότας) in 6:2a. The term "faithful" (πιστούς) recalls its prior cognates throughout the macrochiasm in reference to those "in faith" (ἐν πίστει, 1:2, 4; 2:7, 15; 3:13; 4:12) who have accepted the "faithful" (πιστός) word (1:15; 4:9; cf. 3:1) by coming "to have-faith" (πιστεύειν) upon Christ Jesus (1:16), namely "the faithful" (πιστοῖς) who have knowingly-embraced the truth (4:3b), those "of the faithful" (πιστῶν) for whom God is the Savior (4:10), and "those of the faithful" (τῶν πιστῶν) for whom Timothy must be an example (4:12). Undoubtedly, then, where Paul shifts his focus to "faithful masters" (πιστούς . . . δεσπότας), the audience not only understand that that the "masters" in view of 6:2a are Christians but also—and significantly—that they are "in faith" with the Christian slaves in the very same way that Timothy is Paul's genuine child "in faith" (1:2). Thus the overall force of the participle phrase "those who have faithful masters" underscores a common *familial* bond: both the Christian slave and Christian master in 6:2a live in God's household; they both have come "to have-faith" upon Christ Jesus (1:16) and thus received the salvific blessings of grace, mercy, and peace from God the Father and Christ Jesus, their common Lord (1:2). Such an integral bond between the Christian slaves and their Christian masters would be emphasized by the participle "having" (ἔχοντες), which recalls its use throughout the macrochiasm in reference to clinging.[229] Where slaves are "having" faithful masters, Paul is highlighting that their familial bond is not to be relinquished at any time or in any way.

The verb "look-down" (καταφρονείτωσαν) in 6:2a recalls for the audience Paul's command that none must "look-down-on" (καταφρονείτω) on Timothy's youth (4:12), which was referring to the prideful activity of the young-plant false teachers toward Timothy. Here in 6:2a, then, Paul is clearly addressing a current issue in Ephesus wherein the Christian slaves are mimicking the ungodliness of "some."[230] Furthermore, that Christian slaves must "not (μή) look-down" in 6:2a strengthens the rhetorical

---

229. For English readability purposes, the participle ἔχοντες in 6:2a was translated as "having" instead of "holding," which is the consistent translation for the verb throughout the letter.

230. The present tense of the imperative καταφρονείτωσαν indicates that Paul is addressing a real and present issue.

connection to 4:12 wherein "None (μηδείς) must look-down-on." Given that "not" and its cognates have carried forward a reference to the activity of the false teachers, Paul's implication here in 6:2a is to the point: by continually looking down on their masters who are family members "in faith," Christian slaves are imitating the deplorable conduct of the being-puffed-up, young-plant false teachers (3:6) who look-down-on Paul's genuine child Timothy (4:12).[231]

In sum, the movement from the "b" to "b'" sub-element communicates the reprehensible nature of this specific situation. The parallel repetition of the terms "masters" (δεσπότας) and "not" (μή) in the "b" and "b'" sub-elements would carry forward an emphatic command by the apostle Paul, the sense being: "Consider unbelievers worthy of all honor, and do not dishonor believing masters." Again, Paul seems concerned to help Christian slaves come to grips with the significance of their actions: both God's name and the teaching that exhibits his radiance are on the line, and not one person among the faithful in Ephesus can afford to act like the false teachers by blaspheming (1:20; 6:1a) or looking-down (4:12; 6:2a).

1 Timothy 6:2b: They Are Brothers, Faithful and Beloved Receive the Beneficial-Work

("a'" sub-element)

The concluding "a'" sub-element of the minichiasm and final phrase in the A' element of the fifth microchiasm begins by explaining why Christian slaves must not look-down on their Christian masters: "because they are

---

231. It may be worth noting that the parallel symmetry between the "b" and "b'" sub-elements not only confirms that Paul's command intends for the Christian slaves to act in an antithetical manner as the false teachers but also—and significantly—corroborates that Paul has in view the false teachers in 4:12. Here, a visual representation of the pairings in the "b" sub-element and "b'" sub-element may be helpful (Similar phrases in the letter have been included alongside to demonstrate the connection to the false teachers):

"b" sub-element:
1:20: "that they might be-disciplined not (μή) to blaspheme (βλασφημεῖν)";
6:1b: "that the name of God and the teaching might not (μή) be-blasphemed (βλασφημῆται)";

"b'" sub-element:
4:12: "None (μηδείς) must look-down-on (καταφρονείτω) your youth";
6:2a: "But those who have faithful masters must not (μή) look-down (καταφρονείτωσαν)."

Given the striking similarity of both pairs of the "b" and "b'" sub-elements (6:1b, 6:2a) to 1:20 and 4:12, it is evident that both pairs allude specifically to the false teachers.

brothers" (6:2b). The term "brothers" (ἀδελφοί) recalls Paul's instructions in the parallel A element for Timothy to exhort younger-men as "brothers" (ἀδελφοῖς). Thus where "brothers" in the A element emphasized the familial theme of the letter—that the church is the household of God—the audience understand that the Christian slaves in the parallel A' element have misapplied their relationship with their "brothers," namely by thinking that the societal structures in Ephesus have been negated by the fact that there is no slave or master in God's household—only family members. In other words, the correct understanding by Christian slaves that their faithful masters should be viewed as "brothers" in the familial realm "in faith" led to an incorrect practice of discounting the socio-economic status of their "brothers" as masters.[232] Furthermore, in regard to the current minichiasm, the rhetorical juxtaposition of "Those who are (εἰσίν) under the yoke as slaves" in 6:1a of the "a" sub-element and "they are (εἰσιν) brothers" in 6:2a of the parallel "a'" sub-element would highlight the corrective force of Paul's commands. That is, Paul is challenging those who "are" (εἰσιν) slaves to be more thoughtful and deliberate about how they relate to masters who "are" (εἰσιν) believers.

Having conveyed what Christian slaves should not do, Paul goes on to spell out what they should do: "rather all-the-more they must serve-as-slaves, because faithful and beloved are those who receive the beneficial-work" (6:2b). Immediately, the audience hear the strong conjunctive-adverbial phrase "rather . . . all-the-more" (ἀλλὰ μᾶλλον), which underscores Paul's positive command in 6:2b relative to his negative command in 6:2a.[233] The verb "serve-as-slaves" (δουλευέτωσαν) here in 6:2b of the "a'" sub-element recalls its noun cognate "slaves" (δοῦλοι) in 6:1a of the parallel "a" sub-element. In effect, the parallelism between "slaves" and "serve-as-slaves" encapsulates everything Paul has expressed in the current minichiasm: to "serve-as-slaves" means accepting one's identity "under the yolk as slaves";

232. See Verner, *Household of God*, 142. Barclay, *1 & 2 Tim*, 180: "Masters and slaves are to be regarded as equals. This should be reflected in their treatment of one another. At the same time, this essential equality does not do away with functional differences in social or economic relationships."

233. It is possible that the force of the comparative adverb μᾶλλον accentuates the difference in attitude and action that Christian slaves should exhibit toward their Christian masters, "instead" (e.g., Marshall, *PE*, 631). However, it is more likely that μᾶλλον functions to intensify the proceeding command, namely that slaves should serve "all-the-more" (e.g., Knight, *PE*, 246); see BDAG, s.v. Verse 6:2 itself makes clear that the current attitude in Ephesus by Christian slaves is wrong *and* that their correct attitude and service toward Christian masters should have an "intensified" quality precisely because their masters are family members "in faith." This echoes what the apostle writes elsewhere—that believers should love all people but especially those that belong to the household of God; see Galatians 6:10.

yet, considering their identity in view of Christ Jesus's ransom on their behalf, those who are "slaves" are to "serve-as-slaves" both missionally by considering their non-Christian masters worthy of all honor and familially by abounding in service to their "faithful masters" because "they are brothers."

Within the "a'" sub-element, the second causal clause—"because (ὅτι) faithful and beloved are (εἰσιν) . . ."—parallels the first causal clause—"because (ὅτι) they are (εἰσιν) brothers." The back-to-back reiteration would likely be heard to reflect Paul's desire for the Christian slaves to better assess the situation, that is, for them to not merely see themselves rightly in terms of their Christian calling but also to rightly see who their faithful masters are from the perspective of the gospel.[234] That is, the phrase "because they are brothers" not only means that such masters are to be viewed by Christian slaves as "faithful" (πιστοί)—family members in God's household—but also, therefore, as "beloved" (ἀγαπητοί). That the Christian slaves are to view their Christian masters as inseparably "faithful and beloved" (πιστοί . . . καὶ ἀγαπητοί) recalls the apostle Paul himself who was the recipient of "the faith and love" (πίστεως καὶ ἀγάπης) that are in Christ Jesus (1:14). Such would underscore that faithful masters who are "beloved" means that they are primarily loved by Christ Jesus and, consequently, are to be loved by other members of God's household—certainly by the Christian slaves.[235] To the Christian slaves, Paul's point is that having been loved, love itself becomes the driving force and persisting exhortation of one's interactions. It is for this reason that "love" (ἀγάπη) is the motivation behind Paul's charge for Timothy to stop the false teachers (1:5); to be sure, where the end of Paul's charge is "love" (1:5), the audience understand beyond any doubt that Paul's exhortation for Timothy to charge "some" not to teach-different (1:3) fully intends that "some" would become "beloved," that is, "faithful"—"brothers" (6:2). Moreover, that Christian slaves are to view their Christian masters as "faithful and beloved" (πιστοί . . . καὶ ἀγαπητοί, 6:2b) in the B' unit of the macrochiasm recalls the women in the parallel B unit who evidence their salvation by remaining in "faith and love" (πίστει καὶ ἀγάπῃ, 2:15). Here, then, the audience understand the full implication of Paul's command: the Christian slaves are to evidence their own salvation—that they are remain-

---

234. Knight aptly describes the rhetorical emphasis: "Both halves of the verse follow the same pattern: imperative with slaves as subject, followed by ὅτι clause with masters as the subject" (*PE*, 246).

235. Marshall, *PE*, 631–32: "The word is frequent in the NT for being loved by God . . . It then expresses, by implication, worthiness of being loved by human beings, i.e., the relationship that should exist between fellow-believers." Knight, *PE*, 247: "God's love for both slave and master has made them brothers and brought them to regard one another as 'beloved.'"

ing "in faith and love" (2:15)—by serving their "brothers" who are "faithful and beloved" (6:2b). Indeed, where Timothy is to be example in "love" (ἀγάπη) for God's household in Ephesus (4:12), the Christian slaves are to demonstrate their allegiance to his leadership by following his example, that is, by viewing their masters as "beloved" (ἀγαπητοί, 6:2b).

It is possible that the participle phrase "those who receive the beneficial-work" would be heard in various ways.[236] The technical way in which the noun "beneficial-work" (εὐεργεσίας) was used in the Greco-Roman patron system often described good deeds done by an influential and powerful benefactor who, in turn, would receive some form of public honor.[237] As such, the audience may have understood the phrase "those who receive the beneficial-work" in the sense that Christian slaves must assiduously serve their Christian masters so that their masters would be honored, which would enhance the church's reputation and advance God's renown.[238] However, given that Paul's immediate focus in 6:2b pertains specifically to Christian relational dynamics, it is more likely that the audience hear "those who receive the beneficial-work" as a rhetorical emphasis, namely that Christian slaves must all-the-more serve-as-slaves for their Christian masters because the latter belong to the household of God and are beloved by Christ Jesus.[239] As such, the impact of the Greco-Roman benefaction language here would likely be understood in a new light.[240] Simply put, to those who are under the yoke as "slaves" (δοῦλοι, 6:1a) and who must all-the-more "serve-as-slaves" (δουλευέτωσαν) for their faithful masters (6:2), it appears that Paul is applying Jesus's teaching that "whoever desires among you to be first must be a slave (δοῦλος) of all" (Mark 10:44).[241] From the perspective of the gospel that

236. The difference is in regard to the noun "beneficial-work" (εὐεργεσίας), which could convey "the receiving of good" or "the doing of good." For example, two modern translations highlight the difference in interpretation:
ESV: "those who benefit by their good service are believers and beloved";
TNIV: "their masters . . . are devoted to the welfare of their slaves."

237. See especially Kidd, *Wealth and Beneficence*, 142–56 and Verner, *Household of God*, 143–44.

238. See Towner, *Letters*, 385–86, who provides an excellent summary of this interpretation, although he provides an altogether different—and more probable—interpretation; see below. See also Towner, "Can Slaves Be Their Masters' Benefactors?," 39–52.

239. This is the interpretation by the majority of commentators.

240. Towner comments: "Paul has been known to co-opt the language and concepts so dominant in his culture in his effort to redefine, challenge, and rather intentionally subvert the 'givens' of his day on the basis of the transforming truth of the gospel he preached" (*Letters*, 387). See ibid. n. 40.

241. The reference to Mark 10:44 here in the B' unit of the macrochiasm may not be insignificant. In the parallel B unit, Paul referred to Jesus's very next statement in Mark 10:45; see volume 1, chapter 4 regarding 1 Timothy 2:6. Where the paired, parallel

exhibits God's radiant glory (1:11), that is, the testimony concerning Christ Jesus who gave himself as a ransom on behalf of all (2:6), Paul's command to Christian slaves would not be surprising but rather expected. With their new identity "in faith that is Christ Jesus" (3:13) and as family members of the household in which Christ Jesus is Lord (1:2), Christian slaves are to live out their high calling as benefactors to their masters while—according to Jesus (Mark 10:44)—being benefactors themselves.[242] Emphasizing this point, the phrase "those who receive" (οἱ . . . ἀντιλαμβανόμενοι) echoes Paul's twice-repeated statement in the prior microchiasm that God created all creation for "reception" (μετάλημψιν) with thanksgiving by the faithful (4:3), that is, nothing is to be rejected, "being-received" (λαμβανόμενον) with thanksgiving (4:4). Heard with this connection, the implication seems to be not only that the faithful masters should be "those who receive" in 6:2b but also that the Christian slaves are working alongside God to provide for "the faithful" (πιστοῖς, 4:3)—in this case, the "faithful" (πιστούς) masters (6:2a)—the "faithful" (πιστοί) and beloved (6:2b).

In sum, here in the performance of the letter, the audience experience Paul's speech as that of a compassionate, firm, and Christ-thinking teacher. He recognizes the plight of Christian slaves who are "under the yoke." Nevertheless, he exhorts them to remember their identity as members of God's household; therefore, they are not to do anything against unbelieving or believing masters that would cause blasphemy against the name of God and the teaching. Still, his commands remind the Christian slaves of their high position: as members of God's household they now possess an exalted identity that enables them to be benefactors in a manner that was typically reserved for the affluent and influential. In short, Paul reminds

---

references to Mark 10:44–45 are intentional in the B and B' units of the macrochiasm, the audience would likely understand that Paul is intending to frame and root their attention upon Jesus.

242. Towner, *Letters*, 390: "Paul has turned the tables. The slaves serve, but in God's surprising *oikonomia* they do so from a position of power; nobility and honor, the rewards of benefaction, are accorded here implicitly to the slaves. In all of this, the privileges of honor which that culture reserved for well-to-do patrons, benefactors, and slave owners are not denied; nor are the obligations of slaves to their masters trivialized. But the meaning and value of life lived at that level are relativized by the more fundamental reality of the universal Lordship of Christ within God's *oikonomia*." Barcley, *1 & 2 Tim*, 180: "The language that Paul uses here is that of benefaction, usually applied to those in positions of power or authority who do beneficent work for those in lesser positions . . . Instead, Paul seeks to transform the way slaves think about their service. They are the benefactors. Their masters benefit from their work." Knight, *PE*, 247: "By the use of this word [εὐεργεσία] Paul turns the service of a slave into an act of bestowing good on another, even his master. Paul has thereby made the difficult role of a slave the means by which the slave can benefit his master." See Marshall, *PE*, 632.

them to participate in the life of Christ Jesus, the Lord upon whom they have-faith (1:16) and in whom they exist (3:13)—the life of a King (cf. 1:17) who served as a slave.²⁴³

The progressive arrangement of the fifth microchiasm has moved the audience toward a climactic end. Beginning in the A element, the focus was the familial reality of those in God's household; in the B element, it was the relation of caring for God's family by caring for one's own family; such familial care was punctuated by tangible works in the C and C' elements, which pivoted around godly care for others in the D element. In the B' element, the audience were directed to the importance of one's own family life in relation to the family of God's household; then in the A' element, the intermingled impact of false-teaching elders and slaves who dishonor their own masters affected both the dynamics of God's household and individual households.

Here, then, in the final statement of the A' element within the fifth microchiasm, Paul issues a climactic command: "These-things teach and exhort" (6:2b). The demonstrative "These-things" (ταῦτα) recalls its prior occurrences throughout the macrochiasm and would refer to what precedes it.²⁴⁴ Thus, "These-things" would likely be understood by the audience to include everything that the apostle Paul has commanded in the fifth microchiasm: the proper disposition that Timothy is to use when exhorting fathers, brothers, mothers, and sisters of God's household (A element); the identification and care of those who are truly widows (B-C-D-C' elements); the discipline and restoration of younger widows (B' element); the honorable treatment of elders who lead commendably—particularly overseers—as well as the process of reproving false-teaching elders and of appointing future qualified elders (A' element); and the godly, missional conduct of Christian slaves toward those-outside and inside the household of God (A' element).²⁴⁵

Furthermore, Paul's command here would effectively pull forward key implications of the entire macrochiasm. The phrase "These-things teach and exhort" (ταῦτα δίδασκε καὶ παρακάλει) in 6:2b echoes Paul's command in 4:11 for Timothy to "Charge these-things and teach" (παράγγελλε ταῦτα

---

243. The gospel principle here is perhaps best articulated in Philippians 2:6–7: "he was in the form of God . . . but emptied himself, taking the form of a slave (δούλου)." The words of Jesus's brother would also echo Paul's apostolic teaching: "Let the lowly brother boast in his exaltation" (Jas 1:9, *ESV*).

244. See 1:18; 3:14; 4:6, 11, 15.

245. Knight, *PE*, 247: "ταῦτα is thus used in a similar formula in 4:11 . . . to refer to what precedes and not to what follows, and the pattern holds here also, where it includes all the material from the last personal section ending at 4:16 or 5:2."

καὶ δίδασκε). Where the concern in 4:11 was to uphold the faithful word concerning the universal offer of salvation, eternal life, and godliness over and against the false teachings of "some" apostates, the audience would likely hear Paul's command in 6:2b to have salvific implications: failure to "teach and exhort" all of the things in the fifth microchiasm would have eternal ramifications.[246] Moreover, given that Timothy is commanded to "teach" (δίδασκε) all these-things in the fifth microchiasm, the audience understand that he is not only to demonstrate what it looks like to toil in word and "teaching" (διδασκαλίᾳ) but also to ensure that "the teaching" (ἡ διδασκαλία, 6:1b) might not be-blasphemed, that is, so that "the (τῇ) sound teaching" (διδασκαλίᾳ)" (1:10)—the gospel—would facilitate the missional calling of God's household. The verb "exhort" (παρακάλει) recalls its prior occurrences in reference to the apostle Paul (1:3; 2:1). That Timothy is to "exhort" would further draw the audience's attention to Timothy's authority in relation to Paul. Moreover, the command "exhort" (παρακάλει) here in 6:2b of the A' element recalls its occurrence in 5:1 of the parallel A element where Paul commands Timothy not to rebuke-violently an elderly-man but rather to "exhort" (παρακάλει) him as a father. The parallel arrangement of "exhort" in the fifth microchiasm, therefore, would be heard not only to advance Timothy's authority but also the way in which Timothy must apply his leadership role in Ephesus, namely with the twofold nuance of authority *and* respect—a combination that must be tempered by wisdom. Thus as the fifth microchiasm concludes, the audience hear a final emphasis of authority—"exhort"—which is purposed for their salvation—"teach." Indeed, the climactic tone of the microchiasm is not one of passive suggestion but of saving significance: Paul, as an apostle of Christ Jesus according to the command of God (1:1), is commissioning Timothy, his genuine child "in faith" (1:2), to enforce among all members of God's household that which accords with the gospel—the sound teaching that leads to mercy and salvation from God's just judgment upon sin (1:8–16; 2:7). At the same time, Paul intends his child Timothy to be winsome and respectful in his leadership as the household's authoritative teacher.

In sum of the fifth microchiasm, Timothy's leadership in God's household at Ephesus involves complex dynamics. While maintaining his respectful authority among family members of God's household (5:1–2) in the A element, Timothy in the parallel A' element must ensure their protection from false-teaching elders (5:20–22) and ensure their compliance

---

246. Such would be apparent from the fifth microchiasm itself: see the B and B' elements regarding younger widows who have turned-aside after Satan; see the A' element regarding false-teaching elders whose sins will be judged; see the A' element regarding the Christian slaves whose actions might blaspheme God's name.

with the the sound teaching of the apostle Paul (5:17–19, 6:1–2). Unlike an elderly-man whom Timothy must exhort as a father (5:1) in the A element, there are false-teaching elders—overseers—in God's household who must be publically reproved (5:20, 24) in the A' element. Furthermore, the proper familial relationships in God's household in the A element (5:1–2) are misapplied and need correction in the parallel A' element (6:2). Inside the framework of the A and A' elements, Timothy in the B element must ensure that godly, elderly widows receive care from the church (5:3, 5, 9) while he simultaneously strives to restore ungodly, younger widows to faith (5:11–16) in the parallel B' element. As a correction to systematic cyclical ungodliness, ungodly children or those-from-parents in the B element must learn to provide for the widows in their own families (5:4, 8) in the same way that ungodly younger widows in the parallel B' element must assist the elderly widows in their own families; failure to do either in the B and B' elements disables God's household from being able to provide for its own family members. Inside the B and B' elements, godly works (10a, c) in the C and C' elements facilitate the pivotal focus of the microchiasm: tangible care for God's household in the D element borne out of humility (5:10:b). Undoubtedly, to care for God's church and to account for differences with regard to age, gender, marriage, and socio-economic status, Timothy must apply Paul's apostolic teaching with interpersonal wisdom in view of the church's missional calling. In short, Timothy is to preserve the teaching and promote godliness so that the name of God and the teaching that displays his radiance—the gospel—would not be-blasphemed but rather honored and upheld among all humans. As the fifth microchiasm carries forward the overall macrochiasm toward its climactic conclusion in the sixth and final microchiasm, the audience are postured to positively align themselves with Timothy's teaching and exhorting in Ephesus.

3

1 Timothy 6:3–21: The Teaching that is According to Godliness Is Great Gain for Eternal Life

(A' Unit)

THIS CHAPTER EXAMINES THE A' unit of the macrochiasm—the sixth and final microchiasm within the 1 Timothy letter.[1] Within the sixth microchiasm (6:3–21), there are three minichiasms (6:6–8; 6:9–11; 6:12–14).

The Sixth Microchiasm

The 6:3–21 microchiasm is composed carefully of seven elements (A-B-C-D-C'-B'-A'); linguistic parallels identifying chiastic arrangements are indicated by the Greek text:

> A. ³ If someone (τις) teaches-different and does not come-toward the sound words of our Lord Jesus Christ and to the teaching that is according to godliness, ⁴ he is puffed-up, grasping nothing; rather having-an-unhealthy-craving regarding (περί) controversies and word-fights, from which become envy, rivalry, blasphemy, wicked suspicions, ⁵ friction of humans who are depraved in the mind and who are deprived of the truth, supposing godliness to be a means-of-gain. ⁶ But godliness with (μετά) contentment is great gain; ⁷ for we brought-in nothing into the world, that to bring-out

---

1. For the establishment of 1 Timothy as a macrochiasm, clarifications of terminology, and an explanation of my translation methodology, see volume 1, chapter 2.

some-thing we do-not have-the-power; ⁸ but holding food and clothing, these we will be-content with.

B. ⁹ But those wanting to be-rich (πλουτεῖν) fall into temptation and snare and many senseless and harmful longings, which plunge humans into ruin and destruction. ¹⁰ For the root of all evils is the affection-of-money, which some—aspiring—have wandered from the faith and have pierced themselves with many pains. ¹¹ But you, O (ὦ) human of God, flee these; but pursue justice, godliness, faith, love, steadfastness, gentleness. ¹² Agonize the commendable agony of the faith, take-possession (ἐπιλαβοῦ) of the eternal life (ζωῆς) to which you were called and to which you confessed the commendable confession in the sight of many testifiers. ¹³ I charge (παραγγέλλω), in the sight of God who provides-life to all-things and of Christ Jesus who testified before Pontius Pilate the commendable confession, ¹⁴ you to keep the commandment spotless, irreproachable until the manifesting of our Lord Jesus Christ,

    C. ¹⁵ª which in his own times the blessed and only (μόνος) Power will display,

        D. ¹⁵ᵇ the King of those who-are-kings and Lord of those who-are-lords,

    C'. ¹⁶ who only (μόνος) holding without-death, housing-in without-approachable light, which no human has seen nor has power to see; to him honor and eternal strength, amen.

B'. ¹⁷ As for the rich (πλουσίοις) in this present age, charge (παράγγελλε) them not to be-haughty, nor to hope upon the without-certainty of riches (πλούτου), rather upon God, the one who brings-about to us all-things richly (πλουσίως) for enjoyment; ¹⁸ to do-good-work, to be-rich (πλουτεῖν) in commendable works, to be generous, liberal, ¹⁹ storing-up for themselves a commendable basis for the inevitable-coming, that they might take-possession (ἐπιλάβωνται) of that which is truly life (ζωῆς). ²⁰ O (ʼΩ) Timothy, the entrustment guard, turning-aside from the vile empty-talk and contradictions of false-named knowledge,

A'.²¹ which some (τινες)—professing—regarding (περί) the faith have swerved. Grace with (μεθ') you-all.

1 Timothy 6:3–8: Different, Depraved, Deprived, and Discontent False Teachers

(A Element)

The A element (6:3–8) of the sixth and final microchiasm (6:3–21) begins with a condition: "If someone teaches-different and does not come-toward the sound words of our Lord Jesus Christ and to the teaching that is according to godliness" (6:3). The phrase "If someone teaches-different" is significant, unifying both the fifth and sixth microchiasms as well as the overall arrangement of the 1 Timothy macrochiasm. The seamless movement of Timothy's authority from the A' element of the fifth microchiasm to "teach . . . exhort" (δίδασκε . . . παρακάλει, 6:2b) would be heard—via transitional words—to carry forward over and against "someone" who "teaches-different" (ἑτεροδιδασκαλεῖ, 6:3) in the A element of the sixth microchiasm.² Immediately in the sixth microchiasm, then, the audience understand that Paul is concerned with, emphasizing, and underscoring that there is a stark dichotomy in regard to what is being taught in Ephesus; as heard throughout the letter, here in 6:3 it is Paul's entrusted representative Timothy versus the false teachers.³ In regard to the arrangement of the macrochiasm, the phrase "If someone teaches-different" (εἴ τις ἑτεροδιδασκαλεῖ) here in 6:3 of the A' unit—the sixth microchiasm—recalls for the audience Paul's initial and main exhortation for Timothy to charge "some not to teach-different (τισὶν μὴ ἑτεροδιδασκαλεῖν) in 1:3 of the parallel A unit—the first microchiasm.⁴ Significantly, the very same issue presented in the beginning of the letter is explicitly reiterated to Timothy and the audience at the end. By rhetoric

---

2. Both verbs (see *italics*) δίδασκε and παρακάλει are heard within the verb ἑτεροδιδασκαλεῖ in the A' unit. Van Neste, "Cohesion and Structure in the PE," 100: "Timothy is to teach (διδάσκω) these things, but there are others who 'teach otherwise' (ἑτεροδιδασκαλέω). By summing up the previous material in terms of teaching (esp. with the use of διδάσκω), a transition is created for addressing those who do not teach these things." Regarding the function of *transitional words*, see volume 1, chapter 2.

3. Marshall, *PE*, 638: "The use of ἑτεροδιδασκαλέω (1.3) is a deliberate contrast with δίδασκε in the previous verse." Knight, *PE*, 249: "It indicates that they 'teach a (completely) different doctrine,' i.e., one different from the apostolic teaching and therefore to be regarded as false (as the context here and in 1:3ff. evidence)." See Barcley, *1 & 2 Tim*, 184.

4. See Bassler, *1 & 2 Tim*, 108.

alone, Paul insists that the false teachers in Ephesus—likely unqualified overseers from among themselves—are a first and last concern.[5]

Furthermore, the audience understand that the conditional formula "If (εἴ) someone teaches-different" (6:3) is not intended to suggest a hypothetical situation or possibility but rather a real and present danger that the apostle has already directly and indirectly addressed throughout the letter.[6] To be sure, the *fact* that Timothy must remain in Ephesus so that he might "charge some not to teach-different" in 1:3 of the A unit parallels the *fact* that "someone teaches-diffferent" in 6:3 of the A' unit. In this way, Paul's consistent cognate pairing of the terms "if" and "some" throughout the macrochiasm would convey a deliberate rhetorical formula that underscores the present situation in Ephesus: "if (εἴ) some-thing (τι) different lies-opposed to the sound teaching (1:10); "if (εἰ) someone (τις) aspires to overseer (3:1); "if (εἰ) someone (τις) does not know how to lead his own household" (3:5); "if (εἰ) some (τις) widow has children or those-from-parents" (5:4); "if (εἰ) someone (τις) does not provide-for those of his own and especially for household-members (5:8); "If (εἴ) some (τις) faithful-woman has widows (5:15); and now "if (εἴ) someone (τις) teaches-different and does come-toward the sound words of our Lord Jesus Christ" (6:3). The consistent combination of the terms "if" and "some" would be understood as highly polemical, the sense being, "*Some* should be not doing this at all!"[7] To be sure, it is because of the present circumstance regarding "some" and their influence within the Ephesian church that Timothy must remain in Ephesus, that he might carry out Paul's charge to preserve the teaching and promote godliness as God's missional household.

The indefinite pronoun "someone" (τις) recalls its use throughout the macrochiasm as an explicit or implicit polemical reference to the false teachers (1:3, 6, 19; 3:1, 5; 4:1; 5:24) and anyone in the church whom they have influenced (5:15, 16; cf. 5:4, 8).[8] Notably, then, Paul's use of "someone"

---

5. That the false teachers in Ephesus are unqualified men in the office of overseer, that is, teaching elders, see volume 1, chapter 1 regarding Acts 20:28–30 and volume 2, chapter 2 regarding 1 Timothy 3:1–7; see also chapter 2 regarding 1 Timothy 5:17, 20.

6. Knight, *PE*, 249: "With the conditional clause, 'if anyone . . . ,' Paul asserts what he regards to be true and thus means '*since* someone . . . does not so assent)." Marshall, *PE*, 638: "εἴ τις introduces a factual premise." Wieland, *Significance of Salvation*, 19: "The letter can be very largely understood as a response to a perceived threat . . . Some—apparently within the church—are teaching something which the author regards as dangerous."

7. To highlight a rhetorical contrast between true widows and younger widows (5:3–16), in 5:10b Paul's use of the term "if" (εἰ) was notably absent from any pairing with the relative pronoun "some"; see chapter 2 regarding 1 Timothy 5:10b.

8. See Gloer, *1 & 2 Tim*, 195. Contra Wall with Steele, *1 & 2 Tim*, 140: "The

(τις) in 6:3 of the A' unit not only corroborates that Paul has in view the false-teaching "some" (τισίν) from 1:3 of the parallel A unit but also encompasses the sustained polemical movement from the beginning to the end of the macrochiasm. Thus where the A and A' units provide the rhetorical framework for the entire letter, the audience are to understand the forward movement of "some" through the B-C-C'-B' units in light of the respective A and A' units.[9] In this way, the cumulative impact of the macrochiasm would be drawn out here in 6:3 with full effect: "some" teach-different in the A unit (1:3) and likely have influenced the women in Ephesus to reject God's creational design in the B unit, namely to teach and govern men in the church (2:12–13); "some" aspire to the commendable office of overseer in the C unit (3:1)—indeed, are in the office of overseer in the B' unit (5:20, 24; cf. 5:17)—without the ability to care for God's church (3:5); "some" apostasy from the faith in the C' unit by holding-toward teachings of demons, that is, by rejecting God's commendable creation rather than receiving God's creation with thanksgiving (4:1, 3); and in the B' unit "some" children, those-from-parents, and younger widows (5:8, 15, 16; cf. 5:4) exhibit the same ungodly behavior as "some" false teachers who sin (5:24; cf. 5:20). Undoubtedly, the cascading presence and impact of "some" throughout the A-B-C-C'-B' units would have a climactic connotation upon "someone" here in 6:3 of the concluding A' unit. In effect, as the letter is being performed in front of the entire church in Ephesian—both false teachers and the faithful among the Ephesian audience—Paul is publically reproving such false-teaching overseers in the sight of all (cf. 5:20), that is, summoning them for repentence (cf. 1:20) and subsequent allegiance to his apostolic authority, namely the authority of Christ Jesus himself (1:1).

As the audience experience the performance of the letter and thus observe Paul's speech being performed in front of them, there can be no mistake about the two available options that he presents. On the one hand, Paul is an "apostle of Christ Jesus according to the command of God our Savior" (1:1), and Timothy is his "genuine child in faith" (1:2) whom he has entrusted to the charge against the false teachers in Ephesus (1:18; cf. 1:3). Both men are faithful servants of Christ Jesus (1:12; 4:6). On the other hand,

---

caricature of 'someone who teaches differently' is illustrative and need not have specific opponents in mind." Cf. Knight, *PE*, 249: "The statement made about them [false teachers] is presented as a general principle (εἴ τις). Thus the rendering 'anyone' for τις is appropriate, but, as in 1:3–11, specific false teachers are undoubtedly in mind with this generic singular."

9. Although there is no occurrence of the indefinite pronoun τις in the B unit of the macrochiasm (2:1–15), its sustained movement throughout the macrochiasm is not affected.

as an antithesis is "someone" who teaches-different (1:3; 6:3): "some" who teach some-thing different that lies-opposed to the sound teaching (1:10b), that is, opposed to the gospel that exhibits God's radiance, with which Paul was considered-faithful (1:11). Presented with this contrast, the audience are reminded that any submission to or even tolerance of false teaching represents a public assertion to the divine courtroom itself (5:21) as both a rejection of Paul and Timothy's role as authoritative teachers in God's household and an allegiance to "some" who set themselves up against Paul through their false teachings, that is, the teachings of demons (4:1). Beyond any doubt, the apostle Paul indicates that there is no neutral ground.

Continuing the opening statement of the sixth microchiasm, the audience hear: "and does not come-toward" (6:3). The conjunction "and" (καί) clearly connects the verb "does not come-toward" (μὴ προσέρχεται) with the preceding clause "If someone teaches-different." Here, the sense of the verb "come-toward" (προσέρχεται) conveys a movement of the heart toward an object, be it a person or anything else—the sense being to "agree with."[10] In effect, therefore, Paul intends the audience to understand that the defining feature of a false teacher is that "someone . . . does not agree." Significantly also, whereas Christ Jesus "came" (ἦλθεν) into the world to save sinners" (1:15) and where the Savior God desires all humans to be-saved, that is, "to come" (ἐλθεῖν) to a knowing-embrace of truth (2:4), it is unmistakably evident that "someone" who does *not* "come-toward" (προσέρχεται) the sound words of Jesus Christ in 6:3 is definitively navigating away from Christ Jesus (1:15) and from God (2:4). Simultaneously, Paul is underscoring the sustained missional impetus of the letter: although the false teachers do not "come-toward" the sound words of the Lord Jesus Christ (6:3), the Savior God still desires for them "to come" and be-saved (2:4), a fact demonstrated by Christ Jesus who "came" into the world to save them (1:15).[11]

Conceptually also, such motion by the false teachers away from Christ Jesus and God echoes Paul's statements in the parallel A unit wherein "some" have actively "turned-aside" from love—from a pure heart, a good conscience, and a without-hypocrisy faith (1:5–6). Moreover, in 1:19 of the

---

10. Knight, *PE*, 250: "προσέρχομαι . . . means generally 'come or go to' and is used here in the special sense of 'agree with, accede to.'" The textual variant προσέχεται, which occurs regularly in the letter (1:4; 3:8; 4:1, 13), supports this interpretation. The sense of the verb is "giving oneself to"; it can also be used to describe "addiction." See Marshall's discussion (*PE*, 638).

11. It is also worth noting that in the same way that Paul intends "to come" (ἐλθεῖν) to Ephesus (3:14) and thus instructs Timothy to lead the Ephesian church until "I come" (ἔρχομαι, 4:13), Paul's movement is missional in nature, that is, toward a situation wherein "some" are not saved and where "some" are influencing others to move away from salvation.

A unit, the net effect of such movement for "some" was that by intentionally "rejecting"—the sense being "casting-aside" or "driving-away"—faith and a good conscience, they have become-shipwrecked regarding the faith.[12]

Thus as in the parallel A unit, the point being highlighted here in the A' unit by Paul is that the problem of the false teachers is not merely—or mainly—ignorance but rather insubordination—"a failure of the heart that involves willful rejection of God's pattern."[13] To be sure, whereas Paul "without-knowing did in unfaithfulness" (1:13), "some" have deliberately moved away from that which they once knew; this fact frames the entire letter in the A unit (1:6, 19) and the A' unit (6:3)—its rhetorical purpose thus conveying a first and last concern. In short, "If someone teaches-different," then they are moving in the opposite direction of truth—they do "not come-toward" the sound words of Jesus Christ (6:3)—and, therefore, cannot be received as reliable guides in God's household. Moreover, combined with the negative particle "not" (μή), which has been associated with the activities of the false teachers in the parallel A unit (1:3, 4, 7, 20), the phrase "does not come-toward" emphasizes precisely what "someone" is doing when they teach-different, namely not agreeing with what is true teaching. Such would certainly be a conceptual echo of Paul's statement in the parallel A unit regarding "some-thing different" that lies-opposed to the sound teaching (1:10b). In effect, then, the audience understand that the hallmark activity of "someone" who "teaches-different" is that they do not agree with the apostle Paul.

Further still, Paul goes on to articulate the full extent of what "someone" who teaches-different does not agree with: "the sound words of our Lord Jesus Christ" (6:3). The participle "sound (ὑγιαίνουσιν)" in 6:3 of the A' unit recalls its only other occurrence in the macrochiasm, which is arranged in 1:10b of the parallel A unit regarding "the sound (ὑγιαινούσῃ) teaching" of Paul. The twofold rhetorical implication would be apparent. On the one hand, the integrated polemical contrast within the A unit itself is strongly underscored here in the A' unit: in the same way that "some . . . teach-different" (1:3), that is, "some-thing different" that lies-opposed to "the sound (ὑγιαινούσῃ) teaching" in 1:10, so also "someone teaches-different" and does not come-toward "the sound (ὑγιαίνουσιν) words" in 6:3.[14] In

---

12. For the implications of "rejecting" (ἀπωσάμενοι) as "cast-aside" or "driven-away," see volume 1, chapter 3 regarding 1 Timothy 1:19.

13. Towner, *Letters*, 393.

14. The parallelism within the A unit—the first microchiasm—is itself striking:
A element: "τισὶν . . . ἑτεροδιδασκαλεῖν" (1:3);
A' element: "τι ἕτερον . . . διδασκαλίᾳ" (1:10b).
Such would enhance the force of Paul's statement in the parallel A' unit of the

short, the effect of not agreeing with "the sound words" is the same as teaching some-thing opposed to "the sound teaching": unhealthy, infectious, and damaging to the well-being of God's household.[15] On the other hand, therefore, "the sound words" of Jesus Christ (6:3) are to be understood in tandem with "the sound teaching" (1:10). Thus Paul's statements within the arrangement of the macrochiasm are even more fully integrated: to teach "some-thing different" that lies-opposed to "the sound teaching" indicates that "someone" does not agree with "the sound words" of Jesus Christ. The effect is devastating for anyone who rejects Paul. Paul is "an apostle of Christ Jesus" (1:1) and was directly appointed for service by "Christ Jesus our Lord" (1:12); as Christ Jesus's very own personally chosen and authorized representative, Jesus and Paul are inseparable.[16] Emphatically, the audience understand that to reject any or all of "the sound teaching" with which Paul was counted-faithful (1:10–11) is to not agree with "the sounds words" of Jesus Christ (6:3); to refuse one is simultaneously and unavoidably to refuse the other.[17]

---

macrochiasm.

15. See volume 1, chapter 3 regarding 1 Timothy 1:10. Cf. Knight, *PE*, 250: "'sound' in the sense of 'correct,' i.e., true in contrast with that which is incorrect or false."

16. For the significance of the term "apostle," see volume 1, chapter 3 regarding 1 Timothy 1:1. Knight, *PE*, 250: "False teachers are not assenting to the words that have come from the source of authority, 'our Lord Jesus Christ.'"

17. Here, it may be worth noting the striking implications that are relevant for the modern-day debate regarding a woman's role to teach and to govern in the church (2:12). In the 1 Timothy letter, there is undoubtedly an association between the false teachers and women, namely the former's influence upon the latter. Yet, while it seems apparent to me that the 1 Timothy text itself clearly testifies that false-teaching overseers—to be sure, male elders in line with the tradition of OT male elders (see discussion regarding 4:14; 5:17; see also volume 1, chapter 1 regarding Paul's prediction in Acts 20:30)—were influencing the women in Ephesus (rather than a situation wherein the false teachers were themselves female overseers), Payne presents a strong case that the women in the first-century Ephesian church were the false teachers (*Man and Woman*, 299–304). Ibid., 304, concludes: "First Timothy's many statements regarding problems caused by women depict a situation where women had become central to the false teaching that was dividing the church."

Payne's conclusion—indeed, all other scholarship suggesting that women were the false teachers in Ephesus—would have profound significance regarding the current debate about women's roles in the church. Particularly, where the false-teaching overseers are women in 1 Timothy, the full implication is that they are the total embodiment of what it means to teach some-thing different than Paul and Jesus Christ (1:3, 10b; 6:3), namely because Paul—and thus Jesus Christ, the one whom Paul authoritatively represents (1:1, 12; 2:7)—clearly states that women are not permitted to teach nor to govern men in the church (2:12). In other words, the insistence that women were the false teachers in no way supports the idea that a woman who teaches and governs as a church overseer is in agreement with the words and teaching of Jesus Christ; much

Regarding the term "words" (λόγοις) here in 6:3, its occurrences throughout the progression of the macrochiasm have prepared the audience for the climactic fact that "the sound teaching" of Paul is "the sound words" of Jesus Christ.[18] Particularly, "the ... words" (λόγοις τοῖς) of Jesus Christ in 6:3 recall "the words" (τοῖς λόγοις) of the faith in which Timothy is being-nourished in 4:6 of the fourth microchiasm. Notably, then, where "the words (τοῖς λόγοις) of the faith" was heard to be synonymous with "the (τῆς) commendable teaching (διδασκαλίας)" in 4:6, the connection between "the sound words" (ὑγιαίνουσιν λόγοις τοῖς, 6:3) of Jesus Christ and "the sound teaching" (τῇ ὑγιαινούσῃ διδασκαλίᾳ, 1:10) of his apostle Paul is unmistakeable.[19] Such would be further corroborated by Paul's statement in 5:17 regarding the teaching elders's toil, where the two terms "word" (λόγῳ) and "teaching" (διδασκαλίᾳ) were understood as synonyms.[20] Moreover, where Jesus Christ is the source of "the sound words (λόγοις)" here in the climactic A' unit of the macrochiasm, its other cognate occurrences throughout the letter are understood with their full impact. It is precisely because "the sound words (λόγοις)" are of Jesus Christ (6:3)

---

rather, the insistence thereof undermines itself. See discussion in volume 1, chapter 4 regarding 1 Timothy 2:12–14.

Fee notes that the "very case-specific instruction Paul gives in 1 Timothy 2:11–12 ... is clearly the 'odd text out,' not the norm. In the context of 1 Timothy, the issue is not church order but false teaching" (*Listening to the Spirit in the Text*, 74). However, where the teaching of Christ Jesus's apostle Paul and of Jesus Christ himself are inseparably connected (1:1, 10, 12; 2:7; 6:3), it is apparent that the two—church order and false teaching—are inseparably connected: rejecting Paul's teaching about church order in 2:11–12 is equally to not agree with Jesus Christ (6:3).

18. See Knight, *PE*, 250. Contra Spencer, *1 Tim*, 144 n. 3: "The phrase in 6:3 can be subjective genitive (*words from our Lord Jesus Christ*) or objective genitive (*words about our Lord Jesus Christ*). Probably the latter fits this context better since it modifies *healthy words* which is parallel to *godly teaching* (6:3)." Cf. Wall, "1 Tim," 658: "Paul's reference to the 'healthy words' of Jesus implies that the congregation already was following a collection of the Lord's sayings—i.e., words spoken by Jesus committed to memory and transmitted orally from congregation to congregation." Ngewa's comments are helpful: "Academics argue about whether this means instruction 'about' Christ or instruction 'coming from' Christ, as the one who originally gave it. Yet these two options overlap, for the content of the gospel is the person and work of Christ, who is also its ultimate source" (*1 & 2 Tim*, 148–49). See discussion in Mihoc, "Final Admonition to Timothy," 140–41.

19. In passing, the phrase "the sound teaching" occurs more regularly in the PE than does "the sound words"; for the former, see 1 Tim 1:10; 2 Tim 4:3; Titus 1:9; 2:1; for the latter, see 2 Tim 1:13; Titus 2:8. Similarly, Towner observes that "the independent use of διδασκαλία for Christian instruction is far more frequent than the plural λόγοις" (*Letters*, 394 n. 6).

20. Notably, the conjuction "and" (καί) functioned epexegetically in 4:6 and 5:17 as a specifying term.

that Paul says, "faithful is the word (λόγος) and worthy of all acceptance" (1:15; 4:9); indeed, the "words" (λόγοις) of Jesus Christ (6:3) are the means by which people "would-inevitably-come to have-faith upon him for life eternal" (1:16); moreover, the "words" (λόγος) of Jesus Christ (6:3) is the very "word" (λόγου) of God (4:5) through which the faithful receive God's commendable creation with thanksgiving (4:3–4). The "words" (λόγοις) of Jesus Christ (6:3) are the source of the "word" (λόγῳ) in which Timothy is to be an example (4:12). Furthermore, where "the sounds words (λόγοις)" of the Lord Jesus Christ (6:3) are the very words that his apostle Paul is "saying" (λέγω) as a divinely appointed proclaimer, apostle, and teacher (2:7) and are the very words that the Spirit "says" (λέγει, 4:1) and the writing "says" (λέγει, 5:18), there is a dire importance for the Ephesian audience to agree with everything that the Lord Jesus Christ's apostle Paul has said in the letter. By not agreeing with "the sounds words (λόγοις)" of Jesus Christ in the A' unit, it seems clear why "some" in the parallel A unit instead hold-toward "genealogies" (γενεαλογίαις, 1:4), have turned-aside for "useless-words" (ματαιολογίαν, 1:6), and are not understanding what "they-are-saying" (λέγουσιν, 1:7); such would explain why the false teachers are "false-worders" (ψευδολόγων, 4:2) in the C' unit.[21]

The phrase "of our Lord Jesus Christ" is significant. Similar to the unique occurrence of "sound" in the A and A' units, the full combination of the terms "Lord," "our," "Jesus," and "Christ" has only been heard by the audience in their parallel arrangement within the macrochiasm. That is, "of our Lord Jesus Christ" (τοῦ κυρίου ἡμῶν Ἰησοῦ Χριστοῦ) here in 6:3 of the A' unit uniquely recalls "Christ Jesus our Lord" (Χριστοῦ Ἰησοῦ κυρίου ἡμῶν) in 1:2 and "Christ Jesus our Lord" (Χριστῷ Ἰησοῦ τῷ κυρίῳ ἡμῶν) in 1:12 of the parallel A unit.[22] Several observations are worth noting. First, Paul clearly intends the audience to understand that the entire letter is framed from beginning to end by the fact that Jesus Christ is "Lord." As in the A unit, the implications of the term "Lord" (κυρίου) here in the A' unit would be evident; Paul wants the entire audience to bear in mind that as "Lord," Jesus Christ is the very God of the OT.[23] Allegiance to Jesus Christ

21. The aural occurrence (see *italics*) of "words" (λόγοις) within each term would be apparent: "genealogies" (γενεαλογίαις, 1:4), "useless-words" (ματαιολογίαν, 1:6), "saying" (λέγουσιν, 1:7), "false-worders" (ψευδολόγων, 4:2).

22. See also 1:14: "our Lord . . . Christ Jesus." It is worth noting that both occurrences of "Christ Jesus our Lord" in 1:2 and 1:12 (as well as 1:14) are themselves in a parallel arrangement within the respective A and A' elements of the first microchiasm; see volume 1, chapter 3. Such would indicate Paul's deliberate use of the phrase on both a microchiastic and macrochiastic level to intentionally arrange the 1 Timothy letter.

23. The LXX Greek translation of the Hebrew OT divine name for God is "Lord" (κύριος); see volume 1, chapter 3. It may be worth noting that where "the name of God"

as "Lord," then, is not to be disregarded. Indeed, given the clear concern of the letter, Paul is again summoning his audience to ensure that they have aligned themselves with the "Lord Jesus Christ" over and against "someone" who "teaches-different and does not come-toward the sound words of our Lord Jesus Christ" (6:3). In no clearer terms, Paul is pitting allegiance to the false teachers against allegiance to Jesus Christ—there is no neutrality. The pronoun "our" (ἡμῶν) further underscores the allegiance in view. That Jesus Christ is "our" (ἡμῶν) Lord in the A' unit (6:3) and "our" (ἡμῶν) Lord in the parallel A unit (1:2, 12) would not only highlight the bond between Paul and the faithful among the audience but also, therefore, would draw attention to "some" who do not share the same bond. In effect, for "some" who do not have-faith upon Christ Jesus as their Lord (1:2, 12, 16), Paul's statement is missional, the sense being, "If you haven't joined us yet, then do!"

Paul's summons for the audience to align themselves with the "Lord" would be emphasized through the sudden and deliberate rhetorical designation of "Christ Jesus" *now* as "Jesus Christ." To be sure, the switch would be very noticeable for the audience. Throughout the 1 Timothy letter, Paul has consistently used the phrase "Christ Jesus" (1:1, 2, 12, 14, 15, 16; 2:5; 3:13; 4:6; 5:21) rather than "Jesus Christ" (6:3). While the word order of "Christ Jesus" may function to describe *Christ* with regard Jesus's saving activity, it seems possible that the word order of "Jesus Christ" may function to describe *Jesus* according to his kingly status as the "'Anointed One' or 'Messiah.'"[24] Indeed, that Jesus's kingly authority is in view would be corroborated by the corresponding change in word order for the placement of "Lord" *prior* to "Jesus Christ" (τοῦ κυρίου . . . Ἰησοῦ Χριστοῦ, 6:3) in distinction from Paul's placement of "Lord" *after* "Christ Jesus" (Χριστοῦ Ἰησοῦ τοῦ κυρίου, 1:2; Χριστῷ Ἰησοῦ τῷ κυρίῳ, 1:12). In short, by the rhetorical switch here in 6:3, the audience would understand that Paul is going out of his way to uphold Jesus Christ's status as their "Lord." To be sure, along with Paul and Timothy (1:2), to be able to say that Jesus Christ is "*our* Lord" (6:3) would require the audience's allegiance to him—and thus his apostle (1:1) *and* the apostle's entrusted representative Timothy (1:18).

Still, rather than a power-hungry summons for submission to a domineering tyrant who wants to be known as "Lord," the cumulative story of

---

(6:1b) references the LXX Decalogue, Paul may have in view the "Lord" Jesus Christ; the full phrase of the LXX Decalogue is "the name of the Lord (κυρίου) your God" (LXX Exod 20:7; Deut 5:11). Where a connection is intended between "the name of God" (6:1) and "our Lord Jesus Christ" (6:3), Paul would be identifying "Jesus Christ" as "the name of God."

24. Belleville, "Christology, the PE," 322. See discussion in volume 1, chapter 3 regarding 1 Timothy 1:1.

the macrochiasm would make clear beyond any doubt what kind of "Lord" Jesus Christ is. Most clearly unlike a tyrant, Paul has taken pains to underscore Jesus's divine, missional, sacrificial love: Jesus Christ is their hope (1:1), the one from whom they have received grace, peace, and mercy (1:2), in whom is the reservoir of grace, faith, and love (1:14); he is the one who came into the world to save sinners (1:15) and gave himself as a ransom on behalf of all (2:5–6); Jesus is the one who is merciful and all patient to those who oppose him (1:13, 16), the one whom Timothy serves (4:6), the one who considered Paul to be faithful and appointed him for service—though Paul was firstly in unfaithfulness (1:12–13). To this sort of "Lord" who surrendered his life to save Paul, Timothy, the audience, and all humans, it would only seem reasonable and appropriate to surrender one's self to him. Thus for "someone" who "does not come-toward the sounds words of our Lord Jesus Christ" (6:3), Paul is challenging them to consider why not.

With such beyond-abounding love that is in Christ Jesus (1:14), it is clear that "some" who are swerving-from and have turned-aside from love (1:5–6) have personally rejected Jesus. To be sure, rather than coming-toward "the sound words" (ὑγιαίνουσιν λόγοις τοῖς) of the Lord Jesus Christ (6:3), that is, the faithful "word" (λόγος) that is worthy of all acceptance (1:15; 4:9), "some" have chosen instead to accept "useless-words" (ματαιολογίαν) (1:6). Here, a further point would not go unnoticed: though love is most certainly in Christ Jesus (1:14), and although the end of Paul's charge intends for the false teachers to be restored to love, that is, to be Paul's very own beloved brothers "in faith" (1:5; 6:2), the audience—and particularly "some"—must also bear in mind that having "turned-aside" (ἐξετράπησαν) from love (1:6) is connected with having "turned-aside" (ἐξετράπησαν) after Satan (5:15). Unsettling as it is, Paul's point is that no neutrality is possible *and* Jesus Christ himself will deliver impartial judgment to all in the final, heavenly court (5:21). In short, the choice of "someone" to not come-toward "the sound words" of the Lord Jesus Christ will result in an end of their own decision; it would be most beneficial, therefore, for "someone" to agree with "the sound teaching" of Paul (1:10). To summarize, the import of the phrase "the sound words of our Lord Jesus Christ" enables the audience to appreciate the weightiness of the attitudes and actions of the false teachers.

Paul's next phrase "and to the teaching that is according to godliness" is heard in direct connection to the previous phrase regarding "the sound words of the Lord Jesus Christ" (6:3). That is, "if someone teaches-different," then that person equally "does not come-toward" or agree with both "the sound words" *and* "the teaching." Given this connection, the conjuction "and" (καί) would likely be heard epexegetically, specifying that "the . . . words (λόγοις τοῖς) of our Lord Jesus Christ" is synonymous with "the teaching (τῇ . . . διδασκαλίᾳ) that is according to godliness." Indeed, such was already indicated by the synonymy between "the sound words" (ὑγιαίνουσιν λόγοις τοῖς) of Jesus Christ (6:3) and "the sound teaching" (τῇ ὑγιαινούᾳη σιδασκαλίᾳ) of Paul (1:10), between "the words (τοῖς λόγοις) of the faith" and "the teaching" (τῆς . . . διδασκαλίας) in 4:6, and between "word" (λόγῳ) and "teaching" (διδασκαλίᾳ) in 5:17.[25] Thus where "the sound words" are understood to be synonymous with "the teaching" in 6:3, the implications of the parallelism between "the sound teaching" of Paul in 1:10 of the A unit and "the sound words" of Jesus Christ in 6:3 of the parallel A' unit is corroborated for the audience. Indeed, "the sound teaching" of Paul (1:10b), that is, "the teaching" of the church (4:13, 16; 6:1; cf. 4:6), is none other than the exact "words" of Jesus Christ (6:3). Positively, then, whereas "someone" who teaches-different is identifiable as "someone" who "does not come-toward the sound words of our Lord Jesus Christ" (6:3), the Ephesian audience understand that a true teacher—a qualified teaching elder, an overseer—is one who *does come-toward* Jesus Christ's very own words and thus toward the sound teaching of Paul and the church (1:10; 6:3).[26]

Here, given the profound, cumulative, polemical emphasis toward the false teachers throughout the progression of the A-B-C-C'-B' units, the climactic effect in the A' unit would be felt among the entire Ephesisan audience. Undoubtedly, if "someone" does not come-toward "the teaching" in 6:3 of the A' unit, then they are rejecting "the sound teaching" (διδασκαλίᾳ) in 1:10b of the A unit; consequently, they do not view Paul as a divinely appointed "teacher" (διδάσκαλος, 2:7), and are likely influencing women "to teach" (διδάσκειν, 2:12) over and against God's creational design (2:13) in the B unit. As such, they are not "able-to-teach" (διδακτικόν, 3:2), that is, are not qualified to be an overseer in the C unit; indeed, in the C' unit they are holding-toward "teachings (διδασκαλίαις) of demons" (4:1), thus standing in direct contrast to Timothy who is being-nourished in "the commendable teaching (διδασκαλίας)" (4:6), who is commanded to "teach" (δίδασκε, 4:11), who is to hold-toward "the teaching" (διδασκαλίᾳ, 4:13), and who must strongly-hold "the teaching" (διδασκαλίᾳ, 4:16). In the B' unit, the false teachers are unlike elders who lead commendably in "teaching" (διδασκαλίᾳ, 5:17); as such, they enable and cause "the teaching" (διδασκαλία) to be-blasphemed (6:1b), and are, therefore, the reason why Timothy is commanded to "teach" (δίδασκε, 6:2b). Thus, cumulatively throughout the macrochasim, the false teachers are clearly those who are

---

25. The epexegetical function of "and" (καί) specified and related "the words . . . and (καί) the . . . teaching" (4:6) and "word and (καί) teaching" (5:17) as synonyms.

26. Belleville, "Christology, Greco-Roman," 227: "Orthodox teaching is that which agrees with 'the sound words of our Lord Jesus Christ' (1 Tim 6:3)."

unqualified to lead the church in teaching as overseers because they are directly opposed to the oversight that is imbedded within "the teaching." Indeed, the climactic contrast could not be any more clear than in 6:3 of A' unit: it is "the teaching" (τῇ διδασκαλίᾳ) of the Lord Jesus Christ versus "someone" who "teaches-different" (ἑτεροδιδασκαλεῖ). The emphatic distance placed between Paul and Timothy, on the one hand, and the false teachers, on the other hand, is a clear summons for the audience to consider wisely whom they will follow as leaders in God's household.

Paul further qualifies "the teaching" in view: "that is according to godliness" (6:3). It is possible that the audience hear Paul referring to a general connection, the sense being, "the teaching that corresponds to godliness." Yet, given the arrangement of the macrochiasm, the audience would also hear a further connotation. The phrase "the teaching (διδασκαλίᾳ) that is according to (κατ') godliness" here in 6:3 of the A' unit recalls "the sound teaching (διδασκαλίᾳ), according to (κατά) the gospel of the glory of the blessed God" in 1:10b–11a of the parallel A unit. In 1:10b of the A unit, the sense was that the "teaching" exhibits God's radiance and results in blessing to him.[27] The rhetorical placement of the same formula here in 6:3 of the parallel A' unit would convey the same, namely that the "teaching" exhibits, leads to, and results in "godliness."[28] What is clear from the letter, then, is that the two—"the teaching" (τῇ . . . διδασκαλίᾳ) and "godliness" (εὐσέβειαν)—are inseparably connected such that one cannot be present without the other.[29] Consequently, the audience understand that there is an inevitable litmus test.

On the one hand, agreeing with "the teaching" of Jesus Christ that results in "godliness" (6:3) will in fact show itself with all of the "godliness" that was heard throughout the macrochiasm: it will result in a peaceable disposition in all "godliness" (εὐσεβείᾳ, 2:2); for women who profess "godliness"

---

27. See discussion in volume 1, chapter 3 regarding 1 Timothy 1:10.

28. Knight, *PE*, 250: "The words describe the truth of Christianity seen as a whole. It is a life-changing message and thus it 'accords with godliness' . . . it is that which 'promot[es] ([is] designed for) godliness' (Robertson . . . this view is more likely than BAGD s.v. κατά II.7, which takes the phrase as adjectival)." Simpson, *PE*, 109: "True teaching is also according to godliness: it must promote a changed life which is pleasing to God."

29. The notably odd grammatical construction of the 6:3 sentence itself seems to highlight this fact. Literally, rather than "the teaching that is according to godliness," the Greek construction is "the according to godliness teaching" (τῇ κατ' εὐσέβειαν διδασκαλίᾳ).

Barcley, *1 & 2 Tim*, 184: "theology and ethics are closely tied to one another . . . Faithful adherence to godliness in doctrine leads to godliness in behaviour." Similarly, Paul correlates "truth and godliness" explicitly in Titus 1:1 (ἀληθείας τῆς κατ' εὐσέβειαν); see my discussions in *To Exhort and Reprove*, 22–26 and in *True Faith*, 8.

(θεοσέβειαν), that is, who profess to agree with "the teaching," it will be consistent-with good works (2:10); it will result in exclaiming the confessedly great truth regarding Jesus Christ who is the mystery of "godliness" (εὐσεβείας, 3:16); it will result in daily, intentional training for "godliness" (εὐσέβειαν, 4:7), that is, for the "godliness" (εὐσέβεια) that showcases the promise of life for the present and for the inevitable-coming (4:8), namely that the living God is their Savior (4:10). On the other hand, it will be evident if "someone" does not come-toward "the teaching": it will result in the absence of a peaceable disposition (2:2), of good works (2:10), of exclaiming Jesus Christ (3:16), and of intentional living here and now that has in view the promise of life for the inevitable-coming (4:7, 8). Indeed, where "the teaching" of Jesus Christ (6:3) is the same as "the sound teaching" of Paul (1:10b), the audience understand the integrated implication. That is, to not agree with Jesus Christ's teaching would be evident by a lifestyle that shows itself to be in any way contrary to Paul's teaching in the 1 Timothy letter: holding-toward myths and genealogies without-limit (1:4), being angry and word-quarreling (2:8); drawing attention to oneself with rich attire more than drawing attention to Jesus Christ (2:9); accepting the false teaching that a woman is permitted to teach and to govern a man in God's household (2:12–14);[30] a man being infidelitous to his wife (3:2, 12); a man not leading his own household (3:1, 4, 5, 12); forbidding marriage and foods (4:3); promoting ascetic bodily practices (4:8); not giving-return repayments to one's parents and widows (5:4, 8, 16); continuing in unrepentant sin and a lifestyle that upholds the influence of false teaching (5:20); and most directly, being "someone" who teaches some-thing that lies-opposed to "the teaching" of Jesus Christ and Paul (1:10b; 6:3).[31] In sum, for the faithful in the audience who claim to agree with "the teaching" of "our Lord Jesus Christ" (6:3), their lifestyle will positively reflect "godliness" by positively accepting "the sound teaching" of Paul (1:10b)—certainly all that Jesus Christ's personally chosen representative and messenger Paul has conveyed in the 1 Timothy letter. Simply, "godliness" shows that a person agrees with, that is, has "come-toward" Jesus Christ.

---

30. Understandably, this aspect of "the teaching" is a very difficult and sensitive topic. Most certainly it is *not* misogynistic. Please see full discussion in volume 1, chapter 4 regarding 1 Timothy 2:12–14.

31. Johnson, "First Timothy," 34: "In sum, the contrast between internal disposition in response to God and external norm as expression of human ambition carries through 1 Timothy, showing that, as in other Pauline compositions, the opening lines set the agenda for the whole." Barcley summarizes Paul's cumulative point: "False teaching fails to build up the church; in fact, quite the opposite, it rips it apart" (*1 & 2 Tim*, 184).

Still, the term "godliness" (εὐσέβειαν) would have further implications here in 6:3, recalling its significant occurrence at the central, pivotal verse of the entire macrochiasm in 3:16.[32] That is, where Paul defines Jesus Christ as "the mystery of godliness (εὐσεβείας)" at the pivot of the macrochiasm, not only does "godliness" (εὐσέβειαν) in 6:3 hinge upon Jesus Christ, but it also originates from his person.[33] Moreover, then, where "the teaching" in 6:3 was heard to be synonymous with "the sound words of our Lord Jesus Christ," it is not only evident that "godliness" originates from Jesus Christ but also that "the teaching" originates from his "words" (6:3). In short, the audience understand that both "the teaching" (τῇ ... διδασκαλίᾳ) and "godliness" (εὐσέβειαν) in 6:3 find their inseparable culmination in the person of Jesus Christ, the one whose teaching it is and whose godliness it exhibits. Thus where the apostle Paul indicates that there can be no dichotomy between "the teaching" and "godliness" (6:3), it is because both are rooted in the "Lord Jesus Christ" (6:3). If the audience intend to lead a life of godliness, they certainly must not align themselves with "someone" who does not come-toward the Lord Jesus Christ (6:3). Clearly, to pursue godliness, the audience must agree with Jesus Christ and, therefore, the apostle Paul and "the sound teaching" (1:10b), which originates in "the sound words" of Jesus Christ (6:3).

Having heard the entirety of verse 6:3 in full, Paul's intentional arrangement of the letter comes forward for the audience in strong rhetorical fashion. To be sure, the entirety of Paul's statement in 6:3 of the A' unit would be understood as a macrochiastic advancement of Paul's statement in 1:10b–11a of the parallel A unit:

> A unit: "if some-thing different (εἴ τι ἕτερον) lies-opposed to the sound teaching (τῇ ὑγιαινούσῃ διδασκαλίᾳ), according to (κατά) the gospel of the blessed God" (1:10b–11a);
>
> A' unit: "If someone teaches-different (εἴ τις ἑτεροδιδασκαλεῖ) and does not come-toward the sound (ὑγιαίνουσιν) words of our Lord Jesus Christ and to the teaching (τῇ ... διδασκαλίᾳ) that is according to (κατ') to godliness" (6:3).[34]

---

32. Verse 3:16 is the pivot of the entire macrochiasm, marking the transition from the C to C' unit. See volume 2, chapter 2 regarding 3:16.

33. The pronoun "he" (ὅς) was used in 3:16 rather than the name "Christ Jesus" or "Jesus Christ." That Jesus is unmistakeably in view, see volume 2, chapter 2 regarding 1 Timothy 3:16.

34. Wolfe, "Sagacious Use of Scripture," 214: 'A close look at 1:3, 10–11 reveals striking similarities with 6:3. The concern in both passages is with those who teach 'other doctrine' (the verb ἑτεροδιδασκαλέω is used in 1:3 and the noun ἑτεροδιδασκαλία

The deliberate rhetorical arrangement of the macrochiasm would be heard in parallel phrases and terms: "If someone teaches-different" (εἴ τις ἑτεροδιδασκαλεῖ) in 6:3 of the A unit recalls "if some-thing different . . . teaching" (εἴ τι ἕτερον . . . διδασκαλίᾳ) in 1:10b of the parallel A' unit;[35] "the sound (ὑγιαίνουσιν) words . . . the teaching (τῇ . . . διδασκαλίᾳ)" in the A' unit recalls "the sound teaching" (τῇ ὑγιαινούσῃ διδασκαλίᾳ) in the parallel A unit; and the teaching that is "according to" (κατ') godliness in 6:3 recalls the sound teaching "according to (κατά) the gospel of the glory of the blessed God" in 1:11a.[36] This full interaction between the A and A' units would draw out the overall structure, purpose, and goal of the letter. Heard in full, several significant observations are worth noting.

First, the polemical significance of the letter would be emphatically highlighted. The nearly identical parallel phrases "If someone teaches-different" in the A' unit and "if some-thing different . . . teaching" in the A unit would draw attention to that fact that the issue of the false teachers frames everything that Paul says in the letter.[37] Undoubedtly, from beginning to end, the letter was intended by Paul and understood by the audience to address the influence and impact of the false teachers upon "the teaching" and "godliness" (6:3), that is, upon the preservation of the teaching and promotion of godliness as God's missional household.[38] Second, in response to the false teachers, the corrective significance of the letter is equally highlighted. The unique parallel phrases "the sound words . . . the teaching" in the A' unit and "the sound teaching" in the A unit would simultaneously draw

---

in 6:3, the only NT occurrences of these terms, followed in each case by similar statements about 'sound teaching' in 1:10 and 6:3).''

35. That the term "teaches-different" (ἑτεροδιδασκαλεῖ) in 6:3 includes both the terms "different" (ἕτερον) and "teaching" (διδασκαλίᾳ) in 1:10b would be apparent. Also, the relationship between these terms would be corroborated by the arrangement within the A unit, wherein "teach-different" (1:3) was heard in a parallel relation to 1:10b. See above; see also volume 1, chapter 3 regarding 1 Timothy 1:10b.

36. The only other occurrence of "according to" in the 1 Timothy letter is within the A unit—"according to" (κατ') in 1:1 of the microchiasm's A element, which itself is parallel with "according to" (κατά) in 1:11 of the A' element. Given that Paul himself is in view in 1:1, the deliberate use of "according to" in 1:10b and 6:3 would enhance the force of Paul's own relation to the "teaching" (1:10b; 6:3).

37. See above analysis regarding the parallel relation of "if someone teaches-different" in 6:3 to "some not to teach-different" in 1:3. The further parallel relation here regarding 6:3 to "if some-thing different . . . teaching" in 1:10b would enhance the connectedness and impact.

38. Mappes articulates the point well: "[T]he word ["godliness" (εὐσέβεια)] points to a contrast between false teachers, false doctrine, and wrong conduct and true teachers, true doctrine, and right conduct. . . true teachers adhere to (and thus model) sound doctrine that conforms to godliness (εὐσέβεια)" ("Moral Virtues," 212–13).

attention to the unhealthy—damaging—influence and impact of the false teachers and, therefore, call upon the audience to agree with "the teaching" that can heal the damage while fostering health and "godliness" among the church in Ephesus. Third, the parallelism between 1:10b–11a and the latter half of 6:3 suggests synonymy:

> A unit: "the teaching (τῇ διδασκαλίᾳ), according to (κατά) the gospel of the glory of the blessed God" (1:10b–11a);
>
> A' unit: "the teaching (τῆ . . . διδασκαλίᾳ) that is according to (κατ') to godliness" (6:3).

Where the identical arrangements of Paul's statements in the A and A' units convey that "the teaching" (1:10b; 6:3) is interchangeably one and the same, the implication seems to be that "according to the gospel of the glory of the blessed God" (1:11a) is to be heard synonymously with "according to godliness" (6:3). In this case, the rhetorical implication is profound: God's radiance is exhibited by godliness. Still, given that "the sound teaching" corresponds with "the gospel," that is, exhibits God's radiance and results in blessing toward him (1:10b–11a), and given that "the teaching" results in "godliness" (6:3), the implication is that "godliness" (6:3) is the outworking of "the gospel"—both showcasing God's radiance and giving blessing toward him (1:11a). In short, the parallelism of the A and A' units demonstrates that "godliness" (6:3) and "the gospel" (1:11a) go hand in hand. Furthermore, given that Jesus Christ was identified as the sole source of "godliness" in 3:16 and thus of "godliness" in 6:3, the implication is that Jesus Christ is also the sole source of "the gospel" (1:11a).[39] Indeed, Jesus Christ is the person who displays God's radiant "glory" (δόξης) and enables blessing toward him (1:11a) precisely because he himself "was taken-up in glory (δόξῃ)" (3:16).

Here, the fundamental points that outline the macrochiasm thus emerge in an organized structure. A chiasm introduces a theme, pivots upon it, and then advances the theme toward a conclusion;[40] as such, the main linguistic and thematic points of the 1 Timothy letter are now heard:

> Introductory A unit: "if some-thing different (εἴ τι ἕτερον) lies-opposed to the (τῇ) sound (ὑγιαινούσῃ) teaching (διδασκαλίᾳ), according (κατά) to the gospel of the glory (δόξης) of the blessed God" (1:10b–11a);

---

39. Ngewa, *1 & 2 Tim*, 149: "the content of the gospel is the person and work Christ, who is also its ultimate source."

40. See discussion in volume 1, chapter 2.

> Pivot C unit: "the mystery of godliness (εὐσεβείας) . . . was taken-up in glory (δόξῃ) (3:16);
>
> Concluding A' unit: "If someone teaches-different (εἴ τις ἑτεροδιδασκαλεῖ) and does not come-toward the sound (ὑγιαίνουσιν) words . . . the teaching (τῇ . . . διδασκαλίᾳ) that is according to (κατ') godliness (εὐσέβειαν)" (6:3).

The polemical implication of the entire letter is clear: false teaching—teaching that is different, opposed, and does not agree with the sound teaching of Paul—does not exhibit God's radiance, nor result in blessing toward him, nor result in godliness because it is different, lies-opposed to, and does not agree with the sound words and the teaching of Jesus Christ, who himself exhibits God's radiance, enables blessing toward him, and is thus godliness itself. To be sure, anything that disagrees with Paul and Jesus Christ is not the gospel. Simultaneously, the positive implication of the letter is clear: the sound teaching of the apostle Paul exhibits God's radiance, results in blessing toward him, and leads to godliness because it is the sound words and the teaching of Jesus Christ. In short, that which agrees with Paul and Jesus Christ is the gospel.

To summarize 6:3, then, Paul strings back-to-back key terms and phrases that convey one, unified message to the audience: "sound" (ὑγιαίνουσιν), "words" (λόγοις), "the teaching" (τῇ . . . διδασκαλίᾳ), and "godliness" (εὐσέβειαν) are all integrated and derived from "our (ἡμῶν) Lord (κυρίου) Jesus Christ (Ἰησοῦ Χριστοῦ)." As each of these terms has progressed throughout the letter, the audience now understand that each term ultimately finds its basis, source, and origin here in the climactic A' unit of the macrochiasm in regard to the person of Jesus Christ. The synonymy between "the sound teaching" (1:10b) and "the sound words" (6:3) is significant, not only consolidating Paul and Jesus Christ's unified message into one interchangeable phrase but also indicating that "the sound teaching" of Paul and "the sound words" of Jesus Christ both equate to "the gospel." The parallelism between the A and A' units of the macrochiasm is cohesive: "the gospel" is that which showcases God's radiant glory and results in blessing toward him; "godliness" is the exhibition of God's radiant glory and gives blessing toward him. Jesus Christ's central significance to "the gospel" and "godliness" is highlighted as the overarching structure of the macrochiasm. Jesus Christ is the gospel and he is godliness: he is the one who definitively exhibits the glory of God and results in blessing toward him. It is for this reason that those who have come to have-faith upon Christ Jesus (1:16) and have "come-toward" his sound words and teaching (1:10b; 6:3) are themselves defined by godliness (2:2, 10; 4:7, 8) precisely because they are "in Christ Jesus" (1:14; 3:13)—indeed, they are and will be with Jesus Christ as he is "in glory" (3:16) and thus exhibit the glory of God here and now in the present as they will in the inevitable-coming (1:11; 4:8).

Paul goes on to complete the statement that began in 6:3: "he is puffed-up, grasping nothing; rather having-an-unhealthy-craving regarding controversies and word-fights" (6:4). Here, the audience understand that Paul is describing "someone" who teaches-different and does not come-toward the sound words of Jesus Christ in 6:3.[41] Paul states that the false teachers are "puffed-up." The verb "puffed-up" (τετύφωται) here in 6:4 recalls that qualified men for the office of overseer must not be a young-plant so that they might not—"being-puffed-up" (τυφωθείς)—fall into the condemnation of the devil (3:6). Notably, where the false teachers are explicitly in view in 6:4, the connection between "someone" who is "puffed-up" (6:3–4) and "someone" who is a young-plant and "being-puffed-up" (3:5–6) corroborates the polemical intention within Paul's discussion of qualifications for the office of overseer in 3:1–7, namely that Paul certainly has the false teachers in view.[42] Indeed, such would affirm the underlying problem in Ephesus regarding the unqualified overseers (cf. 3:1–7) who do not lead commendably (cf. 5:17) and are sinning unrepentantly by leading others in false teaching that opposes Jesus Christ (5:20; 6:3). The connection between the false teachers who are "puffed-up" in 6:4 and the young-plant false teachers who are "being-puffed-up" in 3:6 would convey the same connotations: these false-teaching overseers in Ephesus have been given too much authority and power without having deep roots in a life of humility exhibited by godliness.[43] Indeed, they have been affected by the effects of pride: "someone" who teaches-different and does not come-toward the sound words and the teaching of the Lord Jesus Christ is clearly "blinded" or "deluded" and thus blindly leading others, namely away from Jesus Christ. Still, given that these false-teaching overseers claim to be Christian teachers while explicitly disagreeing with Jesus Christ, the sense of the descriptor "puffed-up" suggests a "delusional stupidity," which comes from an unfettered pursuit of power.[44]

41. Knight, *PE*, 251; Marshall, *PE*, 639; Barcley, *1 & 2 Tim*, 185.

42. The connection would also corroborate that "a young-plant" is a polemical reference to the false teachers; see volume 2, chapter 2 regarding 1 Timothy 3:6.

43. Given the immediately preceding A' element of the fifth microchiasm, the audience would likely have in view Paul's allusion to Mark 10:44: "whoever desires among you to be first must be a slave of all"; see chapter 2 regarding 1 Timothy 6:2.

44. See Marshall, *PE*, 640, who suggests that both connotations of "puffed up" and "foolish" are possible; contra Knight, *PE*, 251, who suggests only the sense of conceit is in view.

Here, the irony of the false teachers throughout the macrochiasm would be underscored: "some" are desiring to be law-teachers, yet not understanding either what they-are-saying or regarding some-things they-are-insisting (1:7); "someone" aspires to overseer without knowing how to care-for the church of God (3:1, 5); "someone" teaches-different in God's household and disagrees with the teaching of Jesus Christ (6:3) and of Paul (1:10), who is Christ's very own personally chosen representative and was commanded by God and Christ Jesus to be a proclaimer, apostle, and teacher (1:1; 2:7). The irony of false-teaching overseers is that their different teaching is not the result of naiveté, that is, not a problem of knowledge but rather is the function of pride: they are "puffed-up" and do not want to submit to Jesus Christ's lordship nor to his apostle Paul.[45]

The second descriptor is equally telling: the false teachers are "grasping nothing" (6:4). The negative particle "nothing" (μηδέν) recalls its cognate occurrences throughout the macrochiasm in reference to the direct activities of the false teachers or activities under their influence. Antithetical to Timothy who is doing "nothing" (μηδέν) according to favoritism (5:21) and is to lay hands quickly on "none" (μηδενί), "nor" (μηδέ) share in others's sins (5:22), the false teachers—those who sin and on whom hands were laid quickly, likely with favoritism[46]—the false teachers are grasping "nothing" (μηδέν). The participle "grasping" (ἐπιστάμενος) connotes "knowing" or "understanding."[47] Combined with the fact that they are "puffed-up" as young-plants who are not grounded by deep roots in the faith, the implication is clear: such men have no ground to grasp as they are puffed-up, drifting higher and farther away from the faith; they are "grasping nothing."

In this context, Paul goes on to state: "rather having-an-unhealthy-craving regarding controversies and word-fights" (6:4). The participle "having-an-unhealthy-craving (νοσῶν) connotes a twisted yearning for sickness.[48] Certainly, then, the conjuction "rather" (ἀλλά) indicates the stark

---

Paul may be following the practice of ancient polemics that related stupidity to a rejection of sound teaching; see Malherbe, *Paul*, 123–24 n. 7; Towner, *Letters*, 395. Such a correlation, however, is not limited to Greco-Roman philosophy. Within the Hebrew Scriptures there is a regular correlation between disregarding God's revelation and folly. Probably the representative verse expressing this point is Proverbs 1:7: "The fear of the LORD is the beginning of knowledge; fools despise wisdom and instruction."

45. Barcley, *1 & 2 Tim*, 185: "Arrogance . . . means failure to submit, or setting up one's teaching over against the teaching of God. This is precisely the problem with the false teachers. False teaching, however sincerely or 'humbly' it may be presented, arrogantly elevates human opinion above the truth of God's Word."

46. See chapter 2 regarding 1 Timothy 5:22a.

47. See Marshall, *PE*, 640.

48. Knight, *PE*, 251: "νοσῶν (the verb is a NT hapax) used here figuratively of

contrast (see *italics*) between the "*sound*" (ὑγιαίνουσιν), healthy words of Jesus Christ in 6:3 over and against "someone" who is "having-an-*unhealthy-craving*" (νοσῶν) in 6:4.[49] The term "controversies" (ζητήσεις) here in 6:4 of the A' unit of the macrochiasm recalls for the audience "controversial-speculations" (ἐκζητήσεις) in 1:4 of the parallel A unit. The arrangement of both terms within the macrochiasm is significant: it is clear that "some" who teach-different (1:3) in the A unit and "someone" who teaches-different (6:3) in the A' unit are engaged in activities that bring-about "controversial-speculations" (1:4) and "controversies" (6:4) rather than the household-law of God in faith (1:4), thus hurting the health of God's household and everyone within it.[50] Indeed, both in 1:4 of the A element and in 6:4 of the A' element the unhealthy, divisive effect of the false teachers is brought to the fore. Still, the term "word-fights" (λογομαχίας) would be heard in stark contrast to the immediately preceding "words" (λόγοις) of Jesus Christ (6:3).[51] Here, Paul's combined rhetoric is forceful: "someone" who does not come-toward "the sound words" (ὑγιαίνουσιν λόγοις τοῖς) of Jesus Christ in 6:3 is dedicated to Christ's antithesis by "having-an-unhealthy-craving" (νοσῶν) regarding controversies and "word-fights" (λογομαχίας) in 6:4. That the false teachers crave "word-fights" (λογομαχίας) in 6:4 of the A' unit is fitting, given that they have turned-aside for "useless-words" (ματαιολογίαν) in 1:6 of the parallel A unit. For sure, the unhealthy-craving of the false teachers for "word-fights" (λογομαχίας) in 6:4 explains why "some" are "false-worders" (ψευδολόγων) in 4:2. Moreover (see *italics*), where the false-teaching overseers in Ephesus crave "word-*fights*" (λογομαχίας) in 6:4, it is certainly evident why Paul includes the explicit statement that qualified overseers must be "without-*fighting*" (ἄμαχον) in 3:3.[52] The sense of the conjuction "regarding" (περί) may suggest the false teachers are "having-an-unhealthy-craving" because of their involvement in "controversies and word-fights," or

---

having a 'sick' or 'unhealthy craving.'" See Marshall, *PE*, 640.

49. Spencer, *1 Tim*, 145: "In contrast to affirming *healthy* words, some at Ephesus were *ailing* (*noseō*). They were 'sick' or 'diseased.'" See Marshall, *PE*, 640; Barclay, *1 & 2 Tim*, 185.

50. To be clear—and emphatic—the apostle's concern is not to unduly silence fruitful discussion but to check divisive and unfruitful debate. The term ζήτησις itself was originally neutral in meaning ("search, inquiry, investigation") and only later connoted "controversy"; see BDAG, s.v. See Knight, *PE*, 251.

51. The noun "word-fights" (λογομαχίας) is a compound term from "word" (λόγος) and "fight" (μάχη) and is commonly understood to convey "quarrels about words" (*ESV*). See Spencer, *1 Tim*, 145; Ngewa, *1 & 2 Tim*, 150.

52. That the false teachers are current overseers in Ephesus, see volume 1, chapter 1 regarding Acts 20:28–30 and volume 2, chapter 2 regarding 1 Timothy 3:1–7; see also chapter 2 regarding 1 Timothy 5:17, 20, 22.

it may be that Paul's intention is that the false teachers's unhealthy-craving is divulged by an involvement in such activities.[53] What is abundantly clear, however, is Paul's overall diagnosis: anyone claiming to be a Christian—particularly "someone"—yet who does not agree with the sound, healthy words of Jesus Christ and instead has-an-unhealthy-craving for controversies and word-fights is in need of deep healing. The remedy requires the false teachers to abandon their unhealthy activities and to come-toward the healthy words of Jesus Christ—in a word, repentance (cf. 5:20, 24). Until then, "someone" is certainly unqualified to oversee in the household of God wherein Jesus Christ is Lord (1:2, 4; 3:15).

The second half of 6:4 initiates a fivefold vice-list, which focuses on the negative effect of controversies and word-fights:[54] "from which become envy, rivalry, blasphemy, wicked suspicions, friction."[55] The verb "become" (γίνεται) underscores that the activities of "someone" who teaches-different—namely controversies and word-fights—are that which produce further dissension.[56] The first vice "envy" (φθόνος) conveys the sense of "covetousness"[57]—a darkening bitterness that overwhelms a person who is fixated on what others have, effectively robbing themselves of joy for what they themselves actually have.[58] Given that the false teachers are "puffed-up," Paul's suggestion may be that the false teachers are envious for greater degrees of authority. That is, although "some" are desiring to be law-teachers (1:7) and aspire to be an overseer (3:1)—indeed, they actually are overseers (3:1-7; 5:17-20; Acts 20:28-30)—such authority will never be enough when there is an authority above them. Such would explain why "some" are teaching some-thing different that lies-opposed to the sound teaching with which Paul was counted-faithful (1:3, 10-11): it is Paul's authority (1:1)—and subsequently Timothy's authority, Paul's entrusted representa-

---

53. The preposition "regarding" (περί) includes a range of meaning and may broadly include both connotations. Knight, PE, 251: "This craving is 'for' (περί) ζητήσεις καὶ λογομαχίας"; such may suggest that the false teachers are unhealthy because of the things they crave.

54. The phrase "from which become" (ἐξ ὧν γίνεται) refers to "controversies and word-fights"; the relative pronoun "which" (ὧν) is genitive feminine plural, clearly including "controversies and word-fights," both of which are also feminine plural.

55. The last of these "friction" (διαπαρατριβαί) is technically part of 6:5.

56. Knight, PE, 251: "From what has been said in vv. 3-4 (ἐξ ὧν) five results 'arise' (γίνεται)." Marshall, PE, 640: "ἐξ ὧν . . . is followed by a catalogue of the vices which develop (γίνεται) from ignorant controversies."

57. See Spencer, 1 Tim, 145.

58. Towner, Letters, 10: "Aristotle described it as 'a certain sorrow' felt by those who lack what others have." For a more extended treatment of the term φθόνος, see Johnson, "James 3:13—4:10," 327-47.

tive (1:18)—that the false teachers envy and view as opposition. In short, the false teachers have a fundamental "envy" regarding any authority above them—ultimately, therefore, regarding the authority of God and Christ Jesus. Such would explain why "someone does not come-toward the sound words of our *Lord* Jesus Christ" (6:3).

Closely related to the first vice, the second vice "rivalry" (ἔρις) connotes "selfish striving, contention, discord."[59] Given these vices flow from controversies and word-fights (6:4a), that is, from activities that negatively impact the health of God's household, the audience are to view the didactic efforts of "some" who teach-different (1:3; 6:3) as outworkings of their "envy and rivalry," which are causing unnecessary division in the household of God and thus hindering the church's ability to fulfill its missional purpose to welcome and invite all humans (2:1, 2, 4, 6; 4:10).

The third vice "blasphemy" (βλασφημίαι) here in the A' unit recalls its cognate occurrences in the parallel A unit: Paul was firstly a "blasphemer" (βλάσφημον, 1:13) before Christ considered Paul faithful and appointed him for service (1:12); the false teachers Hymenaeus and Alexander were given-toward Satan so that they might be-disciplined not "to blaspheme" (βλασφημεῖν) in 1:20. The connection seems to further the polemic against the false teachers: their "blasphemy" (6:4) is the activity of a "blasphemer"— a person "in unfaithfulness" (1:13), that is, not "in faith" (1:2, 4)—and by implication must learn not "to blaspheme" (1:20). Still, where "blasphemy" (βλασφημίαι, 6:4) in the A element of the sixth microchiasm recalls Paul's concern for the name of God and the teaching to not "be-blasphemed" (βλασφημῆται, 6:1) in the immediately preceding A' element of the fifth microchiasm, it is clear to the audience that Paul is highlighting the faithless behavior ultimately directed against God himself.[60] Thus although the context of the false teachers's unhealthy-craving for controversies and word-fights—envy, rivalry, and now blasphemy—certainly indicates that the direct object of such "blasphemy" would be against Paul, Timothy, and the faithful who follow them in the Ephesian church, the far-reaching and equally direct implication is that the "blasphemy" is an unhealthy-craving against God.[61] To be sure, where Paul is an "apostle of Christ Jesus according

---

59. BDAG, s.v.
60. Contra Towner, *Letters*, 398.
61. Marshall's definition (*PE*, 641) is helpful: "βλασφημία, 'defamation' ... refers to abusive speech which can be defamatory and may be true or false ('slander')." In this way and given the opposition of the false teachers to Paul's teaching, the "blasphemy" in view would most likely be "defamatory" toward Paul. Ibid.: "With reference to God and what is closely associated with him it has the narrower sense of 'blasphemy' ... the author would probably have regarded what was said as derogatory to God and Christ."

to the command of God" (1:1), that is, was divinely appointed a proclaimer, apostle, and teacher "in faith" (2:7), any disregard for Paul's apostolic authority and teaching ultimately expresses a disregard for the one who has commissioned him; undoubtedly, such is apparent in itself by "someone" who does not come-toward the sound words and teaching of the Lord Jesus Christ (6:3). Therefore, while on a horizontal plane the "blasphemy" is directed against Paul and his teaching, it is clear that all "blasphemy" ultimately has a vertical trajectory: in the end all envy, rivalry, and blasphemy within God's household are attacks against God, the Father of the household (1:2).

The fourth vice is "wicked suspicions" (6:4). By itself, the term "suspicions" (ὑπόνοιαι) conveys a neutral idea—"supposition, guess, true intent."[62] Yet, heard together with the qualifier "wicked" (πονηραί)—connoting "evil" or even "guilty" or "unsound"[63]—the phrase highlights the pathological mindset of Paul's opposition: the "wicked suspicions" of the false teachers are unfounded or—more strongly put—are evil precisely because such young-plant, unqualified overseers are grasping nothing while they are being-puffed-up (3:6; 6:4), both having turned-aside from love—a pure heart, a good conscience, and a without-hypocrisy faith (1:5–6) and having influenced others who themselves already have turned-aside after Satan (5:15).[64]

The fifth and final vice that comes from controversies and word-fights (6:4) is "friction" (διαπαρατριβαί, 6:5)—or, more precisely, "constant friction"—the nuance being a persistent quality of contention.[65] In effect, then, the outworking of the false teachers's controversies and word-fights is "friction" to a degree that seeks to ignite a flame.

As the vice-list about the activities of "someone" concludes, the audience hear Paul's sustained polemical emphasis as to why it is necessary for an overseer to be "not violent; rather kind, without-fighting, without-affection-of-money" (3:3). What is more, an unrelenting aspect of the false teachers's activities is highlighted—Paul perhaps indicating that their ongoing presence and influence is not about to dissipate anytime soon, nor

---

62. BDAG, s.v. See Marshall, *PE*, 641.

63. BDAG, s.v.

64. Barcley, *1 & 2 Tim*, 186: "'Evil suspicions' also arise, which are contrary to the biblical command to love. Love seeks to attribute positive motivations to others and to read their actions in the best possible light."

65. Thayer, s.v. Knight, *PE*, 251–52: "διαπαρατριβαί (a 'heightened form of παρὰ τριβή "irritation, friction"' [BAGD]; occurring only here in the NT and extrabiblical literature, while παρατριβή is found elsewhere) means 'mutual or constant irritations or frictions.'" See Marshall, *PE*, 641.

that the false teachers will graciously adhere to Timothy's charge (1:3).[66] That is, against "someone" having-an-unhealthy-craving regarding controversies and word-fights, namely envy, rivalry, blasphemy, wicked suspicions, and friction (6:4–5), it is clear that Timothy will have a difficult time making any headway, particularly when he is their antithesis as an example of those of the faithful in word, behavior, love, faith, and purity (4:12). Timothy can expect that the commendable war to which he is to called will not be a short one (1:18).

Paul concludes verse 6:5 with a threefold description of "someone": "of humans who are depraved in the mind and who are deprived of the truth, supposing godliness to be a means-of-gain."[67] The term "humans" (ἀνθρώπων) recalls its occurrence throughout the macrochiasm, specifically in regard to the Savior God's missional desire for all "humans" (ἀνθρώπους) to be-saved (2:3–4); it is for this reason that the church is to missionally pray on behalf of all "humans" (ἀνθρώπων, 2:1) and why the mediator of God and "humans" (ἀνθρώπων), the "human" (ἄνθρωπος) Christ Jesus gave himself as a ransom on behalf of all (2:5–6).[68] Indeed, the living God is the Savior of all "humans" (ἀνθρώπων, 4:10), even of "some" "humans" (ἀνθρώπων, 5:24). Thus here in the concluding A' unit of the letter, the missional impetus of 1 Timothy is climactically upheld for the entire audience to hear: beyond any doubt, God still desires to save "humans who are depraved in the mind and who are deprived of the truth" (6:5)—even "someone" who does not come-toward the sound words and teaching of Jesus Christ (6:3). Clearly, however, these "humans" in 6:5 who oppose the apostle Paul and Jesus Christ have yet to be-saved.

Paul's first description of the false-teaching humans in the Ephesian church who are having-an-unhealthy-craving regarding controversies and word-fights is "depraved in the mind." The term "mind" (νοῦν) here in 6:5 of the A' unit echoes Paul's statement about the false teachers who are not "understanding" (νοοῦντες) in 1:7 of the parallel A unit. Given this arrangement and parallel connection of the macrochiasm, the audience understand that "the mind" of the false teachers is "not understanding": total ignorance is in view. Still, given that "the mind" of the false teachers is described in terms

---

66. Marshall, PE, 641: "The effect is to make the last item in the list particularly significant and to suggest that it is in apposition to the preceding items."

67. It may be worth noting the word order of Paul's statement, literally: "who are depraved humans the mind and who are deprived of the truth" (διεφθαρμένων ἀνθρώπων τὸν νοῦν καὶ ἀπεστερημένων τῆς ἀληθείας). The grammatical construction would likely be notable to the audience, drawing attention to the participle "who are depraved" (διεφθαρμένων).

68. The term "humans" is implied; see volume 1, chapter 4 regarding 1 Timothy 2:6.

of "depraved" (διεφθαρμένων), that is, "corrupted" or "ruined," Paul makes clear that such ignorance is not derived from innocence but from distortion. Indeed, in stark contrast to Paul who "without-knowing" (ἀγνοῶν) was a blasphemer (2:13), the false teachers have a "mind" (νοῦν), and it is "depraved" (6:5); such is why they are engaged in blasphemy.[69] In other words, the blasphemy of the false teachers is categorically different than Paul's: where "the mind" implies the agent through which God's revelation is processed, it is not merely that the false teachers have a "mind" that cannot process God's revelation but rather that processes God's truth in a way that outputs a distortion of the input.[70] The false teachers "who are depraved in the mind" have heard the gospel—the sound teaching of Paul (1:10b), the sound words and the teaching of Jesus Christ (6:3)—and, rather than agreeing, they have twisted what is "sound" into some-thing different (1:3, 10b; 6:3), thereby resulting in unhealthy-cravings (6:4).

The sense of the phrase "who are depraved in the mind" may suggest to the audience that "the mind" of the false teachers is "depraved" because of their rejection of the gospel, that is, because "someone" has distorted the sound words and the teaching into some-thing different (1:3, 10b; 6:3). However, it is more likely that the audience hear Paul's statement to indicate that such a "mind" simply expresses its dysfunctional, "depraved" state by its continued rejection of the gospel; that is, by continually choosing to not come-toward Jesus Christ, "someone" shows that their "mind" is currently and already "depraved."[71] The overall rhetorical effect of "depraved in the mind" underscores the false teacher's glaring inability to lead the household of God wherein Jesus Christ is Lord (1:2; 6:3). Still, it also helps to explain why "some" apostasy from the faith (4:1): it is because "someone" has a "mind" that is "depraved" and, therefore, cannot actually come-toward the sound words and the teaching of Jesus Christ (6:3). Being "depraved in the mind," the false teachers cannot actually accept the faithful word concerning Christ Jesus (1:15); rather, having-an-unhealthy-craving regarding controversies and word-fights (6:4), they can only agree with and come-toward some-thing different (1:3, 10b; 6:3).

The audience hear Paul's second description of the false-teaching humans in the Ephesian church: "who are deprived of the truth" (6:5). The term "truth" (ἀληθείας) recalls its prior occurrences throughout the macrochiasm: within the B unit, the Savior God desires all human to be-saved

---

69. The α- prefix conveys a negation; its occurrence in regard to Paul (ἀγνοῶν, 1:13) is clearly absent in regard to the false teachers (νοῦν, 6:5).

70. See Marshall, *PE*, 210–11.

71. The latter sense is more probable due to the perfect tense of the participle (διεφθαρμένων), which suggests a current state because of a past action.

and to come to a knowing-embrace of "truth" (ἀληθείας, 2:4) in parallel to Paul's divine appointment as a teacher of the Gentiles in faith and "truth" (ἀληθείᾳ, 2:7);[72] in the C unit, the household of God, which is the church of the living God, is a pillar and foundation of "truth" (ἀληθείας, 3:15); in the C' unit, God's creation is received with thanksgiving by the faithful, that is, those who have knowingly-embraced the "truth" (ἀλήθειαν, 4:3). Given that the false teachers are "deprived of" (ἀπεστερημένων)—literally, "robbed of"—the "truth," it is evident that "someone" who does not agree with Paul and Jesus Christ (1:10b; 6:3) has effectively allowed themselves to be robbed of being saved by the Savior God (2:4), of adhering to Paul's teaching by which God desires them to be-saved (2:7), of supporting God's household, the church (3:15), and of receiving God's creation with thanksgiving (4:3).[73] To be sure, though the Savior God "desires all humans to be-saved and to come to a knowing-embrace of truth" (2:3-4)—even "humans who are ... deprived of the truth" (6:5)—it is clear that "humans who are depraved in the mind" and thus distort God's truth have effectively chosen for themselves to be "deprived of the truth" (6:5). Ironically, then, the unhealthy-craving of the puffed-up false teachers has led to a series of divisive activities that demonstrate their willing, deliberate desire to be "deprived of the truth" (6:4-5).

The third and final description of the false-teaching humans in the Ephesian church who crave controversies and word-fights is that they are "supposing godliness to be a means-of-gain" (6:5).[74] Notably, the audience hear a shift in tense: whereas the first two participles "depraved ... deprived" were conveyed in the perfect, Paul now moves to the present in the third and final participle "supposing" (νομιζόντων). That is, the first two descriptors reflect the false teachers's loss of truth, and the last descriptor articulates the ongoing, concrete attitude that flows from such loss.[75] Specifically, where Paul highlighted the inseparability between "the teaching" and "godliness" in 6:3, here in 6:5 he describes its antithetical contrast, namely the inseparability between "someone" who "teaches-different and

72. In the second microchiasm—the B unit of the macrochiasm—the arrangement of "truth" (ἀληθείας) in 2:4 of the B element and "truth" (ἀληθείᾳ) in 2:7 of the parallel B' element would emphasize the false teacher's deprivation of God's truth by their rejection of Paul's teaching.

73. Knight, *PE*, 252: "ἀποστερέω means generally 'steal' or 'rob'; here the perfect passive means 'deprived' or 'robbed.'" See Barcley, *1 & 2*, 187.

74. Dever, *Message of the New Testament*, 352: "The culprits here are false teachers who do not teach sound doctrine and do 'not agree to the sound instruction of our Lord Jesus Christ and to godly teaching' (6:3). They teach because they love money."

75. Perhaps a more nuanced translation of the participle would read "thinking-fallaciously" or "incorrectly-supposing"; see BDAG, s.v.

does not come-toward . . . the teaching" and their corresponding understanding of "godliness." Rather than viewing "godliness" (εὐσεβείᾳ) as a missional activity of the church to attract those-outside (2:2), rather than influencing women to cosmetic themselves in good works as an outward profession of such "godliness" (θεοσέβειαν, 2:10), rather than training themselves for "godliness" (εὐσέβειαν, 4:7), that is, for the "godliness" (εὐσέβεια) that holds the promise of life for the present and for the inevitable-coming (4:8), it is evident that the false teachers have an entirely different and wrong understanding—a "supposing"—of the purpose and goal of "godliness" (εὐσέβειαν, 6:5).[76] Paul's integrated point is clear: by being "depraved" and "deprived," "someone" who teaches-different over and against the teaching of Jesus Christ is therefore "supposing godliness to be a means-of-gain." Most significantly, then, where Jesus Christ himself is identified as the source and origin of "godliness" (εὐσέβειαν, 3:16), the sense here is not only that the false teachers have a wrong undersanding of Jesus Christ but that they also view him "to be a means-of-gain." Thus in contrast to Paul's full understanding that "godliness is toward all profitability" in regard to the present life *and* eternal life (4:8), the incorrect understanding by "someone" in 6:5 is that "godliness" is viewed merely as a "means-of-gain" (πορισμόν), a motive for material or financial prosperity here and now that does not have eternal life in view.[77] Thus the false teachers fail to consider the real benefit of "godliness," namely being with Jesus Christ "in glory" for eternity; for this reason, therefore, they fail to consider the benefit of "godliness" to attract all humans to be with Jesus Christ "in glory" (3:16). Indeed, the false teachers seem to have a complete disregard for the outward purpose of "godliness,"

---

76. Marshall, *PE*, 642: "After godliness has been mentioned positively in v. 3 we now have an allusion to a misunderstanding of it by the deceived people who think that it is a source of gain."

77. Marshall, *PE*, 642: "πορισμός . . . means 'gain' or, as here, 'means of gain.'"
Given Paul's explicit command from Scripture that teaching elders must be "honored" with financial remuneration (5:17–18), it is clear that Paul in 6:5 is addressing what *motivates* an elder to toil in word and teaching. Whereas qualified teaching elders toil with a true understanding of godliness that intends salvation for others, unqualified teaching elders—the false-teaching overseers in Ephesus—toil for themselves. Ngewa, *1 & 2 Tim*, 151: "Here he is focusing on someone's motives. If their motive in their ministry is to get personal benefits, then their ministry is no longer Christian. They are not following in the footsteps of Christ, who did not come to get things for himself, but came to serve and to give his life as a ransom for many (Mark 10:45)." Simpson, *PE*, 110: "There is nothing wrong in receiving payment for work performed, but if receiving payment is one's main motivation there is something seriously wrong, and especially if one pretends to be something one is not in order to achieve this outcome."

namely to advance God's missional household; instead, they view "godliness" inwardly for their personal benefit.[78]

Here in the concluding A' unit of the macrochiasm, the cumulative impact would be clear. By exposing their motivation, Paul publically announces the false teachers's complete dissimilarity to an existence "in faith": they have no interest in the church's calling to be God's missional household (cf. 2:2; 3:7); they do not agree with the sound words or the teaching (1:10; 6:3); and they apparently care even less for their eternal well-being. Bereft of both the truth and any longing for it, they have become-shipwrecked regarding the faith through their avaricious compulsion for financial gain. Such false teachers are a poor influence on the family members in God's missional household.

1 Timothy 6:6–8: A Minichiastic Unit

As a minichiasm in itself, verses 6:6–8 of the A element are composed carefully of four sub-elements ("a"-"b"-"b'"-"a'"); linguistic parallels identifying chiastic arrangements are indicated by the Greek text:

"a". ⁶ But godliness with contentment (αὐταρκείας) is great gain;

    "b". ⁷ᵃ for we brought-in (εἰσηνέγκαμεν) nothing (οὐδέν) into the world,

    "b'". ⁷ᵇ that to bring-out (ἐξενεγκεῖν) some-thing we do-not (οὐδέ) have-the-power;

"a'". ⁸ but holding food and clothing, these we will be-content with (ἀρκεσθησόμεθα).

The first minichiasm of the 6:3–21 microchiasm is framed by the theme of contentment, namely that which is great gain despite having a bear minimum in the "a" and "a'" sub-elements. The minichiasm gravitates around the unified theme of not even having a bear minimum both at the beginning and end of life in the "b" and "b'" sub-elements.[79]

---

78. This tendency, of course, was not unique to just "Christian" (false) teachers. In this period—as is the case today—there was no shortage of false teachers motivated by financial prosperity, a reality that the apostle himself had to combat by purposefully refusing any financial assistance or remuneration (e.g., 1 Thess 2:5).

79. See Marshall's comments regarding the careful arrangement of 6:6–8 (*PE*, 643).

1 Timothy 6:6: Godliness with Contentment is Great Gain

("a" sub-element)

In response to the false teachers's depraved and deprived way of supposing godliness to be a means-of-gain, Paul declares in the "a" sub-element: "But godliness with contentment is great gain" (6:6). The audience hear the disjunctive "But" (δέ) to signify a contrast. In effect, whereas the false teachers are supposing "godliness to be a means-of-gain" (6:5), the sound teaching of Paul is that "godliness with contentment is great gain" (6:6). Significantly, the audience understand that Paul is contrasting the result of the sound teaching (1:10b)—the sound words and the teaching of Jesus Christ (6:3)—against the result of "someone" who teaches-different (6:3; cf. 1:3, 10b). Furthermore, Paul's rhetoric itself would be heard to emphasize the contrast: it is the false teachers's wrong view of "godliness" (εὐσέβειαν) as "a means-of-gain" (πορισμόν) in 6:5 versus Paul's right view of "godliness" (εὐσέβεια) in 6:6 as "great gain" (πορισμὸς μέγας), the comparative sense being "greater gain" or "surpassing gain."[80] Accordingly, then, given that the "means-of-gain" in view for the false teachers was material and bound only to the present life (6:5), the audience understand that the "great gain" in view for Paul is not merely for the present life but also—and much more—for the life that is inevitably-coming (4:8).[81] To be sure, where "great" (μέγας) recalls its only other occurrence in the macrochiasm, namely the confessedly "great" (μέγα) mystery of "godliness," Jesus Christ (3:16), it is evident that the "great gain" of "godliness" in 6:6 points to an eternity with Jesus Christ "in glory" (3:16), the one upon whom people come to have-faith for life eternal (1:16) and thereby give honor and glory to the King of the eternities for the eternities of the eternities (1:17). Indeed, the correct "godliness" that Paul has in view in 6:6 is the same as in 4:8, namely that "godliness is toward all profitability, holding the promise of life for the present and for the inevitable-coming." Life "in glory" with Jesus Christ is the "great gain" of "godliness."

Still, Paul qualifies his statement, clarifying that specifically godliness "with contentment" is great gain. The qualifying phrase "with contentment"

---

80. The verb "to be" (εἶναι) in 6:5 and "is" (ἔστιν) in 6:6 would further the rhetorical connection and contrast between the two verses. Here, it may be helpful to visualize the overall similarities of both verses (see *italics*):
6:5: "*νομιζόντων* πορισμὸν *εἶναι* τὴν *εὐσέβειαν*";
6:6: "*ἔστιν* δὲ πορισμὸς μέγας ἡ *εὐσέβεια* μετὰ αὐταρκείας."

81. Marshall, PE, 644: "The effect is tht by the end of the clause the reader should recognize that he [Paul] has shifted the reference of πορισμός from 'material' to 'spiritual gain', both in this world and the next."

(μετὰ αὐταρκείας) presents a stark contrast to the avaricious disposition of the false teachers, who are clearly not content but rather are motivated to "gain" more—ironically not having the "great gain" that is "with contentment." Significantly, where "godliness" in view of "the teaching" (6:3) is profitable for a person's eternal existence (4:7, 8) and is essential for the advancement of the church's missional calling (2:1, 10), it is the qualification of "contentment" that reflects the means by which "godliness" accomplishes all of its purposes. Deriving from Greco-Roman Stoic philosophy, the term "contentment" (αὐταρκείας)—literally, "self-sufficient," a compound term of "self" (αὐτός) and "sufficient" (ἀρκετός)—carried a twofold sense: a detachment from the material world and a strong sense of independence.[82] Yet, Paul's application here redefines "contentment" in light of the sufficiency of Jesus Christ.[83] By coming to have-faith upon Jesus Christ (1:16), any and everyone from all races or socio-economic backgrounds—Gentiles, slaves, masters (2:7; 6:2)—share a common existence as family "in faith" (1:2; cf. 1:18; 4:6; 5:1–2), that is, as family members in God's household (3:15; cf. 1:4); they are known by God, the Father of the household, and by the Lord Jesus Christ, the one who unites everyone therein (1:2); they are constant recipients of grace, mercy, and peace (1:2); they are able to share in God's missional desire for all humans to come to a knowing-embrace of truth (2:4); they possess a hope who will not fail—indeed, he did not—namely Jesus Christ who was manifested in flesh to identify with the fleshly and who now exists "in Spirit," "in glory" (3:16); indeed, any and everyone who exists "in faith," that is, "in Christ Jesus" (3:13) will be raised to life eternal (1:16) "in Spirit," "in glory" with him (3:16). A life filled with such certainties and blessings as these is a life filled "with contentment." Whether or not the faithful in the audience have many or few material things, they will all be with Jesus Christ in the life that is inevitably-coming, hence they are "with contentment" in the present life—such is true godliness (4:8).[84] In contrast to the false teachers, ironically the "great gain" of "godliness with contentment" enables the faithful in Ephesus to be good stewards of their resources—those who have much may be financially responsible *and* gen-

---

82. See references to Greek moral teaching in Towner, *Letters*, 399 n. 35. See also Malherbe, "Godliness, Part I," 93–96; Marshall, *PE*, 644–45.

83. Witherington, *Letters*, 286: "Paul, then, is drawing on Hellenistic ideas here, but he is giving them a Christian 'spin.'" Simpson's comments are insightful: "*Contentment* is an interesting word. It is literally *self-sufficiency* . . . But in the NT it certainly does not mean *self-sufficiency* . . . the believer's sufficiency is not from himself or herself but from God. So we might more satisfactorily define the word as meaning *God*-sufficiency" (*PE*, 110). Similarly, see Fee, *1 & 2 Tim*, 143; Patterson and Kelley, "1 Tim," 685. See also Barcley, *1 & 2 Tim*, 189. Contra Malherbe, "Godliness, Part I," 392.

84. See Paul's application of this principle to his own life in Philippians 4:11

erous.⁸⁵ Because the faithful have hoped upon the living God (4:10; 5:5), money and the desire to gain more of it no longer dictate their lives. Rather, they are free to give radically to meet the needs of those in God's household and in their own households (5:3–16), to pay the laborer wages (5:17–18; cf. 6:2), and to use their resources to advance the mission of the church (3:2; 5:10).⁸⁶ From this perspective of eternity, it is clear why "godliness with contentment is great gain" (6:6): it is freedom from treating anything or anyone as "a means-of-gain" (6:5).

1 Timothy 6:7a: We Brought-in Nothing Into the World

("b" sub-element)

In the "b" sub-element, Paul provides a further rationale for why godliness with contentment is great gain in comparison to gaining material possessions or abounding in wealth: "for we brought-in nothing into the world" (6:7a). As its prior occurrences throughout the macrochiasm, the audience understand that the conjuction "for" (γάρ) in 6:7a marks the basis for the preceding 6:6 verse. In effect, the audience understand that the reason why godliness with contentment is great gain (6:6) is because "we brought-in nothing into the world" (6:7a).⁸⁷ Although similar to themes in common ancient literature,⁸⁸ the audience would hear an obvious echo of various OT texts, particularly LXX Job 1:21: "I myself came naked from the womb of my mother, and naked shall I return there."⁸⁹ Furthermore, the combination of "nothing" (οὐδέν) and the verb "we brought-in" (εἰσηνέγκαμεν) underscores the totality in view: the faithful are to be content with anything they receive from God because they themselves began with nothing.

The phrase "into the world" (εἰς τὸν κόσμον) here in the A' unit of the macrochiasm recalls the exact phrase wherein Christ Jesus came "into the world" (εἰς τὸν κόσμον) to save sinners in 1:15 of the parallel A unit. Where the implication is that Christ came "into the world" from another place,

---

85. Witherington, *Letters*, 286: "The point is that we do not really own the things that we have in this world; they are not so much possessions as things that we hold in trust for the real owner, God, and things that we are to be good stewards of."

86. For a comprehensive treatment of Christian stewardship, see Blomberg, *Christians in an Age of Wealth*.

87. See Knight, *PE*, 253. Simpson, *PE*, 111: "The point must be that the way our life begins and ends shows that material possessions are *relatively* unimportant."

88. See Towner, *Letters*, 399; Menken, "*Hoti en* 1 Tim 6, 7," 532–51; Knight, *PE*, 253.

89. See also LXX Eccesiastes 5:15.

the audience are reminded that "the world" is not all there is. Furthermore, where the term "world" (κόσμον) in 6:7a recalls that Christ was counted-faithful in the "world" (κόσμῳ) in 3:16—namely, the "world" (κόσμον) into which he came in 1:15—the audience are to also understand that Christ was then taken-up "in glory" in 3:16—namely, back to the place from where he came and where he now is a judge (5:21). In full, then, Paul intends the audience to be reminded that there is a distinction between two places: there is the realm where Christ came from and currently lives, and there is the "world" into which he came and gave himself as a ransom to save sinners (1:15; 2:6). In effect, the audience are to understand that—unlike themselves—Christ Jesus was divinely living in eternity prior to coming into the "world" (1:15); yet—and simultaneously—it is by coming to have-faith upon him (1:16) that all humans may exist "in faith that is in Christ Jesus" (3:13) and thus will be living in eternity after and beyond this "world."

1 Timothy 6:7b: To Bring-out Some-thing We Do-Not Have-The-Power

("b'" sub-element)

In the "b'" sub-element, Paul provides the equal balance for why godliness with contentment is great gain: "that to bring-out some-thing we do-not have-the-power" (6:7b)—the sense being, "we have absolutely no power to bring anything out of the world."[90] The term "do-not" (οὐδέ) here in the "b'" sub-element recalls "nothing" (οὐδέν) in the parallel "b" sub-element. The rhetorical effect is emphatic, the sense being "absolutely nothing." Still, the parallel occurrence of "nothing" (οὐδέν, 6:7a) and "do-not" (οὐδέ, 6:7b) both recall Paul's corrective statement in 4:4 against the ascetic practices of the false teachers, "Because all creation of God is commendable, and nothing (οὐδέν) is to be rejected." In stark irony, then, while the false teachers are accepting "nothing" of God's commendable creation—which God created for reception (4:3)—they are simultaneously trying to "gain" wealth (6:5). Furthermore, where "some-thing" (τι) here in 6:7b of the A' unit of the macro-chiasm recalls "some-thing (τι) different" in 1:10b of the parallel A unit, not only is the polemical force of Paul's statement clearly brought into view, but the audience also hear the irony drawn out even more: although "to bring-out some-thing we do-not have-the-power" (6:7b), the false teachers live in

---

90. The wooden translation here is intentional to maintain the rhetorical effect and recognition of Greek cognate terms, which Paul's audience would have heard in the letter's performance in Greek; see volume 1, chapter 2 regarding translation methodology.

the opposite manner, the sense being: "We have power to bring-out something." Even more, where the verb "we ... have-the-power" (δυνάμεθα) here in 6:7b of the A' unit of the macrochiasm recalls Paul's grace to Christ Jesus who "empowered" (ἐνδυναμώσαντί) him in 1:12 of the parallel A unit, the polemical contrast against the false teachers is dramatically pushed forward: rather than recognizing their need to be "empowered" by Christ Jesus—the Lord who has power and gives it to others such as Paul (1:12)—the false teachers think that they themselves "have-the-power" (6:7b). Such would explain why "someone" who teaches-different does not come-toward the sound words and the teaching of the Lord Jesus Christ (6:3); they suppose that they "have-the-power" in and of themselves, that is, without Christ.[91] In this way, the contrasting irony of "godliness to be a means-of-gain" (6:5) and "godliness with contentment is great gain" (6:6) is underscored. The false teachers seek to "gain" "contentment"—literally, "self-sufficiency"—apart from Jesus Christ. Conversely, the faithful who are "with contentment" and thus sufficient with Christ do not seek gain; indeed, such is "great gain."

The full symmetry of Paul's corrective statement is heard by the verb "to bring-out" (ἐξενεγκεῖν) in 6:7b of the "b'" sub-element, which both recalls and is juxtaposed with the verb "we brought-in" (εἰσηνέγκαμεν) in 6:7a of the parallel "b" sub-element.[92] Thus where we "brought-in" nothing (6:7a) and we do-not have-the-power "to bring-out" some-thing (6:7b), from beginning to end it is evident why "supposing godliness to be a means-of-gain" is a false view of godliness (6:5) and why "godliness with contentment is great gain" (6:6). The former merely has in view "the world"; the latter has in view both "the world" and the place from which Christ came (1:15), that is, the place to which he was taken-up (3:16). In short, while the sense of the "b" and "b'" sub-elements would be heard to the effect of, "The state in which we came is the very state in which we will leave," the statement itself is intended to correctively point the audience—specifically the false teachers—to Jesus Christ, the person in whom is "great gain" when they leave. No human can take any earthly possessions with them; yet, the human Christ Jesus effectively gave up all the wealth that he had when he came into the world (1:15)—indeed, gave himself (2:5–6)—so that those who would-

---

91. This contrast would be enhanced by the unique linguistic arrangements that occur only in the A and A' units regarding "our Lord" in combination with "Christ Jesus" or "Jesus Christ":

A unit: "I hold grace to him who empowered (ἐνδυναμώσαντί) me, Christ Jesus our Lord (Χριστῷ Ἰησοῦ τῷ κυρίῳ ἡμῶν)" (1:12);

A' unit: "If someone does not come-toward the sound words of our Lord Jesus Christ (τοῦ κυρίου ἡμῶν Ἰησοῦ Χριστοῦ) ... we do-not have-the-power (δυνάμεθα)" (6:3, 7b).

92. The rhetorical juxtaposition between the prefixes "into" (εἰς-) and "out" (ἐξ-) would be apparent and highlight that Paul has the full spectrum of life in view.

inevitably-come to have-faith upon him for life eternal (1:16) would share in his gain, that is, "in glory" (3:16).[93] Indeed, whereas the faithful who have come to a knowing-embrace of truth (2:4b; 4:3b) and have come-toward the sound words of the Lord Jesus Christ and the sound teaching of his apostle Paul (1:10; 6:3) will have "great gain" (6:6) because of their existence "in Christ Jesus" (1:14; 3:13), "someone . . . who does not come-toward . . . Jesus Christ" (6:3) will gain exactly what they brought-in into the world: "nothing" (6:7a).

In sum of the parallel "b" and "b'" sub-elements in 6:7, Paul conveys that "the world" stands in distinction to the place from which Christ came and was taken-up; Paul is clear that there is life beyond "the world," another mode of existence "in Spirit," "in glory"; such is the "great gain" that awaits "godliness with contentment" in the present life. To be sure, the faithful may live with "contentment" in Ephesus, that is, in "the world" where nothing was brought-in nor can be brought-out, because there is a far greater place, namely where Jesus Christ is now. At the same time, the faithful in "the world" may enjoy God's commendable creation, receiving it with thanksgiving with the freedom to also give it to others for reception with thanksgiving (4:3b–4); such is why godly children or those-from-parents may freely give to their own parents and widows (5:4, 8, 16), why God's household may freely give to their own godly widows (5:3, 5, 9, 10), why God's household may freely give to qualified overseers who lead commendably and toil in teaching, namely the teaching that is according to godliness (5:17–18; 6:3), and why godly Christian masters may freely give to their godly Christian slaves (cf. 6:2). Indeed, in view of eternity—the life that is inevitably-coming—"godliness" is "great gain" and for all profitability, freeing the faithful to enjoy and be generous in the present life (4:8b; 6:6). Still, as much as the false teachers's view of "godliness to be a means-of-gain" will result in "nothing" at the end of their present life (6:7), Paul's clear emphasis is that eternity is not only for the faithful; rather, even for "someone" who does not come-toward the sound words and the teaching of Jesus Christ that is according to godliness (6:3), their existence does not conclude with their

---

93. It may be worth noting that the straightforward relationship between the "b" and "b'" sub-elements seems to be complicated due to the conjunction "that" (ὅτι), hence there are textual variants that omit the conjunction; see Metzger, *TCGNT*, 576; Yarbrough, *Paul's Utilization of Preformed Traditions*, 132. Towner's proposal (*Letters*, 400) seems most probable: "With some creativity (I adjust the aorist tense of the first verb in translation for smoothness) this might give the right sense: we bring nothing into the world because we cannot bring anything out. The idea would be that human existence is just this way: 'we arrive empty-handed because in fact that is just the way we will leave'; material possession and advantage cannot pass through the veil, and if they could, we would have arrived better equipped." See also Marshall, *PE*, 646–48.

departure from this "world." Paul's overarching point is that all humans will leave fully stripped of anything of this world and will enter either into salvation (1:15–16; 2:4, 6; 4:10) or God's impartial, just judgment (1:8–10; 5:21). It is for this reason that the Savior God desires all humans to be-saved, that is, to come to a knowing-embrace of truth (2:3–4)—indeed, such is precisely his desire for "some" humans who are deprived of the truth (6:5). Thus continuing the missional impetus of the letter, Paul is summoning the false teachers away from God's just judgment and toward salvation—in a word, to what God desires for them (2:4).

1 Timothy 6:8: Holding Food and Clothing, These We Will be Content With

("a'" sub-element)

In the concluding "a'" sub-element of the 6:6–8 minichiasm, Paul clarifies what godliness with contentment looks like in the present life: "but holding food and clothing, these we will be content with" (6:8).[94] As in the parallel "a" sub-element, the audience hear the disjunctive "but" (δέ) to signify a contrast. In effect, just because "godliness" has in view the eternal life to come (6:6), and just because we brought-in nothing into the world and do-not have-the-power to bring-out some-thing (6:7), it does not mean that humans do not require anything in the present life. Rather, where godliness "with contentment" (μετὰ αὐταρκείας) is great gain in 6:6 of the parallel "a" sub-element, Paul makes clear in the "a'" sub-element that "holding food and clothing" are part and parcel to "godlinesss": "these we will be content with (ἀρκεσθησόμεθα)" (6:8).[95] Furthermore, the terms "food" (διατροφάς) and "clothing" (σκεπάσματα) conceptually echo Paul's statements regarding the false teachers who are "forbidding to marry, to avoid foods (βρωμάτων)" in 4:3a and regarding the women of the church in 2:9 who are to cosmetic themselves with cosmopolitan "apparel" (καταστολῇ) with modesty and

---

94. The term "with" is not included in the Greek in 6:8; however, even though "with" is implied, the audience would hear its inclusion through the linguistic and aural word-play of Paul's rhetoric. As an aural parallel of "with contentment" in 6:6, the term "with" occurs as part of the future tense conjugation of the verb "we will be content" in 6:8 (see *italics*):
1 Tim 6:6: "μετὰ αὐταρκείας";
1 Tim 6:8: "ἀρκεσθησόμεθα."

95. The term "these" (τούτοις) would be understood in reference to "holding food and clothing"; see Knight, *PE*, 255.

self-control, not in braids and gold or pearls or rich attire.[96] Here in 6:8, then, a twofold nuance would be heard. On the one hand, Paul's statement guards against any ascetic "hyper-spirituality" that has a complete disregard for the material world and basic necessities, such as food (4:3; 6:8).[97] On the other hand, given that "godliness with contentment" (6:6) is being "content" with merely "holding food and clothing" (6:8), Paul's statement also guards against the false teachers's—and anyone in the audience's—discontented pursuit of financial "gain" (6:5) stemming from a discontentment of not holding more than food and clothing.[98] In short, "godliness" avoids the ungodly, ironic extremes of the false teachers who both deny God's commendable creation and yet pursue financial gain. Unlike "someone" who views things and people as "a means-of-gain"—whether money, or recognition, or fame—the faithful in Ephesus who have come-toward the teaching that is according to godliness (6:3) are content with what they have; they are "with contentment" in the present life "holding food and clothing" because of the "great gain" of eternal life of the inevitable-coming (4:8). Furthermore, the overall impact of the minichiasm would be emphasized by the verb "holding" (ἔχοντες), which recalls its prior occurrences throughout the macrochiasm to connote "clinging to."[99] In the context of the minichiasm, the audience hear Paul's use of "holding" with a jarring rhetorical irony as a polemic over and against the false teachers: whereas the false teachers view godliness as a means-of-gain, that is, gaining more than they already have (6:5), the faithful who are content, that is, who are marked by godliness (6:6) are merely clinging to the bare essentials of food and clothing. In short, "godliness" is not marked by motivation for gain but by thankfulness for what a person already has, the sense being conditional—*if* the faithful only have food and clothing and nothing else, then they will be content.[100] Still, the further force of the irony would not go unnoticed: as much as those who are marked by godliness are content with humble possessions here and now, so too is their "holding" (ἔχοντες, 6:8) of a different sort altogether; it is

---

96. The terms διατροφάς and σκεπάσματα generally refer to "sustenance" and "protective covering," respectively; see Witherington, *Letters*, 287; Marshall, *PE*, 648; Knight, *PE*, 254.

97. See discussion in volume 2, chapter 3 regarding 1 Timothy 4:2–5. See Carter and Carter, "The Gospel and Lifestyle," 135.

98. For example, marriage and foods are commendable creations of God, which he created to be received with thanksgiving by the faithful (4:3–4). Yet, "godliness" may require being content without marriage so long as a person has food.

99. See e.g., 1:19; 3:4, 9.

100. See BDF §418. See also Marshall, *PE*, 648.

"holding" (ἔχουσα) the promise of life for the present and for the inevitable-coming; it is a tangible expression of their training for "godliness" (4:7, 8).[101]

In sum of the 6:6–8 minichiasm, the audience hear a progressive movement: godliness with contentment is of greater value than material possessions (6:6); naked they came and naked they will go (6:7); yet, as they live in-between this world and the next, they cannot be fully naked but require the minimum of food and clothing in order to be content, that is, the contentment in 6:6 will be difficult to attain apart from the bare necessities of life in 6:8. Rather than advocating "the simple life" as the universal standard of living, the undergirding motive for Paul's discussion would be understood in view of the missional purpose of God's household in the 1 Timothy letter: it is "godliness with contentment" that will bring-about the household-law of God (1:4) and thus the missional activities of the church. Rather than the expression of discontent—"having-an-unhealthy-craving regarding controversies and word-fights, from which become envy, rivalry, blasphemy, wicked suspicions, friction" (6:4)—Paul highlights in the 6:6–8 minichiasm that "godliness" undermines discontentment—thus the divisive activities of the false teachers—and fosters health within God's household. Indeed, such "godliness" corresponds with Paul's sound, healthy teaching and the sound, healthy words of Jesus Christ (1:10; 6:3). In the end, Paul intends "someone" who teaches-different to come-toward the teaching of the Lord Jesus Christ that is according to "godliness" (6:3), that is, to come to have-faith upon Christ for life eternal (1:16) and thereby be "content" with "holding food and clothing" (6:8), which is more than they brought-in and more than they have-power to bring-out of the world (6:7). Indeed, as a subtle echo of Jesus's teaching in Matthew 6:24—literally, "you are not powerful to slave for God and also mammon"—the false teachers's discontentment in life—their pursuit of material acquisition and money—is simply unable to simultaneously share and work alongside God's basic desire for all human to be-saved (2:4).[102]

---

101. Given that "godliness with contentment" (6:6) ultimately has eternal life in view as a result of coming to have-faith upon Christ (1:16), Paul may be intending a deeper meaning with the phrase "holding food and clothing" (6:8), namely "holding"—clinging to—Jesus Christ as one's food and as one's clothing—one's sustenance and covering, protection. In this way, Paul's statement in 6:8 may be exclamative, the sense being: "but clinging to Jesus Christ, this we will be content with!" For conceptual echoes of food and clothing in Jesus's teachings, see e.g., John 6:26–58 and Matthew 22:11–14, respectively.

102. Carter and Carter, "The Gospel and Lifestyle," 135: "A missional lifestyle is one of satisfaction in what God has provided, be it much or little . . . Satisfaction and contentment break our bondage to the endless pursuit of more, freeing us *from* anxiety and freeing us *to* bring glory to our Redeemer."

1 Timothy 6:9–14: Those Wanting to Be-Rich

(B Element)

Within the B element of the microchiasm (6:9–14), the audience hear two minichiasms (6:9–11; 6:12–14). In this section, each of the two minichiasms will be examined.

1 Timothy 6:9–11: A Minichiastic Unit

As a minichiasm in itself, verses 6:9–11 are composed carefully of five sub-elements ("a"-"b"-"c"-"b'"-"a'"); linguistic parallels identifying chiastic arrangements are indicated by the Greek text:

"a". ⁹ᵃ But (δέ) those wanting to be-rich fall into temptation and snare

    "b". ⁹ᵇ and many (πολλάς) senseless and harmful longings, which plunge humans into ruin and destruction.

        "c". ¹⁰ᵃ For the root of all evils is the affection-of-money,

    "b'". ¹⁰ᵇ which some—aspiring—have wandered from the faith and have pierced themselves with many (πολλαῖς) pains.

"a'". ¹¹ But (δέ) you, O human of God, flee these; but pursue justice, godliness, faith, love, steadfastness, gentleness.

The second minichiasm of the 6:3–21 microchiasm is framed by contrasting activities in the "a" and "a'" sub-elements. The "b" and "b'" sub-elements emphasize the impact of pursuing the wrong activites, which gravitate around the pivot "c" sub-element regarding the wrong application of affection.

1 Timothy 6:9a: Those Wanting to Be-Rich Fall into Temptation and Snare

("a" sub-element)

In the introductory "a" sub-element of the 6:9–11 minichiasm, Paul declares: "But those wanting to be-rich fall into temptation and snare" (6:9a). As in the prior minichiasm, the disjunctive "But" (δέ) signifies a contrast. In effect, those who are marked by godliness, that is, who are content (6:6, 8) are pitted against those who are discontent, that is, "those wanting to be-rich" (6:9). Furthermore, the great gain of godliness, namely contentment in the present life because of the inevitable-coming life with Christ (6:6, 8; cf. 4:8) is pitted against the great danger of discontentment: "those wanting to be-rich fall into temptation and snare" (6:9). Undoubtedly, the audience would understand that Paul is contrasting true "godliness" over and against "someone" in 6:3.[103] The participle "wanting" (βουλόμενοι) recalls Paul's missional instructions to the church throughout the macrochiasm that intend to bring about salvation for others or for his addressees: "I want" (βούλομαι), therefore, men to pray in all place" (2:8); "I want (βούλομαι), therefore, younger-women to marry" (5:14).[104] The irony here is jarring: in stark contrast to Paul's "want" for missional activity and the salvation of others (2:8; 5:14)—to be sure, that which the Savior God desires (2:3–4)—the false teachers are "wanting" to be-rich (6:9). Significantly also, where "I want" in 2:8 and 5:14 conveyed an authoritative instruction, it is evident that the false teachers's "wanting" also implies authority—yet, not Paul's authority; rather, the authority "to be-rich" (6:9), which compels them to be discontent, thus spreading envy, rivalry, blasphemy, wicked suspicions, and friction within God's household (6:4–5).[105] Moreover, given that the false teachers are supposing godliness to be a means-of-gain (6:5), the implication of such "wanting" is not merely that those who are already rich are "wanting to be-rich"; much rather, Paul is underscoring that "someone" does not necessarily have to be rich in order to be controlled by discontentment, that is, "wanting to be-rich."[106] Notably, where contentment was marked by the bare necessities of food and clothing (6:8), "wanting to be-rich" is not only wanting material gain (6:5) but is being controlled by "wanting" to have more than the

---

103. Barentsen, *Emerging Leadership*, 225: "The charge of being greedy is a standard charge in such a polemical exchange and was undoubtedly directed towards the same individuals who were charged with false teaching."

104. The verb "I want" (βούλομαι) is implicity included in 2:9: "likewise also [I want] women to cosmetic themselves in cosmopolitan apparel with modesty and self-control." See volume 1, chapter 4.

105. Witherington observes "the similarity between the phrase 'wishing to be rich' and 'wishing to be teachers of the law' (1 Tim 1:17). This rhetorical effect or echo suggests that Paul is referring to the same people with both phrases" (*Letters*, 287). To be sure, Paul is referring to the false teachers in both phrases; however, the two phrases do not share cognate terms—"desiring (θέλοντες) to be law-teachers" (1:7); "wanting (βουλόμενοι) to be-rich" (6:9a). Any connection would merely be conceptual.

106. Paul is stating a principle that applies to all people who want to be rich irrespective of their actual circumstances. Here, then, not only is Paul applying the principal as a corrective measure for the discontent false teachers and those under their influence, but he is also applying it to the faithful in the audience as a preventative measure. Cf. Kidd, *Wealth and Beneficence*, 95–97.

minimum necessities for a person to be godly and content, namely food and clothing (6:8).[107]

That such is the case, the verb "to be-rich" (πλουτεῖν) recalls Paul's instructions for women to cosmetic themselves not in "rich" (πολυτελεῖ) attire (2:9). Where "rich" attire in 2:9 conveys wanting more than clothing that is necessary in 6:8, it is evident that "to be-rich" also conveys wanting more than what is necessary. Furthermore, where "wanting to be-rich" (6:9) is antithetical to "godliness with contentment . . . holding food and clothing" (6:6, 8), the audience understand the fuller implication of why Paul wants the women in Ephesus to cosmetic themselves in "what is proper for women who profess godliness, consistent-with good works" (2:10), that is, "not in . . . rich attire" (2:9). Certainly, where "godliness" indicates an agreement with and a movement toward the teaching of Jesus Christ (6:3), it is clear why Paul is concerned with "those wanting to be-rich": not only do they disagree with the purpose of godliness—"supposing godliness to be a means-of-gain" (6:5)—but they clearly disagree with the source of godliness, Jesus Christ. Such is the dire implication of discontentment.

To remove any doubt, Paul states the result of discontentment: those wanting to be-rich "fall into temptation and snare" (6:9). The language here corroborates that Paul has in view "someone"—the unqualified, false-teaching overseers in Ephesus. Paul's sustained polemic in the third microchiasm underscored that it is necessary for a qualified overseer to *not* be like the unqualified Ephesian overseers: "Not a young-plant, that he might not—being-puffed-up—fall (ἐμπέσῃ) into the condemnation of the devil" (3:6). Positively, Paul highlighted that it is necessary for qualified overseers "to hold a commendable testimony from those-outside, so that he"—unlike the unqualified overseers—"might not fall (ἐμπέσῃ) into disgrace and the snare (παγίδα) of the devil" (3:7). In the same way, it would be apparent to the audience in 6:9 that those who "fall (ἐμπίπτουσιν) into temptation and snare (παγίδα)" are clearly the unqualified, false-teaching overseers whom Paul has been addressing throughout the entire macrochiasm, particularly in the third microchiasm in reference to an overseer's qualifications. Moreover, the connection would carry forward key implications. As in 3:7 of the third microchiasm, the connotation of "snare" in 6:9 would epitomize deception—a purposefully disguised the trap by an effective hunter so that the victim will ignorantly step into it. Also, as in 3:6 and 3:7, "fall" in 6:9 would indicate the

---

107. Given our age of affluence, we may hear the verb "to be-rich" to connote "basking in piles of gold." However, in view of the previous minichaism (6:6–8), Paul's indication is that wanting "to be-rich" is on par with wanting more than the bare necessities of life, that is, more than food and clothing (6:8). Contra Marshall's suggestion that "the force could be 'to stay rich'" (*PE*, 649).

result of the prideful blindness by which a person steps into a hidden trap—a "snare." In effect, then, Paul highlights that discontentment—"wanting to be-rich"—is not only caused by pride but also, therefore, leads to the same result: falling into a snare.[108] Here, Paul may intend a further allusion to LXX Proverbs 21:6: "He that gathers treasures with a falsifying tongue pursues uselessness upon the snares (παγίδας) of death." That is, where Paul's polemical implication was that the false teachers are "falsifying" (2:7), are "false-worders" (4:2), and are supposing godliness to be a means-of-gain (6:5), the implication may be that "those wanting to be-rich" not only "fall . . . into snare" (6:9a), that is, "fall . . . into the snare of the devil" (3:7), but also fall into the "snares of death" (LXX Prov 21:6).[109]

Still, where underlying pride stirs "wanting to be-rich"—the sense being, "I deserve better"—it is evident that the false teachers, blinded by pride, choose to disregard the wisdom and warnings of others and, therefore, fall into a snare that is painfully obvious to those around them. Equally evident, however, is the reason why Paul continues to address the false teachers: the end of Paul's charge is love (1:5); his "want" is for the false teachers to see their dire situation so that they might not fall further but instead be ransomed by Christ (2:6) from the condemnation of the devil (3:6). Indeed, Paul's statement here in 6:9 is not preemptive but reactive: those wanting to be-rich—clearly the false-teaching overseers in Ephesus who do not lead commendably (cf. 5:17) and are supposing godliness to be a means-of-gain (6:5)—have already become blinded to the "snare" set before them.[110]

For sure, Paul's use of the term "temptation" (πειρασμόν) would have been understood as the precursor to falling into a snare: it is "wanting to be-rich"—effectively being controlled by pride—that leads a person to fall into "temptation" (πειρασμόν), the full sense being, "those wanting to be-rich succumb to sin."[111] Particularly to the false teachers, then, Paul would be underscoring that a seemingly harmless "wanting to be-rich" is itself a deception, indicating that "someone" has already fallen into "temptation,"

---

108. Marshall, *PE*, 649: "The thought is that the desire for riches leads people into other actions . . ."

109. The linguistic connection between "falsifying (ψευδεῖ) tongue" in LXX Proverbs 21:6 and "falsifying" (ψεύδομαι, 2:7), "false-worders" (ψευδολόγων, 4:2) in 1 Timothy would both strengthen Paul's allusion to LXX Proverbs 21:6 and its polemical effect toward the false teachers.

110. For a helpful discussion on the blinding impact of the desire for money, see Keller, *Counterfeit Gods*, 48–71.

111. Towner aptly describes how the desire for wealth infects a person's being, making them "susceptible to corrupt suggestions and unscrupulous opportunities to advance" (*Letters*, 402).

that is, allowed sin to take hold of them. It is here, then, that "someone" continues forward into a "snare."

1 Timothy 6:9b: Senseless and Harmful Longings, Ruin and Destruction

("b" sub-element)

In the "b" sub-element, Paul articulates a further result of being controlled by pride and wanting to be-rich: "and many senseless and harmful longings, which plunge humans into ruin and destruction" (6:9b). That is, where the first result of wanting to be-rich was falling into temptation, and the second result was falling into a snare, the third result is "many senseless and harmful longings."[112] The noun "longings" (ἐπιθυμίας) recalls the cognate verb "longs-for" (ἐπιθυμεῖ) in 3:1 of the third microchiasm. To be sure, in 3:1 the audience heard "longs-for" to convey a positive sense regarding a man aspiring to an overseer—"a commendable work he longs-for" (3:1). However, the audience also understood "longs-for" within Paul's simultaneous polemic to demonstrate that "someone" who was aspiring to be—indeed already was (5:17, 20)—an overseer is unqualified according to the requirements in 3:1–7. Undoubtedly, then, where "longs-for" was associated with "someone" in 3:1, the audience hear the full, interconnected, rhetorical implication of the "longings" in 6:9b. That is, given that "someone" who teaches-different (6:3) is depraved in the mind and deprived of the truth, is supposing godliness to be a means-of-gain (6:5), is wanting to be-rich (6:9a), and falls into temptation, snare, and many senseless and harmful "longings" (ἐπιθυμίας, 6:9b), it is clear that the same "someone" who "longs-for" (ἐπιθυμεῖ) the commendable work of an overseer in 3:1 does so from a depraved, senseless, harmful, greedy, discontented, prideful disposition. Certainly, this is why Paul specifies that it is necessary for a qualified overseer to be "without-affection-of-money" (3:3). In other words, a person's "longings" in and of itself is not "senseless and harmful" (6:9b).[113] For sure, a man who aspires

---

112. Ibid., articulates the threefold sequence as "a violent chain reaction." The sequence of "temptation" (πειρασμόν), "snare" (παγίδα), and "longings" (ἐπιθυμίας) in 1 Timothy 6:9 is similarly heard in James 1:14–15: "But each person is tempted (πειράζεται) when he is lured and enticed by his own longing (ἐπιθυμίας). Then longing (ἐπιθυμία) when it has conceived gives birth to sin, and sin when it is fully grown brings forth death."

113. Knight, PE, 256: "ἐπιθυμίας, 'desire,' 'longing,' or 'craving,' which is used in both neutral (or positive) and negative senses in the NT." For the former see e.g., 1 Thessalonians 2:17; for the latter, see e.g., James 1:14.

to an overseer "longs-for" a *commendable* task (3:1) in the same way that missional prayer on behalf of all humans and a life in all godliness are *commendable* in the sight of the Savior God (2:1–3). However, a "longing" that stems from discontentment and pride (6:5, 9–10) is not commendable but rather "senseless and harmful." For sure, then, "someone"—the unqualified overseers in the Ephesian church—who aspires to an overseer with such "senseless and harmful longings" is "someone" who "longs-for" the commendable work of an overseer in an entirely wrong way. It is fundamentally for this reason that the false-teaching overseers are unqualified (3:1–7), do not lead commendably (cf. 5:17), and teach-different (1:3, 10; 6:3). Moreover, it is for this reason that the unqualified false-teaching overseers in Ephesus must be reproved by Timothy for the restorative, missional purpose of their salvation (5:20), namely that "someone" would come-toward the sound words and the teaching of Jesus Christ (6:3) and thus begin to exhibit a life in all godliness that shares the Savior God's missional desire for all humans to be-saved (2:2–4).

In view of the false teachers's "longings" that are motivated by "wanting to be-rich" (6:9a), the adjective "many" (πολλάς) would emphasize and reiterate the inordinate quality of "someone" who "longs-for" the commendable work of an overseer in the same way as (3:1).[114] Particularly in view of "someone," the term "senseless" (ἀνοήτους) recalls Paul's earlier cognate description of humans—to be sure, the false teachers—who are depraved in the "mind" (νοῦν, 6:5) and of "some" who are not "understanding" (νοοῦντες, 1:7). Given the context of the macrochiasm, the audience would understand "senseless" not in reference to abstract ignorance but rather a rejection of the sound teaching of the apostle Paul (1:10b)—God's very own gospel (1:11)—and of the sound words and the teaching of Jesus Christ (6:3). That is, unlike Paul who was firstly was "without-knowing" (ἀγνοῶν), the false teachers who are depraved in the "mind" (νοῦν, 6:5) and pridefully discontent are not morally neutral: their being "senseless" (ἀνοήτους) is an expression of a rebellious disposition.[115] Emphasizing this divisive connotation, the adjective "harmful" (βλαβεράς) conveys that which is "noxious."[116]

---

114. Here, it is worth noting the sustained aural impact of Paul's word choice in 6:9. Witherington, *Letters*, 287: "Some sharp rhetorical skill is on display in 1 Timothy 6:9 in some impressive alliteration: *ploutein, empiptousin, peirasmon, pagida, pollas*—all playing on the repetition of the *p* sound." With the addition of "longings" to Witherington's list, the audience would hear back-to-back alliteration: "to be-rich" (πλουτεῖν), "fall" (ἐμπίπτουσιν), "temptation" (πειρασμὸν), "snare" (παγίδα), "longings" (ἐπιθυμίας), "many" (πολλάς).

115. Knight, *PE*, 256: "ἀνόητος, 'foolish,' the primary emphasis being moral rather than intellectual."

116. Ibid.: "βλαβεράς, i.e., 'harmful' or 'injurious' (a NT hapax used in extrabiblical

Such is conceptually reminiscent and antithetical to the "sound"—healthy—words and teaching of Jesus Christ and his apostle Paul (1:10; 6:3). Paul's warning is clear: wanting to be-rich derives from prideful "longings" that are toxic to the core.

Paul concludes the "b" sub-element by describing the comprehensive, dire effects of wanting to be-rich: "which plunge humans into ruin and destruction" (6:9b). The term "which" (αἵτινες) here in 6:9b of the A' unit recalls its occurrence in 1:4 of the parallel A unit regarding the effects of "some" who teach-different, "which" (αἵτινες) bring-about controversial-speculations rather than the household-law of God in faith." In this way, the audience hear the progression of the macrochiasm across the introductory A unit and concluding A' unit: the false teaching that resulted in divisiveness (1:4) eventually leads to "ruin and destruction" (6:9b). Indeed, such is contrasted to the pivotal point of the letter regarding "how it is necessary to behave in the household of God, which (ἥτις) is the church of God, a pillar and buttress of truth" (3:15, C unit). The verb "plunge" (βυθίζουσιν) carries the sense of "sink" or "drag down"—a vivid image of drowning, being overwhelmed by water, sucked down by the undertow into the dark depths of the uncontrollable ocean.[117] Indeed, such is reminiscent of Paul's earlier statement in the parallel A unit regarding "some"—by rejecting the faith—regarding the faith "have become-shipwrecked," particularly Hymenaeus and Alexander (1:19–20). In effect, the false-teaching overseers in Ephesus who are wanting to be-rich (6:5)—"someone" who does not agree with Jesus Christ (6:3) nor with Paul (1:10)—have not only "become-shipwrecked" (1:19) but now "plunge" with pride to their own demise.

Such is emphasized by Paul's following words: the plunging is of "humans into ruin and destruction" (6:9b). The term "humans" (ἀνθρώπους) recalls its occurrence in the immediately preceding A element of the microchiasm wherein Paul was describing "someone"—the false-teaching overseers in Ephesus who does not accept the sound words and teaching of Jesus Christ (6:3)—as "humans" (ἀνθρώπων) who are depraved in the mind and deprived of the truth (6:5). Thus while Paul's principle assertion in 6:9b would apply to humans in general, it is evident to the audience that Paul specifically has in view the "humans," that is, the false teachers in 6:5—indeed, those who have been the subject of Paul's discussion thus far in the sixth microchiasm.

Greek as the opposite of 'useful' or 'profitable'; see LSJM)."

117. Marshall, *PE*, 650: "to plunge something into water or deluge it, 'to swamp.'" Knight, *PE*, 256: "The figure is that of causing someone to drown."

Still and precisely in view of the false teachers, the term "humans" (ἀνθρώπους) in 6:9b recalls its occurrences and, therefore, its overall connotation throughout the macrochiasm regarding God and his household's mission for salvation: Paul exhorts the church to pray on behalf of *all* "humans" (ἀνθρώπων, 2:1) in the same way that the Savior God desires *all* "humans" (ἀνθρώπους) to be-saved (2:3–4), in the same way that the mediator of God and "humans" (ἀνθρώπων), the "human" (ἄνθρωπος) Christ Jesus gave himself as a ransom on behalf of *all* (2:6), in the same way that the living God is, therefore, the Savior of *all* "humans" (ἀνθρώπων, 4:10)—certainly including "some" "humans" (ἀνθρώπων) who sin (5:24; cf. 5:20), certainly including "humans" (ἀνθρώπων) who are depraved in the mind (6:5), and, therefore, most certainly including the same "humans" (ἀνθρώπους) who are discontent, prideful, wanting to be-rich, and plunging themselves into ruin and destruction (6:9b). Beyond any doubt, the first-century Ephesian audience hear the message of Paul's letter loud and clear: God, Christ Jesus, and Paul—the apostle according to the command of God and Christ Jesus (1:1)—have one and the same desire, namely the salvation of all humans, specifically "some"—the false teachers—who have become-shipwrecked regarding the faith (1:19), have apostatized from the faith (4:1), and do not come-toward Jesus Christ's sound words and teaching (6:3). Such is evidenced by the blatant disregard by "some" who teach some-thing different that lies-opposed to the sound teaching with with Paul was counted-faithful by God (1:10b–11) and to which Paul was appointed to proclaim as an apostle and teacher (1:1, 10–11, 12; 2:7).

The encouraging note that the false-teaching overseers in Ephesus are being salvifically sought after by God, Christ, and Paul is juxtaposed against the current destination to which the shipwrecked, plunging false teachers are heading: "ruin and destruction" (6:9b). Given Paul's allusion to eternity in the prior 6:6–8 minichiasm, the audience would likely understand the same implication here.[118] In this way, the conjuction "and" (καί) would be epexegetical, the terms "ruin" (ὄλεθρον) and "destruction" (ἀπώλειαν) both

---

118. Barclay, *1 & 2 Tim*, 191–92: "Some commentators make a distinction between 'ruin' and 'destruction', seeing the first as a reference to present ruin and the second as final destruction. That is possible. But most likely the two words together point to the utter, final, spiritual ruin of those whose minds are set on earthly things. The consequences of greed are dire, and they are eternal." Towner, *Letters*, 403: "Rather, each term occurs in contexts discussing eschatological destruction and judgment, and the thought driven home by their combination here seems to be of the complete moral and spiritual devastation that leads (among other things) to apostasy (v. 10b)." Cf. Marshall, *PE*, 651: "The thought is of the present effects which last into the next life." Contra Knight, *PE*, 256–57, who suggests that the juxtaposition refers to two distinct aspects, present disaster and eschatological judgment.

conveying the same connotation as a rhetorical emphasis, and the collective meaning of the phrase would be a clear summary of the minichiasm thus far. In short, the destination and end result of wanting to be-rich—falling into temptation, snare, and harmful longings—is an unrecognizable wreckage of mind, body, and soul—"ruin and destruction," the opposite of salvation.

1 Timothy 6:10a: The Root of All Evils is the Affection-of-Money

("c" sub-element)

In the pivot "c" sub-element, Paul hinges the movement of "wanting to be-rich" and "ruin and destruction" upon a profoundly personal statement, cutting to the heart of the matter: "For the root of all evils is the affection-of-money" (6:10a).[119] Although "the root" is heard as the first word in Paul's statement, clearly the audience understand that "the affection-of-money" is the subject and, therefore, the emphasis. To be sure, the rhetorical construction of the sentence indicates that a strong emphasis on "the affection-of-money" would be heard, the sense being, "The root of all evils? The affection-of-money!" Indeed, where the conjuction "for" (γάρ) in 6:10a marks the basis for the preceding statements in 6:9, the rhetorical impact is heard in full: the reason why "wanting to be-rich" ultimately results in "ruin and destruction" (6:9a) is because "the root of all evils is the affection-of-money" (6:9b). Simply, in view of Paul's explicit concern for the false teachers who are supposing godliness to be a means-of-*gain* (6:5) and wanting to be-*rich* (6:9a), it is clear that Paul in 6:9b is deeply concerned about their "*affection-of-money*."

Upon hearing the term "the root" (ῥίζα), the literal impression would likely be "*a root*."[120] Certainly, where Paul indicated that discontent, that is, *pride* undergirds the false teachers's concern with gain (6:5) and wanting to be-rich (6:9), the audience would understand that Paul is not conveying

---

119. My choice for the translation "affection-of-money" (φιλαργυρία, 6:10a) is to avoid confusion with the term "love" (ἀγάπη, 1:5; ἀγάπη, 2:15; ἀγάπη, 4:12) and "beloved" (ἀγαπητοί, 6:2). The term φιλαργυρία could equally be translated as "love-of-money," as represented in most translations (e.g., *ESV*, *NIV*). See discussion below.

It may be worth noting that this aphorism was not at all unique to Paul; rather, similar sayings and ideas are heard both in Jesus's teachings (e.g., Mark 4:5–6, 16–17) and ancient literature (see the references provided in Marshall, *PE*, 652 n. 55).

120. The absence of a definite article seems to suggest "*a* root" rather than "*the* root." For support of the former, see Mounce, *PE*, 346; Knight, *PE*, 257; for the latter, Towner, *Letters*, 404; Marshall, *PE*, 651.

that "the affection-of-money" is *the* source and ultimate cause "of all evils" (6:10a); rather, Paul's point here is that "the *affection*-of-money" is "a root" stemming from "*the* root of all evils"—*pride*.[121] Nevertheless, the rhetorical position of the term "root" at the beginning of Paul's statement and the polemical context in the sixth microchiasm to underscore the discontentment and pride of the false teachers would carry the stronger, more forceful connotation—"the root."[122]

The term "the root" (ῥίζα) is straightforward, the connotation being "that from which a plant grows." In this way, the audience understand that "evils" grow from "the-affection-of-money." Still, the further connotation of "the root" would be evident: a root not only fosters growth of a plant but also was itself planted to grow. Here, then, the audience would hear "the root" (ῥίζα) as a conceptual echo of Paul's reference to the unqualified false-teaching overseers in 3:6 whom Paul implicitly referred to as a "young-plant" (νεόφυτον).[123] That is, where "young-plant" conveyed that the false teachers's roots "in faith" did not have enough time to grow deep, it is evident that their young-plant roots "in faith" have died from pride—specifically from "wanting to be-rich"; it is thus from falling into temptation, snare, and harmful longings that they finally plunge into ruin and destruction (6:9).[124] To be sure, "the root" in view of 6:10a was not planted by the

---

121. Witherington, *Letters*, 287: "We must be careful not to mistranslate 1 Timothy 6:10, especially since it is the most often quoted and misquoted line from the Pastoral Epistles (see, e.g., the RSV, which wrongly puts the definite article before 'root') . . . Paul says that the love of money (not money itself) is *a* root, not *the* root . . ." Blomberg, *Neither Poverty Nor Riches*, 211: "It would be difficult to demonstrate that the love of money is *the* most foundational cause of all kinds of evil, but it certainly is *an* important one . . . no scripture ever declares *money* as the root of all kinds of evil, but rather the *love of*, allegiance to or attachment to money in the fashion that led Jesus to declare, 'You cannot serve both God and Money' (Matt. 6:24; Luke 16:13)."

122. Towner describes the nuance: "It is the strongest sense ["*the* root"] that lends the argument the force required to drive home the point that avarice produces devastating results. To tame the translation ["*a* root"] is to soften the indictment of the greedy opponents" (*Letters*, 404). Wall with Steele, *1 & 2 Tim*, 143: "In fact, the placement of 'root' at the head of the proverb . . . only intensifies the truth that greed is the source of every destructive power."

123. While the terms "the root" (ῥίζα, 6:10) and "young-plant" (νεόφυτον, 3:6) are not cognates, there conceptual similarity would be apparent.

124. Given that the false teachers were young-plants (3:6), Paul's use of the term "root" (ῥίζα) and its connotation here echoes Jesus's teaching about a specific group in Mark 4:5–6: "Other seed fell on rocky ground, where it did not have much soil, and immediately it sprang up, since it had no depth of soil. And when the sun rose, it was scorched, and since it had no root (ῥίζαν), it withered away." Such would aptly describe the false teachers quick rise "in faith," hence their quick rise to the office of overseer (cf. 5:22) and then their quick departure—rejecting the faith (1:19), apostatizing from the faith (4:1).

sound teaching of Paul nor the sound words of Jesus Christ (1:10; 6:3); much rather, the audience understand that "the root of all evils" was planted by someone else and by a different hand.[125]

The term "all" (πάντων) within the phrase "of all evils" in 6:10a recalls its occurrences throughout the macrochiasm in regard to missional godliness exhibited by the faithful in the audience (2:1, 2, 3, 8, 11; 3:4, 11; 4:4, 8; 5:10) and to salvation (1:15; 2:4, 6). Here, then, Paul's sudden application of "all" in regard to "evils" would be jarring and rhetorically obvious, drawing the audience's attention to a dire contrast. The false teachers are actively pursuing the root of "all" (πάντων) evils (6:10a) rather than coming to a knowing-embrace of truth, namely of the fact that the Savior God actively desires "all" (πάντας) humans to be-saved (2:3–4) and for this reason Christ Jesus gave himself as a ransom on behalf of "all" (πάντων, 2:6). In effect, Paul is underscoring the false teachers's active refusal of God's continued desire for them to be-saved. Indeed, it is evident for the Ephesian audience that in Paul's letter the Savior God does not desire for "some" humans to be deprived of the truth (6:5); much rather, he desires "all" humans to come to a knowing-embrace of it (2:4).

Moreover, within the phrase "of all evils," the presence of the definite article—literally, "the evils" (τῶν κακῶν)—would likely be heard by the audience to convey a particularly emphatic point rather than a generic, less forceful reference to "all kinds of evil" (e.g., *ESV*). That is, what the apostle Paul seems to be asserting is that "*all* evils"—every single one of them: thought, speech, and deed—can find some connection to "the affection-of-money."[126]

---

125. In view of Jesus's teaching in Mark 4:18–19, the implication may be that "the affection-of-money" entered into the "young-plant" false teachers and began to overtake their roots "in faith"; Jesus explains: "They are those who hear the word, but the cares of the world and the deceitfulness of riches (πλούτου) and the longings (ἐπιθυμίαι) for other things enter in and choke the word, and it proves unfruitful." Indeed, where the false teachers's concern is for "gain" (6:5), "to be-rich" (πλουτεῖν, 6:9a), "the affection-of-money" (6:10a), combined with the fact that they fall into harmful "longings" (ἐπιθυμίας, 6:9b), it is possible that they also overlap into both groups about whom Jesus is speaking—the ones with no root (Mark 4:5–6, 16–17), and the ones whose root is choked by other roots (Mark 4:7, 18–19).

Furthermore, given the connection between "young-plant" (νεόφυτον, 3:6) and "root" (ῥίζα, 6:10a), it may also be worth noting the similarity to Jesus's statement in Matthew 15:13 (note the cognate terms): "Every plant (φυτεία) that my heavenly Father has not planted (ἐφύτευσεν) will be rooted-out (ἐκριζωθήσεται)." Conceptually, then, Jesus's words and teaching in the following verse (Matt 15:14) seem to also be embedded within the implications of Paul's polemical discussion about the false-teaching overseers in the sixth microchiasm (see esp. connotations of "being-puffed up" in 6:4; "fall" in 6:9a): "Let them alone; they are blind guides. And if the blind lead the blind, both will fall into a pit" (*ESV*).

126. Cf. Knight, *PE*, 258: "the proverb says that all sorts of evil have as their root

The term "affection-of-money" (φιλαργυρία) combines the verb "love, affection, devotion to" (φιλέω) and "money, silver metal" (ἀργύριον). Thus "wanting to be-rich" (6:9a) is not merely impersonal or neutral but rather is a deeply personal disposition that cares and thinks about "money" as though it were a person. Indeed, the sense of Paul's statement is that "the affection-of-money" is the dynamic of a relationship.[127] That is, "someone" who is supposing godliness to be a means-of-gain (6:5) and wanting to be-rich (6:9a) falls into harmful longings (6:9b) because they have a personal, affectionate relationship with money (6:10a). In effect, such a personal devotion to provide all that is needed for the growth of *money*—rather than the growth of other *people*—illustrates how "the affection-of-money" is "the root of all evils": the false-teaching overseers in Ephesus are pouring all of their thoughts, words, and deeds into "the root" that benefits themselves—certainly an expression of pride and the antithesis of the life and teaching of Christ, who gave himself as a ransom—a payment of everything that he had—on behalf of all (2:6).[128] Moreover, the term "affection-of-money" (φιλαργυρία) recalls the exact opposite of what is necessary for a qualified overseer to be, namely "without-affection-of-money" (ἀφιλάργυρον) in 3:3. Undoubtedly, such an explicit connection between Paul's discussion about the false teachers thus far in the sixth microchiasm (6:3–10a) and Paul's discussion about an overseer's qualifications in the third microchiasm (3:1–7) corroborates for the audience that Paul is specifically addressing those who are false-teaching overseers in Ephesus. Indeed, rather than being "affectionate-of-stranger" (φιλόξενον, 3:2), the audience understand that "someone" who is marked by the "affection-of-money" (φιλαργυρία, 6:10a), that is, *not* "without-affection-of-money" (ἀφιλάργυρον, 3:3), is clearly not qualified to be an overseer in the Ephesian church. In short, Paul reiterates that the false teachers embody the antithesis of a model leader in

---

source the love of money." To be sure, Knight's assessment is correct; yet, the force of Paul's statement is not adequately captured. Contra Witherington, *Letters*, 287: "every kind or all sorts of evil (not all evil)."

127. Staton, *Timothy—Philemon*, 113, puts it well: "Just what constitutes the love of money? The Greek word translated 'love' here is the word that emphasizes affection ... It is one thing to *have* money, but it is another for it to become the object of our affection."

128. Witherington, *Letters*, 289: "It is the attitude toward money that is being critiqued in this verse. For if we love things like money and use people to get them, then we have exactly reversed the way God intends for us to operate ... It is in the end a form of idolatry, and of trying to find our life, support and sufficiency in something other than God." Swindoll, *Insights*, 110: "God's concern is not with actual wealth, which is neutral, but with our attitude toward wealth ... Money itself is not the root of evil. The *love* of money is the root of all kinds of evil (1 Tim. 6:10a)." See France, *Tim*, 57.

God's household and are unfit to care-for the church of God (3:5): they are affectionate about money, not people, not God's people, not God.[129]

1 Timothy 6:10b: Some Have Wandered from the Faith and Pierced Themselves

("b'" sub-element)

In the "b'" sub-element, Paul identifies the specific people who are marked by the affection-of-money: "which some—aspiring—have wandered from the faith and have pierced themselves with many pains" (6:10b). The relative pronoun "which" (ἧς) in 6:10b carries forward the "the affection-of-money" from 6:10a; however, the audience understand that the referential meaning of "which" simplifies to just "money": it is money—not the affection-of-money—that the false teachers aspire to possess.[130] Significantly also, the indefinite pronoun "some" (τινες) recalls "someone" (τις) who teaches-different and does not come-toward the sounds words of Jesus Christ (6:3). To be sure, given that Paul's discussion throughout the sixth microchiasm has clearly been a sustained discussion of "someone" from 6:3, Paul's inclusion of "some" here in 6:10b is needless and, therefore, emphatic. Beyond any doubt, Paul is identifying that "some" (τινες, 6:10b) and "someone" (τις, 6:3) here in the A' unit of the macrochiasm are exactly the same false teachers in the parallel A unit, namely "some" (τισίν) who teach-different (1:3), "some" (τινες) who—swerving-from a pure heart, a good conscience, and a without-hypocrisy faith—have turned-aside for empty-word (1:5–6), "someone" (τις) who does not know how to use the commendable law lawfully (1:8), and "some" (τινες) who—rejecting faith and a good conscience—have become-shipwrecked regarding the faith (1:19). In short, where the parallel A and A' units frame the arrangement of the entire letter, Paul's rhetorical

---

129. The historical situation recorded in Acts 19 may be significant for Paul's word choice in 1 Timothy. Where the riot in Ephesus in caused by those who clearly do not worship God—namely, a "silversmith" (ἀργυροκόπος) who made temple "silver" (ἀργυροῦς)" for the worship of Artemis (Acts 19:24), Paul's specification that the false teachers are defined by "the affection-of-money" (ἀφιλάργυρον, 6:10)—literally, "the affection-of-silver"—would likely be highly meaningful to the Ephesian audience. As was Demetrius's motivation in Acts 19, Paul seems to be underscoring that the false teachers's motivation is for "abundant-prosperity" (Acts 19:25), that is, "godliness to be a means-of-gain" (1 Tim 6:5), "wanting to be-rich" (1 Tim 6:9). See discussion in volume 1, chapter 1; see also volume 2, chapter 2 (1 Tim 3:3).

130. Knight, PE, 258: "ἥν refers grammatically to its antecedent φιλαργυρία but logically only to the second half of the compound word, i.e., to ἀργύριον." See Marshall, PE, 652.

emphasis regarding "some" and "someone" makes clear that he is not speaking abstractly. Much rather, as the letter is being performed in front of the entire church, the polemical force is effectively drawing all eyes toward the false teaching overseers who disagree with Paul (1:10), disagree with Jesus Christ (6:3), and do not—nor cannot—care-for God's church (3:5). Where the false teachers have prompted the need for Timothy to charge "some" not to teach-different (1:3)—indeed, the need for Paul to send the letter itself—it is evident to the entire Ephesian church that "some" (6:10b) do not have an affection toward them but rather are affectionate for money instead (6:10a). At the most basic level, then, the prideful motivation of "some" who are supposing godliness to be a means-of-gain (6:5), wanting to be-rich (6:9a), and marked by "the affection-of-money" (6:10a) are unfit to exemplify what it looks like to have-faith upon Christ Jesus (1:16), namely what it looks like to model godliness, contentment, and sacrificial selflessness.

As if Paul's three-part rhetorical use of "some" (τινες, 6:10b), "affection-of-money" (φιλαργυρία, 6:10a), and "longings" (ἐπιθυμίας, 6:9b) was not enough to directly link his discussion to the qualifications of overseers (3:1–7) and thus to emphasize that "someone" (τις, 3:1) who is not "without-affection-of-money" (ἀφιλάργυρον, 3:3) but still "longs-for" (ἐπιθυμεῖ, 3:1) a commendable task is completely unqualified to oversee the church, Paul's use of the participle "aspiring" (ὀρεγόμενοι) in 6:10b would certainly pile even further rhetorical emphasis on the fact that Paul has in view the false-teaching overseers in Ephesus. The participle "aspiring" (ὀρεγόμενοι) in 6:10b recalls "someone" who "aspires" (ὀρέγεται) to an overseer in 3:1. Significantly, then, Paul is clearly affirming that his statement in 3:1 is not merely conditional or hypothetical but rather is a situational fact in Ephesus: "If someone aspires (ὀρέγεται) to overseer" (3:1) speaks to the present problem of the false-teaching overseers in Ephesus, namely that "some—aspiring (ὀρεγόμενοι)—have wandered from the faith" (6:10b).[131] To be sure, underscoring even further that Paul has in view the false teachers, the phrase "which some—aspiring—have wandered from the faith" (6:10b) here in the A' unit of the macrochiasm echoes both of Paul's earlier statements in the parallel A unit: "which some—swerving-from—have turned-aside for useless-words" (1:6); "which some—rejecting—regarding the faith have become-shipwrecked" (1:19). In all three instances—1:6 and 1:19 of the A unit and 6:10b of the parallel A' unit—the fourfold combination of the

---

131. The same implication was heard in 6:3 wherein "If (εἴ) someone teaches-different . . ." was not merely hypothetical but representative of the present situation in Ephesus wherein "some . . . teach-different" (1:3). See discussion above regarding 6:3 and Paul's use of "if" (1:10b; 3:1, 5; 5:4, 8, 16; cf. 5:10).

TEACHING THAT IS ACCORDING TO GODLINESS IS GREAT GAIN   179

relative pronoun "which," the indefinite pronoun "some," a participle, and a passive verb is apparent:

> A unit: "which (ὧν) some (τινες)—swerving-from (ἀστοχήσαντες)—have turned-aside (ἐξετράπησαν) for useless-words" (1:6);
>
> "which (ἥν) some (τινες)—rejecting (ἀπωσάμενοι)—regarding the faith have become-shipwrecked (ἐναυάγησαν)" (1:19);
>
> A' unit: "which (ἧς) some (τινες)—aspiring (ὀρεγόμενοι)—have wandered (ἀπεπλανήθησαν) from the faith" (6:10b).[132]

Alongside Paul's use of the participles "swerving" (1:6) and "rejecting" (1:19) in the A unit and "aspiring" (6:10b) in the parallel A' unit, Paul's use of the passive verbs "have turned-aside" (1:6) and "have become-shipwrecked" (1:19) in the A unit and "have wandered" (6:10b) in the parallel A' unit would be notable, the sense being that the false teachers themselves are oblivious to the pernicious effects of their underlying motivations, namely "gain" (6:5), "to be-rich" (6:9), and their "affection-of-money" (6:10a; cf. 3:3). Paul's point draws out the glaring irony of the false teachers: what looks to be an advantageous *motivation*—gain, to be-rich, money—are all causes of one and the same detrimental *movement* toward ruin and destruction (6:9b)—turned-aside, shipwrecked, wandered. Furthermore, in all three instances Paul is clearly focused on the false teachers's relational position to "the faith": where the passive verb "have wandered" (ἀπεπλανήθησαν) in 6:10b conveys a movement away from an object—here, away from "the faith" (τῆς πίστεως)[133]—and the passive verb "have turned-aside" in 1:6 conveyed a movement both away from "faith" (πίστεως, 1:5) and toward "useless-words" (1:6), the audience understand that each and every movement of the false teachers is nothing but catastrophe: they "have become-shipwrecked" regarding "the faith" (τὴν πίστιν, 1:19). What is more, the audience are again confronted with a stark dichotomy: while "some" have wandered from "the faith" (τῆς πίστεως, 6:10b), "some" have turned-aside from "faith" (πίστεως, 1:5), and "some" have become-shipwrecked regarding "the faith" (τὴν πίστιν, 1:19), Timothy is being-nourished in the words of "the faith" (τῆς πίστεως, 4:6) and qualified deacons are holding the mystery

---

132. Note the parallel arrangement of 1:6 and 1:19 within the A and A' elements of the first microchiasm—the A unit. Such would enhance the force of Paul's statement here in 6:10b of the parallel A' unit of the macrochiasm. See volume 1, chapter 3 regarding 1 Timothy 1:19.

133. Knight, *PE*, 258: "ἀπεπλανήθησαν, which in its passive form means 'wander away from.' The preposition ἀπό indicates that from which they have separated . . . namely, τῆς πίστεως."

of "the faith" (τῆς πίστεως, 3:9), namely the same "faith" (πίστεως, 1:5) from which "some" have turned-aside (1:6). For the audience, the implication is obvious: an alignment with "some" leads to destruction, but an alignment with the sound words and the teaching of Jesus Christ (6:3), the sound teaching of Christ's apostle Paul (1:10), and Paul's entrusted representative Timothy (1:18) will certainly lead to salvation.[134]

Still, the audience would likely hear the phrase "some (τινες)—aspiring—have wandered from the faith (τῆς πίστεως)" in 6:10b as an echo of Paul's statement that "some (τινες) will apostasy from the faith (τῆς πίστεως)" in 4:1. Such would corroborate that the apostasy in view—that which the Spirit says explicity regarding "later times" (4:1)—is in fact already happening: the present peril regarding the false teachers signifies that the Ephesian audience are already living in "later times."[135] The false-teaching "some" in the Ephesian church have already apostatized from the faith (4:1).

In the final clause of the "b'" sub-element, Paul states that the false teachers "have pierced themselves with many pains" (6:10b). The pronoun "themselves" recalls its earlier occurrence in the macrochiasm, emphasizing the polemic against the false teachers even further: whereas those wanting to be-rich (6:9a) have an affection-of money (6:10a), that is, "some," have pierced "themselves" (ἑαυτούς) with many pains (6:10b), Christ Jesus gave "himself" (ἑαυτόν) as a ransom on behalf of all (2:6).[136] Here, the contrast is jarring and forceful. By the false teachers's motivation for gain, to be-rich, and money—pride—they have pierced themselves (6:10b). By Christ Jesus's motivation for all humans to be-saved—his missional desire that he perfectly shared with the Savior God (2:4)—he gave himself as a ransom, that is, a full payment, on behalf of all (2:6). The twisted nature of the contrast underscores exactly how much the false teachers are depraved in the mind (6:5): where Christ Jesus was defined as the mystery of "godliness" (3:16) and the false teachers are supposing "godliness" to be a means-of-gain (6:5), they are effectively raking in Christ's ransom payment to fund and grow their affection-of-money—such is the root of all evils, and they are using Christ to grow it.

---

134. The implicit allusion to the results of Timothy's leadership (4:16) would not only highlight that Timothy is completely unlike the false teachers but would also place the onus of the audience's salvation on their own decision to align themselves with Timothy: "Strongly-hold yourself and the teaching, strongly-remain in them; for doing this you will save yourself and those who hear you." See volume 2, chapter 3.

135. For the implication of "later times," see volume 2, chapter 3 regarding 1 Timothy 4:1.

136. The conceptual similarity between "pierced . . . with many pains" (6:10b) and Christ's sacrificial ransom—his painful experience of being pierced through his hands and feet during crucifixion—would be apparent.

Furthermore, the term "many" (πολλαῖς) here in the "b'" sub-element recalls "many" (πολλάς) in the parallel "b" sub-element. In effect, the audience would hear the parallel relation between Paul's statements in each sub-element: just as the false teachers fall into "many (πολλάς) without-sense and harmful longings" in 6:9b of the "b" sub-element, so too they "have pierced themselves with many (πολλαῖς) pains" in 6:10b of the parallel "b'" sub-element. The forward movement of the minichiasm depicts a vivid picture of the "harmful longings" described in 6:9b: those wanting to be-rich "have pierced" (περιέπειραν) themselves as with a spike.[137] The false teachers are not only contumacious toward Jesus Christ and Paul's teaching (1:10; 6:3) but also blinded to their own insanity: they stab themselves not just once (accidentally) but repeatedly "with many pains" (6:10b). To be sure, the "many pains" (ὀδύναις πολλαῖς) in view are figurative, likely alluding to fractured or severed relationships due to their affection-of-money (6:10a) and corruption that occurs when "someone" is not "without-affection-of-money" (3:3).[138] Certainly, the portrait of many self-inflicted pains on account of money—at root, pride—would have been anything but inspiring. Indeed, the twisted irony of the prideful pains of ruin and destruction by "some" (6:10b) over and against the selfless, sacrificial pains of salvation by Christ Jesus (2:6) would resound: anyone in the audience claiming to be a Christian, that is, anyone who has come to have-faith upon Christ Jesus (1:16) simply cannot agree with, follow, or adhere to the false teachers. Indeed, "some" not only distort "the teaching" of Jesus Christ (6:3) by teaching some-thing different (1:3, 10b; 6:3), but they also distort the purpose of his death: Christ died so that they would have the "great gain" of life eternal (6:6; cf. 1:16); he did not die for their material "gain" in the present life (6:5).

1 Timothy 6:11: Pursue Justice, Godliness, Faith, Love, Steadfastness, Gentleness

("a'" sub-element)

In the concluding "a'" sub-element of the 6:9-11 minichiasm, Paul declares: "But you, O human of God, flee these; but pursue justice, godliness, faith, love, steadfastness, gentleness" (6:11). As heard throughout the microchiasm

137. Knight, *PE*, 258: "περιπείρω (a biblical hapax found in Greek literature from the first century BC) means 'pierce through, impale,' here used figuratively to convey a terrible reality . . . Their reaching out after money has brought the previously mentioned foolish and injurious sinful desires into their life (v. 9b)."

138. Knight, *PE*, 258: "In the physical realm ὀδύνη is used of pains like those of a wound, fracture, stabbing, or cut."

(6:6, 9a), the disjunctive "But" (δέ) expresses a contrast. In effect, while "some—aspiring—have wandered from the faith and have pierced themselves with many pains" (6:10b), in stark contrast Paul commands Timothy, "But you, O human of God, flee these" (6:11). Yet, the disjunctive "But" here in 6:11 would be heard with further rhetorical significance: where "But" (δέ, 6:11) in the "a'" sub-element recalls "But" (δέ, 6:9a) in the parallel "a" sub-element, Paul is setting up a clear contrast between "those wanting to be-rich" in the "a" sub-element and "you, O human of God"—namely, Timothy—in the "a'" sub-element. In other words, Paul's employment of "But" here in 6:11 emphasizes a double degree of contrast over and against the false teachers, the sense being: "But you, Timothy, who are so completely unlike 'some' . . ." Such a double degree of contrast was heard in the parallel A unit of the macrochiasm: the false teachers bring-about controversial-speculations (1:4), "But" (δέ) the end of Paul's charge is love (1:5); the false teachers are desiring to be law-teachers, not understanding either what they-are-saying or regarding some-things they-are-insisting (1:7), "But" (δέ) we [Paul and Timothy] know that the law is commendable." Thus framing the letter in both the A and A' units, Paul is underscoring that there are absolutely no similarities between Paul and Timothy versus "some." In short, the audience are presented with an obvious, unconfusing choice between the two antithetical groups: one results in swerving-from love unto ruin and destruction (1:5–6, A unit; 6:9b, A' unit), the other results in love unto salvation (1:5, A unit; 6:9b, A' unit).[139]

The inclusion of the personal pronoun "you" (σύ) in reference to Timothy adds further emphasis to the contrast of this minichiasm, that is, without fail, the audience are to understand that specifically Timothy—not the false teachers—is qualified and entrusted to lead the church.[140] Indeed, the rhetorical "you" (σύ) here in 6:11 of the A' unit recalls its rhetorical occurrence in the parallel A unit to specifically introduce and emphasize Timothy as Paul's uniquely entrusted representative: "As I exhorted you (σε) to remain in Ephesus . . . that you might charge some not to teach-different" (1:3); "This charge I entrust to you (σοι) . . . according to the

---

139. It may be worth noting that the contrasting quality of this letter is evident in a particularly strong and climactic manner within the sixth and final microchiasm. Verses 6:3–5 begin with those who teach-differently than the sound words and teaching of Jesus Christ and are supposing godliness to be a means-of-gain. Verses 6:6–8 highlight the contentment of the godly, which presumably includes Paul and Timothy. Verses 6:8–10 give a vivid portrayal of greedy leaders who pierce themselves with many pains stemming from their affection-of money. Verse 6:11 initiates an extended and climactic exhortation to the "human of God" to pursue a lifestyle that is antithetical to the passions and pursuits of the false teachers.

140. See Knight, *PE*, 260.

prophecies preceding upon you (σέ)" (1:18).¹⁴¹ Still, the rhetorical impact of Paul's contrast here between the false teachers and Timothy is further heightened by the emotive force of the vocative "O" (ὦ).¹⁴² That is, the sudden use of "O" would not be passed over lightly by the audience; its occurrence here would be memorable and emphatic, underscoring the gravity of Paul's personal appeal.¹⁴³

The phrase "human of God" (ἄνθρωπε θεοῦ) would convey several significant nuances. On the most basic level, there is an obvious echo of unique people in the OT who were similarly identified, notably Moses, the "human of God" (ἄνθρωπος τοῦ θεοῦ, LXX Deut 33:1; Josh 14:6) and David, the "human of God" (ἀνθρώπου τοῦ θεοῦ, 2 Chron 8:14). This phrase would be heard as a title, connoting both divine authority from God and exceptional human devotion to God. Here in 6:11, then, the explicit juxtaposition of humanity and divinity within the title would undoubtedly draw attention to its particular significance within the letter: "human of God" (ἄνθρωπε θεοῦ) in 6:11 recalls that "there is one mediator of God and humans (θεοῦ καὶ ἀνθρώπων), the human (ἄνθρωπος) Christ Jesus" (2:5). As the audience experience the performance of the letter, Paul's rhetorical impact here in the climactic A' unit of the letter would be exclamatory, in effect: "Who is the climactic 'human of God' that has total divine authority from God and complete human devotion to him? Christ Jesus!" Here, then, the cumulative impact of not only the letter's macrochiasm but also of the entire biblical narrative would be felt: Moses, David, and Timothy—to be sure, all of the faithful in the audience—are all ultimately and derivatively "humans of God" through their faith upon Christ Jesus, namely their united existence "in faith" (1:2, 4; 3:13), that is, "in Christ Jesus" (1:14; 3:13). Undoubtedly, the audience hear Paul's exclamation that the single, sole, climactic connection between "God" and "human" (6:11) is Christ Jesus. The full salvific impetus of God's missional household in the 1 Timothy letter, therefore, climaxes entirely in the person of Christ Jesus: where "the Savior God (θεοῦ) . . . desires all humans (ἀνθρώπους) to be-saved" (2:4) and "the living God (θεῷ) . . . is the Savior of all humans (ἀνθρώπων)" (4:10), it is evident that in order for Timothy and any human in Ephesus to

---

141. Note the parallel arrangement of "you" in 1:3 and 1:18 within the A and A' elements of the first microchiasm—the A unit. Such would enhance the force of "you" here in 6:11 of the parallel A' unit of the macrochiasm. See volume 1, chapter 3 regarding 1 Timothy 1:18.

142. See Knight, *PE*, 260. Cf. Marshall, *PE*, 656: "it is often, but not necessarily, expressive of emotion." For the use of the vocative marker, see BDF §146.

143. Barcley *1 & 2 Tim*, 195: "The interjection, 'O', carries the sense of urgency and intensity. These are not trifling matters."

be connected to this living Savior God, they must come to have-faith upon Christ Jesus (1:16), who came into the world to save sinners (1:15). To be sure, even for "some humans" (τινῶν ἀνθρώπων) who sin (5:24) and even for "humans" (ἀνθρώπους) who plunge themselves into ruin and destruction (6:9b), it is still entirely possible for them to be emphatically called "O human of God" (ἄνθρωπε θεοῦ) *if* they come to have-faith upon Christ Jesus (1:16)—the mediator of God (θεοῦ) and humans (ἀνθρώπων)" (2:5)—that is, *if* "someone" decides to come-toward the sound words and teaching of Jesus Christ (6:3). In sum, heard with the exclamatory interjection "O," the phrase "human of God" powerfully summons Timothy and the audience—all humans—to remember that they brought-in nothing into the world and do-not have-the-power to bring-out some-thing (6:7); *yet*, by their existence "in faith"—the realm "in Christ Jesus" (1:14; 3:13) wherein Christ is Lord (1:2, 12, 14; 6:3)—they are recipients of grace, mercy, peace, faith, and love from God the Father and Christ Jesus the Lord (1:2, 14), that is, of life eternal (1:16) "in Spirit," "in glory" (3:16).[144]

So positively emphatic is Paul's statement regarding Timothy's identity—certainly the audience, too—as "human of God" that the only appropriate response is summarized by the complementary phrase: "flee these; but pursue justice, godliness, faith, love, steadfastness, gentleness" (6:11).[145] Where 6:11 began with a stark contrast against the activities of the false teachers—"But you, O human of God"—it is clear to the audience that Paul's continued thought—"flee these"—relates to the activities of the false teachers. To be sure, as with its prior occurrences throughout the macrochiasm, the demonstrative "these" (ταῦτα) would refer to what precedes it—in this case, everything that Paul has described of the false teachers in 6:3–10.[146] That Timothy—and the faithful who follow his lead—must "flee" (φεῦγε) the ruinous, destructive activities of the false teachers conveys a determined motion—"avoid" or "run away." Notably, then, the audience understand that Paul's command involves a movement in the total opposite direction than

---

144. In view of Christ as *the* "human of God" (6:11) and an existence "in Christ Jesus" by faith upon him (1:16; 3:13), Barcley's observation (*1 & 2 Tim*, 195–96) applies: "the expression ["human of God"] can also refer to any believer."

145. This "flee/pursue" pairing was not unique to Paul's letters; see Malherbe, *The Cynic Epistles*; Towner, *Letters*, 408. Such ethical teaching in Greek philosophy, however, takes a different basis and motivation for Paul in light of God's eschatological revelation of redemption in Christ Jesus.

146. Given that the previous occurrence of the term occurred in 6:2b—"These-things (ταῦτα) teach and exhort"—the audience would likely hear "these" (ταῦτα) to reach back to Paul's next statement in 6:3. Knight, *PE*, 260–61: "ταῦτα has been used previously in 1 Timothy of everything mentioned in a previous section, and there is no indication that it used otherwise here." See 1:18; 3:14; 4:6, 11, 15; 6:2.

the false teachers. The clear implication is that the result of Paul's command to "flee" (6:11) will have the antithetical result in relation to the false teachers who "have turned-aside (1:6), "have become-shipwrecked (1:19), and "have wandered" (6:10b).[147] Furthermore and doubling the contrast, Paul adds: "but pursue justice, godliness, faith, love, steadfastness, gentleness" (6:11). Here, the disjunctive "but" (δέ) would highlight the full spectrum of Paul's commands: negatively, not only must Timothy and the audience "flee" from the disastrous results of false teaching, "but," positively, they must "pursue justice, godliness, faith, love, steadfastness, gentleness."[148] The verb "pursue" (δίωκε) conveys a sense of running or seeking after, the way a hunter pursues his prey or the way a student follows his master. In short, the intensity of both verbs—"flee" and "pursue"—underscores the dual, ever-active purposefulness that ought to mark a "human of God."[149] The apostle is reiterating for the audience that a knowing-embrace of the truth (2:4; 4:3)—the gospel—necessitates a radically different lifestyle: conversion is not convenient. Specifically, corresponding to Paul's comments in the current 6:9-11 minichiasm, anyone who is a "human of God" by coming to have-faith upon Christ Jesus (1:16) is called to re-appropriate the values and priorities of money and power to the things of God, that is, to the things of Christ Jesus—*the* "human of God."

Verse 6:11 concludes with a list of six virtues that Timothy and the audience must pursue: "justice, godliness, faith, love, steadfastness, gentleness.[150] The first virtue "justice" (δικαιοσύνην) here in the concluding A' unit of the macrochiasm recalls its cognate occurrence in regard to Christ Jesus who "was declared-just (ἐδικαιώθη) in Spirit" at the pivot of the macrochiasm in 3:16. Here, then, for anyone in the audience who is a "human of God" (6:11), that is, who exists "in Christ Jesus" (1:14; 3:13), Paul is commanding them to put into practice the reality of their faith upon Christ (1:16). That is, given that they are "in Christ Jesus" (3:13), and given that Christ Jesus "was declared-just" in Spirit (3:16), so too have the audience been "declared-just

---

147. The OT scene wherein Joseph fled from Potiphar's wife seems relevant here (LXX Genesis 39:12b): "and having left his garments in her hands, he fled (ἔφυγεν), and went forth." It is likely that this is the sort of fleeing Paul has in view: Timothy and the audience must "flee" from everything associated with the false teachers.

148. Knight, *PE*, 261: "Paul joins (δέ) to that negative command its equally necessary positive corollary."

149. For further reflections on this theme in Paul's letters, see Jeon, *Living Intentionally*.

150. Such virtue-lists are common in both the NT (e.g., Gal 5:22-23; 2 Pet 1:5-7) and Greco-Roman ethical teaching. These virtue-lists functioned as helpful summaries of core values expected of those who claimed allegiance to a particular philosophical or religious system. For further comments, see Towner, *Goal*, 160-61.

in Spirit"; thus it is only natural for them to pursue "justice"—a life that is right by the law.[151] Moreover, the term "justice" (δικαιοσύνην) here in 6:11 of the A' unit recalls the cognate term "just" (δικαίῳ) in 1:9 of the parallel A unit for whom the law is not laid. In other words, precisely because a "just" (δικαίῳ, 1:9) person who exists "in Christ Jesus" has been "declared-just" (ἐδικαιώθη, 3:16; cf. 1:14, 3:13), they pursue "justice" (δικαιοσύνην, 6:11). Here, the rhetorical arrangement, unity, and progressive movement of the macrochiasm would be apparent to the audience:

> Introductory A unit: "for the just (δικαίῳ) the law is not laid" (1:9)
>
> Pivot C unit: "[he] was declared-just (ἐδικαιώθη)
> in Spirit" (3:16)
>
> Concluding A' unit: "pursue justice (δικαιοσύνην)" (6:11).

The macrochiasm is framed by the "just" lifestyle (1:9) of those who pursue "justice" (6:11), both of which center and hinge upon the pivotal historical event wherein Christ Jesus "was declared-just" in Spirit (3:16). In stark contrast to "someone" who does not come-toward Jesus Christ (6:3) and is consumed with the root of all evils (6:10a), the lives of Timothy and the faithful among the audience are entirely rooted, grounded, and growing by their faith upon Christ Jesus (1:16), that is, by their existence "in faith that is in Christ Jesus" (3:13; cf. 1:14). In other words, Timothy and the faithful in Ephesus are the "just" (1:9) who pursue "justice" (6:11) because they were "declared-just" by their faith-union with Christ Jesus (3:16; cf. 1:16; 3:13).

In this context, the next three virtues—"godliness, faith, love"—would draw further attention to Christ Jesus and the audience's relationship with him. The term "godliness" (εὐσέβειαν) here in 6:11 of the A' unit recalls its prior occurrences throughout the macrochiasm. Specifically, where "godliness" (εὐσεβείας, 3:16) centers upon the person of Christ Jesus, Paul's point is clear: for those who have come to have-faith upon Christ Jesus (1:16) and have come-toward the sound words of the Lord Jesus Christ and the teaching that is according to "godliness" (εὐσέβειαν, 6:3), they are to pursue

---

151. Marshall, *PE*, 314: "Righteousness [δικαιοσύνη, "justice"] is the quality required by God in human action and represents conformity to his norms, doing what the law requires . . . It thus means conduct in accordance with God's requirements or laws." Knight, *PE*, 261: "δικαιοσύνη, as used of humans in the NT, refers almost always to conduct that is in accord with God's will and pleasing to him . . . Like all Christian virtues, this 'righteousness' is brought about by the transforming work of Christ . . . accomplished by the Holy Spirit . . . so that 'the law's requirement' is fulfilled in those who 'walk according to the Spirit (Rom. 8:3, 4)." Such is precisely conveyed by Paul's integrated use of the cognates "*just*" (1:9), "*was declared-just* in Spirit" (3:16), and "*justice*" (6:11).

"godliness" (εὐσέβειαν, 6:11), which includes everything that has to do with Christ Jesus, who is *the* "human of God" (6:11). Thus for the purpose of exhibiting the godliness of Christ Jesus and attracting all humans to him, the faithful men and women are lead lives in all "godliness" (εὐσεβείᾳ, 2:2); the faithful women who profess "godliness" (θεοσέβειαν) are to cosmetic themselves in good works (2:10); Timothy and the audience are to train themselves for "godliness" (εὐσέβειαν, 4:7b), that is, for "godliness" (εὐσέβεια) that has the promise of life in the present and for the inevitable-coming (4:8b); faithful children and those-from-parents are "to be-godly" (εὐσεβεῖν) to their parents (5:4a); and the faithful are to express the great gain of eternal life by their "godliness (εὐσέβεια) with contentment" in the present life (6:6, 8). In short, the audience's pursuit of "godliness" is what brings-about the missional household-law of God "in faith" (1:4).

Further still, the two terms "faith" (πίστιν), love (ἀγάπην)" in 6:11 of the A' unit recall "the faith (πίστεως) and love (ἀγάπης) that are in Christ Jesus" in 1:14 of the parallel A unit. Thus in the same way that the virtues "justice" and "godliness" derive from Christ Jesus, so too do "faith" and "love" (6:11). The pairing of "faith, love" here in 6:11 recalls their paired occurrences throughout the macrochiasm. In 1:5 of the parallel A unit, the end of Paul's charge to stop the false teachers is "love (ἀγάπη) from a pure heart and a good conscience and a without-hypocrisy faith (πίστεως)"; the parallel implication here in 6:11 of the A' unit, therefore, is that Timothy and the audience's pursuit of "faith" (πίστιν), love (ἀγάπην)" will effectively carry out Paul's charge to stop the false teachers (1:3, 5, 18). It is for this reason, then, that the godly women in Ephesus remain "in faith (πίστει) and love (ἀγάπῃ)" by aligning themselves with the apostle Paul's missional instructions (2:9–15). Moreover, it is for this reason that Timothy is to be an example "in love (ἀγάπῃ), in faith (πίστει)" (4:12). Still, it is for this reason that the Christian slaves in Ephesus who have Christian masters "all-the-more . . . must serve-as-slaves, because faithful (πιστοί) and beloved (ἀγαπητοί) are those who receive the beneficial-work" (6:2). To be sure, where the "faith, love" in 6:11 are exactly the virtues from "which some—swerving-from—have turned-aside" (1:5–6), it is clear that Paul's intent for God's household to pursue "love, faith" in 6:11 is missional and restorative in purpose, namely toward the false teachers.

The final two virtues "steadfastness, gentleness" do not occur elsewhere in the letter; however, in the sequence of the virtue list, both would be heard with particular significance. The term "steadfastness" (ὑπομονήν) carries the sense of "endurance."[152] Notably, then, after hearing Paul's com-

---

152. Knight, *PE*, 262: "ὑπομονή has a wide range of nuances, which include

mand to pursue "justice, godliness, faith, love" (6:11) in stark contrast to the false teachers for whom the law is laid (1:9–10) and who have turned-aside from love and faith (1:6), the audience would likely hear "steadfastness" as a command to continue their pursuit of justice, godliness, faith, and love in view of adversity from the false teachers. Indeed, where the entirety of the letter is framed and sustained by a concern for "some," the command to pursue "steadfastness" echoes Paul's exhortation for Timothy to war the commendable war, holding faith and a good conscience (1:18). Furthermore, Paul's command to pursue "steadfastness" (ὑπομονήν) recalls Paul's cognate exhortation for Timothy "to remain" (προσμεῖναι) in Ephesus that he might charge "some" not to teach-different (1:3).[153] In the same way, it is apparent that godly women who "remain (μείνωσιν) in faith and love" (2:15), Timothy who must "strongly-remain" (ἐπίμενε) in his devotion to the teaching and leadership of the church (4:16), and the godly widow who is "left-remaining" (μεμονωμένη) yet "remains" (προσμένει) in the supplications and prayers night and day (5:5) are all pursuing "steadfastness" (ὑπομονήν) in a way that upholds "justice, godliness, faith, love" (6:11). Negatively, then, if Timothy and the audience do not pursue "steadfastness," then the missional household of God will be overrun by "some" who uphold the opposite of "justice, godliness, faith, and love," namely the without-godly for whom the law is laid (1:9) who are supposing godliness to be a means-of-gain (6:5), who regarding the faith have become-shipwrecked (1:20), and who have turned-aside from love and a without-hypocrisy faith (1:5–6). Here, then, the urgency is clear: if Timothy and the faithful do not pursue "steadfastness," then not only might salvation be lost for those within God's missional household but also, therefore, the salvation of those-outside would be lost.

Perhaps to balance the way in which Timothy and the audience are to pursue "steadfastness" in view of the false teachers, Paul's command to pursue "gentleness" is fitting. The final virtue "gentleness" (πραϋπαθίαν) conveys "meekness," that is, not being driven to argue or fight.[154] Where the faithful in God's missional household are to lead a peaceful and quiet life in *all* godliness and respectability (2:2), the men in *all* place are to pray without anger and word-quarrelling (2:8), and the women are to learn in *all* quietness—a peaceable disposition—(2:11), it is evident that their pursuit of "gentleness" would intend a missional coupling with their "steadfastness."

"patience, endurance, fortitude, steadfastness, perseverance, and expectation (BAGD) ... The word is probably used here in this comprehensive sense."

153. Not only the conceptual similarity but also the aural similarity (see *italics*) between "steadfastness" (ὑπομονήν) and "to remain" (προσμεῖναι) would be apparent.

154. Knight, *PE*, 262: "ὑπομονή and πραϋπαθία are terms for the right ways of acting in relation to a hostile world." See Marshall, *PE*, 659.

TEACHING THAT IS ACCORDING TO GODLINESS IS GREAT GAIN 189

In short, the command to pursue "gentleness" underscores that the urgent need to stop the destructive influence of the false teachers in Ephesus should never morph into a disposition to fight. To be sure, where it is necessary for a qualified overseer to be "kind, without-fighting" (3:3), so too must all of the faithful in the audience who follow his lead.

In sum, verse 6:11 brings the 6:9–11 minichiasm to a conclusion by reminding Timothy primarily and the audience secondarily that, in view of the mediator Christ Jesus (2:5), each may call themselves a "human of God" (6:11) and must, therefore, live contrary to "some" who have wandered from the faith (6:10b) and who thus nurture their affection-of-money over and against Christ (6:10a) by wanting to be-rich (6:9a). Conversely, as God's missional household, the faithful among the audience must pursue justice by living just lives by the law, must express godliness by faith and love, and must endure the ungodly false teachers with gentleness. Indeed, for those who exist "in Christ Jesus" by coming to have-faith upon him (1:16; 3:13), such a lifestyle is to flow organically, missionally, and salvifically.

1 Timothy 6:12–14: A Minichiastic Unit

As a minichiasm in itself, verses 6:12–14 of the B element are composed carefully of four sub-elements ("a"-"b"-"b'"-"a'"); linguistic parallels identifying chiastic arrangements are indicated by the Greek text:

"a". [12a] Agonize the commendable (καλόν) agony of the faith, take-possession of the eternal life to which you were called and to which you confessed the commendable confession (καλὴν ὁμολογίαν)

"b". [12b] in the sight of (ἐνώπιον) many testifiers (μαρτύρων).

"b'". [13a] I charge, in the sight of (ἐνώπιον) God who provides-life to all-things and of Christ Jesus who testified (μαρτυρήσαντος) before Pontius Pilate

"a'". [13b] the commendable confession (καλὴν ὁμολογίαν), [14] you to keep the commandment spotless, irreproachable until the manifesting of our Lord Jesus Christ,

The third and final minichiasm of the 6:3–21 microchiasm is framed by one and the same "commendable confession" in the "a" and "a'" sub-elements, which gravitates around its public testimony in the pivot "b" and "b'" sub-elements.

1 Timothy 6:12: Agonize the Commendable Agony of the Faith, Eternal Life

("a" sub-element)

Continuing Paul's call for steadfastness in view of the false teachers, he begins the introductory "a" sub-element of the 6:12-14 minichiasm with a further command: "Agonize the commendable agony of the faith" (6:12a). The phrase "Agonize the commendable (καλόν) agony of the faith (πίστεως)" here in 6:12a of the A' unit of the macrochiasm echoes Paul's charge to Timothy in 1:18-19 of the parallel A unit: "that you might war in them the commendable (καλήν) war, holding faith (πίστιν)." In both instances, Paul specifically had in view the false teachers: "some—rejecting—regarding the faith have become-shipwrecked" (1:19) in the A unit; "some—aspiring—have wandered from the faith" (6:10b) in the parallel A' unit.[155] Therefore, as much as Paul's concern about the influence of the false teachers frames the entirely of the letter, it is apparent that Paul's charge for Timothy to stop the false teachers in Ephesus—to preserve the teaching and promote godliness as God's missional household—equally frames the entirey of the letter. To be sure, the double repetition of cognate terms—"Agonize . . . agony" (6:12a); "war . . . war" (1:18)—along with the inclusion of "commendable" and the reference to "faith" would highlight the deliberate arrangement, unity, and progressive movement of the macrochiasm:

> A unit: "war in them the commendable (καλήν) war, holding faith (πίστιν)" (1:18-19);
>
> A' unit: "Agonize the commendable (καλόν) agony of the faith (πίστεως)" (6:12a).

The conceptual parallel between "Agonize (ἀγωνίζου) . . . agony (ἀγῶνα)" in 6:12a of the A' unit and "war (στρατεύῃ) . . . war (στρατείαν)" in 1:18 of the A unit sheds light on the nature of Timothy's calling. The "war" in which Timothy is to "war" is not a foolhardy, prideful errand against the false teachers that has Timothy or Paul's personal benefit in view; much rather, it will be "agony"—and despite such, Timothy must "Agonize."[156] The grueling, unrelenting personal strain upon Timothy—mentally, physically,

---

155. For analysis of this parallel, see above regarding 6:10b.

156. As in its verbal occurrence in 4:10 ("we agonize"), the terms "Agonize" and "agony" in 6:12 derive from connotations of either (or both) athletic struggle and weaponized combat—hence, a common translation to the effect of, "*Fight* the commendable *fight*" (e.g., ESV). See Knight, *PE*, 202, 263; Marshall, *PE*, 555, 659; Wiersbe, *Ephesians Through Revelation*, 236. Both connotations would draw attention to the unavoidable difficulty that Timothy must endure.

emotionally—will not be enjoyable, and Timothy must commit himself to it for the sake of God's missional household.[157]

Furthermore, the parallel repetition of "commendable" (καλήν, 1:18; καλόν, 6:12a) in view of "faith" (πίστιν, 1:18; πίστεως, 6:12a) in the A and A' units highlights why the "war" and "agony" must happen. The missional activity of the church was "commendable" (καλόν) in the sight of the Savior God, who desires all humans to be-saved (2:1–4), and for this reason, Christ Jesus came into the world to save sinners—such was the "faithful" (πιστός) word (1:15)—so that those who would-inevitably-come "to have-faith" (πιστεύειν) upon him would be-saved, that is, have life eternal (1:16). Certainly, Paul's point is that the "war" and "agony" are both "commendable" because they are both motivated by salvation, namely so that "some" would-come "to have-faith."[158] To be sure, where Paul and Timothy toil and "agonize" (ἀγωνιζόμεθα) for the sake of the "faithful" (πιστός) word regarding life for the present and for the inevitable-coming and the universal offer of salvation (4:8–10), it is evident that Timothy must "agonize (ἀγωνίζου) the commendable agony (ἀγῶνα) of the faith (πίστεως)" (6:12a) because he—along with Paul—has hoped upon the living God, who is the Savior of all humans (4:10). In short, the salvation of others is at stake: Timothy must endure.

Still, regarding "*the* faith (τῆς πίστεως)," Paul is likely drawing attention to Timothy's personal perseverance rather than a need to preserve "faith" within the Ephesian church.[159] That is, the genitive phrase "of the faith" would likely be understood appositionally and thus conveying a specific application.[160] The command for Timothy—and the audience—to "agonize the commendable agony of *the* faith" is, therefore, a rhetorical echo of Paul's immediately prior command to pursue "faith" and "steadfastness" as part of one's missional, Christian calling (6:11) to be faithful to God's purpose; indeed, they are to do so even amidst "some" who are swerving-from a without-hypocrisy faith and—by aspiring for money—have wandered from the faith (1:5–6; 6:10) and even as others in the Ephesian church succumb

---

157. Knight, *PE*, 263: "The present imperative form of the verb suggests that this [is] a never-ending struggle."

158. Similarly, ibid.: "The struggle is regarded as 'good' (καλόν), both because it is engaged in for God and the gospel and also because it is inherent to the gospel's making its way in an evil world."

159. E.g., the *NASB* translation "fight the good faith of faith"—without the definite article "the"—leaves the impression that Paul is simply reiterating the need to agonize for "faith" in general.

160. Towner's summary is helpful: "With Timothy's stability of faith in mind, it is preferable to translate the genitive qualifying phrase 'of [the] faith' as a reference to the essential quality of the Christian life as contest (= persistent believing; i.e., 'keep competing in the good contest of faith'), rather than as a definition of the object of the contest with the opponents (= the content of what is believed . . .)" (*Letters*, 411).

to the ruinous, destructive influence of "some." Indeed, where Timothy and the audience must pursue "gentleness"—a disposition to not argue or fight—Paul's concern is that they preserve the integrity of their own faith—pursuing justice, godliness, love (6:11)—while they "Agonize the commendable agony" (6:12a). In short, the "agony" will take a toll on Timothy and the audience, but they must intentionally "Agonize" to *not* grow bitter or divisive themselves.[161]

Paul continues his command in the "a" sub-element: "take-possession of the eternal life to which you were called" (6:12a). Noteworthy here is the juxtaposition of divine sovereignty and human responsibility.[162] On the one hand, Timothy himself is commanded to "take-possession (ἐπιλαβοῦ) of the eternal life" (6:12a). Where the sense of the verb "take-possession" is to "overtake" or "take hold of"—to realize a goal, to materialize an ambition—Paul is placing the onus clearly upon Timothy to work at his own faithfulness with all his might. In full, then, Paul's commands in 6:12 would be heard to the effect of: "Agonize heartily the agony of the faith—agonize until you attain the goal of eternal life." On the other hand, that Timothy is to "take-possession (ἐπιλαβοῦ) of the eternal life" (6:12a) recalls his entire dependence upon God—the Savior God, who desires all humans to be-saved (2:3-4)—and upon Christ Jesus—the mediator of God and humans, who gave himself as a ransom on behalf of all (2:5-6). In other words, Timothy is able to "take-possession" (6:12a)—literally, "strongly-receive"—because Christ "gave himself" (2:6) and because God desires for all humans to be-saved, thus to "strongly-receive" eternal life (2:4; 6:12). Such is divine sovereignty. Yet, only Timothy may "take-possession" of that which God desires and Christ gave—such is human responsibility. Here, both are active and inseparable.

Furthermore, the verb "take-possession" (ἐπιλαβοῦ) in 6:12a recalls the cognate terms "reception" (μετάλημψιν) in 4:3 and "being-received" (λαμβανόμενον) in 4:4 wherein Paul highlighted that God's intention is for his creation to be enjoyed by humans. Given this connection, Paul's rhetorical implication would likely convey that the same God who intends all creation for "reception" (μετάλημψιν) and for "being-received" (λαμβανόμενον)

---

161. As many in pastorial ministry can attest, agonizing for the faith can just as much be agonizing against a darkening of the soul. Paul's command is itself very pastoral: one's own faith must be guarded from attack by deliberately fighting for it.

162. This kind of juxtaposition is common in Paul's writing. Probably the best example is Philippians 2:12-13 (*ESV*): "Therefore, my beloved, as you have always obeyed, so now, not only as in my presence but much more in my absence, work out your own salvation with fear and trembling, for it is God who works in you, both to will and to work for his good pleasure."

(4:3–4) is also the God who intends for humans to "take-possession" (ἐπιλάβου)—literally, "strongly-receive"—the eternal life, which is his desire for all humans (2:3–4). Similarly, in the prior microchiasm Paul articulated that Christian slaves are responsible to serve-as-slaves all-the-more for their Christian masters—"those who receive" (ἀντιλαμβανόμενοι, 6:2)—as part of their calling to work alongside God to provide for the faithful. Thus while both divine sovereignty and human responsibility are integrated and must be heard together, the specific nuance here seems to emphasize human responsibility particularly in light of God's overwhelming sovereignty, the sense being: "God actively desires for you to receive all that he offers. He offers you the eternal life? Do everything possible to take-possession of it!"

Still, in view of eternal life, the verb "take-possession" (ἐπιλαβοῦ) here in 6:12a of the concluding A' unit recalls the cognate occurrence wherein Christ Jesus "was taken-up" (ἀνελήμφθη) in glory" in 3:16 of the macrochiasm's pivot. The connection not only highlights Timothy's dependence upon Christ Jesus—Christ had to be "taken-up" in glory (3:16) so that Timothy could "take-possession" of eternal life (6:12a)—but also draws attention to the manner of existence that defines "eternal life" (6:12a), namely one "in glory" (3:16) alongside "the glory of God" (1:11). For the audience, then, the connection paints a vivid picture of the eternal life of which they must "take-possession": radiance upon radiance—their own glory surrounded and engulfed by the radiant glory of Christ Jesus and God.

The phrase "eternal life" (αἰωνίου ζωῆς) here in 6:12a of the A' unit recalls "life eternal" (ζωὴν αἰώνιον) in 1:16 of the parallel A unit.[163] In effect, where coming to have-faith upon Christ Jesus was "for life eternal" (1:16), it is evident that to "take-possesion of eternal life" (6:12a) here in the A' unit is synonymous with coming to have-faith upon Christ Jesus in the A unit. Clearly, the audience understand that Timothy has already come to have-faith upon Christ (1:16), that is, already taken-possesion of eternal life (6:12a)— Timothy is "in faith" with Paul (1:2), the realm "in Christ Jesus" (3:13). Thus, here, the command to "take-possession of eternal life" (6:12a) reiterates the command to "Agonize the commendable agony of the faith" (6:12a), that is, to maintain one's personal faith upon Christ Jesus (1:16). In this way, the phrase "eternal life" (αἰωνίου ζωῆς) would convey two further nuances.

First, in line with Paul's command to "pursue justice, godliness, faith, love, steadfastness, gentleness" (6:11), the goal here is to pursue a mode of life in the present that is commensurate with the values and vision of "eternal

---

163. It is worth noting that both phrases parallel each other in combination with the Greek term εἰς, which would strengthen the parallelism across the macrochiasm:
A unit: 1:16: "for eternal life" (εἰς ζωὴν αἰώνιον);
A' unit: 6:12a: "eternal life to" (αἰωνίου ζωῆς εἰς).

life." To be sure, such was already conveyed in the fourth microchiasm wherein Timothy—and the audience—were commanded to train for "godliness," namely that which has "the promise of life (ζωῆς) for the present and for the inevitable-coming" (4:7–8). Indeed, such "godliness" with contentment—holding food and clothing in the present—was defined as great gain specifically in view of eternal life (6:6, 8). Significantly, Paul's statement here in 6:12a summarizes the cumulative progression, movement, and message of the entire 1 Timothy letter: the audience's pursuit of "eternal life"—life that is "in Spirit," "in glory" with Jesus Christ (3:16)—while living here and now in the present life—"in flesh" (3:16)—is and must be tangibly expressed by "godliness" (2:2, 10; 3:16; 4:7b, 8b; 5:4a; 6:3, 6, 11), which is the tangible result of agreeing with "the teaching" (1:10; 4:6, 13, 16; 6:3; cf. 2:7, 12; 3:2; 5:17; 6:1, 3). In short, as those who already belong to God's missional household by coming to have-faith upon Christ Jesus (1:16), Timothy and the audience's current manner of life should correspond to the already-but-not-yet reality of their "eternal life," that is, their existence "in faith that is in Christ Jesus" (3:13), the one in whom they are able to pursue justice, godliness, faith, love, steadfastness, and gentleness as humans of God (6:11).

Second, the phrase "eternal life" not only highlights Timothy and the audience's human responsibility to live in a manner consistent with "eternal life" but also reminds them of divine sovereignty, namely God and Christ Jesus's mercy. In the parallel A unit of the macrochiasm, Paul's declaration of his own conversion in 1:12–16 not only climaxes with "life eternal" (ζωὴν αἰώνιον) by coming to have-faith upon Christ Jesus but also emphasizes that he "was granted-mercy" to be an example to those who-would-inevitably-come to have-faith upon Christ (1:16). To be sure, Paul's conversion—his faith upon Christ—reiterates the fact that he "was granted-mercy" though firstly being a blasphemer, persecutor, and hubristic-person (1:13). Even more, in the opening of the letter, Paul begins with a statement of God and Christ Jesus's "mercy" in view of his existence "in faith" (1:2). Thus as much Paul places the onus of Timothy and the audience's human responsibility to "take-possession of eternal life" (6:12a) in the A' unit, he also underscores God and Christ Jesus's overarching, sovereign mercy that enables Paul, Timothy, and the audience to act and respond accordingly.

Still, the emphasis on divine sovereignty is reiterated in 6:12a through the clause "to which you were called." The verb "you were called" (ἐκλήθης) conveys that a divine passive is in view, the sense being that Paul's command to "take-possession of eternal life" is simply to receive the gift of salvation from God, namely the grace, mercy, and peace from God the Father and

Christ Jesus (1:2).[164] Furthermore, the verb "you were called" (ἐκλήθης) recalls "the church" (ἐκκλησίας, 3:5; ἐκκλησία, 3:15; 5:16) of God and the "elect (ἐκλεκτῶν) angels" (5:21). Here, the rhetorical emphasis on God's personal activity is underscored: in the same way that those "in faith" comprise "the church of God"—literally, "the called-out of God" (3:5, 15)—and the "elect angels" pointed to the personal reality of being in the full presence of God in heaven (5:21), Paul's point is clear: Timothy, the church, and the angels will one day be fully together in God's presence, notably by God's own doing. Such is God's sovereign grace, mercy, and peace (1:2).

In view of God's divine sovereignty that "called" Timothy, the "a" sub-element concludes by highlighting Timothy's human responsibility: "and to which you confessed the commendable confession" (6:12a). Here, the conjunctive "and" (καί) correlates the eternal life "to which" Timothy was called with a historical confession "to which" Timothy confessed.[165] In other words, God's personal calling to Timothy to take-possession of eternal life was made personally efficacious when Timothy "confessed the commendable confession." To be sure, where the object of Timothy's "confession" is "eternal life," the clear implication for the audience is that the content of what Timothy "confessed" has Christ Jesus in view—the one upon whom humans come to have-faith for "life eternal" (1:16). Given the context of enduring the "agony of the faith" (6:12a), it is Timothy's continual "confession" of what he "confessed"—namely, Jesus Christ as Lord—by which he may fully realize and take-possession of eternal life. To be sure, where the "commendable (καλήν) confession" (6:12a) recalls the "commendable (καλόν) agony" (6:12a), it is clear that Timothy's perseverance will be difficult and trying; yet, it is still part of his missional lifestyle that is "commendable" (καλόν) in the sight of God (2:3).

Significantly, both cognate terms "confessed" (ὡμολόγησας) and "confession" (ὁμολογίαν) here in 6:12a of the climactic A' unit recall the

---

164. See Barcley, *1 & 2 Tim*, 197; Knight, *PE*, 264.

165. The phrase "to which" does not occur in the Greek text but is assumed where "and" joins the two clauses within 6:12a. The inclusion of the bracketed phrase "to which" in my translation highlights that God's calling and Timothy's public confession share the same object, namely "eternal life."

A comparison of common translations illustrates the confusion caused by the syntax and ambiguous use of the conjunction "and" (καί) here in 6:12a (see *italics*):

ESV: "Take hold of the eternal life to which you were called *and about which* you made the good confession in the presence of many witnesses."

NASB: "take hold of the eternal life to which you were called, *and* you made the good confession in the presence of many witnesses."

NIV: "Take hold of the eternal life to which you were called *when* you made your good confession in the presence of many witnesses."

"confessedly" (ὁμολογουμένως) great mystery of godliness regarding Christ Jesus in the pivot point of the macrochiasm (3:16). Where Christ Jesus himself is the "confessedly" great content whom Paul and the audience exclaim (3:16), it is clear that the "confession" that Timothy "confessed" has none other in view than Christ Jesus—to be sure, that "he was manifested in flesh, was declared-just in Spirit, was seen by angels, was proclaimed in the Gentiles, was counted-faithful in the world, was taken-up in glory" (3:16). Moreover, Paul's back-to-back emphasis on "confessed . . . confession" would draw the audience's attention to the rhetorical significance of the words themselves. Here, Paul's rhetorically interwoven message would be apparent (see *italics*): "confessed (ὡμολόγησας) . . . confession" (ὁμολογίαν) in 6:12a and "confessedly" (ὁμολογουμένως) in 3:16 recall their conceptual and linguistic similarity to the faithful "word" (λόγος) concerning his entrance into the world to save sinners (1:15); the "word" (λόγου) of God concerning Christ Jesus by which all creation is made-holy (4:5); the "words" (λόγοις) of the faith, that is the commendable teaching in which Timothy is being-nourished (4:6); the faithful "word" (λόγος) regarding the all-profitability of godliness for both the present life and the inevitable-coming life (4:8–9); the "word" (λόγῳ) in which Timothy is to be an example (4:12); the elders—overseers—who lead commendably and toil in "word" (λόγῳ) and teaching (5:17); and finally, ultimately, climactically, the "words" (λόγοις) of Jesus Christ himself (6:3).[166] In short, Paul's rhetorical impact upon the audience would be interconnected and resounding: that which is "confessedly" (ὁμολογουμένως)—literally, "same-wordedly"—great (3:16) is that which Timothy "confessed" (ὡμολόγησας)—literally, "same-worded"—namely the "confession" (ὁμολογίαν)—literally, "same-word" (6:12a)—regarding the faithful "word" (λόγος) about Christ Jesus (1:15), which are the "words" (λόγοις) of Jesus Christ himself (6:3).[167]

Moreover, by highlighting Timothy's alignment with the *same*, united confession of Paul and the church (3:16), a simultaneous polemical contrast between the *different* content of the false teachers would not go unnoticed. Building upon Paul's rhetorical word-play (see *italics*) between

---

166. The audience have consistently heard Paul's sustained rhetorical use of "word" (λόγος) and its cognates throughout the macrochiasm (see *italics*): "useless-words" (ματαιολογίαν, 1:6), "double-worded" (διλόγους, 3:8), "false-worders" (ψευδολόγων, 4:2), "word-fights" (λογομαχίας, 6:4). Not only would the audience be attuned, accustomed, and habituated to Paul's rhetorical strategy, but they would also be expecting to hear more of it. The rhetorical use of "confessedly" (3:16), "confessed . . . confession" (6:12a) would be apparent. See volume 2, chapter 2 regarding 1 Timothy 3:16.

167. The verb, noun, and adverb "confessed" (ὡμολόγησας), "confession" (ὁμολογίαν), and "confessedly" (ὁμολογουμένως) are comprised of the terms "same" (ὅμοιος) and the root noun "word" (λόγος).

"some" who "teach-*different*" (ἑτεροδιδασκαλεῖ, 1:3), that is, some-thing "*different*" (ἕτερον, 1:10) than the "confessedly" (ὁμολογουμένως)—"*same-wordedly*"—great mystery of godliness, Christ Jesus (3:16), the audience hear a heightened, twofold rhetorical contrast between Timothy and the false teachers here in the A' unit.[168] On the one hand, the false teachers directly oppose the words of Jesus Christ (see *italics*): whereas "someone teaches-*different* and does not come-toward the sound words (λόγοις) of our Lord Jesus Christ" (6:3), Timothy "confessed (ὡμολόγησας)"—"*same-worded*"—the commendable "confession" (ὁμολογίαν)—"*same-word*"—regarding the "commendably" (ὁμολογουμένως)—"*same-wordedly*"—great mystery of godliness, namely everything pertaining to the person of Christ Jesus (3:16). On the other hand, the false teachers subscribe to some-thing *different* than the teaching of Jesus Christ's *same* words (see *italics*): whereas "someone teaches-*different* (ἑτεροδιδασκαλεῖ) and does not come-toward the sound words of our Lord Jesus Christ and the teaching" (6:3), Timothy "confessed (ὡμολόγησας) the commendable confession (ὁμολογίαν) regarding the "commendably" (ὁμολογουμένως) great mystery of godliness, Christ Jesus (3:16). Significantly, it is precisely for this reason that Paul, Timothy, and the faithful in the audience—unlike "some"—share the *same* relationship with Christ Jesus—"*our* Lord" (1:2, 12, 14; 6:3). It is for this reason that Paul, Timothy, and the faithful in the audience—unlike "some"—come-toward "the sound words of our Lord Jesus Christ and the teaching that is according to godliness" (6:3), that is, "the sound teaching, according to the gospel of the glory of the blessed God" (1:10b–11).

Still, as in 3:16, not only do the audience hear a sustained polemical contrast between Timothy and the false teachers, but they also hear the missional impetus of the letter advanced forward as a call for restoration, an invitation for the false teachers themselves to take-possession of eternal life (6:12a) by joining Timothy and God's household. That is, by highlighting the homogeneous agreement of the church and Timothy—"confessedly" (3:16); "confessed . . . confession" (6:12a)—Paul is summoning the false teachers to join him, Timothy, and the faithful among to audience in the *same*—not *different*—words concerning Jesus Christ. It is through the back-to-back rhetorical force of "confessed . . . confession" here in 6:12a that Paul intends for "some" to share the *same* relationship with Jesus Christ—"*our* Lord" (1:2, 12, 14; 6:3)—and thus "take-possession of eternal life (6:12a), that is, to experience the "great gain" of godliness (6:6) by exclaiming the "confessedly great" mystery of godliness (3:16). In short, the weightiness of

---

168. The linguistic contrast between the use of the prefix "same" (ὅμοιος) and "different" (ἕτερος) would be apparent.

Paul's statement is clear: not only Timothy's salvation but the salvation of others—particularly "some"—is tethered to the *confessedly* great *confession* that is *confessed* by those "in faith."

1 Timothy 6:12b: In the Sight of Many Testifiers

("b" sub-element)

In the "b" sub-element, Paul specifies that Timothy confessed the commendable confession "in the sight of many testifiers" (6:12b). The term "testifiers" (μαρτύρων) would convey both a subjective and objective sense and recalls its prior cognates throughout the macrochiasm: Paul stated "I testify" (διαμαρτύρομαι) in regard to Timothy's leadership without prejudice (5:21); only upon two or three "testifiers" (μαρτύρων) may an accusation be accepted (5:19); a godly widow is "testified" (μαρτυρουμένη) in commendable works (5:10); a qualified overseer has a commendable "testimony" (μαρτυρίαν) from those-outside (3:7); and Christ Jesus gave himself as a ransom on behalf of all, the "testimony" (μαρτύριον) in his own times (2:6). In each occurrence, the person was subjectively proven by his or her own actions and was objectively proven by others. Here in 6:12b, then, not only do the "testifiers" subjectively prove by their actions that Timothy "confessed the commendable confession" (6:12a) but Paul is objectively proving it as fact. The rhetorical effect is straightforward, the sense being: "You all know, heard, and saw Timothy's faithfulness to Jesus Christ!"

Still, where Paul's use of "testifiers" had a human audience in view, its combination with the preposition "in the sight of" (ἐνώπιον) may provide a further nuance. In the previous microchiasm, Paul declared "I testify in the sight (ἐνώπιον) of God and of Christ Jesus and of the elect angels" (5:21)—a divine, heavenly assembly comprised God, the mediator of God and humans Christ Jesus, and non-human angels. At the very least, the audience would likely understand that Timothy's confession about Jesus Christ "in the sight of many testifiers" (5:12b) has a final, eschatological significance. Where "testifiers" also has God, Christ Jesus, and the elect angels in view (5:21), the audience are reminded that—regarding Timothy's confession—it is only and ultimately the proof provided by God, Christ Jesus, and the elect angels in the heavenly courtroom that matters.

Furthermore and providing balance between the audience's understanding of the divine and human "testifiers," the preposition "in the sight" (ἐνώπιον) here in 6:12b recalls both divine and human audiences. On the one hand, missional prayer and godliness are commendable and pleasing "in the sight" (ἐνώπιον) of God (2:1–3); children learning to be godly to their own household is pleasing "in the sight" (ἐνώπιον) of God (5:4); Paul testified "in the sight" (ἐνώπιον) of God (5:21). On the other hand, Paul clearly commanded Timothy to reprove those who sin "in the sight" (ἐνώπιον) of all—the entire Ephesian audience—so that the rest might hold fear (5:20). That both divine and human audiences are in view here in 6:12b would likely emphasize the thrust of the "a" sub-element, namely the integrated juxtaposition of divine sovereignty and human responsibility (6:12a). In sum, where both are in view, Paul is clearly referring to an actual historical event in Timothy's present life that has eternal ramifications for the inevitable-coming life.[169]

The inclusion of the adjective "many" (πολλῶν) in 6:12b recalls the "many" (πολλάς) without-sense and harmful longings of the false teachers in 6:9b. Here, then, a twofold nuance would be heard. On the one hand, Paul is highlighting the stark contrast between the end result of Timothy's confession regarding Jesus Christ in the sight of "many" testifiers (6:12b)—namely, eternal life (6:12a)—over and against the result of the false teachers's affection-of-money—namely, "many" harmful longings that plunge them into ruin and destruction (6:9–10a). On the other hand, Paul is underscoring the gravity of Timothy's confession in regard to the Ephesian congregation. That is, Timothy's continued faithfulness to his confession—or lack of—will have edifying—or catastrophic—ripple effects upon the audience. As much as the false-teaching overseers in Ephesus have threatened God's missional household—their own salvation and the salvation of others—with the influence of their leadership positions, Timothy must be reminded of the consequences of his own leadership position. Indeed, Timothy must "flee these; but pursue justice, godliness, faith, love, steadfastness, gentleness" (6:11); he must "Agonize the commendable agony of the faith" and "take-possession of the eternal life" (6:12a). For doing this, Timothy will save himself and those who hear him (4:16).

In sum, the repeated use of the preposition "in the sight" reflects the reality that Timothy—and the audience—are part of a unified whole: family members in God's household. Even as "some" can have a ruinous impact on such a family, Paul is quick to highlight the salvific impact that even one faithful leader may have upon God's family. To be sure, though

---

169. It is impossible to state with certainty whether Paul is referring to the historical event of Timothy's conversion, or perhaps to his appointment as a church leader; see discussion in Knight, *PE*, 264–65, who suggests that ordination is in view. Rather, where the apostle Paul does not seem concerned to provide such detail—the audience perhaps already aware—he is relating God's "ahistorical" (or "trans-historical") sovereign calling with Timothy's historical human confession.

radically personal in one sense, Paul is clear that coming to have-faith upon Christ Jesus (1:16) and confessing the confessedly great, commendable confession about the Lord Jesus Christ (3:16; 6:12a) is by nature always communal—shared, lived, experienced, and upheld with God's very own family—and, therefore, is to be pursued in the sight of both an earthly and heavenly audience.

1 Timothy 6:13a: I Charge in the Sight of God and of Christ Jesus

("b'" sub-element)

In the "b'" sub-element, Paul continues: "I charge, in the sight of God who provides-life to all-things and of Christ Jesus who testified before Pontius Pilate" (6:13a).[170] Notably, Paul's statement includes both a divine and human audience, effectively sustaining the inseparable aspects of divine sovereignty and human responsibility as well as a juxtaposition between the present life and the inevitable-coming life. The inclusion of both divine and human aspects gives further weight to Timothy's need for *the* "human of God"—the mediator Christ Jesus (2:5)—who perfectly pursued justice, godliness, faith, love, steadfastness, and gentleness (6:11). Still, the onus is placed on Timothy—and the faithful in the audience—to act as a "human of God," that is, to agonize for and maintain his faith upon Christ Jesus (6:12a) even as "some" plunge themselves into ruin and destruction (6:9b).

The verb "I charge" (παραγγέλλω) recalls its prior occurrences and cognates throughout the macrochiasm. In the parallel A unit, Paul exhorted Timothy to remain in Ephesus that he might "charge" (παραγγείλῃς) "some" not to teach-different (1:3); such was the same "charge" (παραγγελίας) that intended love as the end goal (1:5) and the "charge" (παραγγελίαν) that Paul entrusted to Timothy (1:18). In the C' unit, Paul commanded Timothy to "Charge" (παράγγελλε) the things concerning the all-profitability of godliness, the promise thereof, and God's inclusive offer of salvation to all humans (4:10–11), and in the B' unit, Paul commanded Timothy to "charge" (παράγγελλε) the ungodly children or those-from-parents to provide for those of their own biological household and the household-members of

---

170. The textual variant (see *italics*) "I charge *you* (σοι) . . ." is not included in my translation; rather, Paul's specification of the second person pronoun occurs in 6:14 and picks up Paul's charge in 6:13; hence, "I charge, in the sight of God . . . you to keep the commandment spotless . . ." (6:13–14).

God's own household (5:7–8; cf. 5:4).[171] In all these instances, Timothy was commanded to "charge" the false teachers (1:3, 18; 4:11) or those who have been influenced by them (5:7).[172] Here, then, the rhetorical switch would be apparent: Paul is now charging Timothy. Consistent with its other occurrences in the letter, Paul's statement "I charge" would emphasize that authority is in view. Thus, while Paul has entrusted the "charge" to Timothy as his authorized representative in Ephesus (1:18), Paul is reminding Timothy—and the entire audience—that all family members in God's household are under authority—including Paul, who is under the authority of Christ Jesus and God (1:1). More importantly, where "charge" underscored the importance of the content thereof—namely, stopping and correcting the false teachers and those associated with them (1:3, 18; 4:11; 5:7)—here the content of Paul's declaration "I charge" in 4:13a is connected and concerned with the immediately preceding context, that is, "the commendable confession" that Timothy "confessed . . . in the sight of many testifiers" (4:12). In short, rather than a remedial function to correct Timothy's actions—as with the false teachers—Paul's authoritative statement to Timothy in 6:13a is intended to amplify the weightiness of his calling as a leader in Ephesus. Paul's statement "I charge" would, therefore, reiterate and re-emphasize everything in 6:11–12, namely to pursue and agonize to maintain a lifestyle that corresponds with his confession about Jesus Christ—particularly in view of the ruinous and destructive influence of the false teachers.

Moreover, the import of Timothy's steadfastness is further underscored by the explicit movement of the minichiasm: Timothy and the audience are not only to maintain their faith "in the sight (ἐνώπιον) of many testifiers"—perhaps including God, Christ Jesus, and the elect angels (5:21)—but they are—beyond any doubt—to maintain their faith "in the sight (ἐνώπιον) of God . . . and of Christ Jesus" (6:13a). In other words, what Paul implied earlier in 6:12 is now made unambiguous: ultimately, it is one's confession "in the sight of God . . . and of Christ Jesus" that matters (6:13a).[173] Notably, however, the audience hear a clear difference between the content of

---

171. That the "children or those-from-parents" (5:4) are the intended recipients of Timothy's "Charge" in 5:7, see discussion in chapter 2.

172. That Timothy's "Charge" to the children or those-from-parents in 5:7 (cf. 5:4) seems to have the false teachers in view, see discussion in chapter 2.

173. Similarly, see Paul's statements in 1 Corinthians 4:3–5 (*ESV*): "But with me it is a very small thing that I should be judged by you or by any human court. In fact, I do not even judge myself. I am not aware of anything against myself, but I am not thereby acquitted. It is the Lord who judges me. Therefore do not pronounce judgment before the time, before the Lord comes, who will bring to light the things now hidden in darkness and will disclose the purposes of the heart. Then each one will receive his commendation from God."

what Paul is presenting "in the sight" of God and Christ Jesus in 5:21 of the previous microchiasm versus 6:13a of the current microchiasm. Whereas Paul's statement "I testify in the sight of God and of Christ Jesus and of the elect angels" (5:21) is concerned with Timothy's vocational calling as a leader in the church, Paul's statement "I charge you in the sight of God ... and of Christ Jesus" (6:13a) is concerned with Timothy's personal faith upon Christ and his ongoing confession thereof. In other words, because God and Christ Jesus will impartially judge each human in the heavenly court for their actions (5:21, 24), judgment will be impartially bleak for all humans except by their coming to have-faith upon the "human of God" (6:11)—the mediator of God and humans, Christ Jesus (2:5)—who gave himself as a ransom on behalf of all (2:6)—effectively paying the price for the just judgment of God from the lawful use of the commendable law (1:8). Indeed, Christ's activity demonstrated the beyond-abundance of his grace and mercy for sinners—even the worst of sinners like Paul (1:14-16)—so that the salvific blessings of grace, mercy, and peace could be received "in faith" from God the Father and Christ Jesus the Lord (1:2). In short, as much as the pairing of "God" (θεοῦ) and "Christ Jesus" (Χριστοῦ Ἰησοῦ) points to judgment (5:21; 6:13a), their colloborative pairing simultaneously and emphatically points to salvation (1:1, 2; 2:3-6). All those who remain "in faith" are called to continue the confessedly great confession that they confessed (3:16; 6:12a); for them, the "one God (θεός)" and the "one mediator of God and humans, the human Christ Jesus (Χριστὸς Ἰησοῦς)" (2:5) continue to remain very personal and close to their heart as "God (θεοῦ) *our* Savior and Christ Jesus (Χριστοῦ Ἰησοῦ) *our* hope" (1:1). By remaining steadfast, it is in the sight of this "God" of salvation and this "Christ Jesus" of hope that Paul charges Timothy (6:13a).

The phrase "God (θεοῦ) who provides-life to all-things (πάντα)" in 6:13a echoes both "our Savior God (θεοῦ), who desires all (πάντας) humans to be-saved" in 2:3-4 and "the living God (θεῷ), who is the Savior of all (πάντων) humans" in 4:10. Here, then, the audience likely understand that Paul is again reiterating God's indiscriminate, missional, salvific disposition toward "all."[174] The intended association between God and salvation is corroborated for the audience by the term "provides-life" (ζῳογονοῦντος), which recalls its cognates throughout the macrochiasm in regard to "life (ζωήν) eternal" (1:16), the "living (ζῶντος) God" (3:15), the "living (ζῶντι) God" (4:10), and the "eternal life (ζωῆς)" (6:11).[175] Thus where God

---

174. Knight, *PE*, 265: "'all things,' τὰ πάντα, used here of 'humankind and everything else that possesses life" (BAGD s.v. 2bβ; cf. Acts 17:25)."

175. In view of the current minichiasm, the cognate repetitions of "eternal life (ζωῆς)" in 6:12a of the "a" sub-element and "provides-life" (ζῳογονοῦντος) in 6:13a

"provides-life" (ζῳογονοῦντος, 6:13a), the sense is not merely "life (ζωῆς) for the present" but also "for the inevitable-coming" (4:8b). It is in this way that Timothy must take-possession of—and continue to pursue—the "eternal life" to which he was already "called" by God (6:12a); such is to agonize the commendable agony of the faith (6:12a).

Moreover, where the sustained perspective of the entire macrochiasm—particularly here in the climactic sixth and final microchiasm (6:6–8, 11–13a)—has held eternal life in view, Paul's statement "in the sight of God who provides-life" in combination with "Christ Jesus" would be heard with significant import. "Christ Jesus" is the one upon whom people come to have-faith for life eternal (1:16) because he himself "was declared-just in Spirit," "was taken-up in glory" (3:16), and currently presides as both a judge with God in the heavenly court (5:21) and a familial mediator of God and humans, namely for those who are "in faith that is in Christ Jesus," that is, in God's household (1:2, 4; 2:5; 3:13). To be sure, Paul is underscoring that where God "provides-life" to all-things—particularly to humans—such is tangibly demonstrated by the human Christ Jesus (2:5) who was provided-life after he gave himself (2:6; 3:16) and is now—literally—living in heaven (3:16; 5:21).[176] Clearly, Paul's thoughts, speech, and actions are rooted, lifted, and formulated by the reality "of God who provides-life to all-things and of Christ Jesus" (6:13a), and he expects Timothy and the audience—those literally living "in Christ Jesus" (3:13)—to do the same. Thus, as much as Paul's statement is made "in the sight of God . . . and Christ Jesus" (6:13a), it is clear that Paul has God and Christ Jesus in his own sight. Such is the perspective in which Timothy and the audience are to heed Paul's "charge."

Still, the phrase "God who provides-life to all-things" (6:13a) would also be heard in view of the sobering statement "for we brought-in nothing into the world, that to bring-out some-thing we do-not have-the-power" (6:7). In the context of humanity's inherent finitude and weakness in the present life, a perspective in view of the inevitable-coming life that the infinite and powerful God provides (6:13a) would be all the more exigent. Here, too, the contrasted perspective of the false teachers in the sixth microchiasm would be drawn out. The false teachers have no roots in the current,

---

of the "b" sub-element both strengthens the minichiasm's cogency and maintains its movement.

It may be worth noting the conceptual similarity to Genesis 1–2, wherein God functionally provides-life to all-things. For linguistic similarities regarding "all" and "life," see LXX Genesis 1:30; 2:7. Lau, *Manifest in Flesh*, 232: "The first formulaic statement about God, 'the One who gives life to all' . . . affirms the biblical belief in God as the Creator and the Preserver of all creation (cf. 1T4.4)."

176. The integrated collaboration of God and Christ Jesus to provide eternal life for humans conveys a high Christology.

heavenly reality of Christ Jesus but rather are living entirely with their roots in things that are antithetical to God—things to which God neither provides-life nor things that are able provide-life: financial gain (6:5), riches (6:9a), money (6:10a). Whereas only God provides-life (6:13a), that is, life eternal by coming to have-faith upon Christ Jesus (1:16), the false teachers have, in effect, come to have-faith upon financial gain, riches, and money for their ultimate security—all of which cannot be brought-out. Given the missional thrust of the letter, Paul is inviting "some" to consider what really matters in life and who is able to provide it.

The final clause in the "b" sub-element regarding "Christ Jesus who testified before Pontius Pilate" (6:13a) further qualifies Paul's charge to Timothy. The phrase "God who provides-life" drew attention to the weakness and inability of humans to earn or provide life for themselves; for this reason, the phrase's combination with "Christ Jesus" highlighted the collaborative way in which God and Christ Jesus together provide eternal life for humans. However, the divine participation of "Christ Jesus" with "God who provides-life" is specifically depicted here in the final clause in terms of his humanity. The phrase "Christ Jesus who testified before Pontius Pilate" carries forward and progresses the christological significance heard throughout the macrochiasm: the preexistent person of Christ Jesus literally "came into the world" (1:15); he was visibly manifested in flesh (3:16); as a human, he visibly gave himself as a ransom on behalf of all (2:5–6), and here, Christ Jesus—the human of God (6:11)—visibly testified as a human "before" (ἐπί) the human Pontius Pilate (6:13a).[177] Indeed, as the "one mediator of God and humans," Paul is underscoring that "the human Christ Jesus" not only has the unique capacity to bridge the gap between God—the without-perishability King of the eternities (1:17)—and finite, perishable humans (6:7) but also has the complete, unhindered ability to empathize with the weaknesses of humanity.[178]

This unique ability on the part of Christ, which is meant to encourage Timothy and the audience as they agonize the commendable agony of the faith (4:12a), is borne out by the descriptor "who testified before Pontius Pilate." The statement would be particularly striking for the audience due to the way it stands in stark contrast to Paul's previous statement regarding "God who provides-life to all-things." The former underscored ineffable power and divinity; the latter weakness and humanity. To be sure, the rhetorical juxtaposition in 6:13a between the divine activity of Christ Jesus

---

177. Knight, *PE*, 265: "ἐπί more likely means 'before' here rather than 'in the time of' . . . since the former fits that actual historical occasion with its direct and personal dimension." See Marshall, *PE*, 663.

178. For further comments, see Towner, "Christology in the Letters," 219–44.

with God to provide-life and the simultaneous human activity of Christ Jesus with Pontius Pilate to testify in a human court would be full-orbed and emphatic. Thus, as much as Paul encourages Timothy and the audience to take-possession of eternal life from the perspective of Christ Jesus "in glory" with God (3:16; 6:13a), he is simultaneously encouraging them from the perspective of Christ "in flesh" with other humans (3:16; 6:13a).

Although it is possible that Paul is simply using rhetorical terminology to arrange and advance the current minichiasm, Paul's language here seems to convey familiarity with the tradition preserved in John 18:37: "Then Pilate (Πιλᾶτος) said to him, 'So you are a king?' Jesus answered, 'You say that I am a king. For this I was born and for this I have come into the world to testify (μαρτυρήσω) to the truth.'"[179] Given this connection, the content about which Christ Jesus "testified" was certainly in regard to himself. Indeed, both Pilate's objective proof concerning Jesus—"Pilate said to him, 'So you are a king?' Jesus answered, 'You say that I am a king'" (John 18:37)[180]—and Jesus's own subjective proof concerning himself—"For this I was born and for this I have come into the world to testify to the truth'" (John 18:37)—are in view. Notably, with regard to John 18:37, the subjective proof to which Jesus "testified" (6:13a) is exactly the same objective proof to which Paul testified (2:7), namely that Christ Jesus "came into the world" (1:15).[181]

It is likely that Paul's word order for the name "Christ Jesus" here in 6:13a was intentional. Just as the audience heard Paul's sudden switch from the consistent use of "Christ Jesus" (1:1, 2, 12, 14, 15, 16; 2:5; 3:13; 4:6; 5:21) to "Jesus Christ" in the opening statement of the current microchiasm (6:3), so too would Paul's sudden switch back to "Christ Jesus" in 6:13a be equally apparent. In the case that the word order of "Christ Jesus" functions to

---

179. See also Mark 15:2; Matt 27:11.
Most scholars date the composition of John's Gospel to the late first-century, undoubtedly after the composition of 1 Timothy in the mid-sixties (see Carson and Moo, *Introduction*, 264–67, 571–72, respectively). However, Paul's apparent allusion to the contents of John's Gospel—at the very least—indicates that the aural tradition recorded in John's Gospel was known by Paul and the Ephesian church that he established.

180. See also John 18:39 ("So do you want me to release to you the King of the Jews?" *ESV*); John 19:14 ("He said to the Jews, 'Behold your King!'" *ESV*); John 19:15 ("Shall I crucify your King?" *ESV*); John 19:19 ("Pilate also wrote an inscription and put it on the cross. It read, 'Jesus of Nazareth, the King of the Jews.'" *ESV*).

181. The linguistic similarity would be apparent:
John 18:37: "I have come into the world" (ἐλήλυθα εἰς τὸν κόσμον);
1 Tim 1:15: "Christ Jesus came into the world" (Χριστὸς Ἰησοῦς ἦλθεν εἰς τὸν κόσμον).
Such would strengthen the notion that Paul's language in 1 Timothy 6:13a demonstrates an intentional allusion to and awareness of the tradition recorded in John 18:37.

describe *Christ* with regard Jesus's saving activity, Paul seems to be underscoring how Christ Jesus (Χριστοῦ Ἰησοῦ) in flesh as a human who testified before "Pontius Pilate" (Ποντίου Πιλάτου) is significant for why he came into the world (1:15; John 18:37): it was Pilate who "gave-over" (παρέδωκεν) Jesus to be crucified (John 19:16), and thereby Christ Jesus gave (δούς) himself as a ransom on behalf of all (2:6).[182] Thus where Christ's ransom was specifically "the testimony" (τὸ μαρτύριον) to which Paul alludes in 2:6, it is clear that Christ Jesus "who testified" (μαρτυρήσαντος) before Pontius Pilate was speaking not only of his identity—King—but his purpose—salvation.

The participle "who testified" would also have rhetorical significance, both for the current minichiasm and the overall macrochiasm. In regard to the minichiasm, the participle "who testified" (μαρτυρήσαντος) in 6:13a of the "b'" sub-element recalls the immediately preceding cognate noun "testifiers" (μαρτύρων) in 6:12b of the parallel "b" sub-element. In effect, the parallelism between the "b" and "b'" sub-elements emphatically widens—and specifies—the scope of the "many testifiers" in the sight of whom Timothy must continue to prove his faithfulness. That is, Timothy must not only keep in mind that his life is observable in full view of many human testifiers—the Ephesian audience (6:12b)—but also in full view of *the* Testifier—Christ Jesus (6:13a)—who now presides with God to bear witness to Timothy's faithfulness. Where the human Christ Jesus can fully empathize and understand Timothy's struggles, emotions, and fatigue (2:5; 5:13a), Timothy is to find comfort as he agonizes the commendable agony of the faith (6:11) before the audience of many and, ultimately, before the audience of One.

In regard to the macrochiasm, the audience would hear the participle "who testified" with a framing effect. Early in the macrochiasm—the B unit—Paul introduced "the testimony" (τὸ μαρτύριον), which was defined entirely by the person and work of Christ Jesus (2:5–6). Here in the concluding, climactic A' unit of the macrochiasm, Paul specifies that Christ Jesus is the one "who

---

182. The cognates "gave-over" (παρέδωκενα, John 19:16) and "gave" (δούς, 1 Tim 2:6) highlight both aspects of salvation: Pilate's sinful act to not pursue righteousness and Christ's sacrificial act to pay the price thereof. See also John 19:11 wherein Jesus alludes to the sin of Judas who "gave-over" (παραδούς) Jesus to Pontius Pilate. Regarding the inseparability of divine sovereignty and human responsibility, see John 19:10 wherein Jesus identifies that Pilate's authority "had been given" (δεδομένον) from above, that is, by God.

It may be worth noting the rhetorical significance regarding Paul's coupling of "Christ Jesus" and "Pontius Pilate" in 6:13a. Knight, *PE*, 265: "Only here [6:13a] and in Lk. 3:1 is he designated by the nomen Πόντιος, the 'middle, gentile, or tribal name' of Pilate (BAGD)." Where Paul may be drawing attention to the full name of "Pontius Pilate"—emphasizing the humanness of *Pontius* with regard to Pilot's sinful activity—the full designation order of "Christ Jesus"—emphazing *Christ* with regard to Jesus's saving activity—seems deliberate and corresponding.

testified" (μαρτυρήσαντος) about himself and his work of salvation (6:13a). The overarching implication is that the introduction of "the testimony" (2:6) and the conclusion of its cognate "who testified" (6:13a) are both encapsulated by "Christ Jesus." Significantly, then, Paul's use of the cognate terms in between this framework would now be fully understood in view of Christ Jesus. It is now apparent why those who are "in Christ Jesus" (1:14; 3:13) would agonize to hold a commendable "testimony" (μαρτυρίαν) from those-outside (3:7), to be "testified" (μαρτυρουμένη) in commendable works (5:10a), to lawfully not accept an accusation against an elder except upon two or three "testifiers" (μαρτύρων, 5:19), and to remain integrous to the commendable confession that they confessed in the sight of many "testifiers" (μαρτύρων, 6:12). In short, where Christ Jesus provides the rhetorical framework for all testimonies in the letter, Paul's point is that all Christian testimony must extol and exhibit Christ's very own testimony. Indeed, such is an expression of agreement with the sound words and the teaching of the Lord Jesus Christ, which promotes godliness as God's missional household.

1 Timothy 6:13b–14: Christ's Confession, Irreproachable, the Manifesting of Christ

("a'" sub-element)

In the concluding "a'" sub-element of the 6:12–14 minichiasm, Paul begins with a further specification of that which Christ Jesus testified before Pontius Pilate: "the commendable confession" (6:13b). The phrase "commendable confession" (καλὴν ὁμολογίαν) in 6:13b of the "a'" sub-element recalls its exact occurrence in 6:12a of the "a" sub-element regarding the "commendable confession" (καλὴν ὁμολογίαν) that Timothy confessed. Significantly, where the commendable "confession" (ὁμολογίαν) that Timothy "confessed" (ὡμολόγησας) in 6:12a was defined by the "confessedly" (ὁμολογουμένως) great mystery of godliness concerning Christ Jesus (3:16), the content of the "confession" (ὁμολογίαν) that Christ Jesus testified before Pontius Pilate in 6:13a is corroborated, namely himself—that he was manifested in flesh and would be taken-up in glory.[183]

---

183. Similarly, Lau, *Manifest in Flesh*, 233: "The deliberate parallel of τὴν καλὴν ὁμολογίαν in 6.12 and 6.13 shows that what Timothy had confessed, Jesus himself had attested by his death and resurrection."
   That Jesus's commendable confession includes his manifestation in flesh, see John 18:37: "For this purpose I was born and for this purpose I have come into the world" (*ESV*). That Jesus's commendable confession includes being taken-up in glory, see John 18:36: "My kingdom is not of this world. If my kingdom were of this world, my servants

Furthermore, as in 6:12a of the "a" sub-element, Paul's polemic against the false teachers would be advanced here in 6:13b of the parallel "a'" sub-element with far greater rhetorical force. That is, rather than pitting Timothy, Paul, and the church's "confessedly" (ὁμολογουμένως, 3:16)—"same-word-edly"—shared "confession" (ὁμολογίαν, 6:12a)—"same-word"—regarding "the sound words (λόγοις) of our Lord Jesus Christ" (6:3) over and against "someone" who "does not come-toward the sound words of our Lord Jesus Christ (6:3), here in the concluding "a'" sub-element of the minichiasm Paul is directly pitting the "confession" (ὁμολογίαν)—"same-word"—of Christ Jesus himself (6:13b) over and against the false teachers who do not agree with his very own sound words (6:3).[184] To be sure, the implication would be climactically striking: not only do Timothy, Paul, and the church all agree with, come-toward, and share the "*same*-words" as Christ Jesus himself (3:16; 6:12a, 13b), but the false teachers explicitly subscribe to some-thing entirely "*different*" (ἕτερον, 1:10; cf. 1:3; 6:3) than the unified confession of Timothy, Paul, the church, and Christ Jesus.[185] Thus, here in the A' unit of the macrochiasm—the climactic conclusion toward which all prior microchiasms have been cumulatively building and progressing—both the underlying situation of the false teachers and the overarching focus on the teaching that promotes godliness as part of God's missional household are simultaneously and concretely experienced by the audience: the false teachers who stand decidedly against Jesus Christ, his apostle Paul, Paul's entrusted representative Timothy, and the entire household of God are being summoned, invited, and welcomed to join Jesus Christ, Paul, Timothy, and God's very own household in a unified, shared existence "in faith" where everyone agrees to the "same-words" and will live eternally together with their author, source, and speaker—the Lord Jesus Christ—fully "in glory."

---

would have been fighting, that I might not be delivered over to the Jews. But my kingdom is not from the world" (*ESV*). The latter assumes being taken-up from this world and into another—the place of his kingdom. Cf. Knight, *PE*, 266: "Christ's 'good confession' was his affirmative answer to Pilate's question 'Are you the king of the Jews?'"

184. The verb, noun, and adverb "confessed" (ὡμολόγησας), "confession" (ὁμολογίαν), and "confessedly" (ὁμολογουμένως) are comprised of the terms "same" (ὅμοιος) and the root noun "word" (λόγος).
In view of John 18:37, the fact that "someone"—the false teachers—"does not come-toward the sound words" of Jesus Christ (6:3) would be especially forceful, given that Jesus himself says, "Everyone who is of the truth listens to my voice" (*ESV*).

185. The rhetorical contrast between the use of the prefixes "same" (ὅμοιος) and "different" (ἕτερος) would be apparent—the former has been exclusively associated with Paul and the church (3:16), Timothy (6:12a), and Christ Jesus (6:13a); the latter has been exclusively associated with "some" and "someone" (1:3, 10b; 6:3).

Significantly also, where the connection between Timothy's "confession" in 6:12a of the "a" sub-element—to be sure, the same as Paul and the church's (3:16)—and Christ Jesus's "confession" in 6:13b of the parallel "a'" sub-element is explicitly made, Paul's preceding commands for Timothy to "pursue justice, godliness, faith, love, steadfastness, gentleness" (6:11), to "Agonize the commendable agony of the faith" (6:12a), and to "take-possession of the eternal life" to which he was called (6:12a) are all to find their derivation and destination in the person and work of Christ Jesus. It was Christ's "commendable confession" before Pontius Pilate that ultimately led to his gruesome, excruciating death. Thus Timothy's encouraging connection to Christ Jesus—the divine collaborator with God who provides-life eternal (1:16; 6:13a); the human who fully identifies and empathizes with all humans (2:5; 6:13a)—is equally marked by a sobering note. The parallelism between Timothy's "commendable confession" (6:12a) and Christ Jesus's "commendable confession" (6:13b) is a weighty reminder that all humans who unite themselves to Christ by faith—"in faith that is in Christ Jesus" (3:13)—must follow the path of the cross prior to being taken-up "in glory" (3:16); it is the "commendable agony" (6:12a) that accompanies the "commendable confession" (6:13a, 13b). In short, Paul's commands in 6:11–12 to pursue, agonize, and take-possession of the eternal life that is commensurate with the "commendable confession" (6:12, 13b) is a call to remain faithful to Christ Jesus even to the point of death—a call that finds both its ultimate expression and inspiration in Jesus's own faithfulness on the road to eternal glory on behalf of all (2:6).

What is more, for the faithful in Ephesus who are united to Christ Jesus by their faith upon him (1:16) and thus exist "in Christ Jesus" (3:13), the audience understand here in the climactic, concluding A' unit that Christ Jesus is the sole root from which all of their "commendable" efforts throughout the macrochiasm grow and derive. It is because of Christ Jesus's "commendable" (καλήν) confession (6:13b) that they know the law is "commendable" (καλὸς, 1:8), that they war the "commendable" (καλήν) war with faith and a good conscience against divisive teachings (1:18–19), that they do what is "commendable" (καλόν) in the sight of the Savior God (2:3), that qualified men long-for the "commendable" (καλοῦ) work of an overseer (3:1) and lead their own household "commendably" (καλῶς, 3:4) and have a "commendable" (καλήν) testimony from those-outside the church (3:7), that qualified deacons are leading children "commendably" (καλῶς, 3:12) and "commendably" (καλῶς) acquire for themselves a "commendable" (καλόν) standing in Christ Jesus (3:13), that the faithful view all creation of God as "commendable" (καλόν, 4:4), that Timothy will be a "commendable" (καλός) deacon of Christ Jesus by correctly instructing the brothers and by being-nourished in the "commendable" (καλῆς) teaching that he has followed (4:6), that godly widows would be testified in "commendable" (καλοῖς) works (5:10a), that elders who toil in word and teaching—overseers—would lead "commendably" (καλῶς, 5:17), that the faithful would agonize the "commendable" (καλόν) agony of the faith (6:11)—all of which being an expression of the "commendable" (καλήν) confession that they confessed regarding Christ Jesus (6:12a). Here in the concluding A' unit of the macrochiasm, the full implication of the Christian life is highly upheld for the entire audience to ponder: their lives are to reflect, showcase, and exhibit Christ Jesus, the one in whom they exist "in faith" (3:13; cf. 1:14).

In verse 6:14, Paul both brings the "a'" sub-element and current minichiasm to a conclusion and completes Paul's charge to Timothy that was initiated in 6:12 of the "b" sub-element: "you to keep the commandment spotless, irreproachable until the manifesting of our Lord Jesus Christ."[186] The verb "to keep" (τηρῆσαί) recalls its occurrence in 5:22 wherein Timothy was to "keep (τήρει) yourself pure." Thus the explicit connotation of Timothy's call to be a protector and guardian would carry forward.[187] Significantly, as much as Timothy is to be the protector and guardian of himself—his own purity (5:22)—so also must he be the same for "the commandment" in 6:14. In effect, Timothy is to view "the commandment" as an extension of himself, which must be kept pure, that is, protected from the devastating impact of the false teachers.[188] Indeed, such would be corroborated by Paul's rhetorical use of the pronoun "you" (σε), which both reiterates that Timothy must "keep yourself (σεαυτόν) pure" (5:22) and emphasizes that he is to do so equally for "the commandment" (6:14).[189] Given that "the commandment" in 6:14 follows the natural progression of Paul's statement, namely the immediate context of "I charge" in 6:13, the specification of "the commandment" (τὴν ἐντολήν) would likely be heard in reference to "I charge," and thus to the main thrust of the entire letter. Negatively, then, "the commandment" would refer to Paul's charge for Timothy to stop "some" from teaching some-thing different that lies-opposed to the sound teaching

---

186. As noted regarding 6:13, Paul's inclusion of "you" (σε) here in 6:14 picks up Paul's charge to Timothy. Cf. Marshall, *PE*, 663: "The construction here is slightly complicated by the inclusion of σε, which is strictly unnecessary..."

187. Cf. Knight, *PE*, 266: "τηρῆσαι is used here... in the sense of 'keeping' or 'observing' a commandment."

188. For the polemical, nuanced implication of "pure" in 5:22 regarding the false teachers (rather than sexuality), see chapter 2.

189. Marshall notes the awkward and unnecessary inclusion of the pronoun "you" (σε) (*PE*, 663).

(1:3, 10; 6:3).[190] Positively, "the commandment" would refer to Paul's charge for Timothy to preserve the teaching and to promote godliness as God's missional houshold.[191]

Timothy's call to protect and guard the commandment is coupled with the descriptors "spotless" and "irreproachable." The term "spotless" presents the idea of being "without stain"; in this way, "spotless" not only echoes Timothy's call to "keep yourself pure" (5:22) but also strengthens the connection between himself and "the commandment" (6:14)—Timothy must keep both pure and spotless. The term "irreproachable" (ἀνεπίλημπτον) recalls its prior occurrences in the macrochiasm: Paul specified that a qualified overseer is "irreproachable" (ἀνεπίλημπτον, 3:2); Timothy's charge to the ungodly children or those-from-parents intends for them to be "irreproachable" (ἀνεπίλημπτοι, 5:7). In both 3:2 and 5:7, "irreproachable" was defined by a lifestyle of godliness pertaining to family life within their own households and thus within God's household. Significantly, then, where Timothy is to keep the commandment—the charge (1:3, 5, 18)—"irreproachable" in 6:14, the implication seems to be that he must do so through his own personal example and conduct. Indeed, such was already implied by the connection between Timothy's call to keep himself and the commandment pure and spotless (5:22; 6:14).[192] In the full context of what Paul has said so far in the sixth microchiasm (6:3-21), the charge "to keep the commandment spotless, irreproachable" would be heard as a summons for Timothy to lead the church by agreeing with the sound words of Jesus Christ, that is, the teaching that is according to godliness (6:3), thereby fleeing from an incorrect view of godliness as a means-of-gain, from wanting to be-rich, from the affection-of-money (6:5–11) and thus pursuing a lifestyle commensurate with his existence in Christ Jesus,

---

190. That "I charge" (6:13) conveys Timothy's call to stop the false teachers, see above.

191. There is much discussion in regard to the meaning of "the commandment"; see Marshall, *PE*, 663–65; Knight, *PE*, 266–68; Smith, *Pauline Communities*, 297 n. 200. See also Eubank, "Almsgiving Is 'the Commandment,'" 144–50, who in view of the Paul's sustained discussion on wealth suggests that "the commandment" in 6:14 refers to caring for the needy.

Given the context of the minichiasm in regard to John 18:37, it may be worth noting the possible allusion that Paul's statement "you to keep the commandment" in 6:14 may have conveyed to the audience, namely John 14:15: "If you love me, you will keep (τηρήσετε) my commandments (τὰς ἐντολάς)."

192. See above. Towner aptly describes the nuance with his interpretation "keep the mandate (and keep yourself) spotless and irreproachable" (*Letters*, 415). Furthermore, ibid., continues: "the latter rendering, though admittedly teased out of the ambiguous syntax, makes better sense of the initial ethical emphasis of the renewed commission (6:11), but the decision is a fine one." See also Marshall, *PE*, 665.

namely by agonizing the commendable agony of the faith, even to the point of death (6:12–13). In short, the audience understand that Timothy's personal faithfulness to Christ is inseparably tied to his vocational faithfulness as the apostle Paul's genuine child "in faith" (1:2), that is, Paul's child Timothy who was entrusted with the charge (1:18).

The phrase "until the manifesting of our Lord Jesus Christ" (6:14) would draw the audience's attention to a final, eschatological reality. The term "until" (μέχρι) indicates that which is yet to happen. Significantly, then, where "the manifesting" (τῆς ἐπιφανείας) recalls Christ Jesus who "was manifested" (ἐφανερώθη) in flesh in 3:16, Paul is underscoring the already-but-not-yet reality in which Timothy and the audience live.[193] On the one hand, Christ was *already* manifested in flesh (3:16), that is, he already came into the world (1:15), lived as a human (2:5), and gave himself as a ransom on behalf of all humans (2:6). On the other hand, where Christ was taken-up in glory (3:16), the audience understand that "the manifesting" of the human Christ Jesus in 6:14 intends brilliant imagery of his return not merely in flesh but in radiant glory—the full manifestation of the glory of the blessed God (1:11); such is *not yet*, and Timothy must protect the commandment "until" it happens—presumably until dies, if need be.[194]

Indeed, Paul's emphasis on the already-but-not-yet status in which he, Timothy, and the Ephesian church live was already heard in the prior two microchiasms. In the fourth microchiasm, Paul highlighted the overlap of two modes of existence for the faithful: the present—namely, "in flesh," on earth—and the inevitable-coming—namely, "in Spirit," in heaven (4:8b). In the fifth microchiasm, Paul upheld the *not yet* reality of final judgment, which had in view the heavenly court—the place where God and Christ Jesus currently preside as impartial judges (5:21). In other words, after the hinging, pivot point of the entire macrochiasm upon Christ Jesus in 3:16, the overall arrangement, progression, and rhetorical function of the macrochiasm to introduce a theme and advance it to a climactic conclusion is heard: while the introductory A, B, and C units drew attention to the *already*, the concluding C', B', and A' units draw attention to the *not yet*:

---

193. Paul's use of "manifesting" (ἐπιφανείας) in 6:14 would also recall that Timothy is to "manifest" (φανερά) his progress to all in 4:15.

194. To be sure, Paul is not indicating that "the manifesting" will happen while Timothy is in Ephesus or even in his lifetime. Knight, *PE*, 268: "μέχρι does not mean that Paul believes that Timothy will be alive when Christ returns. Rather, this is typical NT language of expectancy..."

A unit: "Christ Jesus came into the world to save sinners" (1:15);

    B unit: "Christ Jesus, who gave himself as a ransom on behalf of all" (2:6);

        C unit: "he was manifested in flesh . . . was taken-up in glory" (3:16);

        C' unit: "the promise of life for the present and for the inevitable-coming" (4:8b);

    B' unit: "in the sight of God and of Christ Jesus and of the elect angels" (5:21);

A' unit: "until the manifesting of our Lord Jesus Christ" (6:14).

The parallel movement across the concluding C', B', and A' units draws attention not merely to reality of what Christ Jesus already did in the world on behalf of all humans but also advances, augments, and provides the full spectrum of the reality that he inaugurated by his entrance into and activity in the world in the A, B, and C units. In short, Paul's declaration to keep the commandment "until the manifesting of our Lord Jesus Christ" is a summary reminder for the entire Ephesian audience to live according to the eschatological reality of Christ's first and second appearances.[195] To be sure, by teaching some-thing different that lies-opposed to the sound teaching of Jesus Christ and his apostle Paul (1:1, 10b; 6:3), it is precisely this elliptical eschatological reality that the false teachers do not have in view—"some" live as though Christ is not returning. Contrary to the false teachers, then, alongside and in adherence to Timothy's leadership, the audience are to keep the commandment spotless and irreproachable—to pursue godliness that results from the teaching—until the manifesting of their Lord Jesus Christ, certainly until they die, if need be.

The phrase "our Lord Jesus Christ" (τοῦ κυρίου ἡμῶν Ἰησοῦ Χριστοῦ) here in 6:14 recalls its exact occurrence in the opening statement of the sixth microchiasm (6:3), wherein Paul spoke of "someone" who teaches-different and does not come-toward the sound words of "our Lord Jesus Christ" (τοῦ κυρίου ἡμῶν Ἰησοῦ Χριστοῦ). The immediate contrast would be apparent: precisely unlike and in response to "someone" who does not agree with the Lord Jesus Christ (6:3), Timothy and the faithful among the audience are to do everything in agreement with the Lord Jesus Christ (6:11–13)—indeed, they are to keep the charge against "someone" while waiting for Christ's return (6:14). Furthermore, the sudden switch in word-order from "Christ Jesus" in 6:13 to "Jesus Christ" in 6:14 would certainly be apparent. Again,

---

195. See Gaffin, *By Faith*, 30–32; Jeon, *To Exhort and Reprove*, 77–82.

as in 6:3, rather than highlighting Jesus's saving activity, Paul would likely be upholding Jesus's kingly status as the "Christ"—a rhetorical implication again emphasized by Paul's placement of the term "Lord" *prior* to "Jesus Christ" (τοῦ κυρίου ... Ἰησοῦ Χριστοῦ, 6:3, 14) in distinction from Paul's placement of "Lord" *after* "Christ Jesus" (Χριστοῦ Ἰησοῦ τοῦ κυρίου, 1:2; Χριστῷ Ἰησοῦ τῷ κυρίῳ, 1:12). Indeed, the rhetorical shift in emphasis would draw attention to the full-orbed status that Jesus maintains: in 6:13, the sacrificial death and accomplishment of salvation by "Christ Jesus who testified before Pontius Pilate the commendable confession" was Paul's focus; subsequently, then, in 6:14 Paul's focus is that which corresponds, namely "the manifesting of our Lord Jesus Christ"—the lordship of Jesus over those whom he saved by his sacrificial death. As in 6:3, the pronoun "our" (ἡμῶν) underscores the allegiance and lordship in view: Jesus is "*our* Lord" precisely because he came to save *us* (1:15). It is the divine, missional, sacrificial love of Jesus Christ that both saved those who came to have-faith upon him (1:16) and is to comfort those who surrender themselves to him as "Lord" (1:3, 12; 6:3, 14). Again, as in 6:3, Paul's missional invitation to the false teachers not only continues but is doubly emphasized; indeed, given the explicit accumulation of ungodliness throughout the microchiasm by the false teachers who are supposing godliness—Jesus Christ (3:16)—to be a means-of-gain (6:5), Paul's statement in 6:14 would carry an appeal, the sense being, "Christ Jesus died for you (6:13); along with us, please come-toward him as your Lord (6:14; cf. 6:3)."

Still, as its occurrence in 6:3, the full combination of the terms "Lord," "our," "Jesus," and "Christ" here in 6:14 of the A' unit would draw attention to the only other place in the letter where all four terms are heard together—the parallel A unit. In effect, the double occurrences of the full phrase in both the A and A' units would underscore the unique arrangement in the macrochiasm:

> A unit: "Christ Jesus our Lord" (Χριστῷ Ἰησοῦ τῷ κυρίῳ ἡμῶν, 1:3, 12);
>
> A' unit: "our Lord Jesus Christ" (τοῦ κυρίου ἡμῶν Ἰησοῦ Χριστοῦ, 6:3, 14).

Notably, then, as much as there is an invitation to view Jesus Christ as Lord (6:14) because he died to accomplish salvation (6:13), Paul's emphasis is equally on the fact that Jesus Christ is "Lord"—the very God of the OT, the one and only God who created all things, and the person to whom allegiance is not to be disregarded.[196] Regardless, then, of whether or not "someone"

---

196. See discussion above regarding 6:3.

wants to agree with the sound words of the Lord Jesus Christ, the implication is that they should: not only will they be-saved (1:16; 2:4) but they will enter into and experience a right relationship with the person who created them. The conclusion of the current minichiasm and B element of the microchiasm is heard with a climactic emphasis upon Jesus Christ as the "Lord."

1 Timothy 6:15a: The Blessed and Only Power

(C Element)

In the C element of the sixth microchiasm, Paul qualifies the second manifestation of Jesus Christ: "which in his own times the blessed and only Power will display" (6:15a). The phrase "his own times" (καιροῖς ἰδίοις) in 6:15a recalls "his own times" (καιροῖς ἰδίοις) in 2:6, wherein Paul underscored the sovereignty of God's plan of salvation in relation to Christ—both the salvific act of Christ Jesus in history and the testimony that he gave himself as a ransom on behalf of all. In the same way, the rhetorical purpose of Paul's language here is to highlight God's sovereign governance—"his own" (ἰδίοις) plan—over all of history: history is not a random set of events but that which is providentially orchestrated by God—such is true especially with respect to the person and work of Jesus Christ.[197] To be sure, as the audience heard in the confessedly great Christ-hymn in 3:16, Paul's use of the passive voice of the verbs in relation to Christ Jesus underscored Christ's own passivity—"he was manifested . . . was declared-just . . . was taken-up in glory."[198] This highlighted the divine dynamic between "God the Father and Christ Jesus our Lord" (1:2), the latter of whom is passive relative to the former. The same dynamic holds true with respect to the second manifestation of Jesus Christ in 6:14: it will be in the time that God the Father has appointed.[199]

---

197. Lau, *Manifest in Flesh*, 227: "Each epiphanic occasion is a salvation-historical event initiated and effected by God Himself. This can be pinpointed in the phrase that modifies the ἐπιφάνεια of Christ in 1T6.15a: ἥν καιροῖς ἰδίοις δείξει . . . The stress of καιροῖς ἰδίοις is on the sovereignty of God, who will execute *His* plan of salvation in accordance to *His* predetermined purpose in redemptive history."

198. These verbs are best interpreted as divine passives; see volume 2, chapter 2 regarding 1 Timothy 3:16.

199. Knight, *PE*, 268: "Paul adds an encouragement 'which he will bring about at the proper time.' I.e., God controls and determines the moment when his Son will return as the victor and when the struggle shall be brought to an end . . . For the action of the Father in the epiphany of the Son see Acts 3:20; 1 Thes. 4:14."

Such is the implication of Jesus's own teaching: "But concerning that day or that hour, no one knows, not even the angels in heaven, nor the Son, but only the Father"

The apostle continues his emphasis on God's sovereign rule over all of history by initiating a grand doxological description in regard to the manifesting of Jesus Christ, which "the blessed and only Power will display" (6:15a). Significantly, both adjectives "blessed" and "only" here in the A unit of the macrochiasm recall their exclusive occurrences in 1:11 and 1:17 of the parallel A unit. Undoubtedly, the audience understand that Paul has *God* in view: "blessed" (μακάριος) in 6:15a of the A' unit recalls the "blessed (μακαρίου) God" in 1:11 of the parallel A unit; "only" (μόνος) in 6:15a of the A' unit recalls "only (μόνῳ) God" in 1:17 of the parallel A unit. Furthermore—and notably—Paul's use of the noun "Power" (δυνάστης) would intend a nuanced rhetorical purpose. Not only does "only Power" (6:15a) reiterate Jewish monotheism, but it establishes a parallel synonymy with "only God" (1:17)—the terms "God" and "Power" being heard as synonyms.[200] Notably, then, the audience would hear "only Power"—God—as an antithetical response to the human predicament that "we brought-in nothing into the world, that to bring-out some-thing we do-not have-the-power (δυνάμεθα)" (6:7). In short, God is both the source of "Power" and that which humans in themselves completely lack. Nevertheless, along with Paul, Timothy, and the godly widow who have "hoped upon God" (4:10; 5:5), the faithful among the audience find their comfort in the "only Power" who overcomes their powerlessness by bestowing on them the blessing of life eternal by their coming to have-faith upon Christ Jesus (1:16). Such is entirely unlike the false teachers who find their comfort in gain (6:5), riches (6:9a), and money (6:10a): being devoid of the "only Power," they plunge themselves into ruin and destruction (6:9b).

Paul punctuates God's sovereignty in the C element with the verb "will display" (δείξει). To be sure, the audience understand that God "will display" Jesus Christ's second appearance in the time that he has appointed. Here, then, while the divine dynamic between God the Father and the Lord Jesus Christ is reiterated—the latter of whom is passive relative to the former—Paul's particularly emphasis seems to be that one's salvation—the human responsibility to come to have-faith upon Christ Jesus (1:16)—depends on a strong acceptance of God's sovereignty. Still, the christological significance

---

(Mark 13:32). This, however, does not undermine the implication of Jesus Christ as "Lord," that is, as God. See discussion below regarding the terms "Power" and "will display." In passing, it may be worth noting that Jesus's teaching in Mark 13:32 does anything but undermine his divinity; rather, he explicitly affirms his identity as "the Son" (ὁ υἱός) in direct relation to "the Father" (ὁ πατήρ).

200. Towner, *Letters*, 420: "The following adjective, 'only,' echoes the Jewish (then Christian) claim of monotheism . . . as it restricts to God the states of '[sovereign] Ruler.' The title came to be used of God in Intertestamental Judaism, and it appears in 2 Macc 3:24 in connection with the term 'epiphany.'"

of Jesus Christ as Lord—that is, as equally God—would not be lost. As much as "the blessed and only Power (δυνάστης)" here in 6:15a of the A' unit identifies God, the audience would also recall Paul's explicit statement regarding "him who empowered (ἐνδυναμώσαντί) me, Christ Jesus our Lord" in 1:12 of the parallel A unit. Indeed, the same "Power" who will display the second manifesting of Jesus Christ in his own times (6:15a) is inseparable from Christ Jesus who "empowered" Paul (1:12). Given the arrangement of the macrochiasm, the audience understand that both God and Jesus Christ share and are one and the same "Power" who alone "empowered" Paul. Indeed, such was made explicit in the opening statement of the letter: Paul is an apostle of Christ Jesus according to the command of both God our Savior and Christ Jesus our hope (1:1). Thus while humans do-not "have-the-power" (δυνάμεθα) to bring-out some-thing (6:7), God *and* the human Jesus Christ—the mediator of God and humans (2:5)—together are the only "Power" (δυνάστης) for humans—indeed, the only hope (1:1) upon whom to have hope (4:10; 5:5). Furthermore, that God "will display" (δείξει) the second manifesting of Jesus Christ in his own times here in 6:14–15a of the A' unit, the audience would also recall 1:16 of the parallel A unit wherein Paul received-mercy so that "Christ Jesus might display (ἐνδείξηται) all patience as an example to those who would-inevitably-come to have-faith upon him for life eternal." Indeed, where it was Christ Jesus himself who appointed Paul for service (1:12) in order that Christ Jesus himself might "display" all patience (1:16), the audience understand that the Lord Jesus Christ is in no way isolated from that which God "will display" (6:15a). Undoubtedly, Paul's language in the A and A' units conveys an integrated, equal, and divine collaboration and outworking of salvation by God the Father *and* the Lord Jesus Christ.

1 Timothy 6:15b: The King and Lord

(D Element)

The pivot "D" element of the sixth and final microchiasm further specifies the identity of God as the blessed and only Power: "the King of those who-are-kings and Lord of those who-are-lords" (6:15b).[201] The pivotal phrase here would have a comprehensive significance for the audience. Certainly, Paul's use of OT and Intertestamental formulaic titles for God would be apparent, effectively bolstering the rhetorical force and fact of Paul's mono-

---

201. Knight, *PE*, 269: "He is also (literally) 'the King of those who reign as kings and Lord of those who rule as lords.'"

theistic assertion in the preceding C element: God is "the blessed and only Power" (6:15a) because he is "the King of those who-are-kings and Lord of those who-are-lords" (6:15b).²⁰² In this way, there would be a subversive implication: Paul is emphasizing God as "King" and "Lord" over and against any and all first-century Greco-Roman imperial claims.²⁰³ Indeed, the phrase "the King of those who-are-kings" recalls the clear contrast already heard in the A and B units: immediately prior to acknowledging and exhorting the audience to pray on behalf of "kings" (βασιλέων, 2:2) in the B unit—correspondingly, "those who-are-kings" (τῶν βασιλευόντων, 6:15b)—Paul had made clear that "only God" is "the King" (τῷ ... βασιλεῖ, 1:17) of the eternities in the A unit—correspondingly, "the King" (ὁ βασιλεύς, 6:15b). Notably, where Paul's emphasis on "the King of those who-are-kings" here in 6:15b of the A' unit recalls doxological praise to "the King of the eternities" in 1:17 of the parallel A unit, the audience not only hear the clear arrangement of the macrochiasm but also a clear progression thereof.²⁰⁴ In 1:17 of the A unit, Paul's praise to "the King" was heard with a note of ambiguity: Christ Jesus had been the immediately preceding and sustained subject of Paul's discussion (1:12–16), yet Paul's descriptors of the King—"without-perishability, without-visibility"—seemed to indicate that God the Father was in view. Here, however, in 6:15b of the parallel A' unit, it seems that God the Father is clearly in view—he is the one who "will display" the manifesting of the Lord Jesus Christ "in his own times"

---

202. Compare the Greek texts:
LXX Deuteronomy 10:17: "For the Lord your God, he *is* God of gods (θεὸς τῶν θεῶν), and the Lord of lords (κύριος τῶν κυρίων), the great, and strong, and terrible God";
LXX Psalm 84:8: "The God of gods (ὁ θεὸς τῶν θεῶν) in Zion";
LXX Psalm 136:2–3: "Give thanks to the God of gods (θεῷ τῶν θεῶν) . . . Give thanks to the Lord of lords (κυρίῳ τῶν κυρίων) . . .";
LXX Dan 4:37: "For he is God of gods and Lord of lords and King of kings" (ὅτι αὐτός ἐστι θεὸς τῶν θεῶν καὶ κύριος τῶν κυρίων καὶ βασιλεὺς τῶν βασιλέων).
Note that Nebuchadnezzar's statement in the LXX Daniel 4:37 text is not included in the Hebrew or Aramaic text and thus is not included in the English Bible; see Bowman and Komoszewski, *Putting Jesus in His Place*, 174.

203. See Beale, "The Origin of the Title," 618–20. Montague, *First and Second Tim*, 130: "It reads literally 'King of those reigning and Lord of those exercising sovereignty.' The present tense indicates those who are at the present time exercising power." Knight, *PE*, 269: "The statement in its entirety says that God is the possessor of the highest power over all who possess power and has full control over all who exercise control."

204. Regarding the parallel arrangement of doxologies in 1:17 and 6:15–16, see Keegan, *First and Second Tim*, 12; Spencer, *1 Tim*, 158.

(6:14–15a).²⁰⁵ Still, upon hearing the very next phrase—"Lord of those who-are-lords"—Paul's statement would convey a further nuance.

Paul's use of the phrase "Lord (κύριος) of those who-are-lords (κυριευόντων)" in 6:15b recalls Paul's immediately preceding reference to "our Lord (κύριου) Jesus Christ" in 6:14. Moreover, throughout the entire macrochiasm, Paul has consistently maintained that only "Christ Jesus" in the A unit (1:2, 12, 14) and only "Jesus Christ" in the parallel A' unit (6:3, 14) is "Lord." Still—and emphatically—where Jesus Christ is specifically identified as "*our* Lord" (1:2, 12, 14; 6:3, 14), it is unambiguous that Jesus Christ is the one and only "Lord" of Paul, Timothy, and the faithful among the Ephesian audience. Thus in addition to Paul's monotheistic assertion of God the Father, the explicit christological doxology here in the pivot of the sixth microchiasm would be equally apparent: "our Lord Jesus Christ" (6:14) is unequivocally the "Lord of those who-are-lords" (6:15b). Significantly, then, where Jesus Christ indeed maintains the referential name of God in the LXX OT—"Lord"—the nuanced implication of Paul's pivotal monotheistic assertion here in 6:15b is upheld: Jesus Christ is not only the "Lord of those who-are-lords," but he also shares in God's status as "the King of those who-are-kings" (6:15b). In other words, Paul is asserting that what is true for the Father, namely his kingship, is equally true for Jesus Christ.

Certainly, the rhetorical significance of the pivot D element is heard with full force: here in the climactic A' unit of the entire macrochiasm, Paul hinges everything upon the divine dynamic and relation between Jesus Christ and God the Father—together from whom the salvific blessings of grace, mercy, and peace flow to those "in faith" (1:2), who together reign as "King" (1:17; 6:15b), who together are the "only God" (1:17) and "only Power" (6:15a) to whom are "honor and glory" (1:17), namely the "glory" of the blessed God (1:11; 6:15a) and Jesus Christ who was taken-up in "glory" (3:16). Furthermore, the audience understand that it is for this reason that "someone" who does not come-toward the sound words of the "Lord Jesus Christ" is in a dire situation (6:3). As much is Paul is upholding the identity of God, he is also hinging the climactic conclusion of the letter upon a missional invitation: along with the Savior God who desires all humans to be-saved (2:3–4), Paul does not desire for "some" humans to plunge themselves into ruin and destruction (6:9b) but rather to come to have-faith upon Jesus Christ, the "Lord" who collaborates and shares in God the Father's prerogative to provide-life (6:13)—life eternal (1:16).²⁰⁶

205. See Wiersbe, *Ephesians Through Revelation*, 236; cf. Wall with Steele, *1 & 2 Tim*, 147.

206. It is worth noting that Paul ties eternal life to knowing—and being known by—"the King" and "Lord"; eternal life is never expressed in terms of some abstract

In sum, the progression and emphasis of the sixth and final microchiasm hinges upon a declaration that is not merely subversive against Greco-Roman assertions but is—more significantly—a reminder to Paul's Ephesian audience that salvation comes from the shared collaboration of God the Father and Jesus Christ who equally reign as "the King of those who-are-kings and Lord of those who-are-lords" (6:15b). Indeed, for those among the audience who exist "in faith," who live in God's household, and thus have God as their Father and Jesus Christ as their Lord (1:2), they may live with the ultimate security: the head and ruler of their household is "the King of those who-are-kings and Lord of those who-are-lords" (6:15b). Now, with this climaxing, doxological pivot, the audience are prepared to hear the approaching conclusion of the letter.

1 Timothy 6:16: Holding Without-Death, Housing-in Light, To Him Honor

(C' Element)

As the C' element progresses the microchiasm toward its climactic conclusion, Paul begins with a final doxological description of God: "who only holding without-death, housing-in without-approachable light" (6:16). The adjective "only" is heard with a dual rhetorical implication. On the one hand, within the arrangement of the sixth microchiasm, "only" (μόνος, 6:16) here in the C' element recalls its parallel occurrence in the C element regarding Paul's monotheistic description of God as the "only" (μόνος) Power (6:15a). Thus both before and after the pivot D element, the audience understand that Paul is emphatically extolling the one and "only" God in the surrounding C and C' elements.[207] On the other hand, within the arrangement of the overall macrochiasm, "only" (μόνος, 6:16) here in the A' unit recalls its parallel occurrence in the A unit regarding Paul's doxology of the King of the eternities who is the "only" (μόνος) God (1:17). Thus the

---

existence but specifically—and *personally*—in terms of being united to the ultimate, only Power (6:15a)—the only God (1:17), the King (1:17; 6:15b) and Lord (1:2, 12, 14; 6:3, 14, 15b), namely Jesus Christ (the mediator of God and humans, 2:5) and thus God the Father. Keller with Alsdorf, *Every Good Endeavor*, 159: "In other words, the biblical worldview uniquely understands the nature, problem, and salvation of humankind as fundamentally *relational*."

207. Here, a visual representation may be helpful:
C element: "the blessed and only (μόνος) Power" (6:15a);
    D element: "the King . . . and Lord" (6:15b);
C' element: "who only (μόνος) holding without-death" (6:16).

audience understand that Paul's entire letter is emphatically framed by a repeated monotheistic assertion—indeed, doubly asserted in the climactic, concluding A' unit (6:15a, 16).

Still, the participle phrase "holding without-death" (6:16) would reiterate Paul's monotheistic doxology. The participle "holding" (ἔχων) recalls its occurrences throughout the macrochiasm, conveying "clinging to."[208] Significantly, where Paul underscores that "only" God is "holding without-death" (6:16), the message is clear: no one except for the King and Lord (6:15b)—not Greco-Roman gods, kings, lords, or military heroes—can lay claim to immortality.[209] Indeed, the term "without-death" (ἀθανασίαν) here in 6:16 of the A' unit conceptually echoes Paul's doxological assertion in 1:17 of the parallel A unit regarding the King of the eternities who is "without-perishability" (ἀφθάρτῳ); to be sure, Paul's point is that only God possesses the unique quality of "without-death" (6:16) in the same way that he is "without-perishability" (1:17). Furthermore, Paul's statement that only God is "holding without-death" in 6:16 again speaks to the existential problem of humans that Paul underscored in 6:7, that is, the problem of mortality despite the evident human yearning for immortality. In full, the phrase "who only holding without-death" upholds for Timothy and the audience that while "without-death" belongs "only" to the King and Lord, he will bestow it on those who would-inevitably-come to have-faith upon Christ Jesus for life eternal (1:16), namely those who take-possession of eternal life (6:12) by allowing the one who gave himself as a ransom on their behalf (2:6) to be the Lord of their life (1:2, 12, 14; 6:3, 14, 15b).[210] Indeed, the only God who provides-life (6:13) will provide his without-death to humans (6:16; cf. 6:7) through the the one mediator of God and humans, the human Christ Jesus, who gave himself—died—on their behalf (2:6). For the audience, then, the tight-knit movement from the C element to the C' element across the pivotal D element conveys the powerful encouragement that Timothy and the audience will experience from God's royal and eternal existence.[211] The rhetorical placement of such a future reality is telling. For Timothy and the audience—amidst and unlike "some" who have wandered from the faith by

---

208. See e.g., 1:19 in the parallel A unit regarding Timothy who is "holding (ἔχων) faith and a good conscience."

209. For examples in Hellenistic discourse, see Towner, *Letters*, n. 63.

210. Witherington, *Letters*, 295: "God is the only one who has immortality, 'deathlessness' (*athanasia*), as an essential property, unlike believers, who die and receive eternal life as a gift, and unlike deified emperors, who are fully mortal despite all claims to the contrary."

211. Towner aptly summarizes: "Christian hope is nothing less than participation in God's unique self-generating life" (*Letters*, 421).

pursuing gain (6:5), wanting to be-rich (6:9a), and the affection-of-money (6:10a)—Paul's command to "flee these; but pursue justice, godliness, faith, love, steadfastness, gentleness" (6:11) would likely result in a certain degree of economic loss and hardship here and now in the present life. Yet, Paul reminds the faithful that they indeed may content "holding (ἔχοντες) food and clothing" (6:8), for God is "holding (ἔχων) without-death" (6:16) and in his own times will display the manifesting of their Lord Jesus Christ (6:14–15a): in due time they will be fed by and clothed with the glory of God and Jesus Christ (1:11; 3:16).

The focus of the second participle phrase of the C' element shifts from God's ontological existence to a description of his dwelling: God is "housing-in without-approachable light" (6:16). Paul's use of the term "light" (φῶς) has clear echoes to the way that God is explicitly correlated with the imagery of light in the OT. In Exodus, light expresses God's particular favor toward his chosen people; according to the ninth plague, the Egyptians suffered a deep darkness while "all the children of Israel had light (φῶς) in all the place they lived" (LXX Exod 10:23).[212] Moreover, that the light is "without-approachable" (ἀπρόσιτον) has conceptual echoes of Exodus 19–20: not only did God reveal himself in fire and lightning at Mount Sinai (Exod 19:16–18) but, due to fear, the Israelites refused to approach God's holy presence (Exod 20:18); notably it was God's dreadful, "without-approachable light" that necessitated a human mediator to approach God on behalf of the people—Moses (Exod 20:19–21).[213] In this way, Paul's

---

212. See also LXX Psalm 4:6; it may be worth noting the further linguistic similarities to 1 Timothy:
LXX Psalm 4:6: "Many say, 'Who will display (δείξει) to us the good?' Lift up to us the light (φῶς) of your face, O Lord (κύριε)!";
1 Tim 6:14–16: "our Lord (κυρίου) Jesus Christ ... the blessed and only Power will display (δείξει) ... Lord (κύριος) of those who-are-lords ... without-approachable light (φῶς)."

213. Exod 19:16–18 (*ESV*): "On the morning of the third day there were thunders and lightnings and a thick cloud on the mountain and a very loud trumpet blast, so that all the people in the camp trembled. Then Moses brought the people out of the camp to meet God, and they took their stand at the foot of the mountain. Now Mount Sinai was wrapped in smoke because the LORD had descended on it in fire. The smoke of it went up like the smoke of a kiln, and the whole mountain trembled greatly."

Exod 20:18–21 (*ESV*): "Now when all the people saw the thunder and the flashes of lightning and the sound of the trumpet and the mountain smoking, the people were afraid and trembled, and they stood far off and said to Moses, 'You speak to us, and we will listen; but do not let God speak to us, lest we die.' Moses said to the people, 'Do not fear, for God has come to test you, that the fear of him may be before you, that you may not sin.' The people stood far off, while Moses drew near to the thick darkness where God was."

description of God in terms of "without-approachable light" would have simultaneously pointed the audience toward Christ.[214]

Still, the rhetorical force of the phrase would be heard by Paul's use of the participle "housing-in" (οἰκῶν), which recalls its cognate occurrences and progression throughout the macrochiasm: in the A unit, Paul's concern was for "the household-law (οἰκονομίαν) of God in faith" (1:4), that is, the realm wherein God is the Father and Christ Jesus is Lord (1:2);[215] in the C unit, a man's leadership of his own "household" (οἴκου) qualified him to care-for God's church (3:4, 5), that is, to be a model of godly behavior in "the household (οἴκῳ) of God," which is the church of God (3:15);[216] in the B' unit, children or those-from-parents were to be-godly to their own "household" (οἶκον, 5:4) and to also provide for God's "household-members" (οἰκείων, 5:8) in the same way that younger-women are "to master-households" (οἰκοδεσποτεῖν, 5:14) rather than to be idlers, going-about the "houses" (οἰκίας, 5:13). Here, then, in the concluding A' unit of the macrochiasm, all of Paul's cumulative household language and his deep concern for the care and sustenance thereof points to and derives from the only God who is "housing-in" (οἰκῶν) without-approachable light (6:16). Paul's implication would be multifaceted.

On the most basic level, the participle phrase "housing-in without-approachable light"—heard in tandem with the preceding participle phrase "holding without-death"—strongly emphasizes God's "otherness": there is none like him.[217] Yet, that God is "housing-in" (οἰκῶν) draws explicit attention to the fact that "the household (οἴκῳ) of God . . . is the church of the living God, a pillar and foundation of truth" that exclaims that "confessedly great mystery of godliness" concerning Christ Jesus (3:15-16). In other words, as much as "housing-in without-approachable light" underscores

---

214. Paul's encounter with Jesus on the road to Damascus in Acts 9:3-4 may be relevant: ". . . suddenly shined-around him light (φῶς) from heaven, and falling upon the ground he heard a voice saying to him, 'Saul, Saul, why are you persecuting me? . . . I-myself am Jesus whom you are persecuting.'" As a result of this event, Paul was temporarily unable to see (Acts 9:8). Paul's conception of God's radiant glory—which Paul beheld from Jesus in Acts 9:3-4—may have informed his description of God with the phrase "without-approachable light (φῶς)" in 1 Timothy 6:16.

215. In the B unit, the household theme is implicity carried forward: the summons to remain "in faith" is to remain in God's household.

216. In the C' unit, the household theme is implicity carried forward: Timothy is to be an example "in faith," and thus of what it is to live in God's household.

217. The "otherness" of God is effectively a description of his "holiness." Sproul, *Holiness of God*, 55-56: "When the Bible calls God holy it means primarily that God is transcendentally separate. He is so far above and beyond us that He seems almost totally foreign to us. To be holy is to be 'other,' to be different in a special way . . . God alone is holy in Himself." See volume 2, chapter 3 regarding 1 Timothy 4:6.

God's otherness, the phrase emphasizes that the audience exist in the very same "household" where God is "housing-in." To be sure, Paul is drawing attention to the "mediator of God and humans, the human Christ Jesus" (2:5b): it is by coming to have-faith upon Christ Jesus (1:16) that the audience exist "in faith" (1:2), that is, within "the household-law of God in faith" (1:4). Furthermore, where their existence is "in faith that is in Christ Jesus" (3:13), Paul seems to be specifying that God is "housing-in" (6:16) "in Christ Jesus" (3:13). It is by the audience's shared existence "in faith" that they live together. In short, the audience live where God lives—"the household of God," which is the church of the living God (3:15), is the place where God is "housing-in" (6:16).[218] Thus for those living in God's household—the household of the only Power, the only one who is holding without-death (6:16)—Timothy and the audience are are to be greatly encouraged to agonize the commendable agony of the faith and to take-possession of the eternal life (6:12) because the one in whose household they live provides-life (6:13), and the one in whom they exist (1:14; 3:13) is the mediator for them to receive it (2:5), namely life eternal (1:16). The audience understand that through Christ Jesus the without-approachable light of God has become approachable: by faith upon Christ, the only Power has imparted his without-death—eternal life—to the family members of his household—the place where he is housing. In turn, they are to war the commendable war (1:18) and agonize the commendable agony of the faith (6:12); they are to support Timothy in Paul's *charge to preserve the teaching* that invites all humans into the place where God is housing and *to promote* its subsequent *godliness* that demonstrates what eternal life inside God's household looks like. The place where God is "housing-in"—the church, "the household of God" (3:15)—is intended to exhibit his radiant "light" (6:16); such is *God's missional household*.

God's without-approachable light is further qualified: "which no human has seen nor has power to see" (6:16).[219] Certainly, the juxtaposition between God and humans is emphasized. The verb "has power" (δύναται, 6:16) here in the C' element recalls that God is the only "Power" (δυνάστης, 6:15a) in the parallel C element.[220] Indeed, where "no human (ἀνθρώπων)

---

218. See Barcley, "1 Tim," 374.

219. Again, in the immediate context of Paul's description of God as "housing-in without-approachable light (φῶς)" (6:16), Paul's statement "which no human has seen nor has power to see" (6:16) seems to be an echo of his own experience on the road to Damascus in Acts 9:8: Paul is forcibly unable to see after the "light (φῶς) shown from heaven." Cf. Eastman, *Ancient Martyrdom Accounts*, xix, who regards this as a paraphrase of Speratus, an early Christian whose language seemed to be subversive toward the Roman emperor.

220. The parallelism between these elements, however, is established through the repetition of the adjective "only" (μόνος) because the verb "to have power" also occurs

... has power" (6:16), the fact resounds: *only God* is and has "Power" (6:15a). Furthermore, here within the A' unit of the macrochiasm, the parallelism between the C and C' elements that no human "has seen" (εἶδεν) nor has power "to see" (ἰδεῖν) the only Power (6:15a-16) conceptually echoes and reinforces Paul's parallel doxology in the A unit where the King of the eternities is "without-visibility" (ἀοράτῳ, 1:17).[221] Indeed, Paul's rhetorical back-to-back repetition of "has seen" and "to see" would make his point emphatic: no ordinary human "has power" to see the only "Power." Undoubtedly, Paul is alluding to the Exodus narrative where God declares, "You shall not have the power to see (οὐ δυνήσῃ ἰδεῖν) my face; for no human shall see (ἴδῃ ἄνθρωπος) my face and live" (LXX 33:20).[222] Significantly, however, although Paul has been underscoring God's ineffable nature—that God is wholly other, that there is profound chasm between the Creator and the creature—it is equally the case that God's desire is to close the chasm between himself and "humans." To be sure, the term "human" (ἀνθρώπων) recalls God's explicitly missional desire for all "humans" (ἀνθρώπους) to be-saved (2:4): God is the Savior of all "humans" (ἀνθρώπων, 4:10). Thus, while "no human has seen nor has power to see" God, the inescapable fact is that the one God himself made a way: he came into the world (1:15) to be the one mediator between God and humans (ἀνθρώπων)—the human (ἄνθρωπος) Christ Jesus (2:5). In short, the audience understand that Jesus has made the "without-visibility" visible (1:17) and the "without-approachable" approachable (6:16) through his manifestation in flesh (3:16).[223] In the person of Christ, then, the full implication of Paul's allusion to the Exodus narrative comes in to view: where Moses mediated between God and the people (Exod 20:19-21), ultimately Jesus Christ is the mediator of God and humans (2:5); where Moses could not see God's face (Exod 33:23), ultimately God shows his face to all humans in the person of Jesus Christ (1:15; 2:5; 3:16; 6:14-16). Indeed, where the imagery of "without-approachable light" (6:16, A' unit) echoes the vibrant connotations of the radiant "glory" (δόξης) of the blessed

---

in 6:7, which is part of the A element.

221. While the verbs "has seen" (εἶδεν) and "to see" (ἰδεῖν) in 6:16 are not cognates of "without-visibility" (ἀοράτῳ) in 1:17, the conceptual similarity would be apparent.

222. This notion is upheld throughout the NT, which suggests that it would have been common Christian knowledge:

John 1:18 (*ESV*): "No one has ever seen (οὐδεὶς ἑώρακεν) God; the only God, who is at the Father's side, he has made him known";

John 6:46 (*ESV*): "not that anyone has seen (ἑώρακεν) the Father except he who is from God; he has seen (ἑώρακεν) the Father."

See also Matt 11:27; Luke 10:22; 1 John 4:12, 20.

223. Note esp. Col 1:15; Heb 1:1-3. See also the further NT associations between God, his dwelling place and glory, and his people: John 1:5, 7-9; Eph 5:8; Rev 21-22.

God" (1:11, A unit), Paul's allusion to the Exodus narrative resounds. Where Moses requests of God, "Display (δεῖξον) to me your glory (δόξαν)" (LXX Exod 33:18), it happens that God's "glory" (δόξη) passes by Moses (LXX Exod 33:19), but God only allows a glimpse of his "glory" (δόξα) to be seen (LXX Exod 33:22). In the 1 Timothy letter, however, Paul indicates that God "will display" (δείξει, 6:15a) the manifesting of the Lord Jesus Christ (6:14), the confessedly great mystery of godliness who is now "in glory" (δόξῃ, 3:16)—the one who saved Paul in order to "display" (ἐνδείξηται) all patience as an example to those who would-inevitably-come to have-faith upon him for life eternal (1:16). The glory that Moses requested to see but could not see in full is fully displayed in Jesus Christ. Significantly, where God's radiant "glory" is exhibited by "the sound teaching"—the gospel (1:10b–11)—the audience understand that it is not only Christ's first coming—"he was manifested in flesh . . . was taken-up in glory" (3:16)—but also his second coming "in glory"—"the manifesting of our Lord Jesus Christ" (6:14)—which fully displays the "without-approachable light" of God (6:16).[224] In full, Paul indicates that both manifestations of Jesus Christ—his first and second coming—are God's tangible display of his glory. In short, given Paul's earlier allusion to the tradition preserved in John 18:37 (1 Tim 6:13), it seems that Paul has Jesus's very own declaration in view: although "no human has seen (εἶδεν) nor has power "to see" (ἰδεῖν)" (1 Tim 6:16), Jesus affirms that "Whoever has seen (ἑωρακὼς) me has seen (ἑώρακεν) the Father" (John 14:9).[225]

Through the movement of the microchiasm across pivotal cluster of the C-D-C' elements, Paul pinpoints the key for empowering Timothy and the audience to pursue his commands of what is good in the B element—a life commensurate with the commendable confession concerning Christ Jesus and the eternal life thereof (6:11–14). The central significance of God as the only Power (6:15a, C element), the King and Lord (6:15b, D element), and the only one holding without-death (6:16, C' element) eclipses all the gain (6:5), riches (6:9a), and money (6:10a) that motivate "some." Paul, Timothy, and the faithful among the audience are motivated only by the eclipsing power, kingship, lordship, and without-death of the only God who displays himself in the person of Jesus Christ. Indeed, here the sound teaching with which Paul was counted-faithful—*the gospel* that results in the glory of the blessed God (1:10b–11)—is summarized and upheld: the

---

224. The connection between the "light" and "glory" of God is made explicit in John 1:5–14; notably, it is Jesus Christ who was seen and who reveals both the "light" and "glory."

225. The back-to-back repetition of the verb "to see" (ὁράω) in both 1 Timothy 6:16 and John 14:9 strengthens the connection.

without-approachable light, which no ordinary human can see is now approachable and visible through the one human Christ Jesus. In a word, Timothy and the audience now possess the "power to see" because they have come to a knowing-embrace of the truth (2:4b; 4:3b), namely the sound teaching of Paul, the authorized apostolic teacher "in faith" (2:7) whom Christ Jesus "empowered" and appointed for service (1:12). Along with the apostle Paul, then, Timothy and the faithful among the audience who agree with the sound words of the Lord Jesus Christ and the teaching that is according to godliness (6:3) have seen the risen Lord "in glory" (3:16) through *the teaching*, that is, *the gospel* of the glory of the blessed God (1:10b–11; 6:3). For this reason, the faithful are empowered to agonize the commendable agony of the faith and take-possession of eternal life (6:12)—indeed, at each moment they may envision an eternal life of blessing the King of the eternities for the eternities of the eternities (1:17).

In the final clause of the C' element, Paul affirms that the audience's reception of immortality by the only Power ought to channel their entire thinking: "to him honor and eternal strength, amen" (6:16). To be sure, the rhetorical parallel between the final doxological phrase here in 6:16 of the concluding A' unit and Paul's doxology in 1:17 of the introductory A unit would be apparent:

> A unit: "to (τῷ) the King . . . honor (τιμή) and glory for the eternities (αἰῶνας) of the eternities (αἰώνων), amen (ἀμήν)" (1:17);

> A' unit: "to him (ᾧ) honor (τιμή) and eternal (αἰώνιον) strength, amen (ἀμήν)" (6:16).[226]

The parallel doxologies not only frame the letter but also draw attention to the disposition of praise that ought to mark the faithful in the audience who have received without-death from the only Power (6:15–16) by coming to have-faith upon Christ Jesus (1:16). Indeed, as the letter progresses toward its climactic conclusion in the A' unit, Paul intends to focus the audience's attention upon God and the "honor" (τιμή) due "to him" (ᾧ).

---

226. Keegan, "First Letter to Tim," 698: "Unlike the doxology [at 1:17] and unlike all the other New Testament passages that are commonly identified as doxologies, this one in chapter 6 is the only one that does not use the Greek work for 'glory,' *doxa*." Neyrey, *Give God the Glory*, 142: "1 Timothy 6:16, which does not contain δόξα, is a true doxology. We find τιμή instead of δόξα, which . . . [are] virtual synonyms." That this is the case, see volume 1, chapter 3 regarding 1Timothy 1:17. Ibid.: "Doxologies, moreover, may ascribe to God glory and honor, as well as 'eternal dominion' (1 Tim 6:16) . . . Thus praise, honor, and glory are given to God, which helps us to situate doxologies under the umbrella of epideictic rhetoric, the rhetoric of praise."

Still, Paul's particularly points of emphasis in the introductory A unit and in distinction from the concluding A' unit would highlight the progressive scope of the macrochiasm. Whereas the immediate purpose of the first doxology was to contextualize Paul's apostolic status—that his unique authority as apostle stems from God's mercy, not personal merit—and to demonstrate the subsequent outflow of his reception thereof—giving blessing to God—it is evident that the immediate context of the second doxology is to assert God's incomparable greatness over financial gain (6:5), riches (6:9a), and money (6:10a). Significantly, then, "honor" here in 6:16 would have a forceful impact upon the way the audience—particularly "some" among them—are to view money. In view of the parallel ascription of "honor" (τιμή, 1:17; 6:16) to God in the A and A' units, the clear financial connotations to "honor" (τίμα) widows who are truly widows (5:3), that teaching elders—overseers—must be considered-worthy of double "honor" (τιμῆς, 5:17), and that Christian slaves must consider their own masters worthy of all "honor" (τιμῆς, 6:1) all find their importance within the framework of "honor" to God (1:17; 6:16). Such conveys a stark contrast over and against the false teachers who are effectively devoid of any honor toward God—they are motivated by "gain" (6:5), "wanting to be-rich" (6:9a), and "the affection-of-money" (6:10a) rather than an affection-of-God. In short, Paul's ascription of "honor" to God includes more than a mere attitude or statement of reverence toward God; undoubtedly, for Paul "honor" also includes a tangible expression of such reverence by one's attitude toward money. In short, the faithful are to use their money simply as a means to "honor" God—*not* as a means-of-gain (6:5). Indeed, according to the entire A' unit of the macrochiasm, "honor" toward God is concretely articulated by fleeing from the affection-of-money and all its associated evils—wanting to be-rich, falling into temptation and snares and many senseless and harmful longings—and pursuing justice, godliness, faith, love, steadfastness, and gentleness (6:9-11).[227]

With the phrase "eternal strength, amen" in 6:16, Paul concludes the C' element by underscoring several important truths to Timothy and the

---

227. To be sure, Paul is not advocating the abandonment of all financial resources at the expense of one's health, such as having food and clothing (6:8). In Paul's other letters, it is clear that stewarding financial resources to "honor" God involves a balance of caring for oneself (1 Thess 2:9; 2 Thess 3:7-8) in addition to providing for others and for the church (Gal 6:9-10). The balance of both aspects was also heard in Paul's final speech to the Ephesian overseers in Acts 20:34-35 (*ESV*): "You yourselves know that these hands ministered to my necessities and to those who were with me. In all things I have shown you that by working hard in this way we must help the weak and remember the words of the Lord Jesus, how he himself said, 'It is more blessed to give than to receive.'"

audience. First, the adjective "eternal" (αἰώνιον) not only highlights God's infinite being and existence—"without-perishability" (1:17); "without-death" (6:16)—but also that God's very own personal being is the source of "eternal (αἰωνίου) life" (6:12). Furthermore, Paul's exclusive use of "eternal" and its cognates in the A and A' units—indeed, his rhetorical repetition of cognates in each unit—would be apparent:

> A unit: "to have-faith upon him for life eternal (αἰώνιον) . . . to the King of the eternities (αἰώνων) . . . the eternities (αἰῶνας) of the eternities (αἰώνων)" (1:16-17);

> A' unit: "take-possession of the eternal (αἰωνίου) life . . . to him honor and eternal (αἰώνιον) strength" (6:12, 16).

Thus as much as God's eternal being frames the entire macrochiasm (1:17; 6:16), the eternal life that flow from him to humans (1:16; 6:12) also forms the framework in which everything within the letter is to be understood. Paul, Timothy, and the faithful in the audience "honor" God here and now *and* for the eternities of the eternities (1:17; 6:16) because God's very own "eternal" existence has been bestowed upon them in the form of "eternal life" (1:16-17; 6:12, 16). In full, it is Paul, Timothy, and the audience's reception of eternal life from the eternal God that compels them *to preserve the teaching*—indeed, the very sound words of Jesus Christ himself—namely *the teaching* that enables humans to have-faith upon Christ Jesus for eternal life (1:10b; 4:6, 13, 16; 6:3; cf. 2:7, 12; 3:2; 5:17; 6:1, 2); it is their reception of eternal life through the teaching that compels them *to promote godliness*—indeed, the actual result of agreeing with sound words and teaching of Jesus Christ himself—namely *godliness* that attracts humans to have-faith upon Christ Jesus for eternal life (2:2, 10; 3:16; 4:7b, 8b; 5:4a; 6:3, 6, 11); it is their expression of eternal life through godliness that compels them to live *as God's missional household*—indeed, the actual place where God is housing together with Jesus Christ—namely *God's missional household* that shares a family desire for all humans to have-faith upon Christ Jesus for eternal life (1:4; 3:5, 15; 5:8; cf. 3:4; 5:4, 8, 14). In short, it the gracious gift of eternal life from the eternal Power—that which beyond-abounds from Christ Jesus (1:14, 16)—that alone speaks to and addresses the human condition of coming into and leaving the world naked, vulnerable, and finite. For this reason, Paul, Timothy, and the audience may exclaim "Christ Jesus our hope" (1:1), for they have hoped upon the living God (4:10; 5:5). Where gain, riches, and money can do nothing for eternal life, the faithful in Ephesus are motivated to ascribe and express all honor to the King, only God, only Power.

Second, the noun "strength" (κράτος) connotes "mighty power" or "extraordinarily ability" that may be exhibited against one's enemies or that is the source of inspiration.[228] Given that the focus of 6:16 exclusively pertains to the person of God, Paul's point is clear: God himself is the source of "strength" for Paul, Timothy, and the faithful Ephesians—certainly in general, but specifically in view of the false teachers. Indeed, Paul's doxology seems to echo his words in a prior letter to the Ephesian church: "Finally, be strong in the Lord and in the strength (κράτει) of his might" (6:10).[229] Where such strength is efficacious and unlimited, Timothy and the faithful Ephesians are encouraged to draw from a never-ending reservoir of God's strength; in this way, they may persevere as they war the commendable war (1:18) and agonize the commendable agony of the faith (6:12).

Third, the term "amen" (ἀμήν, 6:16) here in the concluding A' unit recalls its only other occurrence in the letter, namely "amen" (ἀμήν, 1:17) in the parallel introductory A unit. As in 1:17, the concluding "amen" of the doxology in 6:16 is intended to evoke and invite an enthusiastic response of agreement and participation from the audience. Indeed, to the only Power who provides-life—eternal life!—and provides his own "eternal strength" to endure the commendable agony of the faith, Paul is beckoning the entire audience to join him in praise.[230] Moreover, where Paul's "amen" frames the entire arrangement of the letter, the audience understand that from beginning to end—and everything in between—Paul's letter is intended to be one unified invitation to praise the Savior God who desires all humans to be-saved (2:4), the God who came into the world to save sinners (1:15), the God from whom Paul was granted-mercy (1:13, 16), and the God of without-approachable light who makes himself approachable in the person of Christ Jesus (6:16). To be sure, given the overarching missional thrust of the letter, Paul's parallel framing of "amen" would be heard as a further invitation to the false teachers to abandon their motive of money and to experience an existence "in faith," "in Christ Jesus," "in Spirit," "in glory" (3:13, 16), together

---

228. See LXX Gen 49:24; Deut 8:17; Judg 4:3; Ps 58:10; 62:11; Job 12:16.

229. Both Paul's letter to the Ephesians and 1 Timothy are dated to the early to mid-sixties; see Carson and Moo, *Introduction*, 486–87, 572, repectively; see volume 1, chapter 1; see also Knight, *PE*, 54. In the event that the letter to the Ephesians was received prior to 1 Timothy, its contents would be freshly in their minds and the connection would easily be made between Ephesians 6:10 and 1 Timothy 6:16.

230. In passing it may be worthwhile to observe that the apostle seeks to stir Timothy and the audience to faithfulness by shifting their gaze away from their immediate circumstances and toward God, who in turn forces them to reconsider their situation from a different perspective. A survey of Paul's prayers and exhortations suggests that the apostle seemed less concerned about improved circumstances and more concerned with bringing the truths of the gospel to bear on a given situation.

in the place where God is housing-in (6:16)—the household of God (1:14; 3:15) wherein God is the Father and Jesus Christ is the Lord (1:2).

1 Timothy 6:17–19: Charge the Rich in this Present Age

(B' Element)

Immediately following Paul's doxological focus toward God, Paul shifts the audience's attention in the beginning of the B' element: "As for the rich in this present age, charge them not to be-haughty" (6:17). The term "the rich" (τοῖς πλουσίοις) here in 6:17 of the B' element recalls its cognate occurrence in 6:9a of the parallel B element regarding "those wanting to be-rich (οἱ ... πλουτεῖν)."[231] The established parallelism provides the rhetorical framework for the audience's understanding of the B-C-D-C'-B' progression (6:9–17) in the sixth microchiasm. In other words, Paul is making absolutely clear that the doxological focus upon God's greatness in the C-D-C' elements is to be heard as a stark contrast over and against riches and money in the B and B' elements. Significantly, where "those wanting to be-rich" in 6:9a was a part of Paul's continued polemic against "someone"—the false teachers—in 6:3, the parallel arrangement of the B and B' elements carries forward the specific polemical connotation regarding the false teachers.[232] That is, where "those wanting to be-rich" and those who are marked by the affection-of-money are clearly "some" who—aspiring—have wandered from the faith (6:9–10) in the B element, beyond any doubt the audience understand that Paul specifically has in view "some" when identifying "the rich" (6:17) in the parallel B' element. To be sure, throughout the entire A and B elements of the microchiasm Paul was exclusively and explicitly addressing the situation of the false-teaching overseers in Ephesus—not only their disagreement with the sound words of Jesus Christ and the teaching that results in godliness (6:3) but also their corresponding, distorted, discontented view of godliness as a means of financial gain (6:5), thus wanting to be-rich (6:9a)—an outward growth from the root of pride into the affection-of-money (6:10a). Given Paul's sustained emphasis on the false teachers, it would be wildly

---

231. In my perusal of the various commentaries on 1 Timothy, insufficient attention has been given to interpreting 6:11–16 in light of the "bookends" of the B and B' elements, both of which relate to the theme of wealth. See Thurén, "Die Struktur der Schlussparänese," 242–44. Furthermore, insufficient attention has been given to the polemical context of the false teachers in both the B and B' elements.

232. Long, *1 & 2 Tim*, 177: "Many commentators find the closing sections of 1 Timothy to be choppy and somewhat disorganized ... However, as we saw in the commentary on 1 Timothy 6:2b–10, this is actually a passage primarily about the false teachers."

unfitting either for the audience to perceive a rhetorical movement away from "some" or for Paul to suddenly alter the flow of his cumulative polemic against the false teachers. Indeed, the parallel polemical focus on "some" in both the A (1:3, 6, 8, 19; cf. 1:4, 7, 10) and A' units (6:3, 10; 6:9) emphasizes that Paul intends for the audience to understand that the false teachers are in view: from beginning to end, "some" frame the entire letter.

Paul defines "the rich" as those who are "in this present age" (6:17). The statement would have a strong rhetorical implication. The preposition "in" (ἐν) draws attention not merely to their current status but their trajectory, the sense being that "the rich are *stuck* in this present age." Indeed, such would augment the unmistakeable contrast between the "present age" (τῷ νῦν αἰῶνι) here in 6:17 of the B' element and "the eternal (τῆς αἰωνίου) life" in 6:12 of the parallel B element.[233] In effect, whereas Timothy and the faithful among the audience take-possession of "the eternal life" (6:12), the rich, false teachers have taken-possession of "this present age" (6:17). This contrast here in the B' element conceptually echoes the implied contrast in the parallel B element, specifically in the 6:6–8 minichiasm.[234] Where the false teachers do not agree with Jesus Christ and the teaching that is according to godliness (6:3)—thus their distorted view that godliness is merely a means-of-gain for here and now—it is clear that they only have the present life in view. Conversely, for the faithful whose godliness is derived from Jesus Christ and the teaching (6:3), their contentment with holding food and clothing is due to the great gain of godliness—namely, they have eternal life in view.

Further still, the contrast would not only be heard on a microchiastic level in relation to the B and B' element but also on a macrochiastic scale between the A and A' units. Where the rich are exclusively fixed "in the present age (τῷ νῦν αἰῶνι)" (6:17) in the A' unit, it is evident that they do not have-faith upon Christ Jesus for "life eternal (αἰώνιον)" (1:16) nor, then, is it possible for them to ascribe honor and bless "the King of the eternities (αἰώνων) . . . for the eternities (αἰῶνας) of the eternities (αἰώνων)" (1:17) in the parallel A unit. To be sure, it is not possible for the false teachers to honor God "for the eternities of the eternities" (1:17). In short, there is an inseparable connection between the "the present age" (6:17) and that

---

233. Similarly, Collins, *1 & 2 Tim*, 170: "It shifts the readers' attention from the future appearance of the Lord Jesus Christ (6:14) to the present. It recalls the Pastor's earlier reflection that wealth cannot be taken with us (6:7), and it prepares for the contrast with what is to come. As such, it strengthens the antithesis between hope in uncertain riches and hope in God."

234. Papaioannou, *Geography of Hell*, 43: "1 Timothy 6:17 refers to the 'present age' νῦν αιωνι (*nun aiōni*) implying therefore that there is another one in the future." Such was the conceptual implication of 6:6–8.

of eternity (1:17), namely one's relation to the person and work of Christ Jesus (1:16). To be sure, "if someone"—the false teachers—"does not come-toward the sound words of Jesus Christ" (6:3), then they certainly do not have-faith upon him (1:16). In a vicious cycle, then, it is because the false teachers do not have-faith upon Christ that they are completely grounded in—"rich in"—this present age (6:17), and it is because they are grounded in this present age that "some" are supposing godliness to be a means-of-gain (6:5), wanting to be-rich (6:9a), and motivated by the affection-of-money (6:10a). Indeed, where such aspiring of "some" has caused them to wander from the faith (6:10), it is a without-hypocrisy faith upon Christ (1:5, 16) that breaks the cycle and transfers their thoughts, motivations, and actions toward an eternal perspective. Namely, the reality of Christ's first coming—that he came into the present age (1:15), that he himself is the mediating bridge between the one immortal God and all mortal humans (2:5), and that he was literally manifested in flesh, was declared-just in Spirit, was seen by angels, was proclaimed in the Gentiles, was counted-faithful, and was taken-up in glory (3:16)—directs the attention of all humans toward his eternal life—as a human—"in glory." Moreover, the fixed reality of Christ's second coming—the manifesting of the Lord Jesus Christ, which God will display in his own times (6:14)—directs the attention of all humans to purposefully consider how they ought to live in this present age. It is Christ Jesus who both grounds humans in eternity and subsequently transforms their thoughts, motivations, and actions in this present age. Indeed, such articulates "godliness with contentment" (6:8), the godliness that results from the teaching of Jesus Christ (6:3), the godliness that is defined by, originates in, and derives from Christ Jesus himself (3:16); such articulates why training for godliness is toward all profitability, holding the promise *both* of life for the present and for the inevitable-coming (4:7b, 8b). In short, Christ Jesus is the bridge who connects the two distinct sides of the same coin: he confers importance to the "present age" (νῦν αἰῶνι, 6:17), that is, "life for the present" (ζωῆς τῆς νῦν, 4:8b), by mediating "life eternal" (ζωὴν αἰώνιον, 1:16; cf. 6:12), that is, "life ... for the inevitable-coming" (ζωῆς ... τῆς μελλούσης, 4:8b). In view of the King of the eternities—and praising him for the eternities of the eternities (1:17)—life in the present age is of importance, but of temporary importance relative to eternity. Such is the problem of the false teachers—"the rich"—who only have in view "this present age" (6:17): they are guided by principles and making decisions "in this present age" without considering the coming eternal life. In short, the false teachers in view might be "rich in this present age" (6:17), but they do-not have-the-power to bring-out some-thing (6:7) and will be bankrupt in the inevitable-coming life.

Corroborating that Paul is addressing the sustained problem of the false teachers in Ephesus, he commands Timothy: "charge them not to be-haughty, nor to hope upon the without-certainty of riches" (6:17). To be sure, that Paul has the false teachers in view would be most evident by the parallel linguistic arrangement of Paul's statements in the A and A' units of the macrochiasm:

> A unit: "charge (παραγγείλῃς) some not (μή) to teach-different nor (μηδέ) to hold-toward myths and genealogies without-limit" (1:3–4);
>
> A' unit: "charge (παράγγελλε) them not (μή) to be-haughty, nor (μηδέ) to hope upon the without-certainty of riches" (6:17).[235]

In the same way that Timothy is exhorted to remain in Ephesus in order that he might "charge" the false teachers in the introductory A unit, so too must Timothy "charge" them in the concluding A' unit. Such was the "charge" (παραγγελίαν) that the apostle Paul authoritatively entrusted to Timothy (1:18), which had in view of "some" who regarding the faith had become-shipwrecked (1:19). Furthermore, Paul's command for Timothy to "Charge" (παράγγελλε) in 4:11 had a remedial intent, namely to correct the false teachers's delimited scope of salvation by upholding God's inclusive offer of salvation to all humans (4:10). Also, where Paul commanded Timothy to "charge" (παράγγελλε) the ungodly children or those-from-parents that they might be irreproachable with regard to providing for those of their own household and the household-members of God (5:7–8; cf. 5:4), the implication was at the very least that they had been influenced by the false teachers.[236] Such is corroborated here in the A' unit wherein the false teachers are not only explicitly concerned with gain (6:5), wanting to be-rich (6:9a), and the affection-of-money (6:10a) but are also identified as rich (6:17). Thus for "the rich" false teachers who have their sights grounded merely in this

---

235. The rhetorical use of double infinitives in both 1:3–4 of the A unit and 6:17 of the A' unit would be apparent and corroborate the macrochiastic connection of Paul's statements:
A unit: "to teach-different (ἑτεροδιδασκαλεῖν) . . . to hold-toward (προσέχειν)" (1:3–4);
A' unit: "to be-haughty (ὑψηλοφρονεῖν) . . . to hope (ἠλπικέναι)" (6:17).

236. The further implication of 5:7–8 was that Paul was asserting a polemical instruction toward the false teachers; see chapter 2. Indeed, given that the false teachers are clearly marked by an affection-of-money and want to be-rich (6:9–10), it seems possible and likely that their greedy motivations led to their refusal to provide-for those of their own households and especially for household-members of God's household (5:8).

present age and are influencing the Ephesian church to do the same,[237] it is clear why Timothy must "charge" them (6:17): only an agreement with the teaching that is according to godliness (6:3) will enable them to interpret their wealth in view of the inevitable-coming life.

Still, in view of the A' unit itself, Paul's command for Timothy to "charge" (παράγγελλε) those who are rich in 6:17 of the B' element recalls Paul's declaration in 6:13-14 of the parallel B element, "I charge (παραγγέλλω), in the sight of God ... and of Christ Jesus ... you to keep the commandment spotless." Unlike the "charge" toward the false teachers and those influenced by them (1:3, 18; 4:11; 5:7), Paul's authoritative "charge" to Timothy in 6:13 was not remedial but rather intended to amplify the need for Timothy to persist in his leadership of the Ephesian church—particularly in view of the false teachers. Significantly, then, the rhetorical transition from Timothy receiving Paul's charge (6:13) to now once again carrying out a charge (6:17) emphatically reiterates that correct, proper, qualified authority is in view: Timothy has authority because it derives from Paul's apostolic authority, which itself is according to the command of God and Christ Jesus (1:1). That is, over and against the false-teaching overseers in Ephesus—those wanting to be-rich (6:5) and who are rich (6:17)—the audience understand that Timothy's authority overrules and supersedes. Not only are "the rich" to align themselves with Timothy, Paul, God, and Christ Jesus but also, therefore, the entire church must follow Timothy's leadership—including those who were previously aligned with "some."

The back-to-back negative particles "not" (μή) . . . nor (μηδέ)" in 6:17 would be heard with rhetorical intention. At the same time, where the negative conjuctions and their cognates were consistently associated with the activity of the false teachers throughout the macrochiam, here in the concluding A' unit the cumulative connotation would resound with a climactic effect. In the A unit, Timothy is to charge "some not (μή) to teach-different, nor (μηδέ) to hold-toward myths and genealogies without-limit" (1:3-4), namely "some" who are "not (μή) understanding either (μήτε) what they-are-saying or (μήτε) regarding some-things they-are-insisting" (1:7), that is, "some" who must be-disciplined "not" (μή) to blaspheme (1:20). In the B unit, the influence of "the rich" false teachers (6:17) upon the women in the Ephesian church is evident: Paul wants women who profess godliness to "not" (μή) cosmetic themselves in braids and gold or pearls or rich attire (2:9-10). In the C unit, "some" in leadership positions must be "not" (μή) addicted-to-wine and "not" (μή) violent (3:3), "Not" (μή) a young-plant so

---

237. See volume 1, chapter 4 regarding 1 Timothy 2:9-10 (B unit). See also chapter 2 regarding 1 Timothy 5:6 (B' unit). Note the parallel implications thereof.

that they might "not" (μή)—being-puffed-up—fall into the condemnation of the devil (3:6) and "not" (μή) fall into the snare of the devil (3:7). In the C' unit, Paul is emphatic that "None" (μηδείς)—the young-plant false teachers who are being-puffed-up—must look-down-on Timothy's youth (4:12); furthermore, unlike the false-teaching overseers in Ephesus,[238] Timothy is to "not" (μή) be without-concern with the gift that was given to him by God and affirmed by the presbytery (4:14). In the B' unit, Timothy must prevent the events that gave rise to the false-teaching overseers, namely he is to be doing "nothing" (μηδέν) according to favoritism (5:21), is to lay hands quickly on "none" (μηδενί), "nor" (μηδέ) share in other's sins (5:22a); still, in addition to health reasons, as a remedial response to the ascetic practices of the false teachers,[239] Timothy must "No-longer" (μηκέτι) drink only water but also use a little wine (5:23). Now, here in the concluding A' unit, indeed Paul has in view "someone" who teaches-different—the false teaching overseers—who does "not" (μή) come-toward the sound words of the Lord Jesus Christ (6:3) and due to the outworking of their false teaching (6:4–5, 9–11) must be charged "not" (μή) to be-haughty "nor" (μηδέ) to hope upon the without-certainty of riches (6:17).

With the false teachers climactically in view, Paul identifies two characteristics of "the rich" false teachers—indeed, those still wanting to be-rich (6:9a) due to their affection-of-money (6:10a) in the parallel B element—that must be corrected by Timothy's charge: they are "not to be-haughty, nor to hope upon the without-certainty of riches" (6:17). The verb "to be-haughty" (ὑψηλοφρονεῖν) is a combination of the terms "lofty" (ὑψηλός) and "to think or feel" (φρονέω); hence, "to be-haughty" or "to think highly (of oneself)."[240] Conceptually, "to be-haughty" echoes Paul's description of the false teachers as "puffed-up" (6:4); in both cases, pride and a high-estimation are the underlying quality. Here, not only are the young-plant false teachers "being-puffed-up" and already "puffed-up" on account of having too much influence too soon (3:6; 6:4), but as a result of supposing godliness to be a means-of-gain (6:5), wanting to be-rich (6:9a), and being motivated by the affection-of-money (6:10a) they have fallen into the temptation of being "haughty"—thinking-lofty about themselves. In short, the "haughty" false teachers view their success as meritorious and the result of their own doing.[241] Such is antithetical to the sound teaching that results in godliness

---

238. That the false teachers are overseers in Ephesus, see discussion in chapter 2 regarding 1 Timothy 5:20, 22; see also volume 1, chapter 1 regarding Acts 20:28–30.

239. See volume 2, chapter 3 regarding 1 Timothy 4:3, 8a.

240. The verb, however, is rare, found only here in the NT.

241. Harper aptly describes the nuance: "People tend to become arrogant when they believe they are in control of their future. Money creates the illusion of control,

(6:3): it is solely the godliness of Jesus Christ (3:16) who gave himself as a ransom on behalf of all (2:5) that is meritorious. Whereas the "haughty" false teachers praise their own work—themselves (6:17)—Paul underscores that all praise is due to the blessed God and only Power, the King and Lord (1:17; 6:15). Indeed, that the false teachers are "haughty" (6:17) articulates the opposite disposition that results from receiving the undeserved blessings of grace, mercy, and peace from God the Father and Christ Jesus the Lord (1:2) who alone are deserving of grace in return (1:12). Furthermore, where Paul links "to be-haughty" with "the rich" (6:17), the implication seems to be that both characteristics integrally stand in opposition to the reception of grace, mercy, and peace—namely, of salvation.[242] To be sure, though Paul is specifically addressing the false teachers, the remedial effect would be felt by the entire audience: even those who profess godliness and an agreement with the sound words and teaching of Jesus Christ may functionally—quite possibly unknowingly—adhere to a "haughty" disposition and lifestyle commensurate with "the rich in this present age" (6:17) rather than with "contentment" that comes directly from the salvific blessings from God and Jesus Christ (6:6, 8).

The antithetical relation between "to be-haughty" and the reception of salvation—and the expression thereof—is corroborated by the second part of Timothy's charge: "nor hope upon the without-certainty of riches"[243] (6:17). The alliterative play on words is not only apparrent but also telling: "the rich (πλουσίοις) . . . hope (ἠλπικέναι) upon riches (πλούτου)"; simply put, the rich hope in themselves.[244] The prideful disposition "to be-haugh-

---

and the Bible teaches that the greatest danger of wealth is self-dependence rather than God-dependence" ("Discipleship," 230). France, *Tim*, 60: "The danger of wealth is that it may encourage its possessors to worship the creature instead of the Creator. It makes people 'haughty' (v. 17)."

242. The connection here between the affection-of-money and haughtiness as a collective disposition that refuses grace, mercy, and peace echoes Jesus's teaching; see Mark 10:17–27, esp. v. 25: "It is easier for a camel to go through the eye of a needle than for a rich-person (πλούσιν) to enter into the kingdom of God." Like Jesus, Paul implies that "hope . . . upon God" is difficult for "the rich" (6:17).

243. In this sense, the conjunction "nor" (μηδέ) functions almost epexegetically, thus specifying what it means "to be-haughty."

244. See Malherbe, "Godliness, Part II," 75. Paul's alliterative use of the "p" (π) sound was also heard in 6:9 of the parallel B element; see above. Where the parallel alliteration in the B and B' elements would strengthen the rhetorical arrangement and connection, it may also be worth noting the continued "p" alliteration in 6:17 in comparison to 6:9:
B element: "to be-rich" (πλουτεῖν), "fall" (ἐμπίπτουσιν), "temptation" (πειρασμόν), "snare" (παγίδα), "longings" (ἐπιθυμίας), "many" (πολλάς) (6:9);
B' element: "rich" (πλουσίοις), "charge" (παράγγελλε), "to be-haughty" (ὑψηλοφρονεῖν [the "ψ" aurally likely produces a "π-" sound]), "to hope" (ἠλπικέναι), "upon" (ἐπί),

ty" is thus expounded by the fact that the rich false teachers think highly not only of themselves but of their success—"riches." Indeed rather than viewing their "riches" as gracious, merciful gifts from God, instead the false teachers praise themselves. Furthermore, the verb "to hope" (ἠλπικέναι) here in the A' unit recalls its cognate occurrences throughout the macrochiasm. To be sure, the audience hear the statement as a stark contrast to Paul's opening declaration of the letter where Christ Jesus is identified as "our hope" (ἐλπίδος) in 1:1 of the A unit. Indeed, aside from its occurrence in 3:14, the audience have heard Paul use the verb "hope" with a soteriological nuance: "for we have hoped (ἠλπίκαμεν) upon the living God" (4:10); "she . . . has hoped (ἤλπικεν) upon God" (5:5). Paul's implication in 6:17, therefore, is clear: for the rich "to hope" on "riches" means that they find their ultimate hope—their salvation—"upon" (ἐπί) riches—indeed, upon themselves, "the rich"—versus "upon" (ἐπ') Christ Jesus (1:16; cf. 1:1) and "upon" (ἐπί) God (4:10; 5:5).

Furthermore, that Paul defines riches in terms of "without-certainty" (ἀδηλότητι) is immediately pitted against the remedial clause: "rather upon God" (6:17). The conjuctive term "rather" (ἀλλ') highlights the rhetorical juxtaposition, the sense being: "Don't hope upon uncertainty! Instead, hope upon God!" To be sure, given that "the rich" are effectively hoping upon themselves, Paul is effectively pitting the finitude and "without-certainty" of humans against the certain hope "upon God" (ἐπὶ θεῷ, 6:17).[245] In contrast to humans who brought-in nothing into the world and do-not have-the-power to bring-out some-thing (6:7), God is the only Power, the King and Lord, who alone is holding without-death and eternal strength (6:15–16). It is God who provides-life (6:13), that is, eternal life to humans through the person and work of the one mediator of God and humans, the human Christ Jesus (1:16; 2:5; 6:12). Undoubtedly, the implication is clear: "to hope . . . upon God" is to hope upon certainty. The audience understand that "riches"—namely, the "without-certainty" and finite nature of those who are "rich"—cannot provide any hope when they exit "this present age" (6:17); rather, only God can—and he does. Here, then, the missional intention of the charge would not go unheard: along with Paul, Timothy, and the faithful in the audience for whom Christ Jesus is their hope (1:1) because they themselves have hoped upon God (4:10; 5:5), Paul wants the rich false teachers "to hope . . . upon God" rather than upon riches (1:17) and thus

---

"riches" (πλούτου), "upon" (ἐπί), "brings-about" (παρέχοντι), "all" (πάντα), "richly" (πλουσίως), "enjoyment" (ἀπόλαυσιν) (6:17).

245. See Knight, PE, 273. Marshall, PE, 671: "the construction emphasises the thought of insecurity. Earthly wealth belongs entirely to this world and therefore is no basis for security in the world to come."

freely receive grace, mercy, and peace from God the Father and Christ Jesus the Lord (1:2) so that they would-inevitably-come to have-faith upon Christ Jesus for life eternal (1:16).

Still, the immediate contrast between "without-certainty" and "God" reiterates that "to hope" upon riches or oneself is anything but an amoral decision. That is, in the same way that "someone" does *not* come-toward the sound words of the Lord Jesus Christ (6:3), so too their decision to hope upon riches—*not* upon God (6:17)—is the deliberate rejection of a personal, trusting relationship with Jesus Christ and God. The gravity of not hoping upon God represents a personal allegiance.[246] While Paul's statement missionally intends for the rich false teachers to "hope . . . upon God" (6:17), for those in the church who are influenced by the false teachers's "hope upon . . . riches" (6:17) Paul's statement is heard as a warning: if not already, "the rich" are in danger of becoming apostates on account of their "riches." Certainly, for this reason the audience understand that Paul wants the women *not* to cosmetic themselves in "rich" attire (2:9)—more than missional godliness, their salvation is at stake. In full, Paul's command for Timothy to charge the rich false teachers—indeed, anyone in the audience—"not to be-haughty, nor to hope upon the without-certainty of riches, rather upon God" (6:17) would convey the specific sense of, "Charge them not to build their hope for salvation upon anything or anyone else except upon God."

Paul goes on to describe God: "the one who brings-about to us all-things richly for enjoyment" (6:17). The verb "brings-about" (παρέχοντι) here in the A' unit recalls its only other occurrence in the macrochiasm, namely in the parallel A unit wherein Paul described that "some" who teach-different "bring-about" (παρέχουσιν) controversial-speculations rather than the household-law of God in faith (1:4). In effect, the audience hear Paul frame the entire letter upon an explicit rhetorical contrast: that which the false teachers "bring-about"—controversial-speculations (1:4)—seeks to undermine that which God "brings-about"—God's very own household-law (1:4), which results in "to us all-things richly for enjoyment" (6:17). In other words, not only do the false teachers *not* hope upon God, but they do not want what he wants. Moreover, where Paul's use of the dative pronoun "to us" (ἡμῖν) recalls its cognate occurrences throughout the macrochiasm, a further contrast would be apparent: God is "our" (ἡμῶν) Savior (1:1; 2:3); Christ Jesus is "our" (ἡμῶν) hope (1:1) and "our" (ἡμῶν) Lord (1:2, 12, 14; 6:3. 14). Undoubtedly, while Paul's use of "our" highlighted a common bond between himself, Timothy, and the faithful

---

246. Such echoes the Jesus tradition preserved in Matthew 6:24: "No one is powerful to slave for two lords . . . You are not powerful to slave for God and also mammon." See also Luke 16:13.

in the Ephesian church, the audience understand that Paul's rhetorical use of "to us" intends to fully distinguish "us"—who hope upon God—from "some"—who hope upon riches.[247]

Furthermore, that God brings-about to Paul, Timothy, and the faithful "all-things richly for enjoyment" (6:17) would convey several nuances. In view of the current microchiasm, the term "all-things" (πάντα, 6:17) here in the B' element recalls its occurrence in the parallel B element regarding God who provides-life to "all-things" (πάντα, 6:13). Still, "all-things" (πάντα) in 6:17 recalls its cognate occurrences throughout the macrochiasm, which have carried forward a sustained connotation in regard to God's missional desire for "all" (πάντας) humans to be-saved (2:4): such is the fundamental reason why Paul exhorts the church first of "all" (πάντων) to pray on behalf of "all" (πάντων) humans and "all" (πάντων) who are in authority and to lead a life in "all" (πάσῃ) godliness (2:1–2); why Christ Jesus gave himself as a ransom on behalf of "all" (πάντων, 2:6); why Paul wants men to pray in "all" (παντί) place without anger and word-quarreling (2:8) and wants women to exhibit a corresponding disposition in "all" (πάσῃ) submissiveness (2:11); why qualified overseers are to hold children in submissiveness with "all" (πάσης) respectability (3:4) and why deacons's wives are to be faithful in "all" (πᾶσιν, 3:11); why godliness is for "all" (πάντα) profitability (4:8), the faithful word is worthy of "all" (πάσης) acceptance (4:9; 1:15), and Timothy is to manifest his progress to "all" (πᾶσιν, 4:15); and why godly widows have followed in "all" (παντί) good work (5:10), Timothy must reprove those who-sin in the sight of "all" (πάντων, 5:20), and Christian slaves must consider their own masters worthy of "all" (πάσης) honor (6:1).

What is more, the phrase "all-things (πάντα) . . . for enjoyment (εἰς ἀπόλαυσιν)" echoes Paul's earlier statement that "all (πᾶν) creation of God is commendable and nothing is to be rejected, being-received with thanksgiving" (4:4). In both instances, the implication is certainly that the faithful (4:3)—"us" (6:17)—are intended to receive and enjoy all creation (4:3–4)—"all-things" (6:17). However, explicity over and above the reception and enjoyment of creation, Paul draws attention not to "all creation" or "all-things" but rather to the Creator of "all creation" and "all-things," namely "God" (θεοῦ, 4:4; θεῷ, 6:17). Heard in full across the cumulative progression of the macrochiasm, the audience are to understand that "God, the one who brings-about to us all-things . . . for enjoyment" fundamentally intends for the faithful—those who hope upon him—to enjoy *him* in the present life and in the inevitable-coming life. The danger, then, that Paul's charge intends to stave off and correct is an enjoyment of "riches"—God's

---

247. See Towner, *Letters*, 426.

creation—over and above an enjoyment of the God himself—the Creator. Furthermore, where Paul highlights an integral connection between one's "enjoyment" and that which they "hope upon," a stark contrast is emphasized: "the rich . . . hope upon . . . riches . . . for enjoyment"; Paul, Timothy, and the faithful hope "upon God . . . for enjoyment" (6:17). Evidently, the puffed-up, haughty, "rich" false teachers have lost sight of the fact that ultimately God—not themselves—is both the only Power who has provided for them and the only God to be enjoyed.[248]

Still, it is in this context of hope and enjoyment that Paul's use of the adverb "richly" (πλουσίως) would signify a jarring rhetorical contrast. That is, even in this present age (6:17), it is not "rich" (πολυτελεῖ) attire (2:9), nor wanting "to be-rich" (πλουτεῖν, 6:9a), nor being "rich" (πλουσίοις), nor "riches" (πλούτου) that God intends for ultimate enjoyment (6:17). Rather, where God intends for himself to be the ultimate enjoyment, it is hope upon him—the reception of salvation and life eternal (1:16; 4:10; 5:5)—by which the faithful may fully receive "all-things richly (πλουσίως) for enjoyment." The result of Paul's remedial charge against the false teachers is thus apparent: by "hope . . . upon God" for eternal life, "the rich" may "richly" enjoy "riches" "in this present age" as intended, namely as a means to honor, praise, and worship God (6:16).

To be sure, where the faithful understand that godliness equates to being content with "having food and clothing" (6:8), it is clear that "all-things richly for enjoyment" does not in any way convey that God's concern is to provide material "riches" for them; rather, it is to provide "richly" what is necessary for enjoyment that is commensurate with godliness, namely that which has the promise of life for the present *and* for the inevitable-coming (4:8b). In this way, where "richly" (πλουσίως) connotes an abundance,[249] the audience would likely hear a conceptual echo of Paul's statement in the parallel A unit: "the grace of our Lord beyond-abounded (ὑπερεπλεόνασεν) with the faith and love that are in Christ Jesus" (1:14). Not only, then, does "all-things richly for enjoyment" have in view the salvific, divine blessings of grace, faith, and love, but the phrase specifically has in view Christ Jesus, the one in whom God "brings-about to us all-things richly for enjoyment"—indeed, eternal life.[250] In this way, the scope of that which God

---

248. Knight, *PE*, 273, captures the intent: "This is meant to encourage the rich to put their hope in the Giver and not in the gifts."

249. See Marshall, *PE*, 673; Knight, *PE*, 273.

250. The implication is similar to Paul's other letter to the Ephesian church: "Blessed be the God and Father of our Lord Jesus Christ, who has blessed us in Christ with every spiritual blessing in the heavenly places" (Eph 1:3, *ESV*).
It may also be worth noting the linguistic similarity:

"brings-about" is certainly all-encompassing: in Christ, God has already brought-about every blessing for his people—most significantly, salvific blessings that he continually brings-about as his people hope upon him and which will be enjoyed for eternity "in glory" (3:16; cf. 1:16). Indeed, in view of Christ Jesus, the audience understand that God "brings-about to us all-things richly for enjoyment" (6:17).[251]

In verse 6:18, Paul goes on to identify the resultant lifestyle that flows from hope upon God: the rich may richly enjoy their riches "to do-good-work, to be-rich in commendable works, to be generous, liberal." Verse 6:18 would likely be understood in two pairs: a pair of two actions—"to to-good-work, to be-rich in commendable works"—and of two attitudes—"to be generous, liberal."[252] More specifically, the pair of actions would likley be understood as an outward expression of the pair of inward attitudes. Regarding the first pair, linguistically the audience would hear that the common denominator (see *italics*) is an emphasis on "work": "to do-good-*work*" (ἀγαθοεργεῖν) and "to be-rich in commendable *works* (ἔργοις)" (6:18). To be sure, such an evidential lifestyle as a result of hoping upon God was heard throughout the letter: women who profess godliness cosmetic themselves consistent-with "good works" (ἔργων ἀγαθῶν, 2:10); qualified men are fit for the "commendable work" (καλοῦ ἔργου) of an overseer (3:1); godly widows both are testified in "commendable works" (ἔργοις καλοῖς) and have followed in all "good work" (ἔργῳ ἀγαθῷ); indeed, such "commendable works" (τὰ ἔργα τὰ καλά) are conspicuous (5:25). At least implied, then, the audience understand that a life without good or commendable works indicates that one does not hope upon God, that is, has not experienced "all-things richly for enjoyment" (6:17) that are "in Christ Jesus" (1:14).[253]

---

1 Tim 6:17: "God, the one who brings-about to us all-things richly (πλουσίως) for enjoyment";

Eph 1:7: "In him we have redemption ... forgiveness ... according to the riches (πλοῦτος) of his grace."

The implication in both instances is that God's richness toward his people can only be appreciated in view of Jesus Christ.

251. Cf. Downs, "The God Who Gives Life," 253: "That earthly possessions should be employed 'for [the purpose of] enjoyment' (εἰς ἀπόλαυσιν) is often linked to Paul's anti-ascetic affirmation earlier in the letter ... (1 Tim. 4:4–5) ... In this sense, ἀπόλαυσις is realized not in self-indulgence or in greedy consumption but in the humble acknowledgment that God is the one who richly grants all things for the purpose of enjoyment."

252. That the first pair has two distinct infinitives (ἀγαθοεργεῖν πλουτεῖν) while the second pair has one infinitive (εἶναι) and two distinct adjectives would be apparent.

253. For a more explicit treatment of the inseparable tie between faith and work, see Jeon, *Exhort and Reprove*, 110–11.

Furthermore, the specification "to be-rich" in commendable works would convey a twofold implication. On the one hand, Paul intends to identify what it means "to be-rich" with hope "upon God" (6:17–18) in distinction from what it means be "rich" with "hope upon . . . riches" (6:17). The "rich" (πλουσίοις) false teachers "hope upon . . . riches (πλούτου)" (6:17)—upon themselves—and thus are wanting "to be-rich" (πλουτεῖν, 6:9a) as their source of enjoyment—an entirely self-oriented motivation. Conversely, for the faithful who hope "upon God"—not themselves—and thus "richly" (πλουσίως) enjoy all-things in Christ Jesus (6:17), they enjoy "to be-rich" (πλουτεῖν) in commendable works that have an entirely other-oriented motivation (6:18)—namely, God's missional desire for all humans to be-saved (2:4).[254] On the other hand, Paul is inviting the rich false teachers—indeed, anyone influenced by "some"—to see how hope "upon God" fundamentally transforms what it means for them "to be-rich." That is, by hoping upon God, "the rich" (πλουσίοις) in this present age (6:17a) will stop wanting "to be-rich" (πλουτεῖν, 6:9a) and start wanting to to do-good-work and "to be-rich" (πλουτεῖν) in commendable works (6:18) as an overflow of their personal, trusting relationship with God, who has "richly" (πλουσίως, 6:17b) provided all that they need in Christ Jesus, from whom beyond-abounds grace, faith, and love (1:14). Indeed, for the women who profess godliness in the B unit, then, it is clear why Paul wants them to cosmetic themselves in "good works" rather than "rich" attire (2:9–10): such is fitting for women whose hope upon God has transformed their view of riches.[255] Moreover, it is for this reason that the godly widow—unlike the self-indulgent widow (5:6)—is known for commendable "works" (5:10) precisely because she has hoped upon God (5:5).

---

254. Barentsen further describes the implication of the contrast: "Paul connects false teaching with a desire for honor and profit in a description of deviant leadership, while he connects general benefaction as community service with sound doctrine in a description of Christian leadership" (*Emerging Leadership*, 225).

255. Where Paul intends the "rich" false teachers "to do-good-works" (6:17–18) here in the A' unit of the macrochiasm, and where Paul wants the women to not cosmetic themselves in "rich" attire but rather in "good works" (2:9–10) in the B unit of the macrochiasm, it might be suggested that the women in need of correction in the B unit are the false teachers in the A' unit. However, as heard throughout the macrochiasm, the audience would understand that Paul is addressing false-teaching elders—overseers (5:17, 20)—who are unqualified men (3:1–7); the clear association of women to the false teachers is marked by the influence of the latter (2:12; 5:4, 7–8, 15–16). To be sure, to suggest that the false teachers in the A' unit are the women in the B unit does not fit with the 1 Timothy letter: Paul's corrective concern for the creational order of teaching and governing in the church (2:12–13) is notably absent in 6:17–18, undoubtedly because it is assumed by Paul and the audience that male false teachers are in view. See above note regarding 6:3.

Where Paul is concerned about "work" in relation to what it means "to be-rich" as a result of hope upon God (6:17b–18), the audience would understand the specific connotation of the pair "to do-good-work, to be-rich in commendable works." The verb "to do-good-work" (ἀγαθοεργεῖν) here in 6:18 would refer to using one's possessions for the good of others, that is, "to do-good-work" with one's resources.[256] Similarly, for the "rich" (πλουσίοις) who stop hoping upon the without-certainty of "riches" (πλούτου) and begin hoping upon God who provides "richly" (πλουσίως), the resultant motivation "to be-rich" (πλουτεῖν) in "commendable (καλοῖς) works (ἔργοις)" conveys that they are to abound, flourish, and prosper in that which is "commendable"—namely, works that uphold the "commendable" (καλός) law (1:8), that are "commendable" (καλόν) in the sight of the Savior God (2:3), that maintain a "commendable" (καλήν) testimony from those-outside the church (3:7), and that properly receive and use God's "commendable" (καλόν) creation (4:4). In short, Paul has in view actions that are missional in orientation, that is, attracting others to Christ. Notably, then, it is clear that Paul himself is demonstrating to the audience—and specifically to the false teachers—what "commendable works" look like: Paul desires for the false teachers to abandon their hope upon the without-certainty of riches and to definitively come to hope upon the certainty of God (6:17); Paul desires for the false teachers to see that far above any financial "gain" (6:5), the "great gain" of godliness with contentment (6:6) is found in what God "richly" provides (6:18); Paul desires for the false teachers to see that for all humans who hope upon God, God enables them "to be-rich" (6:18) in a way that simultaneously honors him (6:16). Still, for the entire Ephesian audience, Paul is making clear that tangible evidence—a litmus test—of one's hope upon God is "to-do-good-works, to be-rich in commendable works" (6:18)—the absence thereof is telling.

Corresponding to the first pair of actions, the second pair of attitudes that result from hope upon God—"to be generous, liberal"—are functionally epexegetical, specifying the inward qualities of the outward good and commendable works.[257] The adjective "generous" (εὐμεταδότους)—literally, "good-sharers"—is a compound term from the adverb "well" (εὖ) and the verb "to share" (μεταδίδωμι). Given Paul's immediate emphasis that God en-

---

256. Horton succinctly conveys the point: "If God has given you temporal wealth and position, use it for his glory and your neighbor's good" (*Ordinary*, 139). That Paul is referring to God's provisions of wealth for the purpose of enjoyment (6:17) specifically by the actions and attitudes in 6:18, see discussion in Malherbe, "Godliness, Part II," 89.

257. Cf. Harper, "Discipleship," 231: ". . . to do good, be rich in good deeds, and be generous and willing to share. They are three different ways of saying the same thing, that we have been 'blessed to be a blessing' (Gen. 12:3)."

ables those who hope upon him to act in a certain way with one's resources (6:17–18), the audience understand that "generous" is not a quality that can be summoned by sheer individual volition but rather has a twofold source: hope upon God and the experience thereof. God is King of those who-are-kings and Lord of those who-are-lords, the blessed and only Power who has without-death and eternal strength (16:15–16). To hope upon God, then, is to view all of one's resources as that which *the* King and Lord has entrusted and supplied for the purpose of stewardship—proper management of one's resources in view of God's purposes.[258] Indeed, such is a sobering and humbling antidote against being "haughty" (6:17). Still, it is the personal experience of God's generosity of "all-things richly for enjoyment" (6:17)—the beyond-abounding, salvific blessings that God has provided "in Christ Jesus" (1:14; cf. 1:2)—that effects a "generous" attitude within a person. That is, as much as God freely shares his riches, so also those who hope upon him share the riches that God has supplied to them; those who hope upon God are to be "generous" because God is generous to them.

Similarly, the adjective "liberal" (κοινωνικούς) is a term derived from the adjective "common" (κοινός), which carries the sense of, "belongs to the general populace." Given the familial, household language that pervades the letter—particularly that God the Father's generosity of grace, mercy, and peace is experienced in the familial realm "in faith" (1:2)—the charge to be "liberal" would convey a radically different view of one's "personal" possessions, namely as "family" possessions to be stewarded for the church—God's household (3:15)—according to God's purposes, the Father of the household (1:2).[259] Significantly also, where "liberal" (κοινωνικούς) recalls its cognate occurrence regarding Paul's command for Timothy to not "share" (κοινώνει) in others's sins (5:22)—namely to not support the current false-teaching over-

---

258. Packer aptly captures the implication: "See yourself as a manager, steward, and trustee of God's funds, honored by the responsibility you have been given but totally accountable to God who gave it to you" (*Weakness Is the Way*, 58). Similarly, Barcley, *1 & 2 Tim*, 207: "If God is the Giver, all that we have belongs to him."

259. There is probably no better illustration of what the apostle has in mind than the portrait of the early church in Acts 2:43–45 (*ESV*): "And awe came upon every soul, and many wonders and signs were being done through the apostles. And all who believed were together and had all things in common (κοινά). And they were selling their possessions and belongings and distributing the proceeds to all, as any had need." See Wall with Steele, *1 & 2 Tim*, 150.

It is worth noting that Acts 2:43–45 underscores an embrace of God's majesty as the motivation for their action and attitude: it was an understanding—a conviction—of God's grace and power that bore the fruit of generosity and liberality. It is entirely fitting, then, that the actions and attitudes in 1 Timothy 6:18 are similarly preceded with a lengthy description of God's sovereign power and immeasurable mercy as expressed in Christ Jesus (1 Tim 6:13–17).

seers in Ephesus or appoint new false-teaching overseers—the rhetorical implication would be evident. The false teachers are not part of God's family: by the absence of a "liberal" attitude, the implication is that the false teachers do not share their possessions with God's family, thus neither does God's family "share" in the sins of the false teachers. Still, the transformative implication of Paul's missional desire would also be apparent: by coming to hope upon God (6:17), those who were once false-teachers—those who-sin (5:20, 22)—will become "liberal" (6:18) that is, part of God's family who will "share" (cf. 5:22) in good and commendable works with those "in faith."

Heard together, as with the pair of outward actions in 6:18, the pair of attitudes—"generous, liberal"—functions as a litmus test for one's hope upon God. To be sure, where Paul specifically has the false teachers in view, it is evident that their consuming affection-of-money (6:10a) in the parallel B element stems from their absence of hope upon God in the B' element. Indeed, in view of the immediate arrangement of the B and B' elements, Paul seems to be highlighting the issue of security—hope upon God—versus false security—hope upon riches. The false teachers are trapped in a feedback loop of self-oriented motivation: they seek to establish security—"wanting to be-rich" (6:9a, B element)—yet can never be secure—"the without-certainty of riches" (6:17, B' element)—and thus continue the cycle of "wanting to be-rich" (6:9a). It is because the false teachers constantly need to acquire money as the measure of their security that they are devoid of a "generous, liberal" attitude that enjoys "to do-good-works, to be-rich in commendable works" (6:18). Such "hope upon the without-certainty of riches" (6:17, B' element) clearly articulates the trap of hoping upon anything else except God, which is to "fall into temptation and snare and many senseless and harmful longings, which plunge humans into ruin and destruction" (6:9, B element). Not only conceptually but practically, Paul identifies how Christian salvation—the certainty of God and hope upon him as the source of security—has the power to free "those wanting to be-rich" (6:9a) unto an other-oriented, "generous, liberal" attitude that enables them to hold loosely to their possessions and resources, which are repurposed "to do-good-works, to be-rich in commendable works" (6:18). In short, hope upon God (6:17) will transform even the self-absorbed, grudging attitude of "some" into a "generous, liberal" attitude that finds enjoyment "to do-good-works, to be-rich in commendable works" (6:18).

Paul goes on to describe the further result of hoping upon God: "storing-up for themselves a commendable basis for the inevitable-coming" (6:19a). Given the context of riches in 6:17–18, the sense of the verb "storing-up" (ἀποθησαυρίζοντας) would likely convey "storing-up *treasure*."[260] In this way, the audience may have understood "storing-up" (ἀποθησαυρίζοντας) in 6:19 as an echo of the Jesus tradition preserved in Matthew 6:19-21:

> [19] Do not store-up (θησαυρίζετε) for yourselves treasures (θησαυρούς) upon the earth, where moth and rust destroy and where thieves break in and steal, [20] but store-up (θησαυρίζετε) for yourselves treasures (θησαυρούς) in heaven, where neither moth nor rust destroys and where thieves do not break in nor steal. [21] For where your treasure (θησαυρός) is, there your heart will be also.[261]

Here in 6:19, then, the "storing-up" in view would be heard to emphasize the tangible contrast between "hope upon the without-certainty of riches" versus "upon God" in 6:17—with the pairing of actions and attitudes in 6:18 functioning as the demonstration of the latter. That is, as a result of expressing one's hope upon God (6:17), the corresponding actions and attitudes "to do-good work, the be-rich in commendable works, to be generous, liberal" (6:18) are "storing-up" confidence that a person in fact hopes upon God rather than upon riches. Thus where the connotation of "treasure" is in view, Paul's statement in 6:19a carries the sense of, "storing-up as treasure a commendable basis for the inevitable-coming."[262] In other words, rather than earning material treasure in heaven, the audience understand that the actions and attitudes in 6:18 are to be viewed as an assurance—"a commendable basis"—of one's salvation in 6:19 as the outworking their hope upon God rather than upon riches.[263] Such is corroborated by Paul's

---

260. Such is supplied by most translations: *ESV*, "storing up treasure for themselves"; see also *NASB*, *NIV*, *NRSV*; cf. *KJV*, which does not supply "treasures": "Laying up in store for themselves."

Given that the notion of "treasure" is absent in Paul's use of the related related verb θησαυρίζω in the other Pauline letters (Rom 2:5; 1 Cor 16:2; 2 Cor 16:12), the simple translation "storing-up" here in 1 Timothy 6:19 seems appropriate.

261. See also Matt 12:35; 19:21; Mark 10:21; Luke 6:45; 12:21, 33, 34; 18:22.

262. Contra *ESV*, which suggests that "treasure" is the "good foundation." Cf. *NASB* and *NIV*, which suggest a similar understanding in its translation: "In this way they will lay up treasure for themselves as a firm foundation."

Towner comments on the construction of Paul's statement in 6:19: "The compound form of the verb (*apothēsaurizō*) re-creates the Matthean sense . . . But in place of the object 'treasures in heaven' is the odd phrase 'a firm foundation'" (*Letters*, 428).

263. Contra Downs, "The God Who Gives Life," 258. To be sure, in 6:19 the apostle Paul is concerned with gaining the treasure of assurance of salvation.

This idea is also found explicitly in the Jesus tradition where Jesus challenges the rich young ruler: "You lack one thing: go, sell all that you have and give to the poor, and you will have treasure (θησαυρόν) in heaven; and come, follow me" (Mark 10:21 *ESV*; see also Matt 19:21; Luke 18:22). The concern in this exchange between Jesus and the

back-to-back rhetorical language: in the same way that the action of "commendable (καλοῖς) works" (6:18) substantiates the result of hope upon God (6:17), so too do they substantiate a "commendable (καλόν) basis" (6:19) that is established solely by hope upon God. Indeed, this was already heard by the audience in 3:13 wherein "those who serve-as-deacons commendably (καλῶς) acquire for themselves a commendable (καλόν) standing and much confidence in faith that is in Christ Jesus." Certainly, assurance of salvation—not the achievement of salvation—is in view.[264] For the false teachers, then, the negative implication of Paul's charge to Timothy in the B' element is fully integrated: due to their lack of hope upon God, the rich false teachers lack "commendable" works, which affirms their lack of a "commendable" basis, that is, of salvation. Positively, however, the missional force of Paul's statement would be implied: by charging the false teachers to hope upon God (6:17), both "commendable" works and thus a "commendable" basis would ensue from their compliance. Paul's use of the term "basis" (θεμέλιον) conceptually echoes the function of God's household as "a pillar and foundation (ἑδραίωμα) of truth" (3:15).[265] Such would likely convey the inseparable connection between one's own salvation, namely the assurance thereof (6:19), and the proper functioning of God's household (3:15): those who have a commendable "basis" are generous and liberal with their resources to edify the church in its task to safeguard and exclaim the truth concerning Christ Jesus (3:16).[266]

In short, Paul is expressing a profound theological and existential truth: true treasure is the assurance of salvation and such assurance is plainly evidenced in the way one stewards material resources. Indeed, the implication also flows in the reverse direction: the acquisition of one's "commendable

---

rich young ruler is not so much "treasure in heaven" but a person's ultimate trust—God or riches—which is exactly the same central concern expressed in the contrast between the without-certainty of riches versus the certainty of God (6:17).

264. Contra Hanson, *PE*, 115. It would be mistaken to suppose that Paul is suggesting here "salvation by works" given his pronouncement of sovereign mercy in 1:12–17. Marshall aptly articulates: "we have the normal NT teaching that lack of the expression of faith in good works is an indication of the lack of faith itself, and conversely" (*PE*, 673).

265. The terms "foundation" (ἑδραίωμα) in 3:15 and "basis" (θεμέλιον) in 6:19 are not cognates; however, the conceptual similarity would be apparent. Most translations correctly render the term θεμέλιον in 6:19 as "foundation" (e.g., *ESV*, *NIV*). My translation—"basis"—intends to avoid cognate confusion with "foundation" in 3:15.

266. Cf. Towner's observation concerning the use of the term "basis" (θεμέλιον): "In a description otherwise devoid of architectural imagery, the presence of 'foundation' . . . seems puzzling" (*Letters*, 428). Not only as an echo of 3:15 but also due to the sustained use of household imagery throughout the letter, it seems that Paul's use of the term "basis" is fitting.

basis" (6:19) of salvation is plainly expressed by one's "commendable works" (6:18). Notably, then, in contrast to the false teachers's endless feedback loop of insecurity due to their hope upon riches, Paul articulates its antithesis: as the result of a secure hope upon God (6:17), the faithful do good-work and are rich in commendable works (6:18), thus storing-up a commendable basis of their salvation (6:19), thus demonstrating their generous, liberal attitude by sharing what they have for the good of God's family or for the salvation of others (6:18). The lack of generosity would pose a simple question to all of Paul's audience as to whether they possess a commendable basis—or not.

Still, that salvation is in view would be emphasized by the phrase "for the inevitable-coming."[267] The noun "the inevitable-coming" (τὸ μέλλον) recalls its cognate occurrences throughout the macrochiasm: Paul was granted-mercy so that Christ Jesus might display all patience as an example to "those who would-inevitably-come" (μελλόντων) to have-faith upon him for life eternal (1:16); Timothy and the faithful are to train themselves for godliness, which has the promise of life for the present and for "the inevitable-coming" (τῆς μελλούσης, 4:8). In both 1:16 and 4:8, eternal life was in view; undoubtedly, the audience understand that Paul intends the same connotation here in 6:19. Indeed, the implication of eternal life was already implied by Paul's statement in 6:17 regarding "this present age" (νῦν αἰῶνι), which recalled Paul's coupling of "life for the present and for the inevitable-coming (τῆς νῦν καὶ τῆς μελλούσης) in 4:8. In effect, the audience hear a reiteration of the contrast between those who "hope upon the without-certainty of riches" and those who hope "upon God" (6:17): the false teachers have no basis "for the inevitable-coming" (6:19) because they are entirely rooted "in this present age" (6:17). That is, though they brought-in nothing into the world and do-not have-the-power to bring-out some-thing (6:7), the false teachers mistakenly try to make this world and this present age as their lasting abode; they have no view toward the true eternity—"the inevitable-coming" (6:19); hence, their obsession with money and material resources. For Paul, Timothy, and the faithful among the audience, however, it their hope upon God (6:17)—and thus their orientation toward "the inevitable-coming" (6:19)—by which they deliberately and purposefully steward their resources with a generous, liberal attitude that is expressed through good and commendable works (6:18).

---

267. Where the apostle is alluding to the Jesus tradition—"store-up for yourselves treasures in heaven" (Matt 6:20)—there does appear to be a deliberate change from "in heaven" (Matt 6:20) to "for the inevitable-coming" (1 Tim 6:19). Where the two phrases are interchangeable, indeed there is synonymy in regard to salvation.

In 6:19b, Paul goes on to state the ultimate purpose of Timothy's charge to the false teachers: "that they might take-possession of that which is truly life." Within the purpose clause—"that" (ἵνα)—the phrase "take-possession (ἐπιλάβωνται) of that which is truly life (ζωῆς)" here in 6:19b of the B' element recalls its parallel occurrence in 6:12 of the B element wherein Timothy is to "take-possession (ἐπιλαβοῦ) of the eternal life (ζωῆς)." Significantly, the audience not only hear that Paul has eternal life in view but also—and much more—that Paul's missional desire is emphatic: he wants the false teachers to share in eternal life with him, Timothy, and the faithful.[268] Indeed, the parallelism qualifies the entire paraenetic section extending from the B to B' element: where Timothy must agonize the commendable agony of the faith—specifically in view of the false teachers—so that he may "take-possession of the eternal life" in the B element (6:12), here in the parallel B' element the audience understand that that Timothy is to do so by charging the false teachers (6:17) so that they, too, may "take-possession of that which is truly life" (6:19). In other words, Timothy's agony to preserve his own salvation against the attacks of the false teachers is simultaneously missional, intending the salvation of the false teachers themselves. Thus the movement from the B to B' element conveys a transformation: rather than plunging themselves into ruin and destruction (6:9), Timothy must charge the false teachers so that they may have "that which is truly life" instead (6:19). The inclusion of the adverb "truly" (ὄντως) recalls its multiple occurrences in the preceding microchiasm with regard to widows who are "truly" (ὄντως) widows (5:3, 5, 16). As in the fifth microchiasm, "truly" in 6:19b invites the audience—particularly the false teachers—to discern what is "truly life"—to be sure, what is truly eternal life.[269] The rhetorical irony here is apparent: the rich false teachers who are living exclusively in view of this present age do not actually possess "that which is truly life"—they have no commendable basis for the inevitable-coming (6:19). Indeed, to "take-possession" thereof, they must first let go of that which is not truly life—the without-certainty of riches (6:17). It is only by adopting the paradox—to be generous and liberal with one's riches rather than clinging to one's riches—that the false teachers will have an experience of "that which is truly life,"

---

268. Spencer, *1 Tim*, 163: "*Eternal life* (6:12) is *the real life* (6:19)." Knight, *PE*, 274–75: "In light of the reference in the previous clause to 'the future' (εἰς τὸ μέλλον) and the parallelism of this clause with the second clause of v. 12 (which has the singular imperative of the same verb and αἰωνίου in place of ὄντως), τῆς ὄντως ζωῆς, 'real life,' must refer here to 'eternal life.'" Contra Downs, "The God Who Gives Life," 251: "the phrase τῆς ὄντως ζωῆς is not the equivalent of 'eternal life' (cf. 1 Tim. 6:12)"; see ibid., 256–58.

269. See the textual variant αἰωνίου, which seeks to heighten the connection between 6:12 and 6:19.

namely hope upon God (6:17) and the reception of true riches—the grace, mercy, and peace that God richly provides (1:2; 6:17).[270] In sum, Timothy's charge to the false teachers expresses a full participation with God's very own missional desire for all humans to be-saved (2:3-4); such is a tangible demonstration "of that which is truly life" (6:19)—eternal life (6:12)—here and now "in this present age" (6:17).[271]

The B' element concludes with a final exhortation directed explicitly to Timothy: "O Timothy, the entrustment guard, turning-aside from the vile empty-talk and contradictions of false-named knowledge" (6:20). The emphatic vocative "O" (Ὦ) here in 6:20 of the B' element recalls the parallel vocative in 6:11 of the B element, "O (ὦ) human of God" wherein Timothy is commanded to flee that which leads to ruin and destruction and to pursue that which is commensurate with faith upon Christ Jesus.[272] Again, Paul's rhetorical use of the vocative conveys not only the personal appeal but also the gravity with which he addresses Timothy.[273] Still, Paul's rhetorical use of the name "Timothy" here in the A' unit would be apparent, recalling the only other occurrences of Timothy's name throughout the macrochiasm, which were heard in the parallel A unit (1:2, 18).[274] To be sure, Paul's vocative use of "Timothy" (Τιμόθεε, 6:20) in the A' unit and "Timothy" (Τιμόθεε, 1:18) in the A unit would not go unnoticed. Moreover, given that "the entrustment" here in the A' unit recalls its cognate verb in the parallel A unit, the deliberate rhetorical arrangement of the macrochiasm would be apparent:

270. Towner, *Letters*, 429: "This distinction ['true life'] continues the reversal of values motif already expressed by the transitory present-worldly wealth and the divine provision, as well as by the paradoxical assertion that sharing wealth 'now' is in reality an acquisition of heavenly wealth."

271. Marshall, *PE*, 674: "Clearly heavenly life is meant, but the phrase includes spiritual life here and now (cf. 6.12)."

272. The chiastic arrangement between the B element (6:9-14) and B' element (6:17-20) can be appreciated further by observing the following:
6:11: "But you, O (ὦ) human of God . . .";
6:12: ". . . take-possession of the eternal life (ἐπιλαβοῦ τῆς αἰωνίου ζωῆς) . . .";
6:19: ". . . take-possession of that which is truly life (ἐπιλάβωνται τῆς ὄντως ζωῆς) . . .";
6:20: "O (Ὦ) Timothy . . ."

273. Knight, *PE*, 276: "Ὦ, an emotional interjection, is used here to add solemnity and urgency to his personal address to Timothy." See Barcley, *1 & 2 Tim*, 210.

274. The parallelism within the A unit—the first microchiasm—is itself striking:
A element: Τιμοθέῳ (1:2);
A' element: Τιμόθεε (1:18).
Such would strengthen the rhetorical force of Paul's statement in the parallel A' unit of the macrochiasm.

A unit: "To Timothy (Τιμοθέῳ, 1:2) . . . This charge I entrust (παρατίθεμαί) to you child Timothy (Τιμόθεε) (1:18);

A' unit: "O Timothy (Τιμόθεε), the entrustment (παραθήκην) guard (6:20).[275]

Though unstated in 6:20, the familial implication from 1:18—"child Timothy"—would likely be carried forward in the parallel A' unit.[276] Such would not only remind Timothy to fully represent Paul as "Timothy, genuine child in faith" (1:2), but it would also remind the entire audience of Timothy's direct authority to protect and execute "the entrustment" from the apostle Paul (1:18; 6:20), and thus from God and Christ Jesus (1:1). In this way, the integrated rhetorical effect of both "Timothy" (1:2, 18; 6:20) and "I entrust" (1:18) and "the entrustment" (6:20) would prepare the audience to hear Paul's concluding remarks in the letter, namely a condensed summary of his overarching concern.

In 1:18 of the introductory A unit, that of which Paul says "I entrust" (παρατίθεμαί) was the charge for Timothy to preserve the teaching of the gospel over and against the false teachers in Ephesus. Here, then, in 6:20 of the concluding A' unit, Timothy is reminded of the same "entrustment" (παραθήκην) to preserve the teaching of the gospel.[277] Indeed, given the

275. Keegan, *First and Second Tim*, 11: "Both [the opening and closing bracket] . . . focus on the charge entrusted to Timothy (1:18; 6:20), both times using the Greek vocative case (indicating the person addressed, 'Timothy'), a case rarely used in the New Testament and used only these two times in this letter, a clear indication of their parallel and bracketing function." Van Neste, "Cohesion and Structure in the PE," 94: "the vocative Τιμόθεε occurs in 1:18 and 6:20 and nowhere else in the letter . . . 'Deposit' language is found in both 1:18 . . . and 6:20 . . . where Timothy is seen as the recipient of a message or task from Paul."

276. Ames and Miller, "Prayer and Syncretism in 1 Tim," 96: "1 Timothy is case as correspondence between father and son. Paul addresses the letter to Timothy, whom he calls 'my loyal child' (γνησίῳ τέκνῳ) (1:2). Vocatives near the beginning ('my child Timothy' [τέκνον Τιμόθεε], 1:18) and end ('O Timothy' [ʹΩ Τιμόθεε], 6:20) enhance this intimate tone."

277. Witherington, *Letters*, 298: "The word *parathēkē* here refers to something that has been entrusted to another for safekeeping, and that the trustee has a sacred duty to guard or protect . . . Here the deposit surely is the gospel, both in its theological and ethical dimensions." Barcley, *1 & 2 Tim*, 211: "The 'deposit' has been interpreted in various ways, but the most likely reference is to the truth and teachings of the gospel. In context here, it is set over against the false teaching." Cf. Marshall, *PE*, 675: "Here it is clearly the gospel which is meant, i.e., the whole of the apostolic teaching . . . it is not the charge to Timothy expressed in 1.18 but rather that which Timothy is charged to preserve." Contra Marshall, it is evident that both the charge in 1:18 equally has in view the preservation of the teaching, that is, the gospel.

The term "entrustment" (παραθήκην) is also translated as "deposit" (e.g., *ESV*). Barcley explains: "The idea of guarding the deposit is taken from life in the ancient world

rhetorical force of the parallel vocatives "Timothy" (Τιμόθεε, 1:18) and "Timothy" (Τιμόθεε, 6:20) in the A and A' units, the personal nature of Paul's framing concern in the letter—the entrustment (1:18; 6:20)—is emphatically placed upon Timothy.

Still, the verb "guard" (φύλαξον) in 6:20 recalls "you might guard" (φυλάξῃς) in 5:21, wherein the audience heard an echo of Paul's military language to Timothy in the A unit, namely that "you might charge" (παραγγείλῃς) in 1:3 and that "you might war" (στρατεύῃ) in 1:18.[278] Here in 6:20 of the A' unit, then, the same connotation carries forward and parallels the military language of the A unit: as a soldier would, Timothy is to both protect and execute "the entrustment"—that is, to both preserve the teaching of the gospel and to promote its corresponding missional godliness that intends the salvation of all humans, particularly of "some" who actively seek to undermine it. Indeed, given the arrangement of the macrochiasm, the phrase "the entrustment guard" would express an emphatic, all-encompassing summary of Paul's letter.[279] In order to "guard"—protect and execute—"the entrustment"—*the charge to preserve the teaching and promote godliness as God's missional household*—Timothy must: stop the false teachers from teaching some-thing different that lies-opposed to the sound teaching, the gospel, in the A unit (1:3-20); uphold God's creational design for gender roles in his household in the B unit (2:8-15); assert qualifications for leadership in God's household in the C unit (3:1-13); exemplify the truth regarding God's creation and the universal offer of salvation by maintaining proper worship in the church in the C' unit (4:1-16); foster mercy initiatives and godly conduct (5:3-16; 6:1-2) and ensure that false-teaching overseers do not lead God's household (5:17-25) in the B' unit; and demonstrate the missional calling of the church by striving for the salvation of the false teachers in the A' unit (6:3-19). In sum, given the combined rhetorical force of the back-to-back parallel vocatives "Timothy" (Τιμόθεε, 1:18) and "Timothy" (Τιμόθεε, 6:20) and military language "charge" (παραγγελίαν, 1:18) and

---

where one person would be asked by another to care for a treasured possession while he was away. The person entrusted with the deposit was bound, under sacred duty, to protect it" (*1 & 2 Tim*, 210–11). See Saarinen, *PE*, 114–15. Knight, *PE*, 276: "Paul places Timothy under such a trust with regard to the gospel and its teaching."

278. France, *Tim*, 61: "'guard' is again military language."

279. Towner comments on the combination of "the entrustment guard" (τὴν παραθήκην φύλαξον): "The distinctive phrase . . . alludes to the process (in Greco-Roman and Jewish cultures) of entrusting some commodity with a person who is to ensure its safekeeping . . . and eventually return it to its owner. Assumed in the process are the ownership of the commodity and the obligation of faithfulness on the part of the trustee" (*Letters*, 430). See Tomlinson, "Purpose and Stewardship Theme," 52–83; Lau, *Manifest in Flesh*, 18–39.

"guard" (φύλαξον, 6:20) in the A and A' units, the intensely personal nature of Paul's parallel declarations "I entrust" (παρατίθεμαί) and "the entrustment" (παραθήκην) would be fully articulated: the onus is placed on none other than Timothy, and Paul expects to get back nothing less than what Timothy began with.

The B' element concludes with the extended participle phrase: "turning-aside from the vile empty-talk and contradictions of false-named knowledge" (6:20). The participle "turning-aside" (ἐκτρεπόμενος) recalls its earlier cognate occurrences in regard to "some" younger widows who already "have turned-aside" (ἐξετράπησαν) after Satan (5:15) and "some" who "have turned-aside" (ἐξετράπησαν) for useless-words (1:6). To be sure, the sudden application of "turning-aside" to Timothy would be forceful and jarring: in stark contrast to the false teachers and those under their influence who have effectively "turned-aside" from Paul's apostolic teaching, Timothy is "turning-aside" from the activities of the false teachers by implementing Paul's teaching. In this way, Paul is underscoring the completely divergent movement of the false teachers in relation to Timothy: whereas the false-teaching overseers in Ephesus "turned-aside" from salvation toward ignorance and destruction (1:6; 5:15), Timothy is "turning-aside" from ignorance and destruction toward salvation (6:20). Indeed, Paul's language explicitly identifies that Timothy's movement is specifically opposite of the false teachers. The phrase "vile empty-talk" (τὰς βεβήλους κενοφωνίας) echoes Paul's polemic against the false teachers. In 1:9 of the parallel A unit, Paul states that the law is laid for the "vile" (βεβήλοις), namely for "some" who desire to be law-teachers without knowing the purpose of the law (1:6–8). Similarly, the compound term "empty-talk" (κενοφωνίας)—taken from the adjective "empty" (κενός) and the noun "voice" (φωνή)—conceptually echoes "some" who have turned-aside for "useless-words" (ματαιολογίαν, 1:6).[280] Furthermore, the phrase "vile (βεβήλους) empty-talk" (6:20) recalls Paul's command for Timothy to reject "vile (βεβήλους) and silly myths" in 4:7, which was undoubtedly heard as a direct reference to the false teachers (cf. 1:4). To be sure, that Timothy is to guard the entrustment while "turning-aside from the vile empty-talk" is not a disengagement with the false teachers; much rather—and much more difficult—Paul's sustained indication throughout of the macrochiasm is clear: "turning-aside" from "vile empty-talk" requires engaging "some"

---

280. Knight, *PE*, 277: "Here Paul is apparently returning to his evaluation in 1:6, now using κενοφωνίας as a synonym for ματαιολογία." Spencer, *1 Tim*, 164: "*Kenophōnia* (empty talk) appears to be a synonym of *mataiologia*. *Mataiologia* are words that have no value because the content is not true . . . *Kenophōnia* are sounds (*phōnē*) that are empty (*kenos*), without a truthful, real goal, therefore, they deceive (Eph 5:6)."

for the purpose of their salvation and without sharing in their sins (5:22). Such is the risk of missional love, namely the end of Paul's charge (1:5) that desires "some" to hope upon God (6:17), to take-possession of that which is truly life (6:19), and thus join Paul, Timothy, and the faithful in Ephesus as part of God's missional household to do-good-work, to be-rich in commendable works, to be generous, liberal, storing-up for themselves a commendable basis for the inevitable-coming (6:18–19).

Given Paul's culminating focus on the false teachers, the phrase "contradictions of false-named knowledge" would be heard by the audience as a further specification of their activities. In this way, the conjunction "and" (καί) would function epexegetically: the synonymy between "contradictions of false-named knowledge" and "vile empty-talk" thus highlighting the climactic juxtaposition between Timothy and the false teachers. Still, the rhetorical nuances would not go unnoticed. Built upon the verb meaning "to put" (τίθημι), the term (see *italics*) "contradictions" (ἀντιθέσεις) recalls its cognates throughout the macrochiasm: "This charge I entrust (παρατίθεμαί) to you (1:18); "Instructing (ὑποτιθέμενος) these-things to the brothers" (4:6); "the-laying (ἐπιθέσεως) of hands of the presbytery" (4:14); "Lay (ἐπιτίθει) hands quickly on none" (5:22); "the entrustment (παραθήκην) guard" (6:20).[281] All five cognate occurrences were specifically in view of and in response to the presence and influence of the false teachers in Ephesus. Here, then, in the climactic A' unit of the macrochiasm, Paul's deliberate use of the term "contradictions" (ἀντιθέσεις) would dramatically summarize the sustained tension of the entire letter—the ἀντι prefix highlighting the completely opposite and destructive activities of the false teachers (cf. 1:10b).[282] In other words, it is directly and entirely because of the "contradictions" imposed by the false teachers that Paul must "entrust" the charge to Timothy (1:18), that Timothy must be "Instructing" the brothers with the correct teaching (4:6), that Timothy must be concerned with his divine gift that was publically affirmed with "the-laying" of hands of the

---

281. See Schlarb, *Die gesunde Lehre*, 62–66. Commenting on Schlarb's work, Towner (*Letters*, 432 n. 66) highlights Paul's rhetorical flair: "Schlarb . . . has shown that the selection of the term ἀντίθεσις corresponds to the author's predilection for placing the apostolic mission and faith in opposition with the heresy by means of words built on the τίθημι verb . . . and by use of the negating a-privative prefixes ἀντί and ἀπό. These observations suggest that the term ἀντίθεσις fits neatly within the polemical lexical repertoire."

282. Spencer, *1 Tim*, 264: "According to Aristotle, an *antithesis* is a syllogism in which contraries are placed side by side." In this sense, and given that "some" who teach-different (1:3, 10; 6:3) are in view, the second phrase "the vile and empty-talk and contradictions of false-named knowledge" could be loosely translated to the effect of, "the ruinous teachings of false-named knowledge."

presbytery (4:14), and that Timothy must not "Lay" hands quickly in the appointment of future overseers. Indeed (see *italics*), where "contradictions" (ἀντιθέσεις) in 6:20 conveys that which is entirely against its cognates "This charge I entrust (παρατίθεμαί) to you, child Timothy" in 1:18 and "O Timothy, the entrustment (παραθήκην) guard" in 6:20, it is clear to the audience that the "contradictions" are specifically in view of the teaching of the gospel and Paul's charge to Timothy for the preservation thereof.[283] At the conclusion of the letter, then, Paul wants the entire audience to be certain: the false teachers are the cause of the problem and the reason for Paul's letter.

The "false-named knowledge" (ψευδωνύμου γνώσεως) further emphasizes and echoes Paul's polemic against the false teachers throughout the macrochiasm. The term "false-named" (ψευδωνύμου) is a composite of the adjective "false" (ψευδής) and the noun "name" (ὄνομα).[284] Regarding the first part of the term (see *italics*), "*false*-named" (ψευδωνύμου) echoes is cognates throughout the macrochiasm as indirect or direct polemical references against the false teachers: in the A unit, the law is laid down for "*falsifiers*" (ψεύσταις, 1:10); in the B unit, unlike the false teachers, Paul is saying the truth, he is not "*falsifying*" (ψεύδομαι, 2:7); and in the C' unit, the apostate "some" are "*false*-worders" (ψευδολόγων, 4:2). Regarding the second part of the term (see *italics*), Paul seems to be underscoring a stark contrast: that which is "false-*named*" (ψευδωνύμου, 6:20) contradicts and does not accurately represent "the *name* (ὄνομα) of God" (6:1)—indeed, it blasphemes the renown of God (6:1), for which reason the false teachers Hymenaeus and Alexander must be-disciplined not to blaspheme (1:20). Emphatically and unmistakably, then, here at the end of the letter Paul wants the entire audience to understand that "some" are *false* teachers. Moreover, that Paul specifically has false-named "knowledge" in view of the false teachers furthers the polemical force of Paul's statement in 6:20.[285] That is, where the term "knowledge" (γνώσεως) recalls its cognate occurrences throughout the macrochiasm, in combination with the adjectival qualifier "false-named" (ψευδωνύμου) the audience understand that Paul is underscoring a complete and total contrast (see *italics*): in 2:4, the Savior God desires all humans to

---

283. Barcley, *1 & 2 Tim*, 211: "the heart of both the words 'deposit' (*parathēkē*) and 'contradiction' (*antithesis*) comes from the same Greek root. Paul is again using wordplay to present the false teaching as that which opposes the truth of the gospel."

284. Marshall, *PE*, 677: "ψευδώνυμος is 'falsely bearing a name, falsely called.'"

285. There is much scholarly discussion regarding Paul's use of the term "knowledge." That the term is connected with later Gnosticism, see Rudolph, *Gnosis*, 302–3; Schmithals, "The Corpus Paulinum and Gnosis," 116; France, *Tim*, 61. That "knowledge" relates to an over-realized eschatology that is described in 2 Timothy, see Towner, *Letters*, 433–34; see also Schlarb, *Die gesunde Lehre*, 120–22.

be-saved, that is, to come to "a *knowing*-embrace" (ἐπίγνωσιν) of truth; in 4:3, Paul identifies the faithful—those who have been saved—as those who "have *knowingly*-embraced" (ἐπεγνωκόσιν) the truth. Still, in combination with the adjectival qualifier "false-named," the audience understand that Paul is underscoring a complete contrast (see *italics*): rather than coming to "a *knowing*-embrace (ἐπίγνωσιν) of *truth* (ἀληθείας)" as God so desires for them (2:4), the false teachers are pursuing "*false*-named (ψευδωνύμου) *knowledge* (γνώσεως)" (6:20). In short, the false teachers are not saved.[286] Such articulates why the false teachers are "depraved in the *mind* (νοῦν) and . . . deprived of the *truth* (ἀληθείας)" (6:5). To be sure (see *italics*), such "*false*-named (ψευδωνύμου) *knowledge* (γνώσεως)" (6:20) is completely at odds with "the church of the living God, a pillar and buttress of *truth* (ἀλήθειαν)" (3:15) and thus is completely at odds with "the faithful and those who have *knowingly*-embraced (ἐπεγνωκόσιν) the *truth* (ἀλήθειαν)" in the Ephesian church (4:3).[287] In climactic fashion, then, the audience understand that the false teaching overseers in Ephesus are completely against God's desire (2:4), against the purpose of the church (3:15), and against the faithful in the church (4:3). Significantly also, Paul is highlighting the dire situation of the false teachers: due to their willing decision to agree with and espouse "false-named knowledge" over and above "a knowing-embrace of truth," the clear implication is that the false teachers are not saved. Thus, here at the conclusion of the letter, the missional implication of Paul's statement resounds: where the Savior God desires *all* humans to be-saved, God is desiring for "*some*" to be-saved—certainly right now, even as the false teachers are hearing Paul's words in the performance of the letter. In sum, as the B' element moves the audience forward to the climactic A' element, the forceful polemic against the false teachers *and* the missional impetus of Paul's letter are both progressed with definitive momentum. The false teachers of "false-named knowledge" are refusing the Savior God's desire, and yet God's desire still remains.

---

286. Regarding the connection of "knowing" and salvation, see Sell, *Knowledge of the Truth*, 3–31.

287. While these connections may allude to the false teachers's rejection of the "confessedly great mystery of godliness" (3:16) and their practice of asceticism (4:3, 7), Paul's concern here is not the details of the "false-named knowledge" but rather that it has no place in the household of God.

1 Timothy 6:21: Some Have Swerved, Grace With You-All

(A' Element)

Paul's final statement of the letter in the concluding A' unit of the macrochiasm upholds its climactic, rhetorical expectation: "which some—professing—regarding the faith have swerved. Grace with you-all" (6:21). The rhetorical placement of the indefinite pronoun "some" is significant. Within the concluding sixth microchiasm, "some" (τινες) in 6:21 of the A' element recalls "someone" (τις) in 6:3 of the parallel A element who teaches-different and does not come-toward the sound words of the Lord Jesus Christ. Moreover, "some" (τινες) in 6:21 recalls "some" (τινες) who have wandered from the faith in 6:10. Beyond any doubt, the audience understand that Paul is framing the entire sixth microchiasm—the climax of the entire macrochiasm—with the explicit presence and influence of the false teaching overseers.[288] Still, the rhetorical placement of "some" in 6:21 would have a far greater impact upon the audience. Paul's deliberate reference to "some" (τινες, 6:21) here at the end of the concluding A' unit recalls "some" (τισίν, 1:3) at the beginning of the parallel introductory A unit. From beginning to end, then, not only do the false teachers frame the entire climax of the letter (6:3, 21), but they also frame the entire letter itself (1:3; 6:21). Given the framing effect of the macrochiasm, the polemical implication of the letter is climactically corroborated for the audience: everything within the A and A' units is to be understood in view of the cumulative presence and influence of the false teachers.[289]

Indeed, here in the A and A' units, the climactic emphasis on the false teachers would be further upheld by the consistent, deliberate, fourfold arrangement of phrases within the A and A' units. Upon hearing the phrase "which some—professing—regarding the faith have swerved" (6:21), the fourfold combination of the relative pronoun "which," the indefinite pronoun "some," a participle, and a passive verb would recall the prior three phrases that were composed in the exact same manner:

---

288. See Thurén, "Die Struktur der Schlussparänese," 242–43. Similarly, Mihoc, "Final Admonition to Timothy," 152: "1 Timothy is brought to its conclusion with a final exhortation to Timothy that calls on him to 'guard the deposit' and warns him once again about the severe dangers of false teaching (vv. 6:20–21a). Thus Paul returns to the concerns with which he opened the letter (1,3ff), concerns that are sustained throughout (1,18–20; 4,1ff; 6,3ff) and which unambiguously demonstrate the unity of 1 Timothy."

289. Collins, *1 & 2 Tim*, 173: "These anonymous 'some' are a leitmotif of the entire epistle, populating its negative horizon."

A unit: "which (ὧν) some (τινες)—swerving-from (ἀστοχήσαντες)—have turned-aside (ἐξετράπησαν) for useless-words" (1:6);

"which (ἥν) some (τινες)—rejecting (ἀπωσάμενοι)—regarding the faith have become-shipwrecked (ἐναυάγησαν)" (1:19);

A' unit: "which (ἧς) some (τινες)—aspiring (ὀρεγόμενοι)—have wandered (ἀπεπλανήθησαν) from the faith" (6:10b);

"which (ἥν) some (τινες)—professing (ἐπαγγελλόμενοι)—regarding the faith have swerved (ἠστόχησαν)" (6:21).

The integration of linguistic and conceptual commonalities in each parallel phrase would be apparent. In short, the futile, destructive movement and motion of "some" structures and anchors the progression of the entire letter. With such a full perspective of the actions, motivations, devotions, and ramifications of the false teachers, Timothy—along with the faithful adherents to *the teaching*, that is, the gospel (1:10–11)—must guard the entrustment. Such is the apostle Paul's *charge to preserve the teaching and promote godliness as God's missional household*.

The participle "professing" (ἐπαγγελλόμενοι) recalls its earlier occurrence in 2:10 regarding women "who profess" (ἐπαγγελλομέναις) godliness. As in 2:10, the participle expresses a deep commitment.[290] Here, then, Paul's point is that "some" have effectively made an oath of allegiance to "vile empty-talk and contradictions of false-named knowledge" (6:20).[291] Still, the linguistic connection between 2:10 and 6:21 does not merely point to a destructive fact but a critical contrast. Whereas the women in Ephesus "who profess" godliness are those who cosmetic themselves consistent-with good works (2:10), the false teachers who are "professing" (6:21) false-named knowledge (6:20) are those who do not do-good-work (6:18). Indeed, the further implication would be apparent: where Paul is concerned for the women who do not cosmetic themselves in good works (2:9–10), it is because he is concerned about the evident influence of the false teachers upon their lives and, thus, the unavoidable result thereof—no hope upon God (6:17), no commendable basis for the inevitable-coming (6:19), and no possession of that which is truly life (6:19).

Indeed, the end result of "some" who are professing false-named knowledge is clear: "regarding the faith have swerved" (6:21). Paul's statement about "some" who "regarding the faith (περὶ τὴν πίστιν) have swerved (ἠστόχησαν)" (6:21) here in the A' unit recalls Paul's nearly identical

---

290. See discussion in volume 1, chapter 4.
291. Knight, *PE*, 277: "The antecedent of ἥν is 'falsely called knowledge.'"

statement in the parallel A unit about "some" who "regarding the faith (περὶ τὴν πίστιν) have become-shipwrecked (ἐναυάγησαν)" (1:19).[292] The rhetorical arrangement of the phrases would likely convey synonymy. The framing effect of the macrochiasm would thus be emphatic: all activity of the false teachers results in the same outcome, swerved and shipwrecked—in a word, lost and ruined—regarding the faith. As in 1:19 of the parallel A unit, the phrase "regarding the faith" here in the A' unit would be understood in the comprehensive sense of the false teachers's salvation—in effect, "regarding their faith upon Christ Jesus, they have swerved."[293] In short, their devotion is their destruction. Indeed, for anyone in the audience who subscribes to the different teaching of "some," the overarching implication is the same: they, too, will have lost and ruined their salvation. In effect, Paul's words would have left a powerful impression upon the audience, in effect: "*Some are lost and ruined. Don't you get get ruined, too!*"

Moreover, within the sixth microchiasm, Paul's use of the preposition "regarding" (περί, 6:21) here in the concluding A' element recalls its parallel occurrence in the introductory A element wherein Paul explicitly described the false teachers—"someone" who teaches-different (6:3)—as having-an-unhealthy-craving "regarding" (περί) controversies and word-fights (6:4). The parallelism not only reinforces that the false teachers are the framing concern of the climactic A' unit of the macrochiasm but also qualifies why "some" crave controversies and word-fights (6:4): it is because "some . . . regarding the faith have swerved" (6:21). Indeed, framing the entire letter, it is climactically clear that "some" (τισίν, 1:3, A unit; τινες, 6:21, A' unit) are marked by "controversial-speculations" and "controversies" (ἐκζητήσεις, 1:4, A unit; ζητήσεις, 6:4, A' unit) because "some" (τινες, 1:6, A unit; τινες, 6:21, A' unit) are "swerving-from" and "have swerved" (ἀστοχήσαντες, 1:6, A unit; ἠστόχησαν, 6:21, A' unit) from "faith" and "the faith" (πίστεως, 1:5, A unit; τὴν πίστιν, 6:21, A' unit). In short, the emphatic, summarizing, and insightful implications of 6:21 reaffirm Paul's motivation and concern for dictating and sending the letter to be publically performed in front of the entire Ephesian church: the ruinous influence of "some" in Ephesus obligates a *charge to preserve the teaching and promote godliness as God's missional household.*

---

292. See Marshall, *PE*, 678.

293. The same connotation was also heard in 6:10: "some—aspiring—have wandered from the faith," that is, their personal faith upon Christ. Cf. Knight, *PE*, 277: "'The faith' (τὴν πίστιν) is used in the same setting and with the same sense here as it is [in] 1:19 . . . i.e., to designate both the gospel one believes, the Christian faith, and the belief that one has regarding its truth and in the one presented therein."

Paul's last statement to the first-century church in Ephesus is: "Grace with you-all" (6:21). Compact and impactful, the audience hear this final statement as a rhetorical, salvific, and missional climax.[294] The term "grace" (χάρις) here in 6:21 of the A' unit recalls its threefold occurrences in the parallel A unit: "grace" (χάρις) from God the Father and Christ Jesus the Lord (1:2); "grace" (χάριν) that Paul holds to Christ Jesus the Lord for empowering him and appointing him for service (1:12); and the "grace" (χάρις) of the Lord that is in Christ Jesus (1:14). In view of the false teachers in 6:21a, Paul's use of "grace" in 6:21b would not only remind the faithful in Ephesus about the salvific blessings that that they received, but it would also be an encouragement to support Timothy in the protection and execution of the entrustment (6:20)—the *charge to preserve the teaching and promote godliness as God's missional household*. Indeed, it is solely by such divine "grace" (1:2, 14; 6:21b) that Timothy and the faithful among the audience will be enabled to carry out the charge.[295]

Furthermore, not only is Paul's deliberate arrangement of the macrochiasm definitely apparent, but it is evident that the three occurrences of "grace" in the A unit (1:2, 12, 14) have progressively moved throughout the macrochiasm into one climactic occurrence of "grace" in the A' unit (6:21b). Indeed, rhetorically climactic, over and above "some" who frame the entire letter in 1:3 and 6:21a, the audience understand that it is "grace" in 1:2 and 6:21b that both precedes and succeeds the false teachers. In short, Paul is emphatic that "grace" has the first and final word—not the false teachers. Thus where "grace" frames both the introductory and concluding words of the introductory and concluding A and A' units of the macrochiasm, Paul intends for the audience to undersand one fundamental fact: from the beginning to the end, it is "grace."[296]

---

294. Regarding the unique brevity of Paul's final statement in 1 Timothy, Barcley's comments are apt: "It is significant that there are no final greetings in this letter. The lack of a greeting section corresponds to the lack of thanksgiving at the beginning of the letter. Only one other letter of Paul, Galatians, has no thanksgiving section and no final greetings. It seems no coincidence that Galatians also deals with false teaching. As Paul has begun, so he closes. He dispenses with niceties. The urgency of dealing with the false teachers is too great. The truth of the gospel is too important" (*1 & 2 Tim*, 212). In the other Pastoral Epistles—2 Timothy and Titus—Paul does not include an introductory greeting, but he does include a concluding greeting (2 Tim 4:19–21; Titus 3:12–15). See also Collins, *1 & 2 Tim*, 174.

295. Knight, *PE*, 277: "For the ongoing life of believers the grace of Jesus is absolutely essential."

296. Barcley, *1 & 2 Tim*, 211: "He has begun with grace (1:2) and he ends with grace."

Still, the explicit rhetorical commonality heard in each of the threefold occurrences of "grace" in the A unit would be apparent and significant for the audience's understanding of the single occurrence of "grace" in the A' unit, namely the person of Christ Jesus as Lord:

> A unit: "grace (χάρις) . . . from God the Father and Christ Jesus our Lord (Χριστοῦ Ἰησοῦ κυρίου ἡμῶν)" (1:2);
>
> "I hold grace (χάριν) to him who empowered me, Christ Jesus our Lord (Χριστῷ Ἰησοῦ τῷ κυρίῳ ἡμῶν)" (1:12);
>
> "the grace (χάρις) of our Lord (Χριστῷ Ἰησοῦ) . . . in Christ Jesus (Χριστῷ Ἰησοῦ)" (1:14);
>
> A' unit: "Grace (χάρις) with you-all (ὑμῶν)" (6:21b).

Where the clear emphasis on the person of "Christ Jesus" as "our Lord" encapsulates and defines all "grace" in the introductory A unit, it is evident that "grace" in the concluding A' unit is also encapsulated and defined by him. As Paul's final words, the audience are not to remember that "grace"—in an abstract sense—has the first and final word over and above the false teachers, but rather that it is specifically "grace" in view of Christ Jesus that has the first and final word.[297] In this way, the salvific implication of "grace" as a divine blessing in the A unit progresses to a climax in the A' unit. It is Christ Jesus who came into the world to save sinners (1:15), who gave himself as a ransom on behalf of all (2:6), who was manifested in flesh, was declared-just in Spirit, and was taken-up in glory (3:16), who resides as a judge in the heavenly court (5:21), and whose second manifesting will usher forth an eternity (6:14–16) of eternal life for those who would-inevitably-come to have-faith upon him (1:16; cf. 6:12). In short, it is the "grace" beyond-abounding from Christ Jesus (1:2, 14) by which the audience are to have an eternal perspective—salvation, yes, but even more, a life together with Jesus Christ that is richly for enjoyment (6:17).

To this same point, Paul's final emphasis on eternity would be conveyed through the unique occurrences of the preposition "with" (μεθ') in 6:21b of the A' element and in 6:6 of the parallel A element: "godliness with (μετά) contentment is great gain." In the A element, over and against the incorrect

---

297. Knight, PE, 277: "This χάρις is explicitly said to be 'of (our) Lord Jesus (Christ)' in all Paul's letters except the last ones, Ephesians, Colossians, and the PE, in which χάρις is unqualified and the blessing is written as here, with only slight variations. At this stage Paul apparently thought it would be evident whose grace he intended." To be sure, in view of Paul's explicit association of "grace" with Christ Jesus in the A unit, it would be evident that Paul intended "grace" to be associated with Christ Jesus in the parallel A' unit.

view of the false teachers that "godliness" is a "means-of-gain"—that which is material and bound only to the present life (6:5)—Paul underscored that "godliness with (μετά) contentment is great gain" (6:6)—not merely for the present life but also—and much more—for the inevitable-coming life. In effect, where the audience heard Paul's use of "contentment" and "great" to point to the sufficiency of Christ in the present life in view of an eternal existence with Jesus Christ "in glory" (3:16), the imbued connotation of "with" (μετά) in the A element conveys an entire perspective of eternity that is rooted in the person of Jesus Christ. It is thus in the immediate context of "grace" in the the parallel A' element that the audience hear "with" (μεθ') in 6:21b as a rhetorical exclamation of what awaits all humans who would-inevitably-come to have-faith upon Christ (1:16), come to a knowing-embrace of truth (2:4), and come-toward the sound words of the Lord Jesus Christ (6:3): that which is truly life, eternal life (1:16; 6:12, 19) from God who provides-life (6:13) by his eternal strength (6:16).

Completely integrated with the rhetorical and salvific climax of the macrochiasm, it is Paul's very last word to the Ephesian audience—the plural pronoun "you-all" (ὑμῶν)—that climactically upholds the missional impetus of the letter for everyone in the audience to hear.[298] Notably, in 6:20 Paul's emphatic declaration "O Timothy" clearly placed the onus of the letter upon Timothy—namely to guard the entrustment, that is, Paul's *charge to preserve the teaching and promote godliness as God's missional household*. Here in 6:21b, however, Paul's final word of the letter emphatically broadens the scope of his audience to include "you-all"—an explicitly inclusive group for whom he intends "grace with."[299] Significantly, where the plural pronoun "you-all" (ὑμῶν) recalls Paul's sustained use of the cognate plural pronoun "our" (ἡμῶν) throughout the macrochiasm, a rhetorical juxtaposition would resound for each and every person listening to and experiencing the performance of Paul's dictated speech in the

---

298. The second person plural pronoun "you-all" (ὑμῶν) is not a cognate of the term "all" (πᾶς) that was consistently used with a missional connotation throughout the letter (e.g., 2:1, 2, 4, 6). Instead, the English translation "you-all" reflects a derivation from a single Greek word (ὑμῶν) that addresses a plural audience.

The textual variant "with you" (μετά σου) that changes the plural "you-all" (ὑμῶν) is likely an attempt by scribes to reflect the letter's address to Timothy in 1:2. However, the plural pronoun is not only well-supported but is also more probable; see Metzger, *TCGNT*, 577. See also Marshall, *PE*, 679.

299. Spencer, *1 Tim*, 165: "He uses the plural *you* (6:21), which shows that, although he writes to Timothy (1:2), he does so in the context of the whole church." See Heil, *Letters of Paul*, 168; Keegan, "First Letter to Tim," 698. See also Fee, *Listening to the Spirit in the Text*, 153.

letter.³⁰⁰ That is, Paul's consistent rhetorical use of "our" (ἡμῶν) throughout the letter established camaraderie between himself, Timothy, and the faithful among the audience; yet, it simultaneously highlighted a polemical distinction. On the one hand, "our" (ἡμῶν) applied exclusively to those for whom Jesus Christ is "our (ἡμῶν) Lord" and "our (ἡμῶν) hope" (1:1, 2, 12, 14; 6:3, 14) and those for whom God is "our (ἡμῶν) Savior" (1:1; 2:3)—namely Paul, Timothy, and the faithful among the audience. On the other hand, "our" (ἡμῶν) distinguished "some" who do not agree with the sound words of "our (ἡμῶν) Lord Jesus Christ" (6:3)—namely the false teaching overseers.³⁰¹ Rhetorically, salvifically, and missionally climactic, then, it is Paul's sudden, explicit, and apparent linguistic switch from the exclusive, inward "our" (ἡμῶν) to the inclusive, outward "you-all" (ὑμῶν) that marks the culmination and tangible outworking of Paul's *charge to preserve the teaching and promote godliness as God's missional household.* Indeed, where the distinctive force of the pronoun "our" was concurrently a missional invitation for the false teachers to join Paul, Timothy, and the faithful among the audience, Paul's sustained, mutually shared desire with

---

300. Alikin, *Christian Gathering*, 163: "The plural suggests that the addressees of the benediction were hearers in a church gathering . . ." Knight, *PE*, 277: "Plural ὑμῶν indicates that Paul expected this letter to be read to the believers, and it further indicates that all along he has had them, not just Timothy, in view." See Montague, *First and Second Tim*, 134; Wiersbe, *Ephesians Through Revelation*, 238; Patterson and Kelley, "1 Tim," 690.

Wall with Steele, *1 & 2 Tim*, 153: "Even though the majority of mss. have the benediction in the singular, Ἡ χάρις μετὰ σοῦ (*hē charis meta sou*, 'Grace be with you'), the critical text rightly retains the plural μετὰ ὑμῖν *(meta hymin)*, 'with you.' Copyists expected the farewell to repeat the letter's individual address when it does not." Hahn and Mitch, *Letters*, 41: "Since the best Greek manuscripts have 'you' in the plural, many have reasoned that the letter, while primarily sent to Timothy, was also intended to be read before the Ephesian congregation." Regarding the first-century practice of publically performing letters—and thus the intention of the 1 Timothy letter—see volume 1, chapter 1.

301. Given the historical context of Paul's final words to the Ephesian overseers in Acts 20, Paul's use of the plural pronoun "you-all" here at the conclusion of 1 Timothy may be deliberately relevant. In Acts 20:28–30, Paul says: "Hold-toward yourselves and all the flock, in which the Holy Spirit has appointed *you-all* (ὑμᾶς) overseers to care-for the church of God, which he made-about through his-own blood. I know that with my departure fierce wolves will come into *you-all* (ὑμᾶς), not sparing the flock, and from *you-all* (ὑμῶν) yourselves will arise men saying twisted-things pulling-away the disciples after themselves" (emphasis added).

In view of the overarching concern for and missional impetus in 1 Timothy toward the false teachers in the Ephesian church, the missional aspect of Paul's final words to the Ephesian church in 6:21b—"Grace with you-all (ὑμῶν)—seems intentional. At the very least, then, it is likely that the original overseers to whom Paul addressed in Acts 20 would recall the connection and thus the prophetic implication that had been realized in Ephesus just as Paul predicted.

God for all humans to be-saved (2:4) is unambiguously thrust forward as his climactic, final note to "you-all" (6:21b).[302]

"Grace with you-all" (6:21b): the lasting invitation of Paul, the divinely appointed proclaimer, apostle, and teacher (2:7)—the former blasphemer himself who was-granted-mercy solely by the beyond-abounding grace of Christ Jesus (1:13-14). It is this apostle Paul, this representative of Christ Jesus, who speaks to "you-all," desiring for the same "grace" to be received and experienced not only by the faithful in Ephesus but also—and emphatically—by "some." As the performance of the letter concludes, the false teachers are not only aware that they are the motivating cause of the letter but also that they themselves are being directly welcomed with an open invitation from the source of grace itself, the Lord Christ Jesus. It is the Lord Jesus Christ himself who—along with God, Paul, Timothy, and the faithful among the audience—desires that "some" would-inevitably-come to have-faith upon him for life eternal (1:16), hope upon God (4:10; 5:5; 6:17), and thus join the faithful in eternity, in God's household, wherein as a family they will altogether honor the King of the eternities for the eternities of the eternities (1:17; 6:15-16). With such an invitation, it is only reasonable for "some" to agree with Paul—and thus with the Lord Jesus Christ—that "the end of the charge is love" (1:5). Here at the end, Christ's love is climactically heard in the final words of his apostle Paul: "Grace with you-all" (6:21b).

---

302. Paul's final words to the Ephesian church in Acts 20, which were spoken roughly ten years prior to the 1 Timothy letter, are worth noting here. In Acts 20, Paul calls together the "elders" of the Ephesian church (20:17), whom he specifically addresses as "you-all (ὑμᾶς) overseers" (20:28). In this way, it may be that Paul's final word in his letter to the Ephesian church in the mid-sixties—"you-all" (ὑμῶν, 1 Tim 6:21b)—specifically has in view the false-teaching elders (1 Tim 5:17; cf. Acts 20:17), that is, overseers (1 Tim 3:1-7; cf. Acts 20:28) whom Paul foresaw would be in the Ephesian church (Acts 20:29). If so, then the missional impetus of the 1 Timothy letter—his desire for the salvation of "some"—is his final, climactic note. For further discussion regarding the relevance of Acts 20:28-30 to the 1 Timothy letter, see volume 1, chapter 1.

Bibliography

Volume 3

Alikin, Valeriy A. *The Earliest History of the Christian Gathering: Origin, Development and Content of the Christian Gathering in the First to Third Centuries*. Boston: Brill, 2010.

Ames, Frank Ritchel, and J. David Miller. "Prayer and Syncretism in 1 Timothy." In *Women in the Biblical World: A Survey of Old and New Testament Perspectives 2*, edited by Elizabeth A. McCabe, 94–111. New York: University Press of America, 2011.

Amundsen, D. W., and C. J. Diers. "The Age of Menopause in Classical Greece and Rome." *HB* 42 (1970) 79–86.

Andria, Solomon. *Romans*. ABCS. Grand Rapids: Zondervan, 2012.

Barcley, William B. *1 & 2 Timothy*. Webster, NY: Evangelical, 2005.

———. "1 Timothy." In *A Biblical-Theological Introduction to the New Testament: The Gospel Realized*, edited by Michael J. Kruger, 357–75. Wheaton, IL: Crossway, 2016.

Barentsen, Jack. *Emerging Leadership in the Pauline Mission: A Social Identity Perspective on Local Leadership Development in Corinth and Ephesus*. PTMS. Eugene, OR: Pickwick, 2011.

Barrett, C. K.. *The Pastoral Epistles*. NCBNT. Oxford: Clarendon, 1963.

Bartchy, S. Scott. "Slave, Slavery." In *DLNT*, edited by Ralph P. Martin and Peter H. Davids, 1098–102. Leicester: InterVarsity, 1997.

———. *First-Century Slavery and 1 Corinthians 7:21*. Eugene, OR: Wipf & Stock, 1973.

Bartsch, Hans-Werner. *Die Anfänge urchristlicher Rectsbildungen: Studien zu den Pastoralbriefen*. Hamburg: Herbert Reich, 1965.

Bassler, Jouette M. *1 & 2 Timothy and Titus*. ANTC. Nashville: Abingdon, 1996.

———. "Limits and Differentiation: The Calculus of Widows in 1 Timothy 5.3–16." In *Feminist Companion to Paul: Deutero-Pauline Writings*, edited by Amy-Jill Levine with Marianne Blickenstaff, 122–46. New York: T. & T. Clark, 2003.

Bauckham, Richard. *The Testimony of the Beloved Disciple: Narrative, History, and Theology in the Gospel of John*. Grand Rapids: Baker, 2007.

Bauer, Walter et al. *A Greek-English Lexicon of the New Testament and Other Early Christian Literature* (BDAG). 3rd ed. Revised by F. W. Danker. Chicago: University of Chicago Press, 2000.

Beale, G. K. "The Origin of the Title 'King of Kings and Lord of Lords' in Revelation 17.14." *NTS* 31 (1985) 618–20.

Belleville, Linda L. "Christology, Greco-Roman Religious Piety, and the Pseudonymity of the Pastoral Letters." In *Paul and Pseudepigraphy*, edited by Stanley E. Porter and Gregory P. Fewster, 221–44. PS 8. Boston: Brill, 2013.

———. "Christology, the Pastoral Epistles, and Commentaries." In *On the Writing on New Testament Commentaries: Festschrift for Grant R. Osborne on the Occasion of his 70th Birthday*, edited by Stanley E. Porter and Eckhard J. Schnabel, 317–38. Boston: Brill, 2013.

———. "Women in Ministry: An Egalitarian Perspective." In *Two Views on Women in Ministry: Revised Edition*, edited by James R. Beck and Craig L. Blomberg, 77–104. Grand Rapids: Zondervan, 2005.

Blass, F., and A. Debrunner. *A Greek Grammar of the New Testament and Other Early Christian Literature* (BDF). Translated by R. W. Funk. Chicago: University of Chicago Press, 1961.

Blomberg, Craig L. *Christians in an Age of Wealth: A Biblical Theology of Stewardship*. Grand Rapids: Zondervan, 2013.

———. *Neither Poverty Nor Riches: A Biblical Theology of Possessions*. NSBT. Downers Grove, IL: InterVarsity, 1999.

Bowman, Robert M., Jr., and J. Ed Komoszewski. *Putting Jesus in His Place: The Case for the Deity of Christ*. Grand Rapids: Kregel, 2007.

Bryant, K. Edwin. *Paul and the Rise of the Slave: Death and Resurrection of the Oppressed in the Epistle to the Romans*. Boston: Brill, 2016.

Carson, D. A., and Douglas Moo. *An Introduction to the New Testament*. 2nd ed. Grand Rapids: Zondervan, 2005.

Carter, Alan, and Katherine Carter. "The Gospel and Lifestyle." In *Theology and Practice of Mission: God, the Church, and the Nations*, edited by Bruce Riley Ashford, 128–44. Nashville: B&H, 2011.

Cavill, Paul. "Anglo-Saxon Saints' Lives—and Deaths." In *Visions and Revisions: The Word and the Text*, edited by Roger Kojecký and Andrew Tate, 79–108. Newcastle upon Tyne, UK: Cambridge Scholars, 2013.

Coleman, Paige. *Delivering Women from the Snares of Death: Purging Sin to Prosper the Soul*. Bloomington, IN: WestBow, 2013.

Collins, Raymond F. *1 & 2 Timothy and Titus: A Commentary*. NTL. Louisville: Westminster John Knox, 2002.

Couser, Greg A. "The Sovereign Savior of 1 and 2 Timothy and Titus." In *Entrusted with The Gospel: Paul's Theology in the Pastoral Epistles*, edited by Andreas J. Köstenberger and Terry L. Wilder, 105–36. Nashville: B&H, 2010.

Dever, Mark. *The Message of the New Testament: Promises Kept*. Wheaton, IL: Crossway, 2005.

Dewey, Joanna. "1 Timothy." In *Women's Bible Commentary: Revised and Updated*, edited by Carol A. Newsom et al, 595–601. 3rd ed. Louisville: Westminster John Knox, 2012.

Downs, David J. "The God Who Gives Life That Is Truly Life: Meritorious Almsgiving and the Divine Economy in 1 Timothy 6." In *The Unrelenting God: God's Action in*

Scripture: Essays in Honor of Beverly Roberts Gaventa, edited by David J. Downs and Matthew L. Skinner, 242-60. Grand Rapids: Eerdmans, 2013.

Early, Joseph, Jr. *A History of Christianity: An Introductory Survey*. Nashville: B&H, 2015.

Eastman, David L. *The Ancient Martyrdom Accounts of Peter and Paul*. WGRW. Atlanta: SBL, 2015.

Easton, Burton Scott. *The Pastoral Epistles: Introduction, Translation, Commentary and Word Studies*. New York: Scribner's, 1947.

Edwards, Ruth B. "The Christological Basis of the Johannine Footwashing." In *Jesus of Nazareth: Lord and Christ: Essays on the Historical Jesus and New Testament Christology*, edited by Joel B. Green and Max Turner, 367-83. Grand Rapids: Eerdmans, 1994.

Eubank, Nathan. "Almsgiving Is 'the Commandment': A Note on 1 Timothy 6.6-19." *NTS* 58 (2012) 144-50.

Fee, Gordon D. *1 & 2 Timothy, Titus*. NIBC 13. Peabody, MA: Hendrickson, 1988.

———. *Listening to the Spirit in the Text*. Grand Rapids: Eerdmans, 2000.

Ferguson, Everett. *Backgrounds of Early Christianity*. 2nd ed. Grand Rapids: Eerdmans, 1993.

Frame, John M. *Systematic Theology: An Introduction to Christian Belief*. Phillipsburg, NJ: P&R, 2013.

France, Dick. *Timothy, Titus and Hebrews*. Peabody, MA: Hendrickson, 2001.

Frandsen, Paul John. *Incestuous and Close-Kin Marriage in Ancient Egypt and Persia: An Examination of Evidence*. Copenhagen: Museum Tusculanum, 2009.

Fuller, J. William. "Of Elders and Triads in 1 Timothy 5.19-25." *NTS* 29 (1983) 258-63.

Gaffin, Richard B., Jr. *By Faith, Not By Sight: Paul and the Order of Salvation*. 2nd ed. Phillipsburg, NJ: P&R, 2013.

Gench, Frances Taylor. *Encountering God in Tyrannical Texts: Reflections on Paul, Women, and the Authority of Scripture*. Louisville: Westminster John Knox, 2015.

Getz, Gene A. *A Biblical Theology of Material Possessions*. Eugene, OR: Wipf & Stock, 1990.

Gloer, W. Hulitt. *1 & 2 Timothy-Titus*. Macon, GA: Smyth & Helwys, 2010.

Grady, J. Lee. *The Truth Sets Women Free: 25 Tough Questions About Women and the Church*. Lake Mary, FL: Charisma, 2014.

Grudem, Wayne. *Evangelical Feminism and Biblical Truth: An Analysis of More Than 100 Disputed Questions*. Wheaton, IL: Crossway, 2012.

Guthrie, Donald. *The Pastoral Epistles: An Introduction and Commentary*. TynNTC 14. Grand Rapids: Eerdmans, 1990.

Hahn, Scott, and Curtis Mitch. *The Letters of Saint Paul to the Thessalonians, Timothy, and Titus*. San Francisco: Ignatius, 2006.

Hanks, Thomas D. *The Subversive Gospel: A New Testament Commentary of Liberation*. Translated by John P. Doner. Eugene, OR: Wipf & Stock, 2000.

Hanson, Anthony Tyrrell. *Studies in the Pastoral Epistles*. Eugene, OR: Wipf & Stock, 2015.

Harper, Todd W. "Discipleship as a Tool to Transform Hearts toward Generosity." In *A Revolution in Generosity: Transforming Stewards to be Rich Toward God*, edited by Wesley K. Willmer, 223-42. Chicago: Moody, 2008.

Harrill, J. Albert. "The Bible." In *The Historical Encyclopedia of World Slavery, Volume 1 A-K*, edited by Junius P. Rodriguez, 78-80. Santa Barbara, CA: ABC-CLIO, 1997.

———. "Paul and Slavery." In *Paul in the Greco-Roman World: A Handbook*, edited by J. Paul Sampley, 575–607. New York: Trinity, 2003.

Hearon, Holly E., and Linda M. Maloney. "Listen to the Voices of the Women." In *Distant Voices Drawing Near: Essays in Honor of Antoinette Clark Wire*, edited by Holly E. Hearon, 33–56. Collegeville, MN: Liturgical, 2004.

Heil, John Paul. *The Letters of Paul as Rituals of Worship*. Cambridge: James Clarke, 2011.

Horrell, David G. "Disciplining Performance and 'Placing' the Church: Widows, Elders and Slaves in the Household of God (1 Tim 5,1—6,2)." In *1 Timothy Reconsidered*, edited by Karl Paul Donfried, 109–34. COP 18. Leuven: Peeters, 2008.

Horton, Michael. *Ordinary: Sustaining Faith in a Radical, Restless World*. Grand Rapids: Zondervan, 2014.

Instone-Brewer, David. "1 Corinthians 9:9–11: A Literal Interpretation of 'Do Not Muzzle the Ox.'" *NTS* 38 (1992) 554–65.

Jeon, Paul S. *Living Intentionally before God: Expository Reflections on 1 Thessalonians*. Eugene, OR: Wipf & Stock, 2013.

———. *To Exhort and Reprove: Audience Response to the Chiastic Structures of Paul's Letter to Titus*. Eugene, OR: Pickwick, 2012.

———. *True Faith: Reflections on Paul's Letter to Titus*. Eugene, OR: Wipf & Stock, 2012.

Johnson, Luke Timothy. "First Timothy 1,1–20: The Shape of the Struggle." In *1 Timothy Reconsidered*, edited by Karl Paul Donfried, 19–39. COP 18. Leuven: Peeters, 2008.

———. "James 3:13—4:10 and the *Topos* περὶ φθόνου." *NovT* 25 (1983) 327–47.

Kartzow, Marianne Bjelland. *Destabilizing the Margins: An Intersectional Approach to Early Christian Memory*. Eugene, OR: Pickwick, 2012.

Keegan, Terence J. *First and Second Timothy, Titus, Philemon*. NCBC 9. Collegeville, MN: Liturgical, 2006.

———. "The First Letter to Timothy." In *New Testament*, edited by Daniel Durken, 678–98. NCBC. Collegeville, MN: Liturgical, 2009.

Keller, Timothy. *Counterfeit Gods: The Empty Promises of Money, Sex, and Power, and the Only Hope that Matters*. New York: Penguin, 2009.

Keller, Timothy, with Katherine Leary Alsdorf. *Every Good Endeavor: Connecting Your Work to God's Work*. New York: Penguin, 2012.

Kelly, J. N. D. *A Commentary on the Pastoral Epistles*. HNTC. Peabody, MA: Hendrickson, 1987.

Kesich, Veselin. *Formation and Struggles: The Birth of the Church AD 33–450, Part 1: The Birth of the Church AD 33–200*. TCH 1.1. Crestwood, NY: St Vladimir's Seminary, 2007.

Kidd, Reggie M. *Wealth and Beneficence in the Pastoral Epistles: A "Bourgeois" Form of Early Christianity?* SBLDiS 122. Atlanta: Scholars, 1990.

Kirk, J. Andrew. "Did 'Officials' in the New Testament Church Receive a Salary?" *ExTim* 84 (1973) 105–8.

Knight, George W., III. *The Pastoral Epistles: A Commentary on the Greek Text*. NIGTC. Grand Rapids: Eerdmans, 1992.

Koenig, John. *New Testament Hospitality: Partnership with Strangers as Promise and Missions*. Eugene, OR: Wipf & Stock, 2001.

Krause, Deborah. *1 Timothy*. RNBC. London: T. & T. Clark, 2004

———. "1 Timothy." In *Theological Bible Commentary*, edited by Gail R. O'Day and David L. Petersen, 435–38. Louisville: Westminster John Knox, 2009.
Lau, Andrew Y. *Manifest in Flesh: The Epiphany Christology of the Pastoral Epistles.* WUNT 2/86. Tübingen: Mohr Siebeck, 1996.
Lea, Thomas D., and Hayne P. Griffin Jr. *1, 2 Timothy, Titus.* NAC 34. Nashville: B&H, 1992.
Long, Thomas G. *1 & 2 Timothy and Titus.* BTCB. Louisville: Westminster John Knox, 2016.
MacArthur, John. *1 Timothy.* MNTC. Chicago: Moody, 1995.
Mackay, Christopher S. *Ancient Rome: A Military and Political History.* New York: Cambridge University Press, 2004.
Malherbe, Abraham J. "Godliness, Self-Sufficiency, Greed, and the Enjoyment of Wealth: 1 Timothy 6:3–19, Part I." *NovT* 52 (2010) 376–405.
———. "Godliness, Self-Sufficiency, Greed, and the Enjoyment of Wealth: 1 Timothy 6:3–19, Part II." *NovT* 53 (2011) 73–96.
———. *Paul and the Popular Philosophers.* Minneapolis: Fortress, 1989.
———, ed. *The Cynic Epistles: A Study Edition.* SBLSBS 12. Missoula, MT: Scholars, 1977.
Mappes, David A. "Moral Virtues Associated with Eldership." *BSac* 160 (2003) 202–18.
Marshall, I. H. *The Pastoral Epistles.* ICC. Edinburgh: T. & T. Clark, 1999.
McCabe, Richard A. *Incest, Drama and Nature's Law, 1550–1700.* Cambridge: Cambridge University Press, 1993.
Meier, John P. "*Presbyteros* in the Pastoral Epistles." *CBQ* 35 (1973) 323–45.
Menken, Maarten J. J. "Ὅτι ἐν 1 Tim 6, 7." *Bib* 58 (1977) 532–51.
Merkle, Benjamin L. *40 Questions about Elders and Deacons.* Grand Rapids: Kregel, 2008.
———. *Why Elders? A Biblical and Practical Guide for Church Members.* Grand Rapids: Kregel, 2009.
Methuen, Charlotte. "The 'Virgin Widow': A Problematic Social Role for the Early Church." *HTR* 90/3 (1997) 285–98.
Metzger, Bruce M. *A Textual Commentary on the Greek New Testament (TCGNT).* 2nd ed. Stuttgart: Deutsche Bibelgesellschaft, 1994.
Middleton, Paul. *Radical Martyrdom and Cosmic Conflict in Early Christianity.* New York: T. & T. Clark, 2006.
Mihoc, Vasile. "The Final Admonition to Timothy." In *1 Timothy Reconsidered*, edited by Karl Paul Donfried, 135–52. COP 18. Leuven: Peeters, 2008.
Montague, George T. *First and Second Timothy, Titus.* CCSS. Grand Rapids: Baker Academic, 2008.
Mounce, William D. *Pastoral Epistles.* WBC 46. Nashville: Thomas Nelson, 2000.
Neyrey, Jerome H. *Give God the Glory: Ancient Prayer and Worship in Cultural Perspective.* Grand Rapids: Eerdmans, 2007.
Ngewa, Samuel M. *1 & 2 Timothy and Titus.* ABCS. Grand Rapids: Zondervan, 2009.
Oden, Thomas C. *First and Second Timothy and Titus.* Interpretation. Louisville: Westminster John Knox, 1989.
Osiek, Carolyn, and David L. Balch. *Families in the New Testament World: Households and House Churches.* Family, Religion, and Culture. Louisville: Westminster John Knox, 1997.

Packer, J. I. *Weakness Is the Way: Life with Christ Our Strength*. Wheaton, IL: Crossway, 2013.

Papaioannou, Kim. *The Geography of Hell in the Teaching of Jesus: Gehenna, Hades, the Abyss, the Outer Darkness Where There is Weeping and Gnashing of Teeth*. Eugene, OR: Pickwick, 2013.

Patterson, Dorothy Kelley, and Rhonda Harrington Kelley, eds. "1 Timothy." In *Women's Evangelical Commentary: New Testament*, edited by Dorothy Kelley Patterson and Rhonda Harrington Kelley, 654–90. Nashville: B&H, 2006.

Payne, Philip B. *Man and Woman, One in Christ: An Exegetical and Theological Study of Paul's Letters*. Grand Rapids: Zondervan, 2009.

Pearce, Sarah J. K. *The Land of the Body: Studies in Philo's Representation of Egypt*. WUNT 208. Tübingen: Mohr Siebeck, 2007.

Phillips, John. *Exploring the Pastoral Epistles: An Expository Commentary*. Grand Rapids: Kregel, 2004.

Plessis, Paul du. *Borkowski's Textbook on Roman Law*. 5th ed. Oxford: Oxford University Press, 2015.

Portefaix, Lilian. "'Good Citizenship' in the Household of God: Women's Position in the Pastorals Reconsidered in the Light of Roman Rule." In *Feminist Companion to Paul: Deutero-Pauline Writings*, edited by Amy-Jill Levine with Marianne Blickenstaff, 147–58. New York: T. & T. Clark, 2003.

Rudolph, Kurt. *Gnosis: The Nature and History of Gnosticism*. Translated by Robert McLachlan Wilson. Edinburgh: T. & T. Clark, 1983.

Saarinen, Risto. *The Pastoral Epistles with Philemon and Jude*. BrazTCB. Grand Rapids: Brazos, 2008.

Schlarb, Egbert. *Die gesunde Lehre: Häresie und Wahrheit im Spiegel der Pastoralbriefe*. Marburg: Elwert, 1990.

Schmithals, Walter. "The Corpus Paulinum and Gnosis." In *The New Testament and Gnosis: Essays in Honour of Robert McL. Wilson*, edited by Alastair H. B. Logan and Alexander J. M. Wedderburn, 107–24. Edinburgh: T. & T. Clark, 1983.

Sell, Jesse. *The Knowledge of the Truth—Two Doctrines*. Frankfurt: Lang, 1982.

Simpson, Graham. *The Pastoral Epistles: 1–2 Timothy, Titus: An Exegetical and Contextual Commentary*. ICNT. Bangalore, India: Primalogue, 2011.

Smith, Claire S. *Pauline Communities as "Scholastic Communities": A Study of the Vocabulary of "Teaching" in 1 Corinthians, 1 and 2 Timothy and Titus*. WUNT 2/335. Tübingen: Mohr Siebeck, 2012.

Spencer, Aída Besançon. *1 Timothy: A New Covenant Commentary*. NCCS. Cambridge: Lutterworth, 2013.

Spicq, C. *Saint Paul: Les Épîtres Pastorales*. 2 vols. EBib. Paris: Gabalda, 1969.

Sproul, R. C. *The Holiness of God*. Wheaton, IL: Tyndale, 1985.

Staton, Knofel. *Timothy—Philemon*. Eugene, OR: Wipf & Stock, 2001.

Swindoll, Charles R. *Swindoll's Living Insights: James, 1 & 2 Peter*. NTC 13. Carol Stream, IL: Tyndale, 2014.

Swinson, L. Timothy. *What Is Scripture? Paul's Use of* Graphe *in the Letters to Timothy*. Eugene, OR: Wipf & Stock, 2014.

Tamez, Elsa. "1 Timothy." In *Global Bible Commentary*, edited by Daniel Patte, 508–15. Nashville: Abingdon, 2004.

Thayer, J. H. *A Greek-English Lexicon of the New Testament: A Dictionary Numerically Coded to* Strong's Exhaustive Concordance. Grand Rapids: Baker, 1977.

Thurén, Jukka. "Die Struktur der Schlussparänese 1 Tim. 6,3–21." *TZ* 26 (1970) 241–53.

Thurston, Bonnie. "1 Timothy 5.3–16 and the Leadership of Women in the Early Church." In *Feminist Companion to Paul: Deutero-Pauline Writings*, edited by Amy-Jill Levine with Marianne Blickenstaff, 159–74. New York: T. & T. Clark, 2003.

———. *The Widows: A Woman's Ministry in the Early Church*. Minneapolis: Fortress, 1989.

Tomlinson, F. Alan. "The Purpose and Stewardship Theme within the Pastoral Epistles." In *Entrusted with The Gospel: Paul's Theology in the Pastoral Epistles*, edited by Andreas J. Kostënberger and Terry L. Wilder, 52–83. Nashville: B&H, 2010.

Towner, Philip H. "Can Slaves Be Their Masters' Benefactors? 1 Timothy 6:1–2a in Literary, Cultural, and Theological Context." *CTST* 182/183 (1997) 39–52.

———. "Christology in the Letters to Timothy and Titus." In *Contours of Christology in the New Testament*, edited by Richard N. Longenecker, 219–44. Grand Rapids: Eerdmans, 2005.

———. *The Goal of Our Instruction: The Structure of Theology and Ethics in the Pastoral Epistles*. JSNTSup 34. Sheffield: JSOT, 1989.

———. *The Letters to Timothy and Titus*. NIGTC. Grand Rapids: Eerdmans, 2006.

Van Neste, Ray. "Cohesion and Structure in the Pastoral Epistles." In *Entrusted with The Gospel: Paul's Theology in the Pastoral Epistles*, edited by Andreas J. Kostënberger and Terry L. Wilder, 84–104. Nashville: B&H, 2010.

Verner, David C. *Household of God: The Social World of the Pastoral Epistles*. SBLDiS 71. Chico, CA: Scholars, 1983.

Wagner, Walter H. *After the Apostles: Christianity in the Second Century*. Minneapolis: Fortress, 1994.

Wall, Robert W. "1 Timothy." In *The Bible Knowledge Background Commentary: Acts–Philemon*, edited by Craig A. Evans, 643–60. Colorado Springs: Victor, 2004.

Wall, Robert W., with Richard B. Steele. *1 & 2 Timothy and Titus*. Grand Rapids: Eerdmans, 2012.

Waltke, Bruce K., with Charles Yu. *An Old Testament Theology: An Exegetical, Canonical, and Thematic Approach*. Grand Rapids: Zondervan, 2007.

Watson, Kelly L. *Insatiable Appetites: Imperial Encounters with Cannibals in the North Atlantic World*. New York: New York University Press, 2015.

Wieland, George M. *The Significance of Salvation: A Study of Salvation Language in the Pastoral Epistles*. Eugene, OR: Wipf & Stock, 2006.

Winter, Bruce W. *Roman Wives, Roman Widows: The Appearance of New Women and the Pauline Communities*. Grand Rapids: Eerdmans, 2003.

Witherington, Ben, III. *Letters and Homilies for Hellenized Christians*. Vol. 1, *A Socio-Rhetorical Commentary on Titus, 1–2 Timothy and 1–3 John*. Downers Grove, IL: IVP Academic, 2006.

Wolfe, B. Paul. "The Sagacious Use of Scripture." In *Entrusted with The Gospel: Paul's Theology in the Pastoral Epistles*, edited by Andreas J. Kostënberger and Terry L. Wilder, 199–218. Nashville: B&H, 2010.

Yarbrough, Mark M. *Paul's Utilization of Preformed Traditions: An Evaluation of the Apostle's Literary, Rhetorical, and Theological Tactics*. New York: T. & T. Clark, 2009.

www.ingramcontent.com/pod-product-compliance
Lightning Source LLC
Chambersburg PA
CBHW071241230426
43668CB00011B/1530